DUMBARTON OAKS COLLOQUIUM

ON THE HISTORY

OF LANDSCAPE ARCHITECTURE

XV

Regional Garden Design
in the United States

Edited by

THERESE O'MALLEY

AND

MARC TREIB

To Brinck –
with continuing admiration
and friendship.

[signature] MARC.

I
16
96

Berkeley

Dumbarton Oaks Research Library and Collection
Washington, D.C.

Printed in the United States of America

Library of Congress Cataloging-in-Publication Data

Regional garden design in the United States / edited by Therese
    O'Malley and Marc Treib.
        p. cm.
    Collected papers from the 15th Dumbarton Oaks Colloquium on the
History of Landscape Architecture, held in 1991.
    Includes bibliographical references and index.
    ISBN 0-88402-223-4
    1. Gardens, American—Congresses.   2. Gardens—United States—
Design—Congresses.   3. Landscape design—United States—
Congresses.   I. O'Malley, Therese.   II. Treib, Marc.
III. Dumbarton Oaks Colloquium on the History of Landscape
Architecture (15th : 1991)
SB457.53.R44   1994
712'.0973—dc20   93-23720
                                                                        CIP

Contents

Appendix

Foreword

The symposium on the regional garden was originally conceived as a pendant to the Vernacular Garden symposium held at Dumbarton Oaks in 1990. This earlier meeting attempted to investigate the common gardens of world cultures from diverse places and times. In contrast, the Regional Garden colloquium focused solely on the designed landscape of the United States. The Senior Fellows Committee of Studies in Landscape Architecture began discussion on the topic with fundamental questions: What were the gardens, with regional varieties, of the Native American peoples? What landscape traditions did the French, Spanish, Dutch, and English bring to their New World colonies, and, more particularly, how were these archetypes adapted in response to the new cultural and ecological contexts? Finally, what effect did time, with its second, third, and fourth waves of immigration, exert upon European and colonial ideas and the evolving effect of urbanization?

Typically for meetings of this sort not all of these questions and issues could be addressed in a single symposium of two days' duration. The papers delivered at the symposium and the edited and expanded versions presented in this book, however, lay a foundation for examining the topic of regionalism in American garden design. The symposium program was divided by geographic region: the West Coast, the Midwest, the South, and New England; an organization that has been replicated in this published form. The definition of region and its application to landscape design is central to Marc Treib's introductory essay. He asks if a region is a geographical, biological, environmental, or cultural area, or, more complexly, a cognitive entity based on the interaction of these factors? While the United States as a whole could be taken as a region, it is more commonly subdivided into areas such as New England, the Tidewater Atlantic, the Southwest, and the Pacific Northwest. The factors of climate, plant ecology, and physical geography as well as cultural attitudes give shape to Treib's evolving definition. Regionalism, he argues, is not static, but a dynamic attitude that changes over time, and he tests his thesis with an attempt to define the modern California garden. Providing a historical background for the contemporary California garden, Dianne Harris focuses on the San Francisco Bay area at the turn of the century, in particular the influence of the architect Bernard Maybeck and his relation to the aesthetic and philosophical milieu of the period.

Robert Grese and Lance Neckar examine the contributions of three landscape architects who formulated a midwestern landscape type: Jens Jensen, Ossian Simonds, and

Horace Cleveland. Jensen's naturalistic design and emphasis on native plants paralleled the Prairie School in architecture. He established a foundation for what today is termed an ecological approach to landscape design. Cleveland worked as a planner as well as a landscape architect. His *Landscape Architecture As Applied to the Wants of the West* addressed communities developing at the turn of the century on the edge of established settlements and stressed the importance of landscape design within the city. To complement these two essays, we have reprinted Wilhelm Miller's seminal essay of 1915, *The Prairie Spirit in Landscape Gardening,* as an appendix. Miller's essay, which is often cited but rarely seen, was an important formulation of both ideas and practical plant selection. We have taken this opportunity to make it available once again to students of landscape history. Christopher Vernon has written an introduction to this appendix in which he situates Miller's contribution to midwestern landscape practice and theory.

The Virginian piedmont was one region in the English colonies to develop a defined variant of the "Old World" landscape, a theme explored by C. Allan Brown. James Ackerman discusses the subtle transformation of British models in the creation of nineteenth-century public parks. Louisiana notarial documents, a product of the imported French legal system, provide a wealth of pictorial evidence for Suzanne Turner's discussion of domestic gardens in New Orleans. In essays by Charles Beveridge and Laurie Olin, the attention turns to practice, the interplay between the standard approach to design that develops over time in office practice, and the responsive variations demanded by regional conditions. Beveridge discusses the work of Frederick Law Olmsted in the East, the Midwest, and California. He suggests that when challenged by a new environment Olmsted responded with his most creative designs—his project for Stanford University being his most splendid example. Laurie Olin, a practicing landscape architect, suggests that in contemporary landscape architecture the designer must explore regional variations in order to withstand the prevailing forces of homogenization and to imbue design with specific iconographic associations.

As a whole, these essays suggest that regionalism will always remain, to some degree, in the eyes of the beholder, the designer, and, above all, those of a cultural group of a specific place and time. While acknowledging environmental conditions in landscape design is critical in today's world—for example, as seen in the evolving xeriscape approach in areas with limited rainfall—the interpretation of these conditions into garden form will remain personal, various, and potentially rich in environmental and aesthetic effect.

We wish to thank not only the authors for their diligent efforts, but also John Dixon Hunt, former Director of Studies in Landscape Architecture, who convened the original symposium, and his successor Joachim Wolschke-Bulmahn for his subsequent help and support. We should also acknowledge Elizabeth Kryder-Reid who helped prepare the manuscript for publication.

Therese O'Malley
Marc Treib
June 1993

Introduction

JOHN DIXON HUNT

In planning this symposium, the Senior Fellows Committee asked each speaker to address the idea of regionality: not only to define the region that each was exploring but also to try and answer such questions as what is a region? what is regionality? how exactly does it affect and effect garden design?

Now the region addressed might well be North America itself, as opposed to, say, Europe; that was certainly how many of the first colonists viewed their new territory. Gradually, the different parts of the East Coast—for a while, of course the only region—came to be distinguished as having each its own special character from New England down to Georgia. Then, as more and more of the country was opened up, both the vastness and the variety of its territory became one of the ineluctable facts of the American experience. We shall be reading much about how eastern landscape architects went west and were faced with new regional characteristics that enforced changes in the ideas and designs they had carried with them from Boston, New York, or Philadelphia.

It is not difficult to register regional difference. For an Englishman, the Lake District is not Devonshire—neither in its climate, topography, geology, flora, and fauna—all aspects that obviously determine gardens—nor in its social and economic profile. These last will certainly determine the shape and use of the larger cultural landscape of fields and roads, for instance, and arguably, therefore, also the smaller and more concentrated interventions into the physical world that we call gardens.

However, I am curious as to when a region slips into being a locality, or conversely, when a locality graduates into a region. Both, presumably, have centers that give them being and shape and *raison d'être*, and these centers—they may be villages, towns, cities, simply the natural center of a glacial valley floor, or a prominent mountain—determine the region that spreads around them like ripples across a pond hit by a stone.

Use is probably one of the most important determinants of regional character in landscape architecture as well as in landscape: hillsides for sheep are walled in different ways than hillsides terraced for crops. But we have also perhaps to remind ourselves not to be positivistically utilitarian—"use" can also refer to intellectual, ideological, and contemplative use of landscape and garden space. Here we enter the far more intangible world of mental habits, though these in their turn may be conditioned by environmental, social, and economic factors.

The patron for whom Andrea Palladio designed a villa in the Veneto foothills did not live there; his base was a palace in the city of Venice, Vicenza, or Verona, and the villa was a villa-cum-working farm. His whole attitude toward its space, how that space could be decorated and used, would be different from a similarly wealthy and important figure in England in the following century. Here the country seat was primary, the power base in a quite literal fashion—hence came the wealth and the local authority to decide how the surrounding area was governed and who should represent it in the House of Commons. Given this wholly different use—in the broadest sense of the word—of an English country seat, the ways in which its immediate environment was constructed would be very different from those of a villa used only at weekends or at harvest time.

One aspect of regionality that will concern us, though it is not obvious at first sight, is the region left behind; the lost, abandoned, or mythical world carried into another new and maybe hostile region and sometimes imposed upon a new one. Early colonists in this country necessarily sought to make the New World habitable by recreating domestic spaces, including gardens, similar to what they had known back home. But soon there were other notions of region to imitate or adapt in the eastern colonies—not just, say, some part of England or even England now thought of—as through a reversed telescope—as a region itself, but Renaissance Italy, revolutionary France, or classical Rome. These regions had their tangible shapes and forms, susceptible to physical recreation, but they were also just as importantly regions of the mind that could be found in approximate equivalents elsewhere; equivalents that sometimes seemed to deny or bypass the actual regions where these visions were set down. Nothing speaks more eloquently of this than the penchant in the late nineteenth- and early twentieth-century United States for Italianate villas and gardens. Here it is as much the "regions" that are imported as the regions in which these foreign ideas are settled that must concern us.

Regionality has a strong appeal today as a plausible weapon to fight off the homogenized visions of the modern world, provided we do not elevate some taste for vernacular idioms into a "neo-regionalist" style all of its own. Thus, beyond the historical concerns, which are at the center of most of the essays gathered here, is the present and future theme of how contemporary landscape architecture can adapt its strategies to regional differences.

Wallace Stevens's "Anecdote of the Jar," a poem now somewhat in vogue with landscape architects, tells of drawing out the potential of some Tennessee hillside by placing a jar on it. This American version of the classical urn, avatar of a powerful region of the western mind, elucidates for the modern poet a fresh view of some native habitat, the region of his song. This parable speaks perhaps to the contemporary landscape architect who must use the full (nowadays international) resources of his craft to signal the essential mystery of locality, place, and region.

Aspects of Regionality and the Modern(ist)
Garden in California

MARC TREIB

The Dewey Donnell garden, just north of San Francisco, has come to represent the epitome of the modern California garden (Fig. 1). *House Beautiful* magazine, like *Sunset*, the Magazine of Western Living, featured its ultra-contemporary kidney-shaped pool on its pages,[1] and both publications contributed to popularizing the garden's idiom. While at root a regional enterprise, the modern(ist) California garden was widely propagated by popular home journals and widely emulated across the nation in at least diluted form. It became, in some ways, part of American suburban lore.[2] Designed in 1948 by Thomas Church, the Donnell garden displayed virtually all the desirable characteristics of the postwar suburban garden. Most importantly, its design suggested that contemporary Californian family life took place out of doors, and that leisure was the reward for triumph during the war years and continued hard work in the present. Although striking in its modern idiom and reinterpretation of spatial design, the garden was not only to be looked at: more importantly, it was to be used. Living in the garden or yard was the central idea—whether gardening, playing, swimming or engaging in other sports, or for the ubiquitous gathering of family and neighbors around the barbecue on weekends. Of course, outdoor activity required a temperate and clement weather, and both were provided abundantly by the California climate.

Although this paper will address the origins and form of the California garden in the years 1945–60, it is also intended as a vehicle to advance a definition of regionalism applied to garden design. First, we need to accept that regionalism is a dynamic rather than a static entity; that is, it evolves over time. Second, regionality can not be ascertained

All photographs by the author except as noted.

[1] The garden's fresh-looking design quickly entered the public imagination, furthered by the new possibilities for color reproduction in magazines after the war. In the early photographic images used to illustrate the articles, people are included, often in bathing suits, enjoying the benefits of the California climate as well as those of the modern garden and its pool.

[2] For example, the catalog cover for Claes Oldenburg's first major European exhibition in Stockholm used variants of pool shapes that could probably be traced to Church's Donnell design. See *Claes Oldenburg: Skulpturer och teckningar*, Stockholm, 1966.

1. Donnell garden, Sonoma County, California, 1948. Thomas Church, landscape architect. View of the pool area looking south

by examining garden form and materials alone; on the contrary, it encompasses cultural and aesthetic concerns as well as ecological and environmental parameters. While the ecological characteristics of a place remain relatively constant or are modified only slowly over time, other aspects of regionalism may change rapidly, causing consequent modifications in garden form.

ASPECTS OF REGIONALITY I: ECOLOGY

It would seem that all gardens must inherently reflect the region in which they are located, and to some degree this is true. Given horticultural materials that depend upon climatic and nutritional systems, sunlight, and water particular to the place, local environmental conditions control the very existence of its plantings. We could also invert the phrasing of the issue, however: Can gardens ever escape having regional traits, given their dependence upon and response to their immediate physical situation? If gardens were purely ecological entities, the answer might be "no," or at least a qualified "no." But gardens are neither wilderness nor natural landscapes, and they require the human

6

presence for their creation and maintenance.[3] Botany, horticulture, and agriculture have all extended the range of climates and terrains hospitable to plant life and have induced greater yields from indigenous species or imported species sharing sympathies with native families. Modifying the land to support cultivation through horticulture is the first impact of the human mind upon the field.

The garden also represents the human will as an environmental, as well as a horticultural, construct. One need not rehearse in detail the long and full host of purposes that gardens have served: from providing pleasure through order, sound, texture, fragrance, and even taste; to their use as symbols of power and suppression; or their roles as carriers of cosmologies and religious belief. Yet any consideration of the intentions behind garden making and the physical characteristics of plants leads to a consideration of their formal consequences. Form, in turn, manifests an order, even if materials native to the site are employed. A simple diagram (Fig. 2), then, could chart those factors subject to manipulation through design, yielding a matrix that lists native and non-native plants along one axis; natural ordering and non-natural ordering along the other. Native plants in a native order would mesh imperceptibly with the existing landscape; the non-native, used in a non-natural order would constitute the other extreme: a formally structured botanical garden might be a convenient example of this latter type (Fig. 3). However, in the remaining two categories—non-native materials in a natural order or especially native materials in a non-natural order—one finds the strongest suggestions for a designed regional garden. For here, one can accept the limitations of the environment while reshaping it to suite prevalent cultural assumptions.

	Natural Ordering	*Non-Natural Ordering*
Native Materials	Existing site; Landscape	Drought-tolerant plants in formal arrangement
Non-Native Materials	Landscape garden with specimens	Botanical garden; Patio de los Naranjos

2. The interaction of indigenous materials and types of design order

[3] The garden could be defined as a zone of constructed nature, where cultural idea may be allowed to outweigh natural process. The dry gardens of the Japanese Zen tradition are not as dependent upon their ecosystem as they are upon the human thought and energy used to create them. Still, a culture is related to its region. In the science fiction novel, *Garden on the Moon* (trans. X. Fielding, New York, 1966), by Pierre Boulle, the plot centers on the idea that to reach the moon is not the real problem for humankind: it is the return to Earth. A Japanese scientist, using this space accomplishment to bolster national pride, lands on the moon on what will be a suicidal journey. As he awaits the depletion of his oxygen and his ultimate death, he begins to arrange the moon rocks to be more in accord with his enculturated idea of garden. That idea has been brought with him, through space, to the moon.

3. Patio de los Naranjos, Seville, Spain, tenth century. This enclosed garden court embodies horticultural techniques raised to the level of an art

4. Mission, Santa Barbara, California, 1786; 1815–20. The garden of the Franciscan mission took the form of an enclosed quadrangle, ideally with a fountain at its center. An arcade enclosed the garden on two or more sides and softened the boundary between architecture and cultivated landscape

THE MODERN(IST) GARDEN IN CALIFORNIA

Aspects of Regionality II: Idea

It would seem obvious that this schematic attempt to define what is regional, however, is limited. While it does address issues of ecology and horticulture and their manipulation through design, this rough definition acknowledges the *cultural* aspects of gardens in only a very limited way. Thus, we should add a consideration of culture. Culture is an elusive word that possesses a variety of meanings as it appears in differing contexts and in different disciplines. Among Webster's definitions one finds: "the integrated pattern of human knowledge, belief and behavior that depends upon man's capacity for learning and transmitting knowledge to succeeding generations." In sociology, culture expresses a value system, societal form, and its structuring. Here "culture" is used simply, or even simplistically, to include the collective social idea of the garden and the uses to which the garden is put as an improved ecological zone. Societies change with time; they evolve and at times are suppressed by foreign invasions. But even within a single social group, aspirations and influences may be mutable, and they may be dominated by either indigenous or imported ideas and values. This was certainly the case in the Golden State.

In California, the native peoples were seminomadic hunters and gatherers, and prior to their contact with the Spanish missionaries and colonists in the late eighteenth century they practiced virtually no cultivation but lived, instead, from the fruits of the land. The Spanish brought beans and other vegetables new to California, wheat and barley, and grapes for wine and the table.[4] From Central America they also brought certain species of palm trees alien to Alta California (Fig. 4).[5] During the first period of settlement, ornamental gardens were restricted to the interiors of the missions' quadrangles, and even here, plant specimens within the precinct were not strictly limited and could include fruit-bearing trees. The garden structure itself employed a familiar medieval monastic model—a fountain positioned at the intersection of four paths. Thus, patterns of Iberian agriculture and, later, garden design were overlaid upon the indigenous ecology.

---

[4] "To their mission gardens, the Franciscans brought from Mexico all the garden and orchard seeds and plants which they thought would grow. . . . Early accounts record that the missionaries grew lemons, oranges, figs, dates, olives, pomegranates, limes, and grapes successfully, as well as peaches, pears, cherries, apples, walnuts, almonds, plums, quinces, apricots, raspberries, and strawberries. Some of the fruits still grown in the state are direct lineal descendants of those planted by the padres, notably the Mission grape, Mission fig, and Mission olive" [p. 192]. At Santa Barbara, flowers were plentiful: "lilies, hyacinths, daffodils, and jonquils, are listed, as well as many of the favorites of long ago—the cornflower, larkspur, peony, marigold, sweet Williams, gillyflower, violet, carnation, Marguerite, honeysuckle, jasmine, rose, and buttercup" [p. 193]. V. Padilla, "The Franciscan Missionaries in Southern California," in B. Marranca, ed., *American Garden Writing: Gleanings from Garden Lives Then and Now,* New York, 1989.

[5] "Besides the date palm, the Franciscans raised the Mexican fan palm *(Washingtonia robusta)* and the native fan palm *(Washingtonia filifera),* the seeds of which were brought by the padres from the California desert and planted in their gardens" Padilla, "Franciscan Missionaries," 196. Being a symbol of the perceived cultural inferiority of southern California, palm trees are not appreciated as a cultural norm in northern California. A recent proposal to plant a row of Canary Island palms along the Embarcadero has met with many cries of "Palm trees are not San Francisco!"

5. "Sunny Cove" brand orange crate label. The idealized California landscape of the first half of the twentieth century: a
Spanish-style house set amid fecund orange groves and against
the majestic mountains

Over time, as the *pueblo* (civil settlement) developed, the gardens of Spain and Mexico found their descendants in the ornamental plantings of Alta California; the gardens
were planted with bougainvillea, apples, figs, pomegranates, geraniums, citron, oranges,
and climbing vines. With the exception of the mission churches, the early architecture
was mud-built, whitewashed, one story, and mostly flat-roofed, although pitched tile
roofs came to replace the flat earthen roofs as technical and economic means allowed.
Apertures in the forms of wooden doors or small windows were limited, and arcades
provided a transitional zone that was used frequently when weather allowed. The garden
extended the domain of the arcade and was usually enclosed by a girdling wall, a descen-
dant of the enclosed gardens of Spain. The irrigated planting within that wall contrasted
dramatically with the golden grasses of the hillsides in summer.

During the California boom years in the early decades of the twentieth century,
agriculture in general, and the citrus industry in particular, flourished with increased
irrigation resources and the rapid shipment provided by the railroad (Fig. 5). To provide
a sense of history and to re-establish its right to land tenure, California sought its roots
in its Spanish past. Like most tales of Spanish California, Helen Hunt Jackson's *Ramona*,
published in 1884, was a fabulous conflation of lives lived in anachronistic settings.[6] In

[6] H. Hunt Jackson, *Ramona*, New York, 1884. Harold Kirker explains: "For the Californians were un-
certainly discovering that they had a past of their own. As one of them put it: 'Give me neither Romanesque
nor Gothic; much less Italian Renaissance, and least of all English Colonial—this is California—Give me
Mission.'" (As quoted in Felix Rey, "A Tribute to Mission Style," *Architect and Engineer* [October 1924], 78).

spite of its historical inaccuracies, the novel became a prime source of romantic imagery and invigorated the search for an appropriate architectural and cultural image.

Santa Barbara, for example, promulgated a municipal ordinance in 1925 that required buildings in the central area to be built in the "Spanish" style. Its definition of Spanish was open to broad interpretation, however, and accepted some strange stylistic concoctions providing they were at least vaguely Mediterranean in influence. Garden images constituted an important element of the myth; one can hardly picture the time without at least one wall pigmented by the branches of a magenta bougainvillea. The major works of the period such as James Osborn Craig's El Paseo shopping complex of 1923 (Fig. 6) or William Moser's Santa Barbara County Courthouse of 1928 compensate in exuberance what might have been lacking in stylistic verity. Each of these projects featured planted or paved open spaces (Fig. 7). As David Gebhard has shown, the use of garden style in Southern California later in the 1920s, whether in the romantic Spanish or the emerging modern idiom, was not the critical ingredient in terms of its net effect on the garden.[7] Whether Iberian, non-specific Romantic, Modernist, or any other vocabulary, the garden provided vegetation, amenity, and the imprint of civilized living on the California wilderness. This idea of garden as the setting for outdoor living transcended any particular stylistic predilection.

Perhaps the burgeoning of the movie industry, an industry which thrived on the creation of impressions rather than truths, allowed this flexibility and downplayed the urge toward stylistic accuracy. Indeed, several of the major estates with lavish gardens, such as that for Harold Lloyd designed by A. E. Hanson from 1925–29, were created for wealthy movie stars and others made *nouveaux riches* by the cinema machine. In general, whether large or small, eclecticism reigned in the garden of Southern California. In the northern part of the state, on the other hand, the rich favored the Italianate and other Beaux-Arts styles, a good example of which is Bruce Porter's Filoli in Woodside from 1914 on (Fig. 8). The Bay Area intelligentsia developed a local version of the more naturalized Arts and Crafts that also drew to some extent from A. J. Downing, though twice removed (in time and space) from the sources.[8]

More succinctly: "An immigrant society is always culturally conservative." *California's Architectural Frontier: Style and Tradition in the Nineteenth Century*, Santa Barbara, 1873. 130.

[7] "If we look closely at their response to Southern California, we will readily see that there was little in the end to distinguish their approach from the designs of their traditionalist colleagues. In the twenties, they adopted the view that place was to be transformed—whether as a new vision of the Mediterranean world or of the jungles of Yucatan; in the thirties, they and their traditionalist colleagues played down these romantic and exotic intimations and instead maneuvered the landscape so that it seemed 'normal,' i.e. what one would have encountered throughout the rest of the United States." D. Gebhard, "The Modernist and the Landscape in Southern California, 1920–1941," unpublished paper presented at the annual meeting of the Society of Architectural Historians, 1989. See also D. Streatfield, "The Evolution of the California Landscape: 3. The Great Promotions," *Landscape Architecture* 67 (May 1977), 229–39, 272, and idem, "The Evolution of the California Landscape: 4. Suburbia at the Zenith," *Landscape Architecture* 67 (September 1977), 417–24.

[8] Dianne Harris discusses turn-of-the-century gardens in "Making Gardens in the Athens of the West: Bernard Maybeck and the San Francisco Bay Region Tradition in Landscape and Garden Design," included in this volume.

6. El Paseo, Santa Barbara, California, 1923. James Osborn Craig, architect. This interlocking network of paths, arcades, and courtyards adapted a Mediterranean style of architecture to the myth of Southern California

7. Steedman garden, Santa Barbara, California, 1925. George Washington Smith, architect. The garden represents the Spanish sensibility applied to the California landscape and temperament

8. Filoli, Woodside, California, 1914. Bruce Porter, landscape architect. One of the great estates of California designed in an Italianate style adapted to the local topography and climate

With the completion of hostilities in 1945, California turned from waging war to regaining the American Dream. Federal housing programs provided low interest loans to veterans to purchase single-family houses in the developing suburbs. During the war years, thousands of workers had moved to the Golden State for employment in the aircraft and war materiel industries centered in Southern California. After the war ended, they stayed. The freeway system superseded the successful red cars of the Pacific Electric Railway, allowing even greater personal mobility and the ever-increasing distance from the city center.[9] More and more of what had been desert or agricultural land became the sites of single-family homes and the suburban pattern that supported them.[10] Although Californians were creatures of mobility, they sought permanence in their homes, and they turned again to the colonial revival styles, and even more enthusiastically to the so-called "California ranch house." But the house was little without land, and the land was little without a planted landscape. Limited in size by the pattern of subdivision, the site was usually treated as a totality: the land and the garden were the setting for the home. Given the numbers of houses needed to meet the appetite of the market, construction became more rationalized and rapid.[11]

[9] See R. Banham, *Los Angeles: The Architecture of Four Ecologies,* Baltimore, 1971.
[10] E. W. Soja, *Postmodern Geographies: The Reassertion of Space in Critical Theory,* London and New York, 1989, 194–95.
[11] Here would have been the great opportunity for the factory-built house; although implemented in part, it never was realized at a scale at which it would have made an impact of the direction of housing. The image of the traditional architectural style overcame the necessity for rationalized production. See G. Her-

Thus, we can see in the California garden and its accompanying architecture that the social attitudes—whether Spanish or American—have undergone continued modifications. Principal among these was the change from the walled garden to the broadened limits of the suburban tract. This continued evolution limits our ability to define a regional garden or architecture precisely because we must always confine a specific review of regionality to a specific time as well as place. Instead, cultural ideas, whether historically received or newly imported, must be treated as a fluid overlay upon the more or less static conditions of climate and plant ecology that comprised Aspect I.

ASPECTS OF REGIONALITY III: FUNCTION

Gardens are not visual entities alone, and even those austere examples which admit no physical passage—the dry Zen gardens of Japan, for example—still address the question of use, even if use should be taken as contemplative. Accompanying the dynamic social attitude toward the garden is a continually evolving idea about its function. As the cultural concept of the California garden developed over time, its use shifted from the pharmaceutical, symbolic, meditative, and experiential space of the mission, to the cultivated and productive zone of the colonial, to the pleasure zone of the early part of the twentieth century. In the postwar period, however, the use of the garden for individual and family activity rose to the forefront of its purposes.

The argument for a social landscape of health, sports, and utility had continued in the United States for the better part of a century. From the great parks of the later nineteenth century, of which Olmsted and Vaux's Central Park is the most prominent example, the argument for contact with natural open space as a form of social and moral improvement had occupied a prominent position in the attitudes of Americans toward parks and gardens. As the embrace of urbanism increased in the twentieth century, the idea that our wilderness areas could become circumscribed, and finally decimated, gained increasingly greater currency, leading to a renewed interest in the mythical pastoral life.[12] Settlement patterns just after the war strengthened the American predilection for finding the benefits of both the urban and the rural in suburbia. Building technology, the automobile, and favorable financing patterns in the late 1940s provided the ticket to the suburbs, particularly in areas such as Southern California, which burgeoned after the war. From a land area of forty-three square miles at the beginning of the century, Los Angeles had multiplied to over ten times that size by 1930; its population had skyrocketed from some thirty-five thousand in 1880 to about two million by 1940.[13]

The landscape and architecture of the single-family home evolved, but slowly. While

bert, *The Dream of the Factory-Made House: Walter Gropius and Konrad Wachsmann*, Cambridge, Mass., 1984, and T. Hine, "The Search for the Postwar House," in *Blueprints for Modern Living: History and Legacy of the Case Study Houses*, Los Angeles and Cambridge, Mass., 1990.

[12] See B. Novak, *Nature and Culture: American Landscape and Painting 1825–1875*, New York, 1980, and L. Marx, *The Machine in the Garden: Technology and the Pastoral Ideal in America*, New York, 1969.

[13] Soja, *Postmodern Geographies*, 194–95.

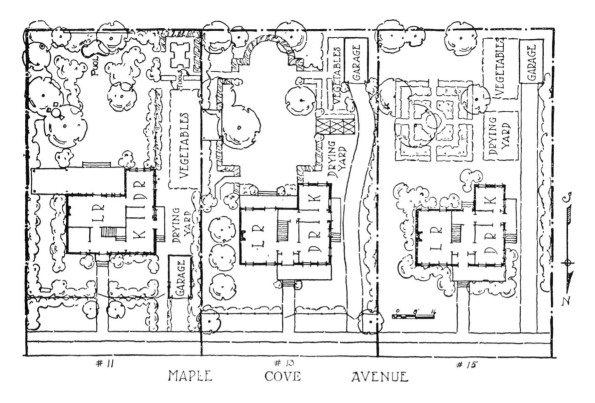

9. Site plan of a hypothetical suburban block. This site plan illustrates Fletcher Steele's argument for a
house plan that moves the kitchen to the street side of the lot, allowing a greater connection between
the living and dining spaces and the garden. Formality has been avoided as restrictive, and the design
of the garden has been developed to maximize the sense of space (photo: from F. Steele, *Design in the Lit-*
tle Garden, Boston, 1924)

the house would admit technological improvements in building materials and methods,
it steadfastly maintained patterns from the past. Federal housing agencies, for example,
provided loans only for houses that followed an approved disposition of rooms; these, it
was believed, would retain their economic value at the time of resale. This planning of
internal spaces confined the development of exterior ground. In one of his best writings,
Design in the Little Garden of 1924, landscape architect Fletcher Steele methodically demonstrated how moving the kitchen from the back of the house to the street side would
allow a much more efficient and flexible utilization of space both within and without the
house (no. 11 in Fig. 9): in place of small divided plots, the full extent of the site could
be enjoyed, and the garden rendered a more vibrant part of the domestic enclave. At
the time he wrote, however, Steele's choice of house plan would not have been eligible
for many bank loan programs, and thus, impractical for widespread application to subdivisions.[14]

To effect a radical rethinking of the suburban garden, changes in house plans were
crucial. They were prompted by the tenets of the Modern Movement in architecture,

[14] F. Steele, *Design in the Little Garden*, Boston, 1924.

15

which in Europe had argued for increased contact with greenery, air, and light. While these were more critical issues in Europe where urban patterns and housing stock could be traced, in places, to medieval times, they were less important in American suburbia. And yet the move to suburbia was predicted to some degree on similar desires; one should recall, for example, the fears of polio epidemics through the 1950s that drove many children to rural camps during the summers and ultimately their families out of the cities to the suburbs. The open plan, the challenge to traditional architectural types, the flat roof, the inter-penetrating spaces that replaced static and distinct rooms, all influenced the design of the postwar Californian home.

The changes in architecture and living pattern demanded a consequent change in the outdoor spaces around the house. The ordering and styles of the landscape architecture will be examined in greater detail in the fourth and concluding section of the evolving definition of regionalism in gardens. At this point, however, we should underscore the notion of use related to the living pattern of California in the late 1940s and 1950s, much of it modified by the changes in family life and mobility caused by the war or in its aftermath—women working outside the home, for example.[15] Broadly sketched, one could say that the evolving lifestyle was far more informal, reflecting a deterioration of the patriarchal hierarchy, with women and ultimately children having a greater share in the daily life of the house. (This swing in family governance reaches a culmination in the domination and tyranny of the teenager during the 1950s, but that is another story.)

Because the sites of many of these houses were limited in size, it was necessary to utilize every square foot of the lot. This restriction led to the design of an integrated site plan that could foster multiple uses or readings, rather than distinct units for specialized purposes. Site plans of the late 1940s included functional areas such as the detached garage and laundry drying yards; in time, with the gas or electric dryer provided by the resumption of the production of consumer goods, these zones disappear, giving over more space for other purposes.[16] This is admittedly a rather breathless treatment of a complex issue, and one that in itself changes with time. However, the importance of use and activity derived from social patterns as another factor in determining the regionality of any particular garden design should be located.

ASPECTS OF REGIONALITY IV: AESTHETICS AND STYLE

Finally, let us address the issue of design style, a term which these days has such negative connotations that it demands further clarification. Style can be taken as both the concrete expression of values as well as the specific characteristics of form. It should

---

[15] See *Blueprints for Modern Living: History and Legacy of the Case Study Houses,* Los Angeles and Cambridge, Mass., 1990, in particular, essays by Thomas Hine and Dolores Hayden.
[16] For example, all three plans discussed by Steele in *Design in the Little Garden* include areas of drying laundry. This use continued in several of the Case Study Houses. With the increased availability of washing machines and dryers, the need of this space declined and was eventually turned to other purposes.

be taken to include structural and spatial orders, in addition to the formal vocabulary. Style is not negligible, and its personal and social expressions produce considerable consequences.[17]

Of course, one could adopt radical structural and spatial changes and still remain conservative in terms of formal vocabulary. This was quite common, for example, in the so-called ranch houses of Cliff May and their attendant landscapes (Fig. 10). May's first works, circa 1940, followed the early California prototype quite closely, although he built in wood instead of adobe. But under the influences of the Modernists working in California in the 1950s, he gradually adopted a freer and more open internal arrangement—to the point of radicality in one of his own houses—while retaining a singularly conservative exterior (Fig. 11).[18] Planting around the house was requisite, but romantic clumpings of natives and flowering exotics were predominant characteristics. The 1963 offices for *Sunset* magazine in Menlo Park, California (Fig. 12), which came late in May's career, adapted the residential ranch house type to office use, employing a similar plan and attitude towards internal and external spaces common in his residential designs. Its single story fostered direct connections between building and garden, and its enclosed courtyards continued the Spanish pattern of the patio—the outdoor space for family living, even if the building serves as publication offices. The site is planted with a variety of native and non-native specimens, and a projecting lawn informally extends the line of garden out from the offices. Interestingly, Thomas Church was the landscape architect for this project, furthering *Sunset's* presentation of the apotheosis of the suburban lifestyle on its pages.[19] The question of style again brings us to the question of regionality, and before returning to the particulars of modern landscape design in California, the condition of local versus imported ideas in other contexts needs to be addressed.

To begin, the dictionary description of the word region tells us that it is an "indefinite area," the boundaries of which can be determined only by establishing the criteria for definition, be they homogeneous land form, climate, fauna, or flora. Geographers distinguish between single and multiple factor regions, for example, those that might be defined by climate alone, or those that require a congruence of climate and population type.[20] Let us also try to distinguish between the adjectives *regional* and *provincial*. Although certain aspects of their definitions may overlap, regional tends to be a geographic term whereas provincial is an administrative term. More importantly perhaps, in terms of art forms, provincial almost always bears a negative connotation. The dictionary includes in its definitions "limited in outlook," and offers "unsophisticated" as a synonym. It suggests an inferior variation of a higher cultural pattern, for example, those patterns

[17] For a discussion of the role and importance of taste, see P. Lewis, "American Landscape Tastes," in M. Treib, ed., *Modern Landscape Architecture: A Critical Review*, Cambridge, Mass., 1993.

[18] See *Sunset* magazine editorial staff, *Western Ranch Houses by Cliff May*, Menlo Park, Calif., 1958.

[19] See P. Lewis, "The Making of Vernacular Taste: The Case of *Sunset* and *Southern Living*," in J. D. Hunt and J. Wolschke-Bulmahn, eds., *The Vernacular Garden*, Dumbarton Oaks Colloquium on the History of Landscape Architecture 14, Washington, D.C., 1993, 107–36.

[20] In spite of the collection of essays on regionalism in various disciplines, a symposium on the subject came to no generalized definition of the term. See M. Jensen, ed., *Regionalism in America*, Madison, 1952.

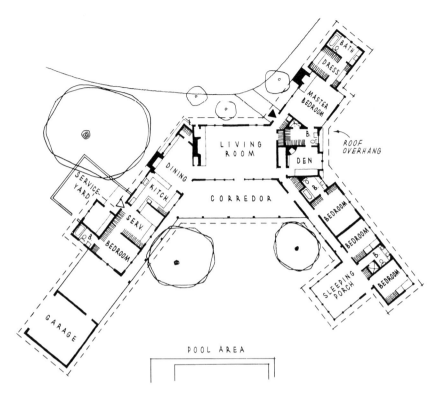

POOL AREA

10. Plan, ranch house, Keene, California, no date. Cliff May, architect. May's early designs centered on the living room and *corredor*, with residential and service wings extending from this nexus (photo: from *Western Ranch Houses by Cliff May*, 1958; courtesy of Lane Publishing Company)

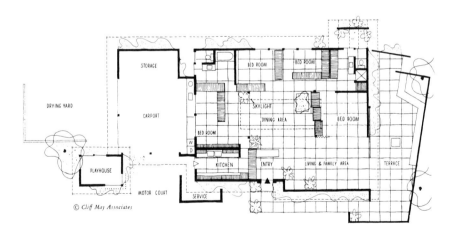

11. Plan, May Residence, West Los Angeles, California, no date. Cliff May, architect. In this later house for the architect's family, the openness of the internal plan parallels the free connection between interior and exterior space (photo: from *Western Ranch Houses by Cliff May*, 1958; courtesy of Lane Publishing Company)

12. *Sunset* magazine headquarters, Menlo Park, California, 1963. Cliff May, architect; Thomas Church, landscape architect. Like an enlarged ranch house, the lanai breezeway links the interior spaces to the garden

established by the cosmopolitan culture of the city. A comparison results, and the provincial is usually cast as a lesser imitation and comes up short. Regional, on the other hand can be regarded positively; a strong regional variant could possibly create a valid alternative to the alien prototype. A regional model might even, in time, establish itself with equal validity and ultimately independence. The provincial is hampered by its distance from its source; the regional is fertilized by its locale.

The Swiss linguist Ferdinand de Saussure distinguished between two basic modes of human communication. The first he termed *langue,* or language, a system of utterances based on an arbitrary connection between the phonic sign and its referent.[21] A language constitutes a system of generalized linguistic conventions in such a form that all its speakers may understand the grammar and vocabulary they hold in common. Language is shared by society as a whole. *Parole,* or speech, on the other hand, is personal and devised by the individual. In some ways we could say that *parole* is to *langue* as the regional may be to the parent idea: as speech reflects the individual reading of the language, the regional garden may reflect more general landscape design idea. The interplay between *langue* and *parole* guarantees that each speaker of the language may create utterances

[21] F. de Saussure, *Course in General Linguistics,* trans. W. Baskin, New York, 1966.

19

13. Drottningholm Palace, Sweden. Nicodemus Tessin the Younger, 1662–86. The gardens at Drottningholm modify the French formal idea to Swedish geological and climatic conditions

that have never been so formed previously and yet would be mutually intelligible nonetheless. It is true, however, that there can also be an indigenous regional expression, although today this would assume that there was virtually no contact with sources beyond the local. In spite of that qualification, it is possible to have a particular phenomenon affected by a broader trend rather than vice versa; indeed, this may be the manner in which ideas of regional origin become more influential through wide distribution.

In some ways the relationship between language and speech parallels the relationship between a parent language and its dialects, which are local or regional variations. At first, slang or elements of a particularized vocabulary might enter the language through carelessness or habit. But over time, assuming sufficient distance from the parent tongue, a dialect develops variations in pronunciation, grammar, and at times, even basic structure—although this is usually the last to appear. At some point, a new language emerges, related to the parent but sufficiently different from it to warrant an identity as a new "language." The family of Latin-derived Romance languages is our most familiar example.

One can also find similar—though not coincidental—patterns in the origins of certain garden design. One must say similar because it is possible for identical environmental and horticultural conditions and technological procedures to nurture to similar forms although the cultures maintain no contact. Or they can be substantially modified by their interaction with an alien context—to the point that they may almost be considered a

14. Vizcaya, Miami, Florida, 1914. F. Burrell Hoffman, architect; Diego Suarez, landscape architect. An Italianate-French formal style adapted to the mangrove swamp and the hot humid climate of south Florida

new "language." Witness, for example, the borrowing of the French formal model—accompanied by various Italian influences—in such diverse locations as Drottningholm in Sweden (Fig. 13) and Vizcaya in Miami (Fig. 14). The respective designers, Nicodemus Tessin the Younger and Diego Suarez found their inspiration, at least to some degree, in the work of French landscape designers such as Le Nôtre and those of Renaissance Italy. While gardens share a common formal ordering, each was modified by site conditions: the Swedish granite bedrock that admitted changes in ground plane only by fill, or the limits imposed by the mangrove swamp on Biscayne Bay. The product of this give and take between formal ideal and local conditions contributed to the making of a hybrid—regionalized, if not completely regional—garden form that still bears a genetic resemblance to its parent.

In recent years, the notion of regionalism, and even a *critical* regionalism has come to occupy a prominent place in architectural discourse. That a building should reflect or comment upon its particular place in time and space is seen as a means of mitigating the homogenizing force of technology and corporate capitalism. By accepting a national or international idea and adapting it to its place, a dialogue is established between the micro- and macrocosms in which we dwell. The claim is that this will help root the human being in a particular place.[22]

[22] See K. Frampton, "Towards a Critical Regionalism: Six Points for an Architecture of Resistance," in H. Foster, ed., *The Anti-Aesthetic: Essays on Post-Modern Culture*, Port Townsend, Wash., 1983.

Read it

MARC TREIB

The architectural critic Kenneth Frampton has proposed that the purpose of regional architecture is to provide a critique of the international tendencies that spread, leveling differences, almost as an epidemic across the world. "Architecture can only be sustained today as a critical practice," Frampton writes, "if it assumes an *arrière-garde* position, that is to say, one which distances itself equally from the Enlightenment myth of progress and from a reactionary, unrealistic impulse to return to the architectonic forms of the preindustrial past. . . . It is my contention that only an *arrière-garde* has the capacity to cultivate a resistant, identity-giving culture while at the same time having discreet recourse to universal technique."[23] The architect thus sees the international idea from the perspective of the region; local forces—be they climate, topography, architectural tradition, and even culture—inform and influence the imported idea and re-form it to suit the regional culture and the particular conditions of the site. Thus, it is through the act of questioning that a critical regionalism emerges.

Of course, one can question whether criticism should be a conscious and/or central concern of environmental design in general, and architecture in particular. Vernacular traditions, for example, are rarely critical, and yet few would dismiss their status as viable modes to accommodate living and work. Landscape architecture, on the other hand, can hardly avoid engaging its site at a very profound level. While the basic elements of landscape design may be vegetation, landform, and site materials such as rock and water, the exigencies of temperature, soil conditions, exposure, rainfall, wind, and a host of other factors will direct the formulation of vocabulary to a strong degree. Even the most alien design idea must necessarily adapt to its particular site conditions, and will thus inform—if not openly critique—the relationship of that local variant to the more general concept, and at times can actually spawn a new idiom. Using this framework, one could view the modernist California garden as a regional entity, embodying the three components of social, spatial, and architectural currents taking root in a specific climate, topography, and era.

Although design ideas may originate precisely from a particular place and time, most are transmitted and transformed over a broad geographic area far beyond the borders of the region, a tendency augmented by the increase in print and electronic media in the last forty years. Those aesthetic trends that influenced the modern California garden derived from two basic sources: European Modernist architecture and the art currents of cubism and surrealism. These ideas, however, were transmogrified, adapted, and enriched by the California setting, and the very fact that landscape architecture is at base an ecological practice utilizing living materials. While these ideas informed modern landscape architecture throughout Europe and the United States, the lifestyle and climate of California directly influenced the allowable plantings, making the resulting gardens regional.

[23] K. Frampton, "Place-Form and Cultural Identity," in J. Thackera, ed., *Design After Modernism*, New York, 1988, 20.

THE MODERN(IST) GARDEN IN CALIFORNIA

One could speculate that theory about the form that landscape architecture takes has lagged well behind those in the arts and architecture because landscape is seen primarily as a physical amenity rather than as an artistic medium. That five trees soften the confines of a backyard or add to the vista or improve the play space appears to be irreproachable. Although the selection of plant species reflects regional as well as personal preferences, the formal relationship of those trees or the particular species chosen seem less important to all but those most informed about design or horticultural matters. Only in the architectural armature—the walls, the fountains, the paving materials, etc.— would it appear that we find much of an argument for a particular style or even stylistic development in general. This could be the reason that the most extreme expressions of garden art are often the most architectural.

The argument for modern landscape design lagged decades behind the argument for a modern architecture, and through the 1930s, landscape architecture in California drew primarily on the Spanish and Italianate traditions for the design of major estates, and the English landscape garden and cottage garden for park and small residential design respectively. In architecture, as early as 1923, in *Towards a New Architecture*, Le Corbusier had claimed that building must respect and reflect the technological advances of the era. For these, neither the Beaux-Arts civic edifice nor the ecclesiastical Gothic were acceptable models. Today, wrote Le Corbusier, one must look instead to the ocean liner and the airplane for viable sources.[24] Architecture must address the evolving social patterns as well as the new technology and materials. In response to these constraints, Le Corbusier formulated his five points for the new architecture, among them the roof terrace that would return to human utility the ground displaced by the building's footprint. As to the form of the landscape, however, the architect was strangely mute. Instead of shaped landscape, natural greenery was treated almost as an abstract condition rather than an actuality; trees and vegetation became the buffer between buildings rather than their extensions or the links between them.[25]

Le Corbusier's proposal of the open plan, that is, a structural network of concrete columns and slabs that allowed the erasure of the hard edges of rooms, evidenced the Modernist concern for space. While the Villa Savoye of 1929—with its free plan, its light ground story of columns, its roof terrace, and free handling of stair and ramp circulation—became, in time, the archetype of Modernist villa, it sat on the meadow as an inert object disengaged from its landscape. Its ribbon windows and composed wall openings framed views of the landscape as if to create a new interpretation of the picturesque.

On the other hand, it was Mies van der Rohe's German Pavilion for the 1929 Barcelona exhibition that became the archetype of the new *spatial* conception between interior

---

[24] Le Corbusier was enamored with the modern machine, but he also devoted his attention to the standard object and its straightforward attitude toward function and form. Beneath a photo of the ocean liner *Aquitania*, he wrote: "The same aesthetic as your English pipe, your office furniture, your limousine," it should be extended to contemporary architecture as well (*Vers une architecture*, 1923; repr. Paris, 1977, 74).

[25] See D. Imbert, *The Modernist Garden in France*, New Haven, 1993.

15. German Pavilion, World Exposition, Barcelona, Spain, 1929 (reconstructed, 1986). Mies van der Rohe, architect. In time this pavilion became the idealized model for inter-penetrating spaces and the linkage between interior and exterior spaces

and exterior (Fig. 15). The building was intended to serve only ceremonial purposes, and free of functional necessity, its architect could approach its design almost as an abstract composition, with planes modulating spaces treated as a continuum. Wall and ceiling planes do not terminate in corners but overlap in space. Emphasizing the plane rather than the mass, and reducing the number of firm corners, the architect has effectively effaced the distinction between interior room and exterior courtyard.

When Modernist architecture arrived in Southern California, it had already lost a considerable portion of its social ideology, becoming in the process more of a body of formal knowledge than a political vehicle. In Europe, Modernism was intended—perhaps in a hopelessly utopian way—as a means for social improvement, both physical and psychological. Certainly, the air and light and greenery called for in Le Corbusier's program for a new urbanism were already found in great abundance. Frank Lloyd Wright was one of the first celebrated modern architects to build in the Los Angeles basin, and he seemed charmed by the environment and the prevailing Spanish myths. The Millard House of 1923 (Fig. 16), the prototype of his concrete block houses, was itself almost a single cell and balcony, but the architect's development of the natural ravine into a sequence of interlocking spaces displayed a remarkable working of the exterior spaces that extended from the central block of the house. Wright's sprawling Barnsdall House of 1920 (Fig. 17) bowed to Mayan precedent in its architectural sheath,

16. La Miniatura (Millard House),
Pasadena, California, 1923.
Frank Lloyd Wright, architect.
This small house of orna-
mented concrete block em-
braces the bowl of the ravine
for privacy and serenity

17. Hollyhock House (Barnsdall House), Los Angeles, California, early 1920s. Frank
Lloyd Wright, architect. The U-shaped plan of the house encloses a courtyard which
gives onto a shallow amphitheater sliced into the hillside

but in its disposition on the site, its series of enclosed courts and semi-circular "amphitheater," and later pergolas and water courses, the house embraced Olive Hill in a manner that effectively wed building to the contour and olive grove of the hillside.

The pergola and children's pool at Hollyhock House were not designed by Frank Lloyd Wright, however, but by two talented Austrian architects, Rudolph M. Schindler and Richard Neutra, who had only recently arrived on the West Coast. In spite of his great architectural accomplishments, Wright would always remain with one foot in the nineteenth century. It was Schindler who opened the interior spaces of the dwelling, and Neutra who completed its spatial integration with the exterior, creating both the opportunity and the necessity of a landscape designed in accord with the Modernist ethic. These would serve as the prototype for the Modernist house in Southern California.

Schindler had come to the United States with hopes of working for Wright, and he remained at Wright's California office when the master left for Japan to build the Imperial Hotel. After the inevitable falling out with Wright, Schindler established an independent practice. From his earliest works, including the twin houses for the Schindler and Chase families in 1922, he engaged the landscape as an active participant in the architectural entity (Fig. 18). Schindler wrote that "Joining the outdoors with the indoors spatially to satisfy a new attitude toward nature and movement cannot be achieved by merely increasing the size of conventional wall openings."[26] Instead, each of the living spaces is completed by a corresponding garden space defined by hedges and a sunken panel; each is given both an indoor and an outdoor fireplace that completes the linkage between house and garden.

As a young man, Richard Neutra had studied garden design in Austria, training which instilled a sensitivity toward nature and the biological metaphor in his design philosophy. Neutra's work from the 1930s on brought architecture resolutely into the twentieth century. Utilizing the steel frame and large panes of fixed or sliding glass only recently made available, Neutra continued—or brought to a logical conclusion—Wright's destruction of the box. Corners were made to disappear through sheets of glass; roof planes and flooring extended outward to disguise the actual line of closure (Fig. 19); planting was brought into the house and the house into the planting. His 1951 apologia, *Mysteries and Realities of the Site,* states that the site "is one miraculous entity. What a site produces on our total being is, in fact, a *combined total impact.*"[27] In his "House in the Wooded Foothills," "[n]o corner post is needed, so the only visible division between indoors and out is the subtle sheen" of the glass sheet.[28] In his work one finds the fusion of interior and exterior characteristic of the new spatial matrix, although in most cases, developers would tame the austerity of high modernism with the image of the ranch house and the use of wood.

Arts and Architecture magazine, under the editorship of John Entenza, also exerted a

---

[26] E. McCoy, *Five California Architects,* New York, 158.
[27] R. Neutra, *Mysteries and Realities of the Site,* Scarsdale, New York, 1951.
[28] Ibid.

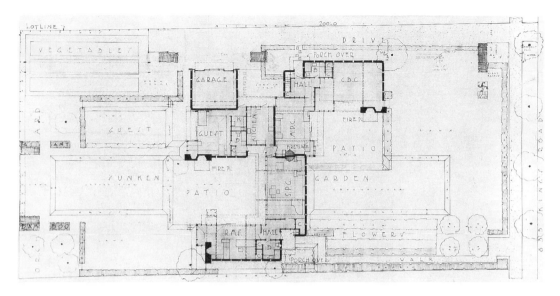

18. Plan, Schindler House, Los Angeles, California, 1922. R. M. Schindler, architect. Each of the living areas of the house is complemented by a banked, sunken patio lined with hedges—extending the realm of the dwelling spaces outdoors (photo: Art Museum, University of California, Santa Barbara)

19. Moore House, Ojai, California, 1952. Richard Neutra, architect. Large glass windows, an extended structural frame, and overhanging roof planes dissolve the boundary between the house and the landscape

20. Eames House (Case Study House No. 8), Pacific Palisades, California, 1949. Charles and Ray Eames, architects. The linear organization of the house derives from the existing row of eucalyptus trees and the slope of the adjacent hillside

considerable influence on the acceptance of new idioms during the late 1940s and 1950s (Fig. 20). The magazine's Case Study House program, initiated in 1948, argued for a modern architecture and landscape in accord with contemporary society and technology.[29] These projects were intended as object lessons that would illustrate what could be accomplished in the Modernist idiom. In these houses, the structure was frankly exposed, and enlarged areas of window glass opened the interior spaces to the yard and garden. As published in the magazine, the drawings for each of the exhibition structures often included at least a schematic presentation of the garden spaces that would extend the interior domain, treating inside and out as a nearly seamless entity. Beyond basic functional areas such as the drying yard or the vegetable garden, space was treated fluidly, erasing the divisions between rooms such as kitchen, living, and dining. In many of the houses, architecture and landscape complemented one another, with screen walls

[29] See E. McCoy, *Modern California Houses: Case Study Houses 1945–1962*, New York, 1962; and *Blueprints for Modern Living: History and Legacy of the Case Study Houses*.

28

extending from the house that grasped bits of space or vegetation. In many of the schemes, the barbecue was a prominent feature of the yard, more an "outdoor living space" than a "garden." Swimming pools were beyond the means of some of the intended clients, but ornamental pools in the work of Neutra, Julius Davidson, and Whitney Smith helped extend the house into the landscape, the interior to the exterior, using the continuous floor plane as the primary visual link. Roofed loggias, paving materials, and patterns used on both interior and exterior furthered the merging of inside and out, and effaced the distinct edge between architecture and garden.

The most radical of the Case Study proposals, the Greenbelt House (Figs. 21, 22) by Ralph Rapson, however, was left unbuilt. A linear garden remained in the center of the home while bifurcating the living zone from the bedroom wing in this extreme example of the popular bi-nuclear plan.[30] Rapson's intentions may be read in the accompanying sketches: the layout of the house allows the child to play under supervision, but the wife manages the home. The appearance of a helicopter suggests that this is the home of the future, but that assigned social roles will remain constant. Although never realized, and regressive in its social vision, Rapson's design addressed the use of space on the suburban lot and the relative functions of architecture and landscape architecture as the vehicles for living. The typical suburban tract home was a house-as-island, surrounded by minimal plots comprising a ceremonial front lawn, narrow, leftover side yards, and a rear yard for the family's use. In contrast, Rapson's garden or greenbelt space would simultaneously join and separate the two wings of the house. Even the name of the project derives from its attitude toward landscape.

What distinguishes each of these Case Study houses and landscapes is not only their uncompromising modernity but their regard for social concerns and the acceptance of the nuclear family. That the house and garden were settings for life is also evidenced in the writings of Thomas Church, the senior figure in modern California landscape architecture. A prolific author, Church wrote for professional journals as well as the popular press, including a series of columns for the *San Francisco Chronicle*. In *Gardens Are for People* [1955] and *Your Private World* [1969], he told potential clients to tell the landscape architect just what they wanted.[31] Form derived from the accommodation of the program; no two gardens should even look alike, he wrote, but should reflect the particulars of the clients and the site.

Despite Church's social orientation, the hundreds of gardens that he designed and built during his long career rely on relatively consistent design ideas. While the particular style could vary from a straightforward almost non-descript vocabulary, Church also

[30] The bi-nuclear scheme was a popular planning idea in the late 1950s and early 1960s. The plan was arranged as a basic H, with entry into the cross-bar. One wing was usually devoted to more public spaces like the kitchen, living and dining rooms; the bedrooms comprised the other wing.

[31] "In any age of reason, it is the owner who finally decides the size of his garden and the purposes for which it shall be used. He analyzes what he really wants as disassociated from what he *ought* to have. Assuming he stays within the vague bounds of good taste, he *can* have just what he wants." T. Church, *Gardens Are for People*, New York, 1955, 2. See also T. Church, *Your Private World*, San Francisco, 1969.

21. Greenbelt House (Case Study House No. 4; unrealized), 1945. Ralph
Rapson, architect. In this scheme, an enframed landscaped zone joined
the two wings of the house (photo: Art Museum, University of California, Santa Barbara)

22. Greenbelt House (Case Study House No. 4; unrealized), 1945. Ralph Rapson, architect. A stone wall
screens the family from its neighbors, allowing visually open walls of shaded glass (photo: Art Museum, University of California, Santa Barbara)

drew upon the latest ideas drawn from the worlds of art and architecture. More commonly, however, the modernity of his designs was not assertive. In the garden for the Henderson Residence (late 1950s) in Hillsborough (Figs. 23, 24), the swimming pool is used to establish a symmetrical armature that structures the overall composition. This formal axis extends perpendicularly to the house and aligns with a courtyard in the building's center. Less formal and more fully planted garden elements on either side of the pool maintain a sense of balance without resorting to symmetry. As a totality, the garden design derives from the tectonic structure of the house. And yet in the softening effect of the planting and the asymmetrical extension of the plan, any sense of a dry formality has been banished.

In other works, usually on tighter sites and tighter budgets, Church used landscape as the foil for the architecture: the sweeping curve building, enclosing a terrace and perhaps part of a lawn (Fig. 25). Enclosure by fence was somewhat inescapable in the suburbs, and Church cleverly showed how one could use the delimitation to advantage, screening while heightening the sense of what lies beyond. The raised planter wall might double as a seat; the zig-zag, the curve, the freely-handled pool were all trademarks that he manipulated to great aesthetic and functional effect.

How do these modern gardens in California relate to national or international ideas? As landscape architecture that utilized new ideas on space and formal vocabulary they were absolutely contemporary. Although their aesthetic vocabulary was heavily influenced at the outset by the work of French "cubist" designers such as Pierre-Émile Legrain, André Vera, and Gabriel Guevrekian (Fig. 26), they ultimately took their spatial concerns from Modernist architecture.[32] The connection between indoor and outdoor sought by the Modernist architects required a response in the landscape. But Californian garden designs rarely exhibited the severity of their European counterparts. There is also a muted tone to much of the work that suggests a Japanese influence, not only in the natural materials used in many of these gardens, but also in the basic spatial sensibility and the suggestion of the human relation to nature.

After graduation from the University of California at Berkeley, Garrett Eckbo first worked in a nursery in Southern California designing gardens for small sites on low budget; he attended graduate school at Harvard thereafter. In a self-generated study published in *Pencil Points* in 1937, Eckbo proposed eighteen contiguous gardens that comprised a single urban block (Fig. 27).[33] The design of each garden varies from the geometric to the curvilinear, the basically flat to those that exploit contour. These studies suggest the parent "language" of Modernism that would be "regionalized" during

[32] Acting as a critic, landscape architect Fletcher Steele reported on recent developments in France in his important essay "New Pioneering in Landscape Design," *Landscape Architecture* 20 (April 1930). Early in his career, Garrett Eckbo traced over a photo of Pierre-Émile Legrain's Tachard garden, its zig-zag edge became a recurring motif in the Californian's designs. See D. Imbert, "A Model for Modernism: The Work and Influence of Pierre-Émile Legrain," in M. Treib, ed., *Modern Landscape Architecture: A Critical Review*, Cambridge, Mass., 1993.

[33] G. Eckbo, "Small Gardens in the City," *Pencil Points* (September 1937).

23. Henderson Residence, Hillsborough, California, 1959. Thomas Church, landscape architect. The swimming pool, set perpendicularly to the plane of the facade, aligns with the internal courtyard and extends the axis into the garden

24. Henderson Residence, Hillsborough, California, 1959. Thomas Church, landscape architect. The view from the covered porch into the garden

25. De Bretteville garden, Woodside, California, ca. 1950. Thomas Church, landscape architect. Where the site allowed—or dictated—Church incorporated existing vegetation such as this California live oak into his garden design

26. Garden, Villa Noailles, Hyères, France, 1927 (re-constructed, 1990). Gabriel Guevrekian, architect. The most extreme, and perhaps the most influential, of the gardens executed in the "cu-bistic" manner

33

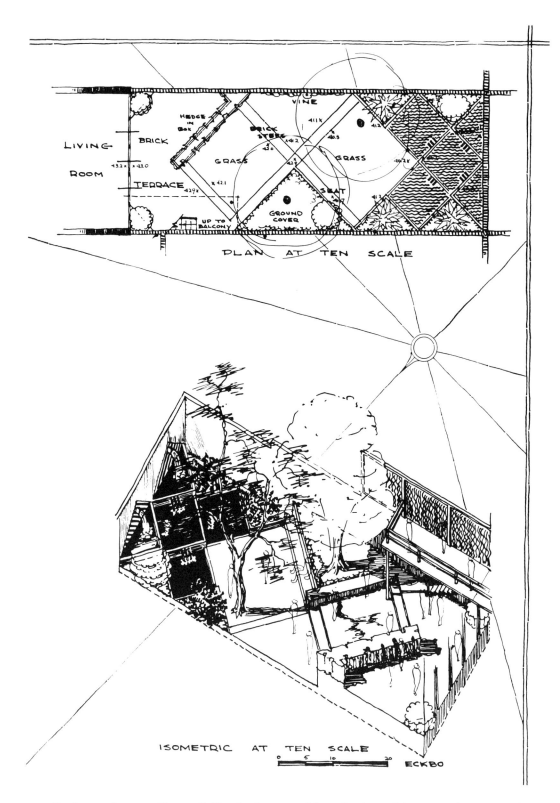

LIVING
ROOM

PLAN AT TEN SCALE

ISOMETRIC AT TEN SCALE

0 5 10 20

ECKBO

27. Garden study, 1937. Garrett Eckbo, landscape architect. In these eighteen garden proposals used to illustrate his article, Eckbo laid out a landscape vocabulary that he would develop for almost fifty years (photo: from G. Eckbo, "Small Gardens in the City," *Pencil Points* [September 1937])

28. Sudarsky House, Bakersfield, California, late 1950s. Garrett Eckbo, landscape architect. The swimming pool as the feature of the rear garden (photo: George Reineking; courtesy of Garrett Eckbo)

Eckbo's long and prolific career (Fig. 28). Like the Church vocabulary, elements of Eckbo's designs were popularized and adopted in backyards and gardens throughout California postwar suburbia. It is interesting to note that within twenty years, popular home journals had adopted most of the modernist precepts as gospel. *Sunset* magazine's *Landscaping for Modern Living,* for example, offered as its preface: "The idea is this: Landscaping offers a way to take the house and garden, building materials and plant materials, the open sky and the stars at night, and blend them all to create a deeply satisfying space for everyday living (Figs. 29, 30)."[34] The gap between High Style and popular gardening had been all but eliminated.

Eckbo became the most prominent modern landscape architect in Southern California, representing the new type of landscape designer emerging during the late 1940s

[34] Editors of *Sunset* magazine, *Landscaping for Modern Living,* Menlo Park, Calif., 1956, no pages given.

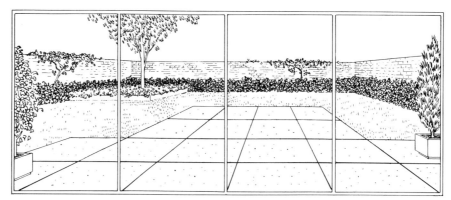

Some think of the floor of a large patio as being by necessity a cold expanse of masonry

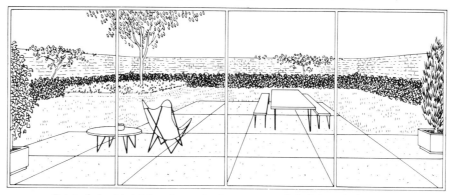

But, partly furnished, it loses its austerity, becomes a part of the indoors, invites you out

People are furnishings, too. They complete the picture—as important to design as plants

29. The link between the interior and exterior (photo: from *Landscaping for Modern Living*, 1956; courtesy of Lane Publishing Company)

and 1950s (Fig. 31). As the creator of over a thousand gardens large and small, Eckbo focused his efforts on the spatial development of the lot as a whole, merging inside and out, fully exploiting the California climate. In most of his schemes, one can clearly perceive the full extent of the site, as Eckbo realized that to subdivide what was already limited space would further reduce the apparent size of the site and its volume. Plants, he declared, should be used to exploit their particular forms and growth characteristics,

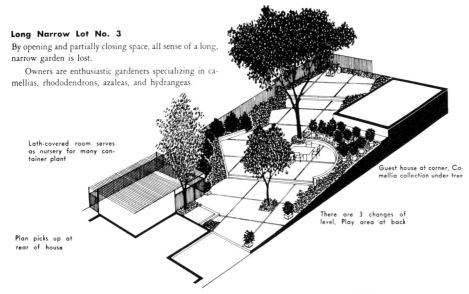

Long Narrow Lot No. 3

By opening and partially closing space, all sense of a long, narrow garden is lost.

Owners are enthusiastic gardeners specializing in camellias, rhododendrons, azaleas, and hydrangeas.

Lath-covered room serves as nursery for many container plant

Plan picks up at rear of house

Guest house at corner, Camellia collection under tree

There are 3 changes of level. Play area at back

30. "Long Narrow Lot No. 3." These series of aerial views presented alternate approaches to the design of lots of differing proportions. The concerns of leading landscape architects were assimilated relatively quickly and popularized through books and magazines such as *Sunset* (photo: from *Landscaping for Modern Living*, 1956; courtesy of Lane Publishing Company)

31. Zimmerman House, Los Angeles, California, late 1950s. Garrett Eckbo, landscape architect. Typically of the postwar Southern California suburban house, the patio extends the living zone of the interior (photo: Julius Shulman; courtesy of Garrett Eckbo)

37

32. Alcoa Forecast Garden (Eckbo Residence), Los Angeles, California, 1958. Garrett Eckbo, landscape architect. Eckbo's experimentation with aluminum is found in overhead grilles, vertical
screens, and the garden fountain (photo: Garrett Eckbo and the
Aluminum Company of America)

and only where spatial enclosure was necessary should they be used in masses.[35] Eckbo
also experimented with new materials, and his most curious exercise in the style was the
modifications to his own garden in Los Angeles sponsored by Alcoa Aluminum, in which
the metal was used for vertical and horizontal screens—and even a fountain (Figs. 32,
33). Most striking about these designs is their use of space as the basic element, creating
a somewhat architectural framework that in many cases would eventually be subsumed
by vegetation. In other instances, a metal screen, exposed masonry wall, or wooden fence
visually extended the zone of the house, while effecting a play of light and shadow. Plants
were used as forms in their own right, and as complements to the architectonics of con-

[35] "Every plant is a specimen, placed where it can develop to the fullest, set in architecture, yet domi-
nating, softening, and loosening the construction lines." Eckbo, "Small Gardens in the City," 574. The ideas
were subsequently developed in Eckbo's *Landscape for Living*, New York, 1950.

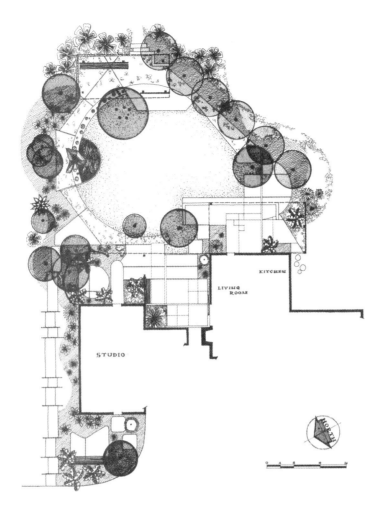

33. Plan, Alcoa Forecast Garden (Eckbo Residence), Los Angeles, California, 1958. Garrett Eckbo, landscape architect

struction. Lawn areas are kept to a minimum (Fig. 34). These concerns—for space, for sympathetic planting, for the contemporary lifestyle, for a modern aesthetic vocabulary—were central to formulating the modern California garden as a regional expression.

Of all California gardens in the modern idiom, Thomas Church's 1948 Donnell garden has become the hallmark (Fig. 35). One reason, and probably the principal reason, is Church's use of biomorphic forms that are read immediately as modern, giving their affinity to the shapes of Jean Arp, Joan Miró, and Isamu Noguchi in art, and those of Le Corbusier and Alvar Aalto—among others—in architecture.[36] But the Donnell garden is also quintessentially Californian in other respects, including those four aspects concerning regionality outlined in the course of this paper. For one, the garden is primarily

[36] See M. Treib, "Axioms for a Modern Landscape Architecture," in *Modern Landscape Architecture.*

34. Garden for The Palo Alto, Palo Alto, California, early 1960s. Robert Royston, landscape architect. In its free shapes, choice of plant materials, and concerns for use, this garden is a nearly ideal example of the modern California landscape idiom (photo: courtesy Royston, Hanamoto, Beck and Abey)

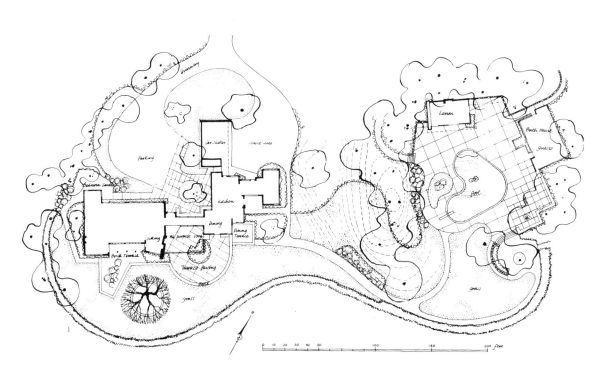

35. Site plan, Donnell garden, Sonoma County, California, 1948. Thomas Church, landscape architect. The house (left) was built several years after the patio and pool, linked by a serpentine hedge that outlines the contour (photo: Michael Laurie; courtesy of Grace Hall and Michael Laurie)

about a regionally directed use, that is, about living outdoors. The garden's construction on a site favored by the family for picnicking actually preceded that of the house to which it is adjacent rather than adjoining. The swimming pool is the focus of the garden's composition as the hearth might be to the home. A lanai serves as a small poolside living unit; and dressing rooms double as guest quarters. If one desired living in the benign outdoors of the Golden State, this garden would provide, both physically and psychologically, an ideal and idyllic setting (Fig. 36). Thus, the first two factors reflecting region, that of the social idea of the garden, and that of use, are well addressed.

In terms of plant materials, one finds a mixture of the native and the imported. Church began with an acknowledgment of the existing pattern of grass-covered hillsides and the stands of California live oaks which provided the structure for the layout. To these, however, were added a line of Monterey cypresses, juniper hedges, bougainvillea, festuca grasses, and simple grass lawns, striking a balance between indigenous ecology and horticultural importation. And finally, in its very biomorphic and constructivist idioms, the Donnell garden suggests the adaptation of a formal vocabulary derived from modern art and architecture, seen as fresh and contemporary, although its inspiration is said to have been the river meanders that feed San Francisco Bay. While spatial develop-

36. Donnell garden, Sonoma County, California, 1948. Thomas Church, landscape architect. The pool with its sculpture by Adaline Kent

37. Donnell garden, Sonoma County, California, 1948. Thomas Church, landscape architect. View from the house toward the pool garden

ments are present in the Donnell design, these are of less consequence than those in the best of Eckbo's work. Instead, like two friends standing side-by-side admiring the view, the house and the garden share the hilltop as adjacent elements, components of one entity. The relationship of garden to house is, to some degree, like that of the Kent garden at Rousham, England, to its historical manor. But the pieces of the Donnell garden are woven more resolutely together by the serpentine hedge and the informal promenade, and the routes by which one may traverse the garden are many—a far more modern structuring of garden space than the preferred linear route of the English landscape garden (Fig. 37).

Looking at the Donnell garden, then, one can see a truly modern garden; one that well represents Roberto Burle Marx's definition of a garden as nature reformed by man for man.[37] But it also well illustrates our evolving definition of regionalism. Regionalism, I have tried to explain, is not alone a concern for native ecology in a natural order, but a far more complex interplay of ecological, social, aesthetic, and functional issues that in their integrated totality provide us with a sense of their geographic region and our place within it.

[37] Although not exactly quoted in this article, see R. Burle Marx, "A Garden Style in Brazil to Meet Contemporary Needs," *Landscape Architecture* 44 (July 1954), for the landscape architect's presentation of his approach to making gardens.

Making Gardens in the Athens of the West: Bernard Maybeck and the San Francisco Bay Region Tradition in Landscape and Garden Design

DIANNE HARRIS

In his 1893 essay, *The Significance of the Frontier in American History,* Frederick Jackson Turner asserted that the key ingredient in the establishment of a unique American cultural identity was the existence of the frontier landscape. Turner's frontier hypothesis, which has reached near legendary status amongst scholars of American Studies who continue to debate its merits, asserted that a type of metabolic change occurs at the frontier on what he called "the savage and the cultured" such that the former gives way to the latter with this process becoming the significant fact in American history. The process, he wrote, is one of "Americanization" that freed the pioneer from dependence upon Europe. The frontier essentially transformed the pioneer's old ways into new American ways, and "subduing nature became the American's manifest destiny."[1] This hypothesis theorized an American identity completely separate from European roots—an entire country with characteristics sufficiently distinct that a new culture could emerge from its landscape; a new, wild landscape that became known as the far western frontier.

Turner's hypothesis continues to be controversial in American Studies due, at least in part, to what many perceive to be an oversimplified thesis that tries to explain American development solely in terms of Western environmental influence. However, I believe the premise can be applied at a smaller scale as a way of understanding regionalism in California, which was the final western frontier, the land that was considered, even as late as 1902, to be "the edge of the world."[2] By looking closely at the works of one man, the

Acknowledgments: The author owes a debt of gratitude to Marc Treib for his insightful comments and editorial wisdom and wishes to thank Dell Upton who was instrumental in determining the direction of the research on this topic in its early phases. Thanks also to John Dixon Hunt and Therese O'Malley for comments on earlier drafts.

[1] F. J. Turner, *The Significance of the Frontier in American History,* edited with an introduction by H. P. Simonson, New York, 1963, 9.

[2] Turner's hypothesis came under serious attack in the 1930s when some historians began to challenge his isolationist theory, which denied the influence of European culture on American democratic develop-

1. Bernard Ralph Maybeck, no date (photo: Documents Collection, College of Environmental Design, University of California, Berkeley)

San Francisco Bay Area architect Bernard Ralph Maybeck (Fig. 1), and at the influences that contributed to his work, we can see that Turner's hypothesis, with all of its flaws, may partially explain regional design in California. In fact, Maybeck's landscape style represents a manifestation of Turner's frontier hypothesis and the attitude toward nature it embodies in its synthesis of the natural landscape and the culture of turn-of-the-century California.

Maybeck's architectural work, which spans a fifty year period from 1892 to 1940, has long been associated with regionalism. His designs are considered by critics and historians to be among the most significant examples of what has become known as the first

ment. His thesis was also criticized for its assumption of a homogeneous American society which would be transformed by the frontier into "stereotyped Americans" (Simonson, 17). His hypothesis has also been seen as racist in its definition of free land in terms of savagery. But as William Cronon has recently made clear, Turner's hypothesis must be understood in context, such that "unexploited natural abundance" must be seen as the central meaning in Turner's frontier hypothesis. Cronon brilliantly explains this and other aspects of the American perception of the Great West in his book, *Nature's Metropolis: Chicago and the Great West,* New York, 1991, 46–54, 150, 424 nn. 8, 9. See also W. Cronon, "Turner's First Stand: The Significance of Significance in American History," in R. Etulain, ed., *Writing Western History: Essays on Classic Western Historians,* Albuquerque, 1991. See also R. Billington, *America's Frontier Heritage,* New York, 1966, and idem, *Frederick Jackson Turner,* New York, 1973. While scholars have recently attempted to analyze the forces at work in American culture that gave credence to the frontier myth and have attempted to uncover the power structure that benefited from the proliferation of the idea of the frontier, such analysis is beyond the scope of this paper. Instead, I am using Turner's hypothesis as a kind of measuring device against which the California scene can be examined within the larger context of American studies. See also, G. Burgess, "On the Edge of the World," *Sunset,* August 1902, 233–34.

44

Bay Region tradition.[3] Yet little has been said about the correspondingly strong tradition in landscape and garden design. By looking at Maybeck's landscape projects and at the work of the Bay Area cultural leaders who influenced him, it becomes clear that a shared, idealized vision of California as a Mediterranean paradise bound this group together, and that Maybeck helped establish an approach to house and garden design that paved the way for Thomas Church and Garrett Eckbo in the next generation. Maybeck was certainly not alone in creating a Bay Region approach to landscape design; with him were architects Willis Polk, Julia Morgan, Charles and Henry Greene, and landscape architects John McLaren, John Gregg, and several others. But Maybeck's work provides one of the most consistent examples of integrated architecture and landscape; an integration that is a key ingredient in the regional tradition.

Bernard Maybeck's architecture must be discussed in relation to his contemporaries—an intriguing group whose lives were affected by the Northern California landscape and by the booster mentality of an emerging geographical power center and who, in turn, helped form the basis for cultural life in the Bay Area at the turn of the century. To call this group a circle of friends would be inaccurate. The exact relationship among this group of artists, naturalists, designers, and spiritual leaders remains uncertain. It was, as Richard Longstreth has pointed out, a fluctuating group; but it is certain that some cross-fertilization occurred among individuals such as writer/naturalist/Sierra Club founder John Muir; poet and naturalist Charles Keeler; painters/publishers/craftsmen Arthur and Lucia Mathews; William Keith, a very successful landscape painter and one of the first artists to capture the Yosemite on canvas; and finally, the Swedenborgian Minister and architectural hobbyist Joseph Worcester, who influenced a generation of architects and artists (Fig. 2).[4] Through their collective works, this eclectic group fostered the romanticized and largely factitious nineteenth-century ideal of Northern California as an arcadian land of plenty. With endless comparisons to the landscapes of Italy and Greece, their Mediterranean visions, while often based more in fantasy than in fact, found direct physical translation in the gardens and landscapes designed by Maybeck. While the vision has been an enduring one, it has not proven to be ecologically sustainable as the current drought and consequent water shortage in the state have made clear. If California is an arcadia, it is an unpredictable one, in which metaphoric rivers of milk, honey, and wine may flow, but where actual rivers of water are neither reliable nor abundant. While Turner himself acknowledged that the scarcity of water on the far western frontier would necessitate a different social and political order than that found on eastern frontiers, the image of bountiful California prevailed.[5] As such, the California/Mediterra-

---

[3] For more on the Bay Region tradition in architecture, see S. Woodbridge, ed., *Bay Area Houses*, Salt Lake City, 1988; R. Longstreth, *On the Edge of the World*, Cambridge, Mass., 1983; E. McCoy, *Five California Architects*, Los Angeles, 1960. There are many other sources, some of which are cited in the notes of this paper, but these three represent a good starting point.

[4] R. Longstreth, *On the Edge of the World: Ernest Coxhead and Willis Polk in San Fransisco during the 1890's*, Ph.D. diss., University of California, Berkeley, 1977, chap. 8; Longstreth, *On the Edge*, 74.

[5] F. J. Turner, "Contributions of the West to American Democracy," *Atlantic Monthly*, 1903. Reprinted in R. Billington, ed., *The Frontier in American History*, New York, 1962, 258, 260, 279. The fact that the Mediterra-

2. Group photo, 1909. Standing, left to right: Charles Keeler, William Keith, Francis Brown (editor of the *Chicago Dial*). Seated, left to right: Naturalists John Muir and John Burroughs (photo: The Bancroft Library, University of California, Berkeley)

nean fantasy can be seen as a combination of civic boosterism intended to attract population and money, and the West Coast version of American pastoralism, that fictitious Jeffersonian-based myth that has plagued the American landscape for over two hundred years. While extremely powerful and enduring, landscape mythologies such as these are often highly detrimental to a region's ecology because they deny the realities of the environment, and foster an exploitive view of nature as commodity.[6]

nean metaphor has endured in California for so long and has prevailed with such currency owes something to both governmental and corporate power structures who stood to profit from the rapid settlement and large-scale agricultural development of the state, achieved through proliferation of the myth. Again, however, these issues are far too complex to be properly dealt with in this paper. For more on this see D. Worster, *Rivers of Empire*, New York, 1985, and M. Reisner, *Cadillac Desert*, New York, 1986.

[6] There are many excellent works that deal with this topic. Among them are Donald Worster's *Dust Bowl*, New York, 1979, and *Rivers of Empire: Water, Aridity and the Growth of the American West*, New York, 1985; William Cronon's *Changes in the Land: Indians, Colonists and the Ecology of New England*, New York, 1983; and Carolyn Merchant's *Ecological Revolutions: Nature, Gender, and Science in New England*, Chapel Hill, N.C., 1989. Henry Nash Smith wrote one of the seminal works on the American pastoral myth in his *Virgin Land: The American West as Symbol and Fiction*, Cambridge, Mass., 1950.

The origin of the pastoral fantasy that historian Kevin Starr has termed "the Mediterranean analogy," and that David Streatfield has called Arcadian California, can be traced to the mid-1800s, and serves as the source of much of the imagery used by Maybeck and his contemporaries.[7] In 1845, John Charles Fremont published his "Report of the Exploring Expedition to Oregon and Northern California," a document that contained extensive comparisons between California and Italy and that Starr considers to be "the founding text of the Mediterranean analogy."[8] These comparisons, based on similarities of landscape and climate, were compelling, developing over time into "a metaphor for all that California offered as a regional civilization. Suggesting new textures and values of living, California-as-Mediterranean challenged Americans to embrace beauty and to escape the Puritan past."[9] California was still the new frontier, and its inhabitants, particularly those with vested financial interests who would gain from the state's rapid settlement and development, needed to show the state to be on a cultural par with the rest of the country, specifically the East Coast. By comparing California to Italy and Greece, countries embodying the cultural achievements of the classical past, Fremont—and Maybeck and the Bay Regionalists fifty years later—claimed some of that cultural importance for themselves. So entrenched was Fremont in this California/Italian imagery, that he tried to create an Italian estate for himself in Mariposa, complete with Indian servants dressed as Italian peasants.[10] He modeled his home after an Italian villa and employed Frederick Law Olmsted, who was to succeed Fremont as manager of the Mariposa mining estate, as his landscape architect, creating together, a house that prefigured Bay Region architecture in its strong connection to the site and use of exposed wood.

Olmsted, who like Turner concerned himself with the effects of the frontier landscape on civilization, described the landscape near Bear Valley, California, as being similar to those he had seen in Italy.[11] His San Francisco Bay Area projects of the mid-1860s were significant in their attempt to find an appropriate regional response that embraced the semiarid environment, and for design solutions he recalled memories of Italian villas he had visited during a European tour.[12] His Stanford campus design of the 1890s shows the influence of those recollections. Olmsted may have been among the earliest to establish the idea that appropriate design for California was a blending of indoors and out.

[7] K. Starr, *Americans and the California Dream, 1815–1950*, New York, 1973, and D. Streatfield, "The Evolution of the Southern California Landscape: 1. Settling into Arcadia," *Landscape Architecture* 66 (January 1976), 39–46, 78; idem, "The Evolution of the California Landscape: 2. Arcadia Compromised," *Landscape Architecture* 66 (March 1976), 117–26, 170; idem, "The Evolution of the California Landscape: 3. The Great Promotions," *Landscape Architecture* 67 (May 1977), 229–39, 272; idem, "The Evolution of the California Landscape: 4. Suburbia at the Zenith," *Landscape Architecture* 67 (September 1977), 417–24.

[8] Starr, *California Dream*, 366.

[9] Ibid., 370.

[10] Ibid., 367.

[11] V. Post Ranney, ed., *The Papers of Frederick Law Olmsted, Vol. 5, The California Frontier 1863–1865*, Baltimore and London, 1990, 105, from letter to wife dated October 1863. See also Olmsted's essay, "Notes on the Pioneer Condition," also published in Vol. 5 of the Olmsted papers.

[12] Ibid., 451.

In a design for his unbuilt home at the Mariposa estate, he called for "deep piazzas or galleries with low shades" to allow for cooling ventilation, and for a "rough hewn character in outline and detail" to fit with the landscape and for the use of wood, which was plentiful and could provide "admirable lights and shadows." He wanted a "chalet" that looked at though it was "knocked up by some mountaineer with a genius . . ."[13]

Olmsted's description of his desired residence is notably similar to the home that John Muir built for himself in Yosemite Valley in 1869; a structure that was to become pivotal in the creation of the Bay Region style and would ultimately influence Maybeck's work, if only indirectly. Muir's Yosemite house, which no longer exists, was constructed entirely of wood, had a stream running through it and ferns growing through the floor. Though no photographs of Muir's Yosemite house have come to light, it was built adjacent to the Hutchings Hotel of the 1860s where Muir was a guest, and the hotel had an enormous cedar growing through the living room floor (Fig. 3). Muir's house, like the Hutchings Hotel, must have seemed remarkable in its time, and it made a strong impression on a man who was very much at the center of the influential Bay Area circle. His name was Joseph Worcester, cousin by marriage to Daniel Burnham, and a Swedenborgian minister with interests in architecture, design, and the arts, among other subjects.

Worcester was greatly influenced by the writings of John Ruskin and William Morris and has been credited with the importation of the Arts and Crafts movement to California.[14] While this may or may not be the case, Worcester did help promulgate the ideals of the movement in Northern California. In 1866, Worcester toured Yosemite with Muir and became enchanted with the cabin, deciding ultimately to build his 1876 house in the East Bay hills of Piedmont to be, like Muir's, "itself almost a thing of nature."[15] Based on Muir's model, Worcester constructed a small, shingled house which became the frequent gathering spot for many of the key figures in Bay Area design.[16] The cottage impressed Maybeck who befriended Worcester when the two men became neighbors. The Reverend Worcester's Piedmont garden was heavily planted with fruit trees, vines, and climbing roses that trailed up the sides of his cottage. Photographs and paintings show that the house had a strong connection to its surrounding landscape in its materials and colors as well as through its lushly planted garden. It is probable that Worcester's house, along with his Swedenborgian Church of the New Jerusalem in San Francisco with its unpeeled Madrone tree trunks supporting the ceiling and wild flowers, shrubbery, and tree branches hanging from the walls as decoration, came to exemplify for Maybeck the importance of architecture integrated with landscape and the attributes of bringing aspects of nature into buildings (Fig. 4).

One of the Reverend Worcester's closest friends and most devoted followers was the prominent Bay Area painter William Keith, whose paintings of the seasons of the Califor-

---

[13] Ibid., 110, 111.

[14] L. Mandelson Freudenheim and E. Sussman, *Building With Nature: Roots of the San Francisco Bay Region Tradition*, Salt Lake City, 1974, 7.

[15] Ibid., 11.

[16] Ibid., 12.

3. The "Big Tree Room" in the Hutchings Hotel, Yosemite Valley, California, ca. 1884 (photo: The Bancroft Library, University of California, Berkeley)

4. Interior of Joseph Worcester's Swedenborgian Church, San Francisco, California, 1894. A. Page Brown, architect (photo: Documents Collection, College of Environmental Design, University of California, Berkeley)

nia landscape still hang in the Swedenborgian church. Even if Keith had not been a close friend of Worcester, Maybeck would eventually have become acquainted with his work since both were members of the Bohemian Club where Keith's paintings were regularly exhibited.[17] Keith and Maybeck shared a common vision of the landscape: a vision that Keith recorded on canvas, and that Maybeck created in three dimensions in architecture and landscapes that led to a California version of the picturesque in landscape design. While the term "picturesque" has taken on multiple meanings and is, to an extent, a loaded term, I am using it here to mean landscape design that attempts to emulate the views portrayed by particular landscape painters.

William Keith was the leading painter in San Francisco for thirty years at the turn of the century, and like Worcester, was close to John Muir who took the painter on an early tour of Yosemite, allowing him to become one of the first artists to portray that wilderness. Keith's paintings portrayed the grand scenery of the West, so newly discovered, and so important in establishing California as a force to be reckoned with, challenging Europe's exclusive claim on "culture."

Several parallels can be drawn between Keith and Maybeck, aside from the fact that the two were often mistaken for each other, having similar physical characteristics.[18] Keith evolved from a "painter of outward facts, a giver of information, to a creator of the spiritual often mystical, moods" that were later to become so important to Maybeck's work as demonstrated by the Palace of Fine Arts, a place primarily intended to evoke moods of sadness softened by beauty.[19] Keith often used a quiet body of water in his paintings to serve as a mirror to reflect the landscape above (Fig. 5).[20] Similarly, Maybeck used water to reflect the sky and the colors of his architecture and landscapes, as demonstrated by both the Palace of Fine Arts and his Oakland Packard Showroom (Figs. 6, 7). So important was the relationship of this auto showroom to the water that in determining its color, Maybeck positioned himself in a boat on adjacent Lake Merrit, and from this vantage point, decided the final color of the building based on its reflection in the lake. There are also strong similarities in the style of Maybeck's rendering techniques and Keith's painted portrayals, particularly apparent in the delineation of oaks, a favorite subject for both men (Figs. 8, 9). This pictorial comparison may at first seem superficial, but it shows the influence on the architect of local painters like Keith. Maybeck incorporated Keith's techniques and subject matter into his architectural studies and renderings and later attempted to create those idealized landscapes in three dimensions. The result was a facet of the regional landscape style that I term the California Picturesque.

Maybeck was often literal in his pictorial approach; his renderings frequently utilize a view of a garden taken through an architectural frame (Fig. 10). In the Senger House of 1907, the architect permanently attached a painting that depicts a view of several redwoods, to the wall of a dining alcove by making the frame a part of the wall. The

---

[17] E. Neuhaus, *William Keith: The Man and the Artist,* Berkeley, 1938, 66.
[18] Brother F. Cornelius, *Keith, Old Master of California,* New York, 1942, 234.
[19] Neuhaus, *William Keith,* 48.
[20] Ibid., 71.

5. William Keith, *Strawberry Creek*, ca. 1890s. Oil on canvas (photo: The Hearst Art Gallery, St. Mary's College of California)

6. Palace of Fine Arts, San Francisco, California (photo: from C. Brinton, *Impressions of the Art at the Panama-Pacific Exposition*, New York, 1916)

7. Oakland Packard Showroom, Oakland, California, no longer extant
(photo: from *California Arts and Architecture,* February 1929)

8. William Keith, *Sinuous Romantic Oaks,* ca. 1899. Oil on canvas (photo: The Oakland
Museum)

9. Bernard Maybeck, untitled, 1915. Watercolor (photo: University Art Museum, University of California, Berkeley)

10. Bernard Maybeck, rendering for Phoebe Hearst Memorial, ca. 1923. Pastel on tracing paper (photo: Documents Collection, College of Environmental Design, University of California, Berkeley)

11. View of painting signed "M. Strauss." Senger residence, Berkeley, California, 1907

12. View through the glass door, opposite the painting in the "erker." Senger residence, Berkeley, California, 1907

painting is opposite a glass door that framed a nearly identical view of a clump of redwoods in the garden (Figs. 11, 12). These redwoods are specifically mentioned in the early design concept for the garden as an important element. The painting acts as a mirror, reflecting an idealized version of the garden beyond. Of course, Maybeck's pictorial approach was not unprecedented, and can be traced back several centuries. What makes Maybeck's work unique to the Bay Region, however, is the fact that the pictorial base upon which he worked was inspired by the romantic, idealized, Mediterranean idea of California depicted by landscape painters like William Keith.

Two additional Bay Area painters may also have influenced Maybeck and contributed to his work with landscape. Arthur and Lucia Mathews, who had their studio in the same building as William Keith in 1906, touched at least the outer edge of the circle that most influenced Maybeck and contributed to the regional culture. Lucia Mathews was an avid gardener, and landscape and botanical themes provided the predominant subject matter in her paintings and decorative arts.[21] Like Keith, the Mathews exhibited their

[21] H. L. Jones, *Mathews: Masterpieces of the California Decorative Style*, Santa Barbara and Salt Lake City, 1980, 79.

13. Arthur Mathews, *Youth*, ca. 1917. Oil on canvas (photo: The Oakland Museum)

work at the Bohemian Club, and their paintings were featured prominently at the 1915 Panama Pacific International Exposition, where Lucia received a silver medal.[22]

Besides their painting activities, the Mathews owned and operated a successful shop where they sold furniture of their own design. The shop was a brown-shingled structure with a stylistic resemblance to Maybeck's architecture, suggesting a certain amount of creative exchange.[23] If Maybeck's shingled structures influenced the Mathews, certainly their paintings of the California landscape filled with live oaks, pines, cypresses, and fruits, affected the architect as much as did those of William Keith. Maybeck's renderings and the Mathews' paintings share similarities in method of depiction: the same twisted oaks, the same soft-focus Mediterranean romanticism, and similar colors that favor warm tones (Fig. 13). Maybeck emulated the Mathews' and William Keith's idealized California landscape of vines, flowers, fruit, and woods, first on paper in his preliminary sketches and presentation renderings using pastels, pencil, and ink, and later on the project site using earth, plant materials, water, and architecture.

[22] Ibid., 65, 23.
[23] Ibid., 67.

It is here then, that Frederick Jackson Turner's essay acquires significance for our purposes. For it is through these paintings that the native frontier landscape affected Maybeck, who in turn, contributed to creating a frontier culture or regional style by transforming part of that landscape. The native California landscape gave rise to an imagined and largely symbolic Mediterranean landscape, that in turn was transmitted through literature and painting, and then absorbed and realized by designers like Maybeck.

A most important member of that frontier culture was Charles Keeler who helped establish the idea of the Bay Area as the "Athens of the West." A Berkeley poet and Maybeck's first residential client, Keeler joined forces with the architect to become one of "the most vocal proponents of an indigenous Arts and Crafts movement in Berkeley."[24] His 1904 book, *The Simple Home*, which he dedicated to Maybeck, borrowed heavily from the principles of the Arts and Crafts movement implying that the entirety of the physical environment should become a work of art, and to this end, the book contains an entire chapter on the design of the garden.[25] Keeler was also a naturalist with considerable knowledge of specific plant species; knowledge he might have shared with his architect friend.

While a more detailed discussion of Keeler's approach to landscape design can be found in *The Simple Home*, the key ingredient of his landscape recommendations is an attitude of inclusiveness that is the hallmark of regional design in Northern California and the Bay Area in particular.[26] This attitude allowed both geometric and naturalistic landscape design, both the native and many exotic species that could be grown in the temperate climate, a profusion of color in the landscape at all seasons, and for an eclecticism of form that echoed contemporary trends in the rest of the country. But above all else, this inclusiveness made architecture and landscape inseparably intertwined. Keeler espoused these qualities in his writings, extolling the bountiful quality of the California landscape and suggesting that the California designer need only bring the features of the existing landscape under control to achieve success.

The common thread that weaves together Maybeck and his circle is the Mediterranean analogy. They collectively created, through their writings, paintings, and works of environmental design, a shared conception of Northern California as a place that was both culturally and climatically the "Athens of the West." Maybeck stated his belief in this Mediterranean ideal in an unpublished essay on regional architecture, written while he was immersed in his 1918 Mills College design, for which he laid out a general ground

---

[24] C. Keeler, *The Simple Home*, repr. Salt Lake City, 1979, xxxi, introduction by Dimitri Shipounoff. Interestingly, Keeler was also involved in the promotion of the Bay Area. His book, *San Francisco and Thereabouts* (San Francisco, 1903), is a classic booster text extolling the geographical and cultural virtues of the city following the 1906 earthquake. While Keeler and the other members of the influential circle I am describing have no direct economic motivations for their boosterism that I am aware of, their works must have been greatly appreciated by railroad and agricultural interests among others.

[25] Keeler, *The Simple Home*, xi.

[26] For more on Keeler, see Keeler, *The Simple Home*, and D. Harris, "Maybeck's Landscapes," *Journal of Garden History* 10 (July-September 1990), 145–61.

plan and made suggestions for tree types. He wrote of the fortunate designer in California who is free of problems from snow and ice arguing that the fundamental principles of design in the region should be based on those developed for areas around the Mediterranean Sea where the climate is similar to that of Oakland. The architect argued further that the style of the Mills College campus landscape should be appropriate to Oakland, which he saw as "a garden spot of the earth" where vines do not freeze and flowering bushes thrive.[27] In likening the climate of Oakland to that of the Mediterranean, and in propounding the image of California as a garden spot, Maybeck joined the vast ranks of Americans who saw the West Coast as a promised land of warmth and bounty. This is the California represented on orange crates and produce labels from the early part of the century, in the paintings of Keith and the Mathews, and it is the California that inspired the dance of Isadora Duncan. Most important, the imagery of California-as-Mediterranean inspired Maybeck's landscapes, filled with elements such as the twisted oaks and dramatic skies; the sculpted, toga-clad women adorning Maybeck's planter boxes; the Italian cypresses and trellises dripping with wisteria or grapes; the golden and warm tones given preference in his renderings—all these combine to create Maybeck's regional landscape designs (Figs. 14, 15).

The Mediterranean imagery is one of three aspects that together constitute Maybeck's regional landscape designs. The pictorial base is the second aspect, and the third is the fact that the distinctiveness of his work as a regional expression lies in the importance of reading it as a total package. Maybeck's outdoor work cannot be looked at as a separate entity with an identifiable style of its own, but must always be seen in relationship to his buildings. His garden designs cannot be studied as those designed by other masters of regionalism such as Jens Jensen, who worked closely with Frank Lloyd Wright. While landscape architects like Jensen may have worked closely with architects to create exterior environments compatible with the architecture, Maybeck's landscape designs are completely dependent on their architectural framework. He did not strive to create gardens or landscapes as separate entities. Instead, the form and style of the garden are site and architecture specific, determined by the individual nature of each project, and it is this intertwining of interior and exterior spaces that has become the keynote in California landscape design.

Having established the regional qualities of Maybeck's work, and having looked at the group of people who influenced that work, we can now look at three projects that exemplify his Bay Region tradition, for the tradition belongs to Maybeck as much as the Prairie School belongs to Frank Lloyd Wright. While others participated in its creation, these men became the acknowledged masters of their respective regional styles.

The James Fagan residence of 1920, located in the San Francisco peninsula suburb of Woodside, is a fine example of Maybeck's contribution to the newly emerging California residential style. Maybeck conceived the house as two separate wings divided by a

---

[27] Bernard Maybeck papers, Documents Collection, College of Environmental Design, University of California, Berkeley. Mills College Office File, unpublished essay on regional architecture, 1918, 6, 7.

14. Bernard Maybeck, rendering for Strawberry Canyon Bath House, University of California, Berkeley, 1911. Watercolor on board. Unbuilt (photo: Documents Collection, College of Environmental Design, University of California, Berkeley)

15. Bernard Maybeck, rendering for University of California Hospital, 1902. Unbuilt (photo: Documents Collection, College of Environmental Design, University of California, Berkeley)

58

central elliptical court. The plan requires the residents to traverse the outdoor space many times each day as they cross from sleeping to living areas, and the outdoor area literally becomes central to their daily life (Fig. 16). The court is of obvious Italian derivation, yet it is distinctly Californian in its relation to the interior spaces and the planting. Maybeck grouped the plants in an informal manner, yet the massing reinforces the architectural plan. He specified areas to be kept clear to preserve views from the interior, as well as areas of dense planting to enclose and shelter the court, substituting heavy planting for walls in this outdoor room.

Maybeck thoughtfully selected the plants to effect this enclosure. For his thick planting around the court he chose Abelia grandiflora and Eugenia myrtifolia, both effective visual barriers which flower or fruit in winter in shades of purple or pink, reinforcing the color scheme of his paving, which was also pink. In this garden, the architect preferred winter blooming plants and drought tolerant species as indicated by his selection of Coprosma, Erica, Myrtus, and Aucuba. For the Fagan residence, Maybeck utilized the trellis, a distinguishing element of his work, to full effect (Fig. 17). The architect generally designed his trellises as a continuation of the structural system of the house, by extending beams or rafters from the building, and he used them so frequently that they are almost a trademark.

The significance of the trellis in Maybeck's work is four-fold. First, it effects a significant transition between architecture and the landscape by extending the house out into the garden, and by allowing the garden to creep onto the house. Second, the trellis, with its vines, helps create Maybeck's Mediterranean pictorial fantasy by recalling the vineyards of the Italian countryside and the significance of the vine as a symbol of fruitfulness through history.

Third, the trellis structure acts as a sort of ruin. Maybeck was enamored with the idea of Piranesian ruins covered with plant life beginning to reclaim the architecture, and the trellises can be seen as a fragment of a hanging garden that helps to create a symbolic representation of this romantic idea. Finally, the trellises, placed adjacent to or over windows, allow the vines and blossoms to hang in front of translucent or transparent glass. In so doing, Maybeck achieved both his desired pictorial effect, with the view through the window from the interior becoming his painting, while modulating the light within his architecture. As the sun shone through the wisteria, for example, it cast either a slightly green or purple glow—depending on the time of year—contributing to the overall lighting scheme while furthering the merging of landscape and architecture (Fig. 18).

For the Fagan residence, Maybeck specified grape vines for the trellis structures instead of wisteria, his more frequent choice. Both vines create shade during the warm summer months and defoliate in winter allowing sun to penetrate and warm both indoor and outdoor spaces. The grape vines also play into the neo-Italianate scheme with their Mediterranean allusions.

The Fagan residence serves as an exemplar for indoor-outdoor living in turn-of-the-century California, with its Mediterranean imagery and courtyard plan. The architect's design for the Palace of Fine Arts of 1915 extended the same typology to his work at a

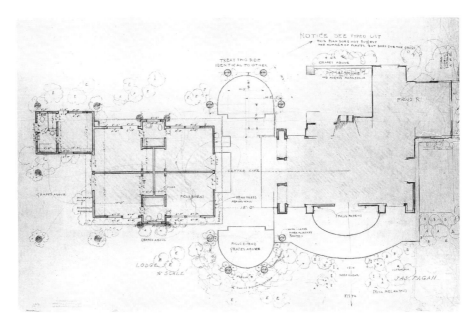

16. Ground plan with planting. James Fagan residence, Woodside, California, 1920 (photo: Documents Collection, College of Environmental Design, University of California, Berkeley)

17. James Fagan residence, Woodside, California, 1920 (photo: Documents Collection, College of Environmental Design, University of California, Berkeley)

18. Side view of Sunday School. Ninth Church of Christian Scientists, San Francisco, California, designed 1935–37. Unbuilt (photo: Documents Collection, College of Environmental Design, University of California, Berkeley)

much larger scale and for a different audience. The "Palace" is less a building than a magnificent, "immense garden structure," built for the Panama Pacific International Exposition.[28] Maybeck's early conceptual drawing of the Palace of Fine Arts reveals his parti for a structure intimately connected with the adjacent lagoon and landscape, and shows the importance of the structure's color in relation to the lagoon. His inscription on the study reads "Palace of Fine Arts without the trimmings—this the main hall" (Fig. 19). While the drawing probably indicates one of the exhibition halls rather than Maybeck's colonnaded structure, it reveals his original intent to play color against the surrounding sky, water, and vegetation, which is so much a part of the Palace of Fine Arts.

Among Maybeck's office records for the Palace of Fine Arts is a letter he wrote stating that "on the whole the lagoon is the crux of the whole composition. . . ." The radius of the colonnade curving around the lagoon is struck not from the center of the rotunda, as one would expect, but from a point in the middle of the lagoon, further strengthening the relationship of the structure to the water.[29]

The conceptual drawing also serves as an example of the Keith-inspired reflecting body of water: a romantic landscape rendered first in pastel on paper and later brought to three-dimensional realization. As Louis Christian Mullgardt stated, "The entire com-

[28] W. H. Jordy, *American Buildings and Their Architects: Progressive and Academic Ideals at the Turn of the Twentieth Century*, New York, 1972, 300.

[29] R. Banham, "The Plot Against Bernard Maybeck," *Journal of the Society of Architectural Historians* 43 (March 1984), 36.

19. Bernard Maybeck, conceptual study for the Palace of Fine Arts, San Francisco, California, ca. 1914. Pastel on tracing paper (photo: Documents Collection, College of Environmental Design, University of California, Berkeley)

20. Palace of Fine Arts, San Francisco, California, ca. 1915 (photo: Documents Collection, College of Environmental Design, University of California, Berkeley)

21. Planter boxes atop the colonnade at the Palace of Fine Arts, San Francisco, California (photo: Marc Treib)

position bespeaks the mind of a romanticist, whose productions are swayed more by nature's glories than by scholastic tradition."[30] The Palace of Fine Arts was one of Maybeck's most romantic creations, a landscape painting come to life, its warm tones reflected in the lagoon (Fig. 20).

Maybeck thoughtfully conceived and considered the planting at the Palace of Fine Arts. The design represented the "natural" style discussed by Keeler in *The Simple Home*, and its manner contrasted sharply with the more formal landscape treatment used for the other portions of the fair. When viewing the Palace of Fine Arts today, one should recall that much of the effect envisioned was never realized. The planting was never installed in the attic-level planter boxes atop the colonnade, ornamented with mysterious, inward-looking female figures (Fig. 21). Budget constraints prevented realization of that scheme, much to Maybeck's great disappointment. The lack of those raised plantings, in the architect's view, detracted from the accelerated "aged" quality of the design he so desired.

In writing about the Palace of Fine Arts, Maybeck revealed his method for achieving a structure thoroughly integrated with its landscape. The architect wrote that to make an agreeable looking plan he used shrubs to fill the vacancies in the walls that are usually

[30] L. C. Mullgardt, *The Architecture and Landscape Gardening of the Exposition*, San Francisco, 1915, 8.

poché, or solid, and that this was possible because of the temperate California climate.[31] In this text, Maybeck again acknowledged the special qualities of the region in which he worked and the importance of its temperate climate, strengthening the Mediterranean imagery, and giving meaning to the words "green architecture" in his conception of the use of vegetation as *poché*.

Remnants of this green architecture remain at the Palace of Fine Arts today, although most of the original planting was destroyed when the plaster Palace was torn down and the concrete Palace built. Originally, blooming plants and shrubs occupied the spaces between the columns of the peristyle. In their place, a few remaining acanthus can be found dotted between the columns, recalling the stylized Corinthian capitals above them. Purple leaf plums stand in striking contrast to the ocher concrete, creating a flickering visual effect that enhances the structure's presence.

In many respects, the Palace was a great success for Maybeck. The project brought him a considerable amount of recognition both within the architectural profession and with the public, greatly enhancing his career. So successful was this monument in the eyes of the public, that long after the exposition had ended, funds were raised for the reconstruction of the Palace in permanent materials, and even today, a fund-raising effort is underway to re-establish the original lighting scheme. Due to those efforts, the rotunda and colonnade stand today as a powerful example of Maybeck's Mediterranean garden/ architecture aesthetic. His use of color recalls Pompeii; the tuscan red and ocher reverberate against the sky and reflect in the lagoon. While these colors were compatible with Jules Guerin's comprehensive color scheme for the exposition, Maybeck's architectural contribution was distinctive. His Palace of Fine Arts conveyed the qualities of the region through its site plan and design, rather than merely storing and displaying the products of California in a decorated warehouse as did other buildings at the fair. Walking through the site, one is simultaneously indoors and out; an experience that is the epitome of the idealized notion of the Mediterranean/California lifestyle, demonstrated on a monumental scale.

One final project rounds out this discussion of Maybeck's regional landscape designs and will illustrate how the architect applied the same design principles to his work regardless of scale, client, or intended user. The Hearst Gymnasium and Memorial complex was a 1926 collaborative effort between Maybeck and his one-time pupil, Julia Morgan. Although principally designed by Maybeck, the gym clearly shows Julia Morgan's influence. The small courtyards are similar in scale to her courtyards in the Berkeley City Club and to those in her Oakland Chapel of the Chimes, but the plan itself is derivative of the Beaux-Arts models that both architects would have studied at the École des Beaux-Arts. According to Kenneth Cardwell, Maybeck used the water gardens at Nimes as a prototype for the gymnasium, but the design remains distinctly Californian in its planting, although the lushness of his original conception is not to be found at the site today.[32]

[31] Documents Collection, College of Environmental Design, University of California, Berkeley. Maybeck Job File, Palace of Fine Arts.
[32] K. Cardwell, *Bernard Maybeck: Artisan, Architect, Artist*, Salt Lake City, 1983, 199.

The dominant plant used at the gymnasium is the California Live Oak, more symbolic of the University of California campus for Maybeck and his contemporaries than the pollarded plane trees now associated with the campus landscape. Maybeck used these oaks everywhere at the gymnasium, planting a small grove of them in one courtyard, using them on the raised terraces at the second-story level, and in the planter boxes located on the marble pool terrace (Figs. 22, 23, 24). These oaks near the pool no longer exist; they died and were not replaced due to the problem of leaf litter falling into the pool. But the oaks were an important part of the design for the architect who sketched the trees in their planter boxes repeatedly and carefully researched soil conditions required for the survival of the oaks growing in planter boxes.[33] The drawings also reveal the consistent use of warm, Mediterranean colors (orange, tuscan red, yellow, and pink) like those at the Palace of Fine Arts. Similarly, the reflections of both building and landscape in a body of water, in this case the marble swimming pool, are of central importance to both complexes.

Directly to the north of the gymnasium was the site for the proposed Phoebe Apperson Hearst Memorial. Commissioned by William Randolph Hearst in memory of his mother who died in 1919, the complex was never built due to a diversion of funds for other campus building projects of greater priority to both the University and the donor.[34] But the pastel renderings Maybeck produced for its design reveal an elaborate landscape scheme in conjunction with the architecture of the memorial (Figs. 25, 26). Maybeck designed an enormous vaulted structure, surrounded by elaborate water courses and raised beds, heavily planted. Vines creep down the walls of the planted areas and the vegetation presses in on the vaulted structure. In these loosely sketched plans, the water features penetrate through the architecture, and there is no clear distinction between exterior and interior. In a manner similar to the Palace of Fine Arts, the water and planting create a framework for the architecture. Certainly, the designs are strongly reminiscent of the Palace of Fine Arts, but even more significant is the characteristic use of water as a surface for reflection, of planting as *poché* to fill out the composition of the ground plan and of architecture and landscape inextricably linked.

The Memorial rendering, with its open air design and hybrid classicism, alludes to Roman baths, further evidence of Maybeck's preference for Mediterranean imagery. Sunlight washes through the drawing, across the architecture, planting, and water creating the warm glow of an idealized California, the Athens of the West.

These projects are but a few of the many completed by Maybeck during his long career, and they represent a small, though indicative, portion of his work in landscape design. They are projects that reveal a deep commitment to regionalism in the best sense of that word. They are not merely the products of provincialism which, as Turpin Bannister has pointed out, "may be quaint, naive and amusing, but lacking in the vitality, spontaneity and promise of future growth characteristic of truly regional products."[35] Quite

[33] Documents Collection, College of Environmental Design, University of California, Berkeley. Maybeck's Hearst Gymnasium Job File, letter dated 9 January 1926.

[34] Cardwell, *Bernard Maybeck*, 198.

[35] Turpin Bannister quoted in essay by Rexford Newcomb, "Regionalism in American Architecture," in M. Jensen, ed., *Regionalism in America*, Madison, Wisc., 1952, 275.

22. Bernard Maybeck, rendering for Hearst Gymnasium swimming pool, University of California, Berkeley, ca. 1926 (photo: Documents Collection, College of Environmental Design, University of California, Berkeley)

23. Hearst Gymnasium, University of California, Berkeley, no date (photo: The Bancroft Library, University of California, Berkeley)

24. Toga clad women adorn a planter box at the Hearst Gymnasium

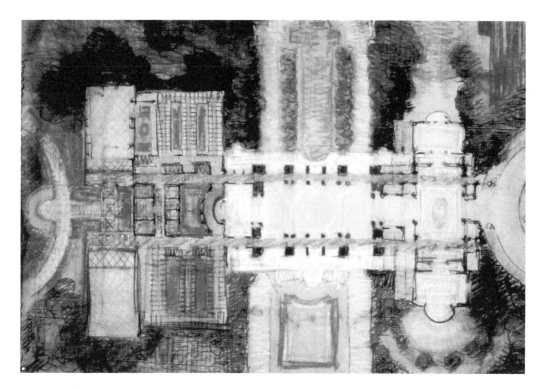

25. Bernard Maybeck, sketch plan for the Phoebe Apperson Hearst Memorial, University of California, Berkeley, 1928. Pastel on paper. Unbuilt. The two parallel, continuous horizontal bands in the drawing are water which is to flow both inside and outside the structure (photo: Documents Collection, College of Environmental Design, University of California, Berkeley)

26. Bernard Maybeck, Phoebe Apperson Hearst Memorial, University of California, Berkeley, 1928. Pastel on paper. Unbuilt (photo: Documents Collection, College of Environmental Design, University of California, Berkeley)

the contrary, the Bay Region tradition has fulfilled its potential for growth, spawning a second and third generation of designers working within its tenets, but expanding its meaning for our own time. Jens Jensen was quick to realize the potential for a distinctive regional design in California, writing that "the Californian is bound to the soil; he belongs, he is happy to belong; his life is influenced by the forceful environments which are his state. No other section of America can portray such outdoor life as California . . . California will be California, and more so as days go by. No one can escape the power of this mountainous country with its striking local color." [36] With this statement, Jensen asserted, just as Frederick Jackson Turner had before him (albeit in a more simplistic way) that the forces of the frontier landscape on the individual are inescapable. So too, it seems, are the forces of the individual on the frontier landscape. The frontier landscape, or at least the cultural construct that arose in the form of the Mediterranean analogy from the perception of a symbolic frontier landscape, did indeed create a unique culture that in turn established a regional tradition in design; a tradition that helped create the basis for garden design in California for the following seventy years.

[36] J. Jensen, *Siftings,* Baltimore and London, 1990, 27.

Fast-Tracking Culture and Landscape: Horace William Shaler Cleveland and the Garden in the Midwest

LANCE M. NECKAR

When Wilhelm Miller of the University of Illinois wrote his essay *The Prairie Spirit in Landscape Gardening* in 1915, he imbued the word "prairie" with symbolic meanings. At one stroke he aligned the midwestern garden with both the growing body of domestic architectural work executed by Frank Lloyd Wright and his contemporaries and the native and emblematic landscapes of the region.[1] This linking was not accidental. Since 1911, Miller had been promoting an aesthetic that would engender "the perfect home amid the prairie states."[2] He drew upon the works of landscape designers, Ossian Cole Simonds (1855–1931), Jens Jensen (1860–1951), and others, including architect and garden city designer, Walter Burley Griffin (1876–1937), to shape his definition of a "middle-western" domestic garden style.[3] From these works he distilled three principles that gave flesh to the "spirit": the conservation of native scenery, the restoration of local vegetation, and the formal repetition of a dominant line, that of the horizon.[4] He illustrated these principles as they applied to eight landscape scenery types which, other than the prairie itself, characterized the Illinois landscape: lake bluffs, ravines, riverbanks,

[1] See particularly F. L. Wright, "A Home in a Prairie Town," *Ladies Home Journal* (February 1901), 17, for an early use of nomenclature, e.g., "prairie"; and H. A. Brooks, *The Prairie School: Frank Lloyd Wright and His Midwest Contemporaries*, Toronto, 1972. Wright himself, at this period, sometimes preferred "New American" and apparently used this term in application to a house designed by him for a childhood friend, Robert M. Lamp, in Madison, Wisconsin (*Madison Democrat,* 6 September 1903).

[2] W. Miller, *The Prairie Spirit in Landscape Gardening,* University of Illinois Agricultural Experiment Station, Circular 184, Urbana, Ill. 1915; and Miller, quoted from a 1 September 1911 article in *Country Life in America,* in M. Gelbloom, "Ossian Simonds: Prairie Spirit in Landscape Gardening," *Prairie School Review* 12, 2 (1975), 38.

[3] Miller, *Prairie Spirit,* 5. Griffin was extraordinarily interested in Ebenezer Howard's garden city ideas. He designed Canberra using these notions, and prior to that, he designed Mossmain, a garden city in Montana. See forthcoming publications on this topic by Paul Damon.

[4] Miller, *Prairie Spirit,* 5.

ponds, dunes, rocks, woods, and roadsides.[5] Using the principles and the formal motifs from the scenery types, Simonds and Jensen brought forth the poetic landscapes that expressed the style, notably the prairie rivers and lagoons edged with native shrubs, sedges, grasses, and the great symbolic clearings where houses commanded quiet open lawns bounded by stratified plants. These simple gardens delighted in the expanse of ground meeting sky. They reveled in windswept winters and suffocating heat hovering above dampened earth; and they celebrated shady escape into hidden ravines and valleys where dogwood danced amid the mayapple.

Horace William Shaler Cleveland (1814–1900), a primal muse of this regional aesthetic, had set forth its precepts in his writings and gardens in the last half of the nineteenth century. Seen from this point of origin, the landscape of the "prairie" spirit was rooted in American romantic literature and Transcendentalism, nourished by Unitarianism and Yankee practicality, and adapted and transplanted to a new and burgeoning landscape in the nineteenth-century West. It was a nonornamental landscape, a designed, or preserved, landscape of common native plants on the unsullied topography of a new region. It was a spare vision that relied on one's feeling for the essential rightness of undefiled nature. Nature, picturesque and bounteous, was the ultimate garden.

Cleveland's reification of the native landscape originated in his deeply held and prescient vision of the role of landscape in cultural improvement. The formal simplicity and economy of the developing style were, in his hands, the products of a strategic idea about how American culture might keep pace with the speculation that clattered along bright new rails and stretched a raw edge of civilization westward. He expressed this vision of a fast-tracked landscape setting for a new American civilization in his book, *Landscape Architecture As Applied to the Wants of the West* (1873), and in his executed works, especially those in Chicago, Minneapolis, and St. Paul from the 1870s, 1880s, and 1890s.[6]

NATURE, POETICS, AND THE PRACTICAL MAN

Horace Cleveland's early life coincided with the flowering of New England literature and thought.[7] His approach to the landscape may be traced to early nineteenth-century preoccupations with the uneasy merging of economy, technology, art, and nature. The shifting ground of this merging was called, normatively, improvement. In a region made rich by the sea trade and the textile industry, Transcendentalist and romantic poets searched for improvement in the realms of myth and nature; and in doing so, raised

---

[5] Ibid., 12.

[6] H. W. S. Cleveland, *Landscape Architecture As Applied to the Wants of the West: With an Essay on Forest Planting in the Great Plains*, Chicago, 1873. The term "fast-track" refers directly here to the compressed process of design and construction used by Cleveland to achieve economies of time and money. Today fast-tracked landscapes (or buildings) are made using this same approach for the same reasons. Generally the process involves beginning construction with only schematic or partially developed plans in hand. More generally the term is used here to connote rapidly advancing developments of all types, growing on the armature of western transportation networks, especially railroad tracks.

[7] The classic work is Van Wyck Brooks, *The Flowering of New England, 1815–1865*, New York, 1936.

nature to a godhead. At the same moment, improvement-minded engineers and scientific agriculturists looked for a resonance between mechanical and artistic interventions into nature as a means of elevating civilization. Grounded in his early life in both the aesthetic and useful, Horace Cleveland's career was destined to be driven by the civilizing necessity of reconciling a practical world with nature and poetics.

Horace Cleveland was born to Richard Jeffry Cleveland (1773–1860) and Dorcas (Cleveland) Hiller Cleveland (?–1854) in 1814 in Lancaster, Massachusetts.[8] His parents were important members of Salem society, where mercantile success spawned a culture that was signified by the literary presence of Nathaniel Hawthorne (1804–64) and the educative leadership of the Peabody family.[9] Mrs. Cleveland, an active Unitarian, with the support of Richard Cleveland's sizable income as a merchant navigator, established schools for the children of the area, and, of course, for the education of their sons, Richard, Henry, and Horace.[10] The Lancaster School was distinctly grounded in the most current educational thinking.[11] In its early years it attracted teachers who set a progressive educational tone, including Jared Sparks (1789–1866), a rising figure in Unitarianism and, later, president of Harvard College; and George Barrel Emerson (1797–1881), a cousin of Ralph Waldo (1803–82) and, later, a leader in education and forestry.[12] Horace also received practical training, in later years, as a surveyor.[13]

[8] Biographical materials on Cleveland tend to be brief and somewhat repetitive; the principal sources used here are W. H. Tishler and V. Luckhardt, "H. W. S. Cleveland: Pioneer Landscape Architect to the Upper Midwest," *Minnesota History* 49, 7 (Fall, 1985), 281–91; idem, "Pioneering with Plans and Plants: H. W. S. Cleveland Brings Landscape Architecture to Wisconsin," *Wisconsin Academy of Arts, Science, and Letters Review* 73 (1985), 63–69; V. Luckhardt, "Horace William Shaler Cleveland: An Overview of the Life and Work of an Early American Landscape Architect, 1814–1900," Master's thesis, University of Wisconsin, 1983; *Dictionary of American Biography*, s.v. "Horace W. S. Cleveland"; T. K. Hubbard, "H. W. S. Cleveland: An American Pioneer in Landscape Architecture and City Planning," *Landscape Architecture* 20 (January 1930), 92; K. Haglund, "The Correspondence of H. W. S. Cleveland," in P. Trowbridge, ed., *Public Space: Environmental Awareness During the Later Nineteenth Century*, Cambridge, Mass., 1975, 162–75; H. W. S. Cleveland, *Landscape Architecture As Applied to the Wants of the West*, ed. R. Lubove, Pittsburgh, 1965; T. Blegen, *Horace William Shaler Cleveland: Pioneer American Landscape Architect*, Minneapolis, 1949.

[9] Hawthorne and Peabody connections and Salem described in H. W. S. Cleveland, *Social Life and Literature Fifty Years Ago*, Boston, 1888, 80–96. See also E. Peabody, ed., *Aesthetic Papers*, Boston, 1849; L. H. Tharp, *The Peabody Sisters of Salem*, Boston, 1950, and E. Peabody, B. Ronda, eds., *Letters of Elizabeth Peabody, American Renaissance Woman*, Middletown, Conn., 1984.

[10] R. J. Cleveland, *Voyages and Commercial Enterprises of the Sons of New England*, New York, 1855, and H. W. S. Cleveland, *Voyages of a Merchant Navigator of the Days That Are Past*, New York, 1886.

[11] D. Nadenicek, "The Literary Landscape of H. W. S. Cleveland," Master's thesis, University of Minnesota, 1991, 60–61, identifies Johann Heinrich Pestalozzi's methods as those emulated by Mrs. Cleveland.

[12] See G. B. Emerson, "The Schoolmaster: The Proper Character, Studies, and Duties of the Teacher, etc.," pt. II in A. Potter and G. B. Emerson, *The School and the Schoolmaster*, New York, 1842; wherein details of school design are offered in addition to advice on instruction. Emerson counseled that "[t]he border of a natural wood may often be chosen for the site of a school. . . ." (p. 527) and proceeded to enumerate appropriate native trees and shrubs to be sought or planted on the site; and idem, *Report on the Trees and Shrubs Growing Naturally in the Forests of Massachusetts*, Boston, 1846; and idem, *Reminiscences of an Old School Teacher*, Boston, 1878; in which he recalls the Lancaster School. See also Luckhardt, "Early American Landscape Architect," 10; and J. Sparks and H. B. Adams, eds., *The Life and Writings of Jared Sparks: Comprising Selections from His Journals and Correspondence*, Boston, 1893, 85–92; wherein C. Thayer names among the other teachers, "Proctor, Emerson, Miles, Wood and Fletcher" (p. 90).

[13] Luckhardt, "Early American Landscape Architect," 12.

It was in this capacity as a surveyor, officially at least, that he took one of his two trips west—to Illinois—in the late 1830s.[14] However, there were obviously other motivations for a young man in a family of travelers and scholars to burst the confines of New England. Among intellectuals of the eastern seaboard in this period, there was particular fascination for the West and for the Native American. Washington Irving (1783–1859) had ventured out to the Oklahoma Territory in 1832 in search of communion with the Osage, Creek, and Delaware and their wilder neighbors, the Commanche and the Pawnee.[15] For the eastern intellectual, the Indian represented the simple nobility of the earth, of America, of the West. The spirits of the Native American and the native landscape became virtually fused. In his journals, Ralph Waldo Emerson mused that "the West is the native American element."[16] This fascination with the West and the Indian would culminate with the publication in 1854 of Henry Wadsworth Longfellow's (1807–82) epic poem, *The Song of Hiawatha*.[17] Hiawatha's struggle was based on the legends collected by Henry Rowe Schoolcraft during his journeys among the Iroquois, Dakota, and Ojibway in the 1820s and 1830s and later published as the *Algic Researches* (1839).[18] Like Schoolcraft, Cleveland undertook his journeys into the West with an admixture of practical and poetic motives. As Cleveland tramped and rode the countryside of this new land, he must have been overwhelmed by its immensity and its promise. Out on this wild landscape, being squared into sections by the Northwest Ordinances and sliced through by prospective rail right-of-ways, he undoubtedly began also to sense his first irritation with the sheer tyranny of this hard-edged organization of a picturesque paradise. Both the grid and the railroad would later become his regular targets as he developed his vision of civilization in the West.[19] In 1888 Cleveland placed some measure of perspective on these early travels when he recalled:

> It was not until my second visit to the West in 1837, that I first heard of the existence of a "right smart town up north on Lake Michigan, called Chicago . . . The sites of . . . St. Paul and Minneapolis could not have been reached in safety by a white man, except by steamboat or with an armed escort. All of the region of the Mississippi, and north of mouth of the Missouri was dream-land.[20]

When he returned home from this trip, in the summer of 1837, he stayed for an ex-

[14] Ibid., 12–13.

[15] W. Irving, *A Tour on the Prairies*, Philadelphia, 1835.

[16] R. W. Emerson, "Index Minor," in L. Allardt, ed., *The Journals and Miscellaneous Notebooks of Ralph Waldo Emerson, 1835–1862*, 12, Cambridge, Mass., 1976, 575.

[17] H. W. Longfellow, *The Song of Hiawatha*, Boston, 1855.

[18] H. R. Schoolcraft, *Algic Researches*, New York, 1839; later republished as *The Myth of Hiawatha, and Other Oral Legends*, Philadelphia, 1856.

[19] Cleveland, *Landscape Architecture*, 11, 29–30, 36–37, 53–55.

[20] H. W. S. Cleveland, *The Aesthetic Development of the United Cities of St. Paul and Minneapolis*, Minneapolis, 1888, 10.

tended visit with his older brother, Henry, who was living in Jamaica Plain, near Boston.[21] Henry Russell Cleveland was associated with four other young local literati, Longfellow, Charles Sumner (1811-74), Cornelius C. Felton, and George Hillard. The group called itself the "Five of Clubs."[22] Horace Cleveland recalled in his book, *Social Life and Literature Fifty Years Ago*, the *zeitgeist* of the period and his direct involvement with many of its formative thinkers and writers.[23] One might surmise from his recollections that the men probably talked the summer through on a wide range of current issues—of poetry, and German Romanticism; of the nascent American literature, dominated by Irving's earthy tales; of Transcendentalism, Emerson and, perhaps, of Hawthorne, who was Longfellow's Bowdoin College classmate; and of travel, especially to the West, where their young visitor had so recently adventured.

Henry Cleveland died in 1843 at the age of thirty-four.[24] In the meantime, Horace had married and resolved to be a scientific farmer.[25] His father's fortunes had sagged disastrously, perhaps explaining Horace's curtailed education; unlike his brothers, Henry and Richard, he did not attend Harvard. Horace contributed letters and articles to Andrew Jackson Downing's (1815–52) *The Horticulturist* in this period, and like his near contemporaries and fellow farmers, Downing, Frederick Law Olmsted (1822–1903), and Robert Morris Copeland, he turned gradually to landscape gardening.[26] In 1854 he formed a loose partnership with Copeland, and they maintained a practice in Salem, Massachusetts. For all of these men, landscape gardening seemed to embody the gathering of diverse concerns that could shape cultural improvement in their times. In other words, for them, the landscape improved would be the realm of an improved human condition.

As he began to develop his own landscape aesthetic in this period, Cleveland seemed to have been sustained broadly by the general spirit of the times, and, more specifically,

---

[21] Luckhardt, "Early American Landscape Architect," 14.

[22] *Dictionary of American Biography*, s.v. "Horace W. S. Cleveland"; Luckhardt, "Early American Landscape Architect," 14; R. Lubove, "Biographical Note," *Landscape Architecture*, 61 (no page given).

[23] Cleveland, *Social Life*, 39–47; H. W. S. Cleveland and G. Hillard, eds., *A Selection of Writings, etc., with a Memoir by George Hillard*, Boston, 1884, vi, includes a short biography of Horace's brother and a recollection by one of the five of the period.

[24] Luckhardt, "Early American Landscape Architect," 16; and Cleveland and Hillard, *Selection of Writings*, xxxvi.

[25] Luckhardt, "Early American Landscape Architect," 16.

[26] Luckhardt, "Early American Landscape Architect," 16–17. Downing's coalescent role as the stimulus for a broad range of improvement activities under the heading of "landscape gardening" in the 1840s and, even after his death, in the 1850s cannot be overestimated. A. J. Downing, *A Treatise on the Theory and Practice of Landscape Gardening Adapted to North America*, New York, 1841, had been continuously in print and updated since its original publication. A clientele for landscape gardening services began to emerge out of the forum provided by his magazine, *The Horticulturist*, beginning with its first number in 1846. Yet at this period, both Cleveland and Olmsted contributed to the magazine as scientific farmers who reported on the successes and failures of farming practices and crops. See, for example, H. W. S. Cleveland, "Description of a Cheap Vinery for Foreign Grapes," *The Horticulturist* 1, 6 (December 1846), 269–70; and many successive articles on mulching techniques. See also, F. L. Olmsted, "A Note on the True Soldat Laboureur Pear," *The Horticulturist* 7, 1 (January 1852), 14–15; by way of comparison of interests at this time, see the following article by James Fennimore Cooper on "The Color of Buildings in Rural Scenery."

by an Emersonian Transcendentalism, a view of nature as the driving motive of improvement on the American continent. His developing ideas bore strong relationships to several of Emerson's essays from the 1830s and 1840s. In *Nature* Emerson had raised the landscape to a level of symbolic deity when he wrote, "we are as much strangers in nature as we are aliens from God. . . . Is not the landscape, every glimpse of which hath a grandeur, a face of him?"[27] By the next decade, however, even the leafy precincts of Concord, Massachusetts, Emerson's home, felt the impact of expansive technology and trade in New England. Emerson began to shift to a more practical strain of writing. In 1844, in an essay entitled "The Young American," Emerson noted the railroad's role in acquainting Americans with their "bountiful continent . . . state on state, and territory on territory, to the waves of the Pacific sea."[28] He hoped that this acquaintance would free the country from its dependence on European culture and would engender in the "nervous, rocky West . . . a new and continental element into the national mind . . . an American genius."[29] "How much better," he declared, "when the whole land is a garden, and the people have grown up in the bowers of a paradise."[30] As Emerson urged "an education and a sentiment commensurate" to the building of a garden nation, he asserted that "even on the coast, prudent men have begun to see that every American should be educated with a view to the values of land."[31] He urged the study of the arts of engineering, architecture, scientific agriculture, geology, and forestry and added that, "with cheap land and the pacific disposition of the people, everything invites to the arts of agriculture, of gardening, and domestic architecture"; especially in the countryside where men would "render a service to the whole continent, and . . . further the most poetic of all occupations of real life, the bringing out by art the native but hidden graces of the landscape."[32] Nature, for Emerson, was "the noblest engineer."[33]

In 1855 Copeland and Cleveland were commissioned to design Sleepy Hollow Cemetery in Concord.[34] Ralph Waldo Emerson was one of the three members of the local steering committee.[35] It was not merely coincidental that Copeland and Cleveland were selected, for it is unlikely that any other landscape gardeners of the period could present such persuasive literary credentials as to justify a commission for this legendary haunt that with surety would be the final resting place of the earthly remains of the Transcendentalists. Like Emerson, Cleveland saw the native landscape as the unplundered medium of American culture, a garden, to be preserved and cultivated with artistic care and

---

[27] R. W. Emerson, "Nature," *Nature Addresses and Lectures*, Boston, 1893, 69.

[28] R. W. Emerson, "The Young American," *Nature Addresses and Lectures*, 341–72. Note also "The Transcendentalist," (1842) *Nature Addresses and Lectures*, 338; wherein the transitory aspect of improvements is compared to "thoughts and principles not marketable or perishable. . . ."

[29] Emerson, "Young American," 349.

[30] Ibid.

[31] Ibid., 345.

[32] Ibid., 346–50.

[33] Ibid., 352.

[34] *Dictionary of American Biography*, s.v. "Horace W. S. Cleveland."

[35] Nadenicek, "Literary Landscape," 108.

practical restraint. Although Cleveland's thinking had been obviously molded by the most progressive spirit of the times, Copeland was probably Emerson's principal contact. Copeland had attended Harvard where he had been Longfellow's student.[36] Emerson had selected him to speak in the Concord Lyceum series of 1854–55 where he delivered a presentation entitled, "the Usefull [sic] and the Beautiful," on 10 January 1855.[37] In the series that included such luminaries as James Russell Lowell (1819–91), Henry David Thoreau (1817–62), and C. C. Felton, Copeland's presence signaled that the way had been prepared for the inevitability of the firm's commission to design Sleepy Hollow.[38]

The commission was the most rigorous test of Copeland and Cleveland's developing formal approach; one in which improvement would be manifested as mediation with a more potent presence. If Nature and God were, after all, conjoined in the landscape, who were Copeland and Cleveland to profess a more profound engineering? The humble curvilinear roadways and paths that led the visitor to Sleepy Hollow were coarse cousins to the improvements mounted in the urbane precincts of Mount Auburn and Green-Wood. The site had become what it was. Intrinsically a wooded natural amphitheater, it was a quiet hollow sheltered from the busy commerce of the town, and only gradually embellished by the simple gravemarkers that marked the lives of its inhabitants. When Emerson delivered his "Address to the Inhabitants of Concord, at the Consecration of Sleepy Hollow," he captured the Transcendentalist sentiment of this "modest spot of God's earth":

> In these times, we see the defects of the old theology, its inferiority to our habit of thought. Men go up and down. Science is popularized. The irresistible democracy—shall I call it—of chemistry, of vegetation, which recomposes for new life every decomposing particle—the race never dying, the individual never spared, have impressed on the mind of the age the futility of the old arts of preserving. We give our earth to earth. We will not jealously guard a few atoms under immense marbles—[scratched out] but we lay our dead in groves, signifying our surrender of it back to the elements, not—selfishly and impossibly sequestering it from the vast circulations of nature. . . .
>
> A grove of trees; what benefit or ornament is so fair and great? They make the landscape, they keep the earth habitable. Their roots run down like cattle, to the watercourses. Their heads expand to feed the atmosphere. The life of a tree is a hundred and a thousand years; its decay ornamental, its repairs self-made; they grow when we sleep. They grew when we were unborn. Man is a moth among these longevities. He plants for the next millenium. Shadows haunt them; all that ever lived about them, clings to them. You can almost see behind these pines the Indian with bow and arrow lurking yet, exploring the traces of the old trail. . . .

[36] Ibid., 107, a reasonable surmise on the author's part.
[37] R. Orth and A. Ferguson, eds., *The Journals and Miscellaneous Notebooks of Ralph Waldo Emerson: 1852–1855*, 13, Cambridge, Mass., 1977, 498–99, 514 (see notes).
[38] Ibid.

Modern taste has shown that there is no ornament, no architecture alone so sumptuous as well disposed woods and waters; where art has been employed only to remove the superfluities, and bring out the natural advantages. In cultivated grounds one sees the opulent and picturesque effect of the familiar shrubs: barberry, lilac, privet, and thorns when they are disposed in masses and in large spaces. What work of man will compare with the plantation of a park? It dignifies life. It is a seat for friendship, counsel, taste, and religion. I do not wonder that they are the chosen badge of pride of European nobility. But how much more are they needed by us anxious, overdriven Americans, to staunch and appease that fury of temperament which our climate bestows! This tract fortunately lies next to the Agricultural Society's ground, to the New Burial ground, to the Court House, and the Town House making together a large block of public ground of permanent property of the town and county—all the ornaments of either adding so much to the value of all . . . Sleepy Hollow. In this quiet valley, as in the palm of Nature's hand, we shall sleep well when we have finished our day. . . . The ground has the peaceful character that belongs to this town; no lofty crags, no glittering cataracts; but I hold that every part of nature is handsome, when not deformed by bad art. . . . But we must look forward a thousand years; and these acorns that are falling at our feet are oaks overshadowing our children in a remote century, this mute green bank will be full of history; the good, the wise and great will have left their names and virtues on the trees; heroes, poets, beauties, sanctities and benefactors will have made the air tuneable and articulate.[39]

In 1856, on the crest of enthusiasm about American public gardens, Cleveland and Copeland wrote a pamphlet about the site of the New York park.[40] A New York circle, with Irving at its nominal center, and William Cullen Bryant (1794–1878), editor of the *New York Post,* as its coalescent force, had established an independent orbit of influence in matters of the landscape.[41] With their own painters and their own landscape designer, Andrew Jackson Downing, this group had focused on the art of their home, the Hudson River Valley. Cleveland and Copeland's New England literary connections meant little to the Hudson River Valley group, and the commission to design the humble burying ground in the "other" Sleepy Hollow was no match for their cosmopolitan expectations. Frederick Law Olmsted, the politically correct farmer-turned-landscape gardener from Staten Island and the author of several books on his travels in England and in the American South, was named superintendent of the park in 1857.[42] He and Calvert Vaux (1824–95), a British architect and Downing's former partner, won the competition for the park design later in the same year. Copeland, probably in partnership with Cleveland, entered

---

[39] J. E. Cabot, *A Memoir of Ralph Waldo Emerson,* Boston, 1887.

[40] H. W. S. Cleveland and R. M. Copeland, *A Few Words on the Central Park,* Boston, 1856.

[41] F. L. Olmsted, Jr., and T. K. Hubbard, eds., *Forty Years of Landscape Architecture: Central Park,* Cambridge, Mass., 1973 (a reprint of *Frederick Law Olmsted, Landscape Architect, 1822–1903*), 21–29; and L. W. Roper, *F. L. O.: A Biography of Frederick Law Olmsted,* Baltimore, 1973, 129.

[42] Roper, *F. L. O.,* 124–31.

the competition but, apparently, did not place.[43] They continued to practice in New England, moving to Danvers in 1857.[44] During the Civil War, with construction at a standstill and the settlement of the West put on hold, Cleveland, too old to serve, wrote pamphlets and articles about marksmanship.[45]

LANDSCAPE ARCHITECTURE AND THE RISE OF THE MIDWEST

For most Americans whose lives spanned the nineteenth century, the Civil War drove a spike in the line between what had been and what would be. Although the war had shattered the idealist zeal of most Americans born in the early part of the century, Cleveland retained a large measure of his vision. His commissions and writings in the 1870s would be the proving grounds of his idealism tempered by a pragmatism that responded to the new conditions of the country. These new conditions were influenced not only by time but by space. With the return of peace, once again the West beckoned, and Cleveland responded.

Nevertheless, in the wake of the war, with few prospects of work, and having lost his partner, Cleveland struggled to pursue his career in landscape design, and his way west was a tortuous one. He armed himself with introductions to Frederick Law Olmsted and Calvert Vaux, from literary figures, George William Curtis (1824–92) and Charles Eliot Norton (1827–1908), the latter a former student of his brother.[46] He became a consulting field employee of the Olmsted and Vaux firm, working first on Prospect Park; in March, 1869, he apparently journeyed to Chicago to work on the South Park System, and, possibly, on Riverside.[47]

In the same year he also made significant initiatives that signaled his independence from Olmsted. He wrote a short pamphlet, "The Public Grounds of Chicago: How to give them Character and Expression."[48] In this pamphlet he regretted the flatness of the region about Chicago and exposed the potential ridiculousness of a rugged, picturesque treatment on such unrelieved topography. All of Chicago, in Cleveland's view, would have to be made, therefore, with extreme skill and sensitivity since so little was naturally given. He suggested, specifically, that boulevards in the city be designed as artistic and scientific arboreta. His idea was to plant masses of varieties of the same or similar species of trees with careful attention to the topographic situation and the drainage regime. It

[43] Roper, *F. L. O.*, 143; *Dictionary of American Biography*, s.v. "Horace W. S. Cleveland"; Tishler and Luckhardt, "H. W. S. Cleveland," author's notes from a paper read by Professor Tishler, First Annual Clearing Institute, Ellison Bay, Wisconsin, September 1990; and subsequent telephone conversation, May 1991, wherein Tishler noted that only Copeland's name appeared in the records of the competition entry.

[44] Luckhardt, "Early American Lanscape Architect," 18.

[45] *Dictionary of American Biography*, s.v. "Horace W. S. Cleveland."

[46] Roper, *F. L. O.*, 333, and Haglund, "Correspondence," 164.

[47] See D. Bluestone, *Constructing Chicago*, New Haven, 1991, 37–44, 52–54, for a recounting of Cleveland's idea for a museum parkway and for commentary on the landscape of Chicago.

[48] H. W. S. Cleveland, *The Public Grounds of Chicago: How to Give Them Character and Expression*, 2nd ed., Chicago, 1869, 1–20, especially 12–20; see also Haglund, "Correspondence," 173.

was his first attempt to find within himself an empathetic response to the making of open space as the armature of urbanization on the barren table land that met Lake Michigan.

Chicago was a far cry from the dreamland of his youth. All around the city, suburban railroad towns sprouted next to gleaming new tracks. Many of these towns were boomed on the illusory strength of rail development. Following in the more idealistic pattern set by the improvers of Lake Forest a decade earlier, the developers of Highland Park commissioned Cleveland and his new consulting partner, William Merchant Richardson French, a civil engineer, to design their community on the north shore of Lake Michigan.[49] Here the topography of the townsite, carved by deep ravines that opened to the lake, drew Cleveland and French more instinctively to a picturesque solution. Curvilinear roadways laced around the ravines in broad arcs, leaving these picturesque features as possible park locations or embellishments of private estates.

By 1870, when he had apparently resolved to stay in Chicago, the West, or more properly, then the Northwest, had already grown spectacularly. Cleveland realized at that point that the region must, in a matter of decades, match three centuries of cultural development on the eastern seaboard. With this realization, Cleveland, then in his mid-50s, set forth to define the landscape of this civilization amid the rough and tumble of Chicago, the capital city of the emerging Midwest.

As a newcomer, Cleveland had some difficulty in carving out his own share of the work of building the region. In 1870 he was, with Swain Nelson and Company, appointed consulting landscape gardener to the General Officers of Graceland Cemetery (Figs. 1, 2), a landscape that Simonds would later make one of the preeminent garden cemeteries of the nation.[50] The Graceland design marked an important point in the evolution of Cleveland's design vision for the midwestern garden. Graceland recalled the simple aesthetic of Sleepy Hollow, and Cleveland transformed it to meet the conditions of a broad, flat-ridged western savannah. When completed, Graceland looked like a country cemetery, laced with curving drives and dotted here and there with limestone markers and low curbs among oak groves and wild shrubs. In 1872 the officers prepared a statement of conditions which recast an Emersonian thought to capture the essence of this oak meadow: "The cemetery has become a garden. . . . We lay the bodies of beloved dead in the bosom of our mother Earth, and they become part of her substance. They return to dust; and from thence, spring flower and leaf and waving grass."[51]

[49] H. W. S. Cleveland, "Advertisement: Cleveland and French, Landscape Architects and Engineers, Chicago, Illinois: Suburban Additions," ca. 1872?, 4; mentions the Highland Park work. M. Ebner, *Creating Chicago's North Shore*, Chicago, 1988, 36–37. The author misunderstands the landscape design intentions of the community's developers and misidentifies French. J. Sniderman and J. A. Nathan, "Reawakening a Spirit of Stewardship," *Landscape Architecture* 77 (September–October 1987), 88–93, illustrate the plan (p. 89) and give Cleveland and French credit for setting the environmental quality of the community by saving the ravines from development. See also E. Chamberlin, *Chicago and Its Suburbs*, Chicago, 1874, 393, wherein the author noted that the Highland Park Company had "called in the aid of good landscape gardeners to lay [the town] out." Much was made of the topographic sensitivity of these "earnest" utilizers of the "natural beauties" of the site, but neither Cleveland nor French was mentioned by name.
[50] Office of Graceland Cemetery, *Catalogue of the Graceland Cemetery: Lot Owners to April, 1870*, Chicago, 1870.
[51] In J. Vinci, "Graceland: Nineteenth-Century Garden Cemetery," *Chicago History* (Summer 1977), 88.

1. H. W. S. Cleveland, O. C. Simonds(?), and others, "reflecting pond," *Views in Graceland*, ca. 1875–85 (photo: E. D. Carr Scrapbook, Chicago Historical Society)

2. H. W. S. Cleveland and others, "four tombstones," *Views in Graceland*, ca. 1875–85 (photo: E. D. Carr Scrapbook, Chicago Historical Society)

Their energies fueled by their successes, Cleveland and French began in earnest to develop their own Chicago clientele. In 1871 Cleveland wrote "A Few Hints on Landscape Gardening as Applied to the Wants of the West," to which French added an essay on civil engineering in relationship to landscape design.[52] The great fire of the same year, 1871, cut some of their efforts short, but they rebounded resiliently in 1872.

One of Cleveland's commissions, Drexel Boulevard, was a child of the fire. He theorized that a city with wide boulevards, in the manner of Paris, would be less susceptible to total conflagration than those that were tightly built in a relentless grid.[53] In 1872 Cleveland executed the Drexel design under the aegis of the South Park Commission.[54] The boulevard, once completed, was an elegant urban street, divided by a restrained ornamental garden. The Drexel Boulevard work united Cleveland with a man whose presence on the Minneapolis scene a decade later would be critical to the realization of the public gardens of that city. William Morse Berry, (1826–1920), a former ship captain and Maine native, joined him as a construction superintendent on the boulevard and in the other projects for the South Parks (Figs. 3, 4).[55]

[52] H. W. S. Cleveland, "A Few Hints on Landscape Gardening in the West," and W. M. R. French, "The Relation of Engineering to Landscape Gardening," Chicago, 1871 (Cleveland and French's essays are bound together). This small volume contains several testimonials by clients in the East and West, such as Simon Brown of Concord, Massachusetts, and W. Robbins of Hinsdale, Illinois. For the latter, Cleveland designed the Robbins Park Addition, a small curvilinear subdivision illustrated in schematic design in the book. Another illustration shows a very simple design for J. Y. Scammon, of Hyde Park, south of Chicago.

[53] Cleveland recommended W. Robinson, *The Parks, Promenades and Gardens of Paris*, London, 1869, regularly in his lectures in St. Paul and Minneapolis in 1872, and he mentioned the idea in *Landscape Architecture*, 69.

[54] Cleveland, *Landscape Architecture*, 46–47; Cleveland reported to Olmsted in a letter, 30 July 1872, that "the proposition has been formally made to me to take charge of the planting & arrangement of the South Park & Drexel Avenue." He conceded that he was still considering the proposition, but by 10 September 1872, he reported in another letter that he has taken the position offered by the Board (Frederick Law Olmsted Papers, Correspondence, Library of Congress, Washington, D. C.) H. W. S. Cleveland, "Landscape Architect's Report," *Report of the South Park Commissioners to the Board of County Commissioners of Cook County, From December 1st, 1872, to December 1st, 1873*, Chicago, 1873, 13, noted that he had been called upon to reduce the width of the "central ornamental ground" of the boulevard, necessitating rearrangement of "the whole design." On 21 September 1871, Olmsted had written to H. H. Honore resisting changes in the design of the "South Open Parkway" (Frederick Law Olmsted Papers). He provided in the letter, nevertheless, a revised section of the roadway. Perhaps Olmsted's reluctance to make changes began to turn the commissioners to Cleveland. Later letters (1893) from Cleveland to Olmsted, cited and partially quoted in Haglund, "Correspondence," 170, might be interpreted to mean that Cleveland attributed this work entirely to Olmsted, but since the later predated the completion of Jackson Park, it surely referred to Washington Park and probably to his own work. Roper (*F. L. O.*, 333) has clouded the issue as well by referring to the "superintendence of the South Park work and of the approach boulevards" in Cleveland's hands. Olmsted and Vaux may have understood the work in this way, but strictly speaking, Cleveland was the landscape architect of all of the work, and William Morse Berry was the superintendent. Cleveland made several significant changes to the executed design while working from the schematic plan, as indicated in the text and in note 57.

[55] I. Atwater, *History of the City of Minneapolis*, New York, 1893, pt. 1, 420–22. See also W. M. Berry, "Superintendent's Report," *Report of the South Park Commissioners, December 1st, 1872, to December 1st, 1873*,

3. H. W. S. Cleveland and others(?), South (Washington) Park, Chicago, Illinois, ca. 1875. Stereograph by Lovejoy and Foster (photo: Chicago Historical Society)

4. H. W. S. Cleveland and others(?), South (Washington) Park, Chicago, Illinois, ca. 1875. Mrs. Whiting and Mrs. George Gage(?) seated on bench. Stereograph by Lovejoy and Foster (photo: Chicago Historical Society)

Prior to the fire, preliminary grading had begun on the Olmsted design for the South Park, later Washington Park, at the inland end of the Midway and at the foot of Drexel Boulevard; however, the costs of the city's reconstruction scaled back expectations for a completed effort.[56] Cleveland was retained in the summer of 1872 as the South Park Commission's landscape architect to execute with "rigid economy . . . the details of ornamental arrangement and planting" for the Olmsted and Vaux plan.[57] This constrained commission would constitute Cleveland and Berry's first experiments with fast-tracking. On 20 December 1873, Cleveland submitted his report to the commissioners in which he detailed the specific actions he had taken to go forward with the modified scheme.[58] He paid special attention to the matters of economies in preserving existing oak groves, moving mature trees among the new plantations, and using native shrubs for a special "ramble" near the northeast entrance of the park from Drexel Boulevard.[59]

He recommended planting these shrubs, "already . . . [collected] from the woods," under the trees proposed in the original scheme "to form thickets and copses."[60] Olmsted and Vaux had proposed an open grove so that park users would be safe from marauders who might hide in the undergrowth, but Cleveland assured the commissioners that since the park was currently in an unsettled region of the city, there would, for some time, be little likelihood of such danger.[61] He further assured them that "the desired effect [would be] speedily secured, and whenever it [became] desirable to carry out the original design, it [would] be easy to remove the shrubbery . . ."[62] In closing his report he specifically commended Berry for his "ready aid . . . in promoting the preparation [and] execution of [his] designs . . . ," and the chairman, L. B. Sidway for his interest in the "wise economy" of the work.[63]

In 1871 and 1872, in pursuit of business beyond Chicago, Cleveland and French had developed the latter's family connections to critical figures close to the President of the University of Minnesota, William Watts Folwell (1837–1929).[64] Folwell asked Cleve-

---

9–11, and "Funeral of W. M. Berry, Park Builder, in Chicago Today," *Minneapolis Tribune* (?) (clipping in Charles M. Loring Papers, Minnesota Historical Society, St. Paul, Minnesota); written in Loring's failing hand next to the obituary, "He planted many thousand trees on the streets of Minneapolis which are living monuments to his memory"; and in another hand, "One of Natures [sic] Noblemen Minneapolis owes much to him for its attractive streets and parks. C. M. Loring."

[56] Cleveland, "Landscape Architect's Report," 12; "Washington Park, Chicago," *Park and Cemetery* 5, 1 (March 1895), 2.

[57] Cleveland, "Landscape Architect's Report," 12. See also Chamberlin, *Chicago and its Suburbs*, 320–21, in which the "Olmstead [sic] & Vaux" plan is described. There is a critical distinction here between the plan as drawn schematically by Olmsted and Vaux and the design as executed by Cleveland. Chamberlain noted further that "Mr. Cleveland, the architect" had developed a new scheme and a cost-saving rationale for a flat open clearing on the south open green, rather than a concave one, "according to the original plan." The entire experience of this broad, flat clearing set the stage for later work by Simonds and Jensen.

[58] Cleveland, "Landscape Architect's Report," 12–20.

[59] Ibid., 18.

[60] Ibid.

[61] Ibid.

[62] Ibid.

[63] Ibid, 20.

[64] *William Watts Folwell: The Autobiography and Letters of a Pioneer of Culture*, ed. S. Buck, Minneapolis,

land to substitute for him in a "Peoples' Course of Lectures" series event in February, 1872, where he delivered a lecture (in both cities) entitled "Landscape Gardening As Applied to the Wants of the West," developing the text of his earlier pamphlet and incipient book.[65] The arguments of the text, which were based on a nonornamental, picturesque aesthetic for the landscape development of western cities, found immediate and enthusiastic response among the residents of St. Paul. In that city, two months later, he was commissioned to prepare his report, "Public Parks, Radial Avenues, and Boulevards. Outline Plan of a Park System," in which he recommended the acquisition of the city's two large country parks, Como and Phalen, several smaller city squares, and parkway rights-of-way from the city center outward.[66] He also began negotiations for the design of Oakland Cemetery (1873); St. Anthony Park (1873), a small suburban town plan; the grounds of the Bishop Whipple School in Faribault (1873?); the University of Minnesota grounds (ca. 1875–92); and several other projects in and near the Twin Cities.[67]

The Oakland Cemetery project demonstrated another development in the aesthetic as it was applied to an archetypal midwestern landscape. The Oakland site was a fairly dense oak grove of some seventy acres. The project involved a major expansion of the site to encompass a small, rectilinearly planned burying ground. The Cleveland and French design exercised a picturesquely light hand in its revelation of the existing landscape qualities of the oak woods. A careful survey of the site allowed the designers to thread curvilinear roads and paths amid the young trees that would later shade the graves of the city's pioneers.[68] Like Sleepy Hollow and Graceland, Oakland Cemetery was a masterpiece of topographic restraint, intended, once again, to let nature's engineering control the mood of the landscape.

1933, 166, records that George Leonard Chase, a Hobart College classmate of Folwell, was also a first cousin to Daniel Chester and William Merchant Richardson French. Chase had married Mrs. W. W. Folwell's sister, and these close ties were important in Folwell's rise to the presidency of the University of Minnesota, as well as in the roles that Cleveland (and French) were to play in the design of landscapes in the Twin Cities. French left the loose partnership before 1883 when Cleveland executed his Minneapolis park work.

[65] H. W. S. Cleveland letter to F. L. Olmsted, 19 January 1872, wherein he reported that his "lecture is on the application of landscape architecture to the wants of the West," and further, that he has prepared a magazine article on the subject, "opening fire on the stereotyped system of laying out towns. . . ." Frederick Law Olmsted Papers, Library of Congress; "Minneapolis and St. Anthony Daily Local News," *Saint Paul Pioneer*, 9 February 1872, 14 February 1872, and "St. Paul City News," *Saint Paul Pioneer*, 17 February 1872; clippings may be found in the files of the Ramsey County Historical Society.

[66] H. W. S. Cleveland, *Public Parks, Radial Avenues, and Boulevards. Outline Plan of a Park System*, Saint Paul, 1872.

[67] "Minneapolis and St. Anthony Daily Local News," *Saint Paul Pioneer*, 17 February 1872; Cleveland wrote to Olmsted to say: "I have engaged so much work that I shall open an office in St. Paul and make my headquarters there for the summer." Although the title block of the Oakland Cemetery drawings indicated that Cleveland and French were located in "Chicago and St. Paul," it is unlikely that Cleveland was able to move to Minnesota for the summer as planned because of the Chicago South Park work that was then only on the horizon. Cleveland mentioned a missed opportunity to preserve a park on Nicollet Island at the Falls of St. Anthony in Minneapolis in *Landscape Architecture*, 81.

[68] At this writing, the Cleveland and French drawings for Oakland Cemetery are housed at the Oakland Cemetery office. Among them are design development drawings with many erasured attempts to site the roads over a topographical grid. The technique of a grid survey employed by Cleveland was described in H. W. S. Cleveland, *A Few Words on the Arrangement of Rural Cemeteries*, Chicago, 1881.

Doubtless, encouraged even by these limited successes, Cleveland gathered his resources and completed his book, *Landscape Architecture As Applied to the Wants of the West*, in 1873. In spite of his expressed ire with the ruthless rectilinear thinking of boomtown developers, Cleveland's professional work was aided immeasurably by his contacts with railroad entrepreneurs. Particularly significant was his relationship to the Chicago, Burlington, and Quincy Railroad. Its president at this period was John Murray Forbes, Emerson's brother-in-law. Cleveland's brother, Henry, had married Sarah Perkins, the daughter of Forbes's business mentor and uncle, James Perkins. This complex family relationship and business mentorship also involved Forbes's nephew, Charles E. Perkins, who was stationed in Burlington, Iowa, to run the western land operations of the Burlington and allied roads. Horace Cleveland's son, Ralph, though at best a distant cousin, was a constant guest at the Perkins home, the "Apple Trees," in the 1870s when he was also a rodman on the road in Iowa, near the towns of Emerson and Hawthorne. Emerson himself also journeyed through Burlington on his western lecture tours. The work and the rewards of building the Burlington line were shared among "family." This sharing, which provided direct job contacts for Cleveland, was deemed the best way to achieve an appropriate level of civilization and economy to sustain rail operations in the west. In his book, Cleveland predicated a balance between nature and basic civilizing improvements. Echoing Emerson, he wrote:

> The vast regions yet lying undisturbed between the Mississippi and the Pacific comprise such resources of wealth and variety of sublime and picturesque features of natural scenery as can be seen on no other portion of the earth's surface, that is accessible to civilization. This is raw material placed in our hands to be moulded into shape for the habitations of a nation. . . . [69]

In defining the role of the landscape architect as the aesthetic arbiter of this process for the frontier, Cleveland added:

> That writers on landscape gardening in this country have heretofore failed to give prominence to the really essential principles which lie at the foundation of the art, may be accounted for by the fact that they have supposed themselves to be addressing a class of readers inhabiting districts already brought to a condition of elaborate culture, and who would be mainly interested in the details of decoration. It is obvious that the new regions of the West require a vast amount of preliminary preparation before much attention can be paid to mere extraneous ornament. My object is to show that this preparatory work is justly the province of the landscape gardener, but that it is in reality the essentially important part of his art which

---

[69] Cleveland, *Landscape Architecture*, 29. Special thanks to the Burlington Archives and the *Guide to the Burlington Archives in the Newberry Library, 1851–1901*, Newberry Library, Chicago, 1949. Edith Perkins Cunningham, daughter of Charles E. Perkins, has summarized some of these critical facts in manuscripts and scrapbooks held by the library and in a series of privately printed volumes of family reminiscences and letters.

gives character and expression to the whole, independently of mere decoration *. . . Landscape Gardening, or more properly Landscape Architecture, is the art of arranging land so as to adapt to it most conveniently, economically and gracefully, to any of the varied wants of civilization.*[70]

During the course of 1873 there was an economic panic which generally dampened the firm's business prospects. In St. Paul, the laboring population rallied behind efforts to kill the parks plan, particularly the scheme to acquire and improve the largest and most distant of the sites, Lake Como, and to provide a park and driveway made possible by laws "in favor of the rich."[71] Park-making in St. Paul halted for fourteen years in the wake of this controversy. However, on the bright side, the book, once published and distributed, received warm review.[72] In 1876 Cleveland was invited back to Minneapolis to address the city's Improvement Society led by the estimable Charles M. Loring, Maine-born businessman and servant of his community.[73]

Nature as Garden: Fast-Tracking Culture in Minneapolis

However warm the response to his 1876 address had been, seven more years elapsed before he was invited to return to Minneapolis, then the emerging capital of a new Northwest. On 2 June 1883, at the age of sixty-eight, Cleveland prepared his famous "Suggestions for a System of Parks and Parkways for the City of Minneapolis."[74] This document envisioned the building of the city on the armature of its public gardens, rapidly and minimally improved as civilizing elements necessary to well-structured growth. Realizing the unique moment, he recast his oft-repeated advice on the economy of the work at hand. In his "Suggestions," he declared that

. . . all expenditures for ornamental gardening as especially for artificial structures in the form of rustic buildings, bridges, grottos, fountains, statues, vases, etc. is not only needless as being out of keeping with the rude conditions of the surroundings, but while so many urgent demands exist for works of actual necessity, would dictate such incongruity and deficiency of taste as that of the individual

[70] Ibid., 16–17.

[71] The early efforts to make a park system in St. Paul are chronicled in a very loose fashion in files that may be found in the offices of the Division of Parks and Recreation, City of Saint Paul. One published account of Lake Como and the political battles is P. Murphy and G. Phelps, "Swamps, Farms, Boom or Bust—Como Neighborhood's Colorful History," *Ramsey County History* 19, 1 (1984), 16.

[72] H. W. S. Cleveland letter to F. L. Olmsted, 28 July 1873, wherein he wrote, "I received your note in due course & am glad indeed that my book gave you pleasure," Frederick Law Olmsted Papers, Library of Congress; and Roper, *F. L. O.*, 339; and Haglund, "Correspondence," 168, wherein he cited Olmsted's review of the book in the *Nation*.

[73] *Minneapolis Tribune* (?) clipping, Charles M. Loring Papers, Minnesota Historical Society, St. Paul, Minnesota.

[74] H. W. S. Cleveland, *Suggestions for a System of Parks and Parkways for the City of Minneapolis*, Minneapolis, 1883.

who adorns his person with jewelry before he is provided with comfortable clothing.[75]

Not surprisingly, many of the principal parks projected by the "Suggestions" bounded the water bodies for which Minnesota was, and is, so well known. In the 1880s, Minneapolis hugged the waterpower on the Mississippi at Saint Anthony Falls, and rolling farms, dotted with marshy lakes skirted the edges of the compact town. The moment was perfect. The transplanted New England millers who had forged the basic civility of the rough city now turned their collective gaze to the future. Horace Cleveland's vision of that future sprang from the same idealistic and practical founts that lay at the heart of the community's being. As he would so often in his work with both Minneapolis and St. Paul, Cleveland emphasized the symbolic centrality of the Mississippi River:

> The grand natural feature which gives character to [the] city . . . the main spring of its prosperity, . . . it is the object of vital interest and the center of attraction to intelligent visitors from every quarter of the globe. . . ."[76]

To secure the preservation of the given gardens of the Mississippi River bluffs he proposed "a broad avenue be laid out on each side of the river."[77] The river parkway would begin atop the steep bluffs at a site just north of the Riverside Park and would continue southward to the legendary Falls of Minnehaha, then in a state of desecration.[78] Mixing the poetic and the practical, Cleveland took care to emphasize the luxuriant growth of native trees and shrubs on the river banks, "material for such picturesque effects at the trifling cost of what nature has merely furnished to your hand. . . ."[79]

The scheme also provided for a system of contiguous lakefront parks and parkways (Figs. 5, 6). Radiating from a small central park, the principal focus of residential development in Minneapolis, boulevards would be built on Hennepin Avenue to the south and Lyndale to the north; Kenwood Parkway was laid out to the head of Lake Calhoun, around its western shore and then around the entire perimeter of Lake Harriet; and connections were also proposed for a boulevard link to the Mississippi along the Lake Street right-of-way.

The scheme commenced immediately. The Park Act of 1883, which had created the Board of Park Commissioners, allowed it to operate with broad powers of land acquisition and park development.[80] In this, the first year, Cleveland prepared schematic de-

[75] Ibid., 4.
[76] Ibid., 6.
[77] Ibid., 7.
[78] Ibid.
[79] Ibid., 8.
[80] Archival Records, Minneapolis Board of Park Commissioners, City of Minneapolis Municipal Reference Library, show the detailed project management of the park and parkway construction. Also in the "Correspondence," records of the board may be found in a letter dated 8 July 1895, from George Kessler, engineer and secretary of the Kansas City Board of Park and Boulevard Commissioners, thanking the Minneapolis Board for information on the Minneapolis method of condemning and purchasing lands for parks. Another follow-up letter, 18 October 1895, written by the Clerk of the Kansas City Board, cited J. C. Olmsted

5. View of Minneapolis from Lowry Hill, site of Loring Park in the foreground, ca. 1878 (photo: Minnesota Historical Society)

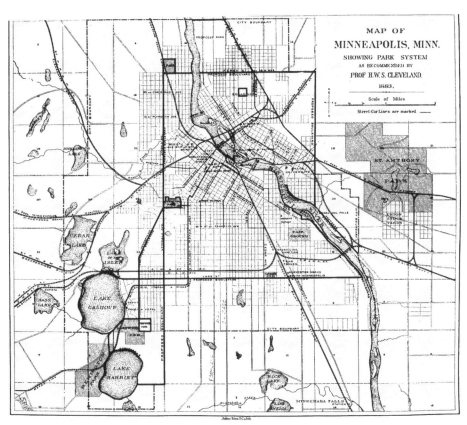

6. H. W. S. Cleveland, "Map of Minneapolis, Minn. Showing Park System," 1883. Suggestions for a system of parks and parkways for the City of Minneapolis, Minnesota

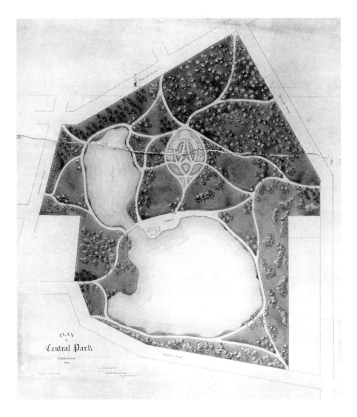

7. H. W. S. Cleveland, "Plan of Central (Loring) Park," 1883(?).
Schematic design. Tempera on watercolor paper (photo: Hennepin County Historical Society)

signs for the Central Park, Riverside Park, and several smaller squares and parks.[81] The
president of the Board, Charles M. Loring, took several years away from his business to
attend to park issues on a day-to-day basis.[82] At first, Loring saw to the construction of

<hr>

as having recommended the Minneapolis model for the acquisition of parks. See also a letter from H. W. S.
Cleveland, "The Danger of Delay in Acquiring Land for Public Use," *Garden and Forest* 5 (16 March 1892),
131, wherein he offers a rationale for rapid land acquisition for park purposes.

[81] *First Annual Report of the Board of Park Commissioners of the City of Minneapolis, For the Year Ending March
13, 1884,* Minneapolis, 1884.

[82] Loring signed off on all procurements at this early period while Rufus Cook was superintendent; see
Archival Records, Minneapolis Board of Park Commissioners, and Charles M. Loring Papers, Minnesota
Historical Society, for Loring's Scrapbook, which includes excerpts from a diary that touches on the daily
work in the parks. The rapid development of Riverside Park illustrated some of the difficulties inherent in
the fast-tracking process. On 7 August 1885 Loring recorded in his diary that he had

> visited Riverside Park with [Commissioners] Geo. A. Brackett, J. C. Oswald, D. Morrison, Col. King,
> (illegible) and Nimocks. After returning to the board rooms, I was greatly insulted by D. Morrison
> because I had permitted an (illegible) stone from a quarry which Mr. Cleveland had recommended
> done (?) to square out the wall. I returned from the rooms and (illegible) tendered my resignation.

He was later persuaded to return to this position (Charles M. Loring Papers, Scrapbook).

8. View of Central (Loring) Park, Wooded Island, ca. 1906 (photo: Minnesota Historical Society)

the parks virtually unaided by the first superintendent, Rufus Cook.[83] Cook was quickly dismissed, and by 1885, William Morse Berry, Cleveland's old partner from the South Park System in Chicago, was hired in his place.[84] The parkway layout was given to Frank Nutter, a young local landscape engineer.[85] With these able men in the employ of the Board, the parks could essentially be built directly from schematic designs.

Central Park, later Loring Park, contained the most ornamental grounds, but they were balanced in the final design by a ramble near the "lake" and a "wild" island that was born of the fast-tracking process (Figs. 7, 8). Cleveland showed in his initial schematic design the development of a conservatory and formal garden as the principal focus of

[83] Charles M. Loring Papers, Scrapbook; see also T. Wirth, *Minneapolis Park System, 1883–1944,* Minneapolis, 1945, 46.

[84] Atwater, *History of Minneapolis,* pt. 1, 420–22, chronicles Berry's hiring and places Cleveland at the center of the decision. See also H. W. S. Cleveland, "Park Construction," *Garden and Forest* 3 (12 March 1890), 129, wherein the author described the advantages, even the necessity of a thoroughly competent park superintendent. Several primary materials, including letters between the Board and Berry may be found in the Archival Records; and clippings from secondary sources, including Berry's obituary, 20 (?) June 1920, may be found in the Charles M. Loring Papers, Scrapbook.

[85] Archival Records, Minneapolis Board of Park Commissioners.

the park. Perhaps modeled on the Parisian parks that he admired, but probably never saw, this park, closest to the city center, was to be its most civilized. As construction commenced immediately upon adoption of Cleveland's plan and schematic designs, Loring superintended the work regularly.[86] Excavation on the lake began in November 1883. In June 1884, as it continued, Loring recorded that he had stopped the work, quickly written to Cleveland about the possibility of preserving an island, and received Cleveland's assent.[87] This island became the locus of the most intense planting of native or "wild" shrubs on the site.[88]

Within just three years of the Park Act and the publication of Cleveland's "Suggestions," Minneapolis had established the momentum that would provide a parkland structure of urban growth for the next four decades. Several of the smaller parks had been well begun, and much of the land of the "Grand Rounds" of connected parks and parkways surrounding Lakes Calhoun, Harriet, and Lake of the Isles had been acquired (Fig. 9).[89] In 1886 the Board of Park Commissioners, perhaps insecure about the results of their swift work, invited Frederick Law Olmsted to review the developments to date.[90] Olmsted refrained from direct critique in his published review, except insofar as he observed that a large park seemed to be missing from the system.[91] Whether this opinion derived from his sense of the whole system or merely his visit to the diminutive Central (Loring) Park was not clearly stated.

If the rapidity of the early park work was one measure of the consanguinity of the Minneapolis group, the preservation of the state's essential literary garden, the Falls of Minnehaha, was the ultimate test of fast-tracked civilization (Figs. 10, 11). At the core of Cleveland's success in Minneapolis was a shared mythology, inculcated in the poetic ideals of young men and women born and educated in the full flower of New England letters. For these transplanted Yankees, many of whom hailed from Longfellow's home state, Maine, *The Song of Hiawatha* was etched in their hearts. Cleveland, who had known

[86] Charles M. Loring Papers, Scrapbook, diary extract from 12 June 1884. See also H. W. S. Cleveland, "Park Construction," 129. See Cleveland's appraisal of J. C. A. Alphand's work at Buttes-Chaumont in *Landscape Architecture*, 64.

[87] Charles M. Loring Papers, Scrapbook.

[88] The plants are listed as "261 wild shrubs from the woods," in the *Third Annual Report of the Board of Park Commissioners of the City of Minneapolis, For the Year Ending March 14, 1886*, Minneapolis, 1886, 9.

[89] The naming of the connected circuit of parks, the "Grand Rounds," was suggested by William Watts Folwell at a much later date, in 1891; see the *Eighth Annual Report of the Board of Park Commissioners of the City of Minneapolis*, Minneapolis, 1891, 22–28. The boulevards on Hennepin and Lyndale and the Lake Street connector to the river had been abandoned, the latter in favor of a connecting piece along Minnehaha Creek.

[90] Olmsted's official report was published as "Letter of Professor Olmsted Relative to the General Duties of Park Commissioners in Incidental Matters," *Fourth Annual Report of the Board of Park Commissioners of the City of Minneapolis, For the Year Ending March 14, 1887*, Minneapolis, 1887, 15–25; but manuscript versions also exist in the files of the Frederick Law Olmsted Papers, Library of Congress. In one of these manuscripts, Olmsted assured the Park Commissioners that "Mr. Cleveland" was an able consultant, and they should have no qualms about his work. Perhaps sensing that he was damning his colleague with faint praise, he omitted this section in the final report.

[91] *Fourth Annual Report of the Board of Park Commissioners of the City of Minneapolis, For the Year Ending March 14, 1887*, Minneapolis, 1887, 23–24.

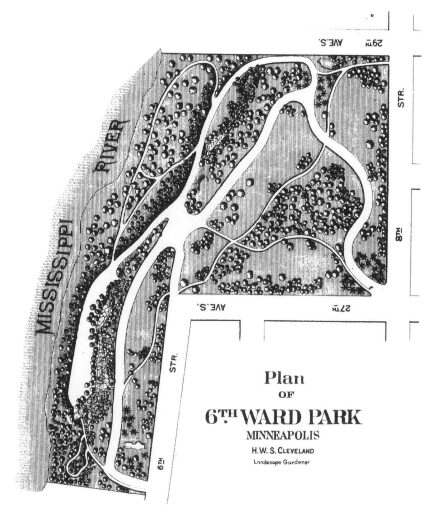

9. H. W. S. Cleveland, "Plan of 6th Ward Park," 1884 (photo: from *First Annual Report of the Board of Park Commissioners of the City of Minneapolis, For the Year Ending March 13, 1884*, Minneapolis, 1884)

Longfellow as his brother's close friend in the days of their youth, was deeply affected by the poem. Set in the old Northwest, it was a parable of the Native American and of primeval landscape at the precipice of change. The mythical story of Hiawatha and Minnehaha, who survived the adversities of the native landscape only to be supplanted by the white "visitors," was given specific locus at the falls. Longfellow's researches, including his use of a daguerreotype of the falls brought to him by a relative of Charles Sumner, gave the extended poem the resonance of geographic and historical reality, and thereby projected a larger realm of affect among the myth's adherents.[92]

[92] The daguerreotype, one of two, was made by Alexander Hesler of Galena, Illinois. See W. Welling, *Photography in America: The Formative Years, 1839–1900*, New York, 1978, 82–83, for Hesler's account of George Sumner's purchase of the image and its conveyance to Longfellow.

10. View of Minnehaha Creek, Glen, and Falls, Minneapolis, Minnesota, ca. 1880 (photo: Minnesota Historical Society)

11. View of Minnehaha Falls, Minneapolis, Minnesota, ca. 1880 (photo: Minnesota Historical Society)

Longfellow died in 1882. In 1885 a commission was formed to examine the preservation of Minnehaha Falls and its environs as Minnesota's first state park.[93] One bright afternoon that year, Charles Loring, the commission's president, led a party aboard the steamboat "Henry W. Longfellow" up the Mississippi River from Saint Paul to the mouth of Minnehaha Creek; here some thirty-five of the state's most public-spirited men and women alighted from their craft and trekked with Loring and "Professor H. W. S. Cleveland, of Chicago," along the Mississippi's banks and up the creek, to the falls.[94] Following this event, the commission brought forward a plan to acquire and preserve the site.[95] Cleveland moved to Minneapolis in 1886 to be closer to the significant work at hand.[96]

In 1888, when he delivered his Minneapolis Society of Fine Arts address entitled "The Aesthetic Development of the United Cities of St. Paul and Minneapolis," the scheme had yet to be completed.[97] In his lecture, Cleveland reflected upon the fortunes of Paris, Boston, and New York, and as he considered Saint Paul and Minneapolis, he called forth memories of the rapid changes in the region within his own lifetime.[98] He talked about gifts to the present culture that had been made by "Longfellow, Emerson, Irving, Everett, and Webster," and, by analogy, likened these literary contributions to the work at hand.[99] For Cleveland, Minnehaha Falls was the preeminent symbol of these "gifts of nature which will provide for the wants of those that come after us. . . ."[100] He declared:

> I would have the city itself such a work of art as may be the fitting abode of a race of men and women whose lives are devoted to a nobler end than money-getting and whose efforts shall be inspired and sustained by the grandeur and beauty of the scenes in which their lives are passed. Nature offers us such advantages as no other city could rival and such as if properly developed would exhibit the highest attainment of art in appropriating the natural elements on which all art is founded. If we fail to secure these natural features and suffer them to be destroyed no power on earth can restore them, and instead of being the chief feature of attractive interest, they will become simply a hideous scene of desolation, a blot that can neither be erased or kept out of sight.[101]

[93] Charles M. Loring Papers, Scrapbook; see also Wirth, *Minneapolis*, 49–62.

[94] "Minnehaha Park," *Minneapolis Tribune* (?), ca. 1885, clipping in Charles M. Loring Papers, Scrapbook.

[95] See *Report of the Commissioners for the State Park at Minnehaha*, Minneapolis, 1885, for a description of the park.

[96] Tishler and Luckhardt, "Pioneering with Plans and Plants," 67.

[97] See the private printing of Cleveland, *Aesthetic Development*, to which is appended a reprint of a letter to the *Northwestern Review*, 1886, pleading the case of preservation of the falls environs. Many clippings related to the work on the falls, including a letter by H. W. S. Cleveland, "The Park System," *Minneapolis Tribune*, ca. 1889, which recounts the narrative of the *genius loci* of the site, are in the Charles M. Loring Papers, Scrapbook.

[98] Cleveland, *Aesthetic Development*, 10–11.

[99] Ibid., 12.

[100] Ibid.

[101] Ibid., 12–13.

The next year, 1889, the park was secured with the help of the heirs of Franklin Steele, an early Minneapolis miller.[102]

CIVILIZATION AMID THE NATIVE LANDSCAPE: THE MIDWESTERN GARDEN

Cleveland's ideas of American civilization, cultivated in the flowering of culture in one region, were well transplanted in the landscape of another. They defined a native landscape aesthetic that suffused the next generation of garden design, a generation in which the Midwest came to its own identity. As the raw conditions of the region gave way to more polished urbanity, Ossian Simonds and Jens Jensen projected the poetry of native plants and archetypal forms onto the landscape with finesse and energy. Paradoxically, urbanization (and agriculture) had, as Cleveland predicted, despoiled much of the native landscape, and at the turn of the century there was a nearly frantic movement to preserve what was left in the region. Jensen in particular was identified with this work, and both he and Simonds executed a large number of commissions for gardens, public and private, that looked to the restoration and symbolic rendering of a native landscape condition.[103] These simply wrought gardens, when considered with the spare forms of the domestic architecture of the period, provided a formal setting that defined the space of a new way of life in the Midwest.

[102] See Charles M. Loring Papers, Scrapbook. See also D. Empson, "The History of the Mississippi River Boulevard in St. Paul", ca. 1975, which may be found in the "Historical" files of the division of Parks and Recreation, City of Saint Paul, which chronicles generally the struggle that Cleveland had in that city after the park work had come to a halt in 1873. On 25 February 1887, the State Legislature established a Board of Park Commissioners for the City of St. Paul. They met on 28 March and at that first meeting extended an invitation to Horace Cleveland to speak again to them as he had more than a dozen years earlier. On 10 May 1887, in the old state capitol building, he delivered an address that previewed the Minneapolis Society of Fine Arts Address; that is, it was a plea for park systems united along the seam of their shared treasure, the Mississippi River, "the grand topographical feature of the whole region between the two cities." He proposed that the land from the city's boundary at the Chicago and Milwaukee Railway bridge to Fort Snelling be acquired.

In the same year the Board authorized a survey of the lands outlined in Cleveland's lecture. Work proceeded immediately on the condemnation of the property. In the late summer of 1888, Cleveland was retained by the Board to execute the principal work at hand, the design of the river parkway and shortly thereafter, the much delayed design of Como Park. The river parkway was not realized in Cleveland's lifetime, but Como Park went ahead quickly.

Frederick Nussbaumer was chosen as the gardener for Como Park and later as its superintendent. He was responsible for much of the floral display, such as the immensely popular "Gates Ajar," mimicking a similar work in Washington Park in Chicago. These floral displays angered Cleveland. See a letter from H. W. S. Cleveland, "Flower-beds in Chicago Parks," *Garden and Forest* 2 (31 July 1889), 370, in which he despaired about the public taste for the "monstrosity" of the gaudy effects of such figurative floral displays.

In 1890 Cleveland, then seventy-six years old, was retained to design the extension of Summit Avenue. The divided parkway to the river is a result of his work. While the connection between the two cities that Cleveland envisioned at Summit Avenue did not occur, the Ford Parkway has made an important connection to Minnehaha Falls that surely Cleveland would have delighted in.

[103] L. K. Eaton, *Landscape Artist in America: The Life and Work of Jens Jensen*, Chicago, 1964. See also R. E. Grese, *Jens Jensen: A Maker of Natural Parks and Gardens*, Baltimore and London, 1992.

The archetypal expressions of this aesthetic seemed, for some, to have sprung fully formed from the minds' eyes of the young designers identified by Wilhelm Miller. However, neither the vast array of direct stimuli on these designers nor the ground that was prepared before them could be exactly charted. Horace Cleveland's general apologias for native landscape had an undeniable, groundbreaking influence, but they have completely overshadowed his development of critical icons of the prairie style. Obscured by the lost documentation of his designs for landscapes familiar to the next generation, (but almost unknowable to ours,) Cleveland's connections to the formal conventions of the prairie spirit have been all but lost. Still, Cleveland rendered a forceful word picture of the open clearing edged by dense woods, an essential icon of the work of Simonds and Jensen, in his statement on his design intentions at Graceland in 1870:

> However beautiful a lawn may be, it is only by contrast with the surrounding wood that its beauty is developed. If extended indefinitely, it becomes monotonous . . . it is like an extended sheet of water whose beauty can only be appreciated by contrast to its shores. On the other hand, . . . the true beauty of a wood can only be secured by viewing it across an open lawn.[104]

He returned to this image in his designs for the copse-like meadow edges in Washington Park and again twenty years later in a letter to *Garden and Forest* adding the caution to preserve the "sacred" foliage of wild shrubs and trees. He declaimed:

> Any one who will look across a meadow or lawn at a line of wood the outer edge of which still retains its fringe of wild shrubbery presenting a mass of foliage impervious to sight from the ground upward, and will then contrast it with the more common case, in which all the shrubbery and low-growing limbs have been cleared, and the eye penetrates perhaps the whole breadth of wood through the maze of bare trunks, will appreciate the superior beauty of the former . . . I have grown tired of hearing the announcement from proprietors . . . that they "have had all the underbrush grubbed out. . . ." Many men who have a genuine love of natural beauty . . . acknowledge with surprise that they had never before analyzed the nature of the obviously superior beauty of a mass of foliage as compared with an open wood when seen across a lawn.[105]

Were these clearings influential for Simonds' and Jensen's formal explorations? It was, and is, impossible to say with certainty. Simonds, in his essay "Appreciation of Natural

---

[104] *Catalogue of Graceland Cemetery*, 11. Compare a piece by O. C. Simonds written in 1899 in a series of articles on "Home Grounds" for the *House Beautiful*, especially 5, 6 (May 1899), 275–79. In the third of this series, he described the essence of the open lawn:

> The lawn should form a large open space, bounded more or less on all sides by a plantation of trees and shrubs. The open space is required to insure a feeling of repose or restfulness arising from the lawn itself, fresh air, the graceful shapes, delightful coloring, and perfume of the things planted, the company of birds, and the extended view of the sky and clouds (p. 276).

[105] H. W. S. Cleveland, "Shrubs on Tree Borders," *Garden and Forest* 3 (17 September 1890), 459. Compare Simonds's views on shrubs at the edges of cemetery lawns in an article for *Park and Cemetery* 10, 8

Beauty," presented in 1898 at the annual meeting of the American Park and Outdoor Art Association in Minneapolis, directly acknowledged Cleveland, (among others, including Olmsted) as having prepared the ground for the present and the future.[106] However, he offered few specifics in spite of direct experience with many landscapes prepared by Cleveland in one decade and brought to a further stage of improvement in his own work. And Jensen knew and appreciated the "open ground" of the great meadow at Washington Park, but he too offered little record of the relationship between his experience of

---

(October 1900), 176–77. Here Simonds expressed the functional and aesthetic qualities of shrubberies as masses which defined spaces:

> It follows, therefore, that the masses of shrubbery covered with foliage reaching from the ground to points above the eye are exceedingly useful in producing the desired effect. It sometimes happens that the trees with foliage coming to the ground serve the same purposes as masses of shrubs, but in too many cases the branches of trees have been cut away. . . . [t]hey make the most pleasing boundaries of lawns, forming a background in one place, carrying a point of foliage in another, so as to give a prominent point of light in contrast with deep shade, and everywhere varying the outline so that it is as beautiful as the margin of a summer's cloud.

[106] In 1898 Simonds referred directly to Cleveland in an essay presented in Minneapolis during the 1898 convention of the American Park and Outdoor Art Association. It was reprinted in O. C. Simonds, "Appreciation of Natural Beauty," *Park and Cemetery*, 8, 5 (July 1898), 92–93. The only other essay from that convention reprinted in that issue of the journal was Cleveland's own, "The Influence of Parks on the Character of Children," 95. Cleveland had become too frail by this time—he was eighty-three—to make the trip from Chicago. The paper was read by Charles M. Loring, his collaborator in the Minneapolis park development and the preservation of Minnehaha Falls.

There are both tangible and intangible historical connections between Cleveland and Simonds, arguably the originator of the natural landscape style that is associated with the Midwest in the period at and just after the turn-of-the-century. Simonds was trained as a civil engineer at the University of Michigan. He was a student of the architect-engineer, William Le Baron Jenney, the originator of the application of the steel frame to the design of tall, light-filled buildings that scraped the skies of Chicago in the last decades of the nineteenth century. Simonds worked for Jenney upon graduation, and in his employ, he made his first survey of the lagoon at Graceland Cemetery, originally laid out by Nelson and Cleveland. In 1881 he returned to Graceland to execute his master work. In the tradition of Adolph Strauch at Spring Grove in Cinncinati, he worked as a superintendent from 1881 until 1898. In 1895 Simonds began a series of commissions in Quincy, Illinois. Cleveland had preceded him there.

Cleveland and Simonds shared an approach to design which looked without question to the essential rightness of nature, the native conditions of the landscape, as an aesthetic of dwelling. In *Landscape Architecture*, 14, Cleveland expressed this approach in the context of an anecdote about the client who "calls upon me for advice in regard to the arrangement of his grounds, and tells me he has built his house and made various improvements by grading and clearing, and now wants me to tell him how to finish it off." Cleveland proceeded in exasperated tones to describe how this philistine had improperly sited the house, expended a large sum of money grubbing out the "beauty of a natural wood," and graded the slopes in the most disastrous and ugly manner:

> . . . after destroying the natural beauty of the place, looks to me to make it attractive by the introduction of artificial decorations, and not infrequently proceeds to give me directions as to the kinds of ornaments he would like, and where and how they are to be bestowed. . . .

In the same anecdotal form, Simonds's apologia for the "Appreciation of Natural Beauty," 92–93, contained several accounts of the follies of men who had laid waste to their native landscapes. One Michigan farmer was reserved for Simonds's special scorn. This man's fields were bounded by luxuriant growth of pines, native larches, and

> perfect specimens of red maples, while in front along the fence and almost hiding it were masses of Carolina roses with their shining red fruits and, brighter still, groups of winterberry bushes with their

this landscape and his designs.[107] In the ethereal world of subliminal influences on design, the "records" of the direct experience of landscape phenomena present themselves as filmy apparitions. Yet, consider the icon of the "wild" wooded islands, the ironic products of the fast-tracked economies of the Chicago and Minneapolis work in the 1870s and 1880s. They had an unmeasurable, but possibly seminal legacy to the prairie lagoons and rivers in Simonds' and Jensen's work, and perhaps to the larger realm of the "prairie" aesthetic. In 1888 the planting on the Minneapolis island was described in detail in an article in *Garden and Forest*. Had Simonds read this article? This possible connection to Cleveland's aesthetic would help explain their shared preferences for certain wild plants, especially sumac, red-twigged dogwood, snowberry, button bush, and red-berried elder. Olmsted, who experimented with wild water gardens himself in the 1880s, saw Loring's little island in Minneapolis in 1886, perhaps read about it again in 1888, and enlarged and reprised the idea in Chicago in 1893 as the celebrated "Wooded Isle" at the World's Columbian Exposition.[108] Seen there, certainly by Simonds, but probably, by all of the other protagonists of the prairie spirit—Jensen, Griffin, and Wright among them—in the context of the Japanese pavilion of the Hoo-den and Sullivan's Transportation Building, its probable effect on the developing regional aesthetic was portentous.[109]

holly-like berries. . . . [t]hese were mostly scarlet, so intense as to attract one's attention from the brow of the hill on either side . . . [y]ou can imagine my disappointment when on looking for this place one spring, I found all the trees and bushes had been cut down . . . [i]f the farmer who owned this bit of roadside beauty . . . had derived half as much pleasure from it during the year as I did during the half dozen times I passed by it, he would have taken his winter exercise in some other way.

[107] See Robert E. Grese's article on Jensen in this volume.
[108] In a short article on "Central Park, Minneapolis," *Garden and Forest* 1 (3 October 1888), 374, the plants on the small island were enumerated:

Conspicuous among them is the Red-berried Elder, whose arching branches admirably fit it for a position on the border of the water. Among other shrubs which overhang the lake are Sumachs and Red-twigged Dogwoods, while further back are Snowberries, Button-bushes and other wild shrubs.

Compare O. C. Simonds, "The Use of Shrubs in Cemeteries," *Park and Cemetery* 10, 8 (October 1900), 178, to this enumeration:

Frequently the greater portion of shrubs needed for boundaries and margins of ponds can be taken from the surrounding country. The panicled dogwood with its rich foliage and white berries on little red stems, the red-branched dogwood, the witch hazel, the viburnums of different kinds, the common hazel, the elderberries, both red and the black-berried species, the spireas of different kinds, the chokeberry, the different sumachs, varying in size from the small aromatic to the staghorn which is almost a tree, the prairie, swamp, and meadow roses, and the New Jersey tea are examples of attractive shrubs that are found almost everywhere in the northern states.

[109] In 1891–92 Frederick Law Olmsted laid out the plans for the World's Columbian Exposition in Chicago. A quintessentially fast-tracked project, the fair had a famous "Wooded Isle" of largely native shrubs and herbaceous materials gathered from the wild. The process is well documented in letters from Rudolf Ulrich to Olmsted in the Frederick Law Olmsted Papers, Library of Congress, and in two articles: C. S. Sargent (?), "The General Design of the Columbian Exposition," *Garden and Forest* 6 (30 August 1893), 361–63; and J. G. Jack, "The Columbian Exposition: Plants Around the Lagoons of Jackson Park," *Garden and Forest* 6 (4 October 1893), 419. See also K. Haglund, "Correspondence," 170, who indicated that Cleveland visited the Exposition in 1893 and corresponded subsequently with Olmsted, declaring appreciatively, "the Wooded Island, . . . the effect of the whole scene was to me such a vision of beauty as I had never dreamed of."

Among the stimuli that barraged these young designers, who could gauge the power of this landscape or of any other in the region, and, more to the point, who could draw a line to Horace Cleveland? There was, and is, no easy chronological or stylistic diagram, but can we imagine, for a moment, the subliminal influence of Cleveland's spare landscapes on the next generation of designers: on Simonds during his first site visits to Graceland Cemetery as a young engineer surveying the lagoon nestled in its wooded meadow; or on Jensen out in the savannah of Washington Park and then into the imaginary valley of his "hidden garden of the prairie country"?[110] Can we also discern with hindsight, but in the same view, Horace Cleveland, at seventy years, with Charles Loring at his side, two pilgrims trudging up the poetic valley of Minnehaha Creek to the classic falls; or the younger man, rambling down a wooded path into the clearing of Sleepy Hollow with his partner, Copeland, and his client, Emerson? If we can, Horace Cleveland's vision of a new American culture in the West and the prairie spirit became one substance in the steamy summer vapors and crystalline quietude of the midwestern garden.

---

[110] O. C. Simonds, in the same article on shrubs for cemeteries in *Parks and Cemetery* 10, 8 (October 1900), 177, referenced earlier, commented that

> We certainly have enough native shrubs to make any locality as beautiful as the fairest park. I have seen prairie roses make ravine in which they were at home more beautiful even than the "wooded island."

J. Jensen, "I Like Our Prairie Landscape," *Park International* 1 (1920), 64.

The Prairie Gardens of O. C. Simonds
and Jens Jensen

ROBERT E. GRESE

In the late 1800s and early 1900s, Ossian Cole Simonds (1855–1931) and Jens Jensen (1860–1951), two landscape gardeners from the Chicago area, experimented with the native flora of the region and developed an approach to garden design that was described by University of Illinois Professor of Landscape Horticulture Wilhelm Miller in 1915 as the "prairie style." Miller, who served as the editor of *The Garden* and a frequent contributor to *Country Life in America,* cast the prairie style as "an American mode of design based upon the practical needs of the Middle-Western people and characterized by preservation of typical Western scenery, by restoration of local color, and by repetition of the horizontal line of land or sky, which is the strongest feature of prairie scenery.[1] Miller saw Simonds and Jensen as leaders of this style, which he regarded as analogous to the prairie school of architecture developing at this same time.[2] A careful examination of the work of Simonds and Jensen demonstrates a reliance on compositional principles of naturalistic design that had been promoted by other landscape designers such as Andrew Jackson Downing and Frederick Law Olmsted. However, in their reliance on the native flora, spatial patterns, and dominant forms of the landscape of the Midwest, Simonds and Jensen effectively developed what can now be understood as a regional style of garden design (Figs. 1–3).

In geographical terms, the Midwest is ill-defined; many garden writers during Simonds and Jensen's time defined the region as extending from the Appalachian Mountains on the east to the Rockies on the west. While some writers included the southern

[1] A response by Wilhelm Miller to John H. Small via a letter to the editor in "The Prairie Style of Landscape Architecture," *The Architectural Record* 40, 6 (December 1916), 591. Miller (1869–1938) wrote widely on landscape gardening topics and had served as assistant editor with Liberty Hyde Bailey of the *Cyclopedia of American Horticulture* from 1897 to 1901. In 1914, Miller became head of the Division of Landscape Extension at the University of Illinois.

[2] In addition to Simonds and Jensen, Miller also mentions Walter Burley Griffin as a contributor to the prairie style. Griffin practiced both in architecture and landscape architecture. W. Miller, *The Prairie Spirit in Landscape Gardening,* University of Illinois Agricultural Experiment Station, Circular 184, Urbana, Ill., 1915, 2–3.

1. W. Miller, *The Prairie Spirit in Landscape Gardening,* University of Illinois Agricultural Experiment Station, Circular 184, Urbana, Illinois, 1915

2. O. C. Simonds at Graceland Cemetery, Chicago, Illinois, ca. 1920 (photo: Morton Arboretum, Lisle, Illinois)

3. Jens Jensen at Columbus Park, Chicago, Illinois, ca. 1920 (photo: Department of Landscape Architecture, University of Massachusetts, Amherst)

states of Texas, Oklahoma, and New Mexico as part of the Midwest, most considered its northern boundary to be the Great Lakes and the Canadian border and its southern boundary to be the Ohio River and Ozark uplands of southern Missouri.[3] For this paper, Illinois and the adjoining states will be considered the heart of the Midwest region. Neither Simonds or Jensen worked exclusively in the Midwest, but, because of their familiarity with the region, it was here that their work seemed most at home.[4]

The economic and social conditions that prevailed in Chicago from the 1870s through World War I provided a fertile ground for artists like Simonds and Jensen. During the post Civil War era, Chicago rapidly grew to become the industrial hub of the Midwest; it was the most active railroad center in the country and the center for the meat-packing industry, for lumber and milling, for manufacturing farm machinery, and increasingly for retail trade.[5] Many of the families who benefited from this new-found wealth ultimately became patrons of the likes of Simonds and Jensen as they built second homes and later permanent estates in the North Shore area along Lake Michigan. These individuals also supported the city's growing cultural institutions: the Art Institute of Chicago, the Chicago Academy of Science, the Field Museum of Natural History, and places of higher learning such as Northwestern University and the University of Chicago. The Columbian Exposition of 1893 helped to confirm Chicago's place as a cultural center; Hull-House and the social reform work of other settlement houses demonstrated that many Chicagoans had a conscience as well. As a result of concern over the lack of play spaces for children, particularly by Jane Addams of Hull-House, in 1899 the Chicago City Council organized a Special Park Commission and charged them with making a systematic study of the parks and recreation grounds of the entire metropolitan area. The commission, which at times included both Simonds and Jensen as members, made sweeping recommendations for creating a region-wide system of parks and preserves. This interest in parks helped to fuel the support for Simonds's work at Lincoln Park (1903–11) and Jensen's work for the West Parks (1905–20).[6]

Other arts also experienced a renaissance of sorts. Miller pointed to "a new and virile school of western art" that included the sculptor Lorado Taft; poets Hamlin Garland, Nicholas V. Lindsay, Harriet Monroe, and Carl Sandburg; and the painters Frank C. Peyraud and Charles Francis Browne.[7] The turn of the century also saw the establish-

[3] For boundaries of the Midwest, see K. B. Lohmann, "Landscape Architecture in the Middle West," *Landscape Architecture* 16 (April 1926), 161; P. B. Wight, "County House Architecture in the Middle West," *The Architectural Record* 40, 4 (October 1916), 291; [F. A. Waugh], "Chapter 18: Landscape Architecture in North America (United States and Canada)," in M. L. Gothein, *A History of Garden Art*, ed. W. P. Wright, 2, New York, 1966, 448–49.
[4] "Ossian Cole Simonds, 1855–1931," *Civic Comment* 36 (November-December 1931), 24; for a listing of Jensen's known projects, see R. E. Grese, *Jens Jensen: A Maker of Natural Parks and Gardens,* Baltimore and London, 1992.
[5] J. Brinkerhoff Jackson, *American Space: The Centennial Years, 1865–1876,* New York, 1972, 72.
[6] D. Heald Perkins, *Report of the Special Park Commission to the City Council of Chicago on the Subject of a Metropolitan Park System,* Chicago, 1904; Chicago Park District, Office of Research and Planning, *Lincoln Park Restoration and Management Plan,* 1991, 19–21.
[7] W. Miller, *The "Illinois Way" of Beautifying the Farm,* University of Illinois Agricultural Experiment Station, Circular 170, Urbana, Ill., 1914, 3–4.

4. The Avery Coonley House (1908–17) in Riverside, Illinois, marks one of several collaborations between Jensen and Frank Lloyd Wright (photo: Morton Arboretum, Lisle, Illinois)

ment of Chicago's Prairie School of architecture with Louis Sullivan as a mentor and Frank Lloyd Wright as its leading spirit. Jensen had particularly close ties to the Prairie School architects, having shared office space with many of them in Steinway Hall, just east of the Loop in downtown Chicago, from 1908 until the end of World War I. Dwight Perkins, the designer of Steinway Hall (1896), leased the loft floor and offered to share the space with several of his architect friends. Although the Steinway Hall group changed over the years, Walter Burley Griffin, Robert Spencer, and Frank Lloyd Wright each spent time there. Jensen collaborated with these prairie architects on such projects as Wright's Coonley House in Riverside, Illinois (1908) (Fig. 4), and Spencer's Magnus House in Winnetka, Illinois (1904).[8] Simonds worked with Dwight Perkins on park structures within Lincoln Park and with other architects on the many estates he designed on the North Shore area of the Chicago region; the lack of records makes it difficult to document the full extent of his practice, however.[9] Both Jensen and Simonds were mem-

[8] H. A. Brooks, *The Prairie School: Frank Lloyd Wright and His Midwest Contemporaries*, Toronto, 1972, 28; E. G. Gillette, interview by Patricia Frank, tape #16c: 14, Gillette Archives, Bentley Historical Library, University of Michigan, Ann Arbor, Mich.; L. K. Eaton, "Jens Jensen and the Chicago School," *Progressive Architecture* 41, 12 (December 1960), 144–50.

[9] Gelbloom notes many of Simonds's projects, including twenty-seven estates in Winnetka, Illinois, alone. M. Gelbloom, "Ossian Simonds: Prairie Spirit in Landscape Gardening," *The Prairie School Review* 12, 2 (1975), 8.

5. Graceland Cemetery, plantings designed by Simonds. Simonds fully
intended that the monuments not detract from the overall landscape of the cemetery. Many native trees and shrubs were used here
to provide a rural feeling to the cemetery. Simonds worked on various parts of Graceland from 1881 until his death in 1931 (photo:
Morton Arboretum, Lisle, Illinois)

bers of Chicago organizations such as the City Club and the Cliff Dwellers during the
same years. Here they rubbed shoulders with prairie architects as well as the writers and
artists who contributed to Chicago's cultural renaissance. Jensen was a frequent contributor to the Chicago Architectural Club's exhibitions and served as jury member on several
local design competitions.

PROFESSIONAL TRAINING

As noted by Mara Gelbloom in her article, "Ossian Simonds: Prairie Spirit in Landscape Gardening" (1975), Simonds began experimenting with his version of the prairie
style at Graceland Cemetery in Chicago several years before Jensen had even set foot in
the United States. Simonds, trained as a civil engineer at the University of Michigan, also
took classes in architecture with William Le Baron Jenney. After graduation in 1878, he
joined the staff of Jenney's office in Chicago. Simonds left the firm about 1880 to form
an architectural partnership with William Holabird. By 1881, Simonds left what had
become Holabird, Simonds, and Roche to assume the role of superintendent of
Graceland Cemetery. At Graceland, Simonds honed his skills as a landscape gardener
and, as Miller notes, laid the groundwork for "the 'middle-western movement' in landscape gardening"[10] (Fig. 5).

[10] Miller, *Prairie Spirit,* 2; R. E. Grese, "Ossian Cole Simonds," in W. H. Tishler, ed., *American Landscape
Architecture,* Washington, D.C., 1989, 74–75.

Jensen, by contrast, started his career in landscape architecture somewhat later. With training from Tune Agricultural School in Denmark, Jensen came to the United States in 1884 and, after a few short stints at farming, began his work with the Chicago West Parks as a street sweeper. Gradually, he seems to have been given more responsibility and was allowed to try his hand at design. His first documented design, which he called the "American Garden," was a small garden of wildflowers in a corner of Union Park in 1888. In the years that followed, Jensen experimented with various styles of design in the parks on the west side of Chicago and residential properties on the North Shore of Chicago and in southeastern Wisconsin.[11]

Despite the obvious differences in their training and backgrounds, Simonds and Jensen eventually pursued parallel careers, developing similar approaches to landscape design. Nonetheless, it is difficult to characterize the exact nature of their personal relationship: no correspondence between them has been found, and other documents provide scant clues. Many of Jensen's office records burned in a fire at The Clearing in the early 1930s; only limited records from Simonds's office still exist. Assuredly, there had to have been some cross-fertilization between these two men. Obviously, each was aware of the other's work, and there is some indication that there was informal interaction between them as well as a mutual respect for each other's work. Their personalities, however, seem to have been markedly different. Simonds has been characterized as quiet and unassuming; Jensen, in contrast, was outspoken and flamboyant. Simonds and Jensen seem to have developed their work individually as separate artists; what they shared was a personal knowledge of, and obvious love for, the native landscape of the Middle West that served as a model for their designs.[12]

Like those Chicago architects who strove for a clean break with Beaux-Arts styles, Simonds and Jensen eschewed Renaissance Revival traditions and chose instead to adapt Olmstedian styles to the peculiarities of the landscape of the Midwest. Like H. W. S. Cleveland, they struggled to develop a landscape art that reflected the needs of the rapidly growing region around Chicago and through the Midwest in general. In many of his writings, Simonds expressed a clear debt to both Olmstead and Adolph Strauch, the designer of Spring Grove Cemetery in Cincinnati, and acknowledged the writings of Humphry Repton, John C. Loudon, Andrew Jackson Downing, William Kent, William Robinson, Samuel Parsons, and Mrs. Schuyler Van Rensselaer.[13] Jensen, in contrast, expressed no such debt to landscape gardening traditions. He acknowledged Louis Sulli-

---

[11] For Jensen's description of the "American Garden," see J. Jensen and R. B. Eskil, "Natural Parks and Gardens," *The Saturday Evening Post,* 8 March 1930, 18–19.

[12] Miller, "Prairie Style," 590–91.

[13] In many of his talks, Simonds quoted extensively from Olmsted and others such as Charles Eliot and Andrew Jackson Downing. See O. C. Simonds, "The Landscape Gardener and His Work," *Park and Cemetery* 7, 1 (March 1897), 3–5; idem, "Parks and Public Grounds," *Park and Cemetery* 13, 2 (April 1903), 21–22; idem, "Landscape Design in Public Parks," *Park and Cemetery* 19, 4 (June 1909), 50–52. For his expressed debt to Adolph Strauch, see O. C. Simonds, "The Planning and Administration of Landscape Cemetery," *Country Life in America* 4, 5 (September 1903), 350, and idem, "Progress and Prospect in Cemetery Design," *Park and Cemetery* 30, 1 (March 1920), 18–19.

6. The Refectory Building in Chicago's Humboldt Park, designed by Hugh M. G. Garden, illustrates the emphasis on horizontal lines so predominant in the prairie style of architecture. Garden was a close friend of Jensen and collaborated with him on several projects in the West Parks and elsewhere (photo: Department of Landscape Architecture, University of Massachusetts, Amherst)

van as a mentor of sorts and noted an aversion to the French garden architecture he had experienced while serving in the German military in Berlin. The French Garden, with its geometric order, spoke to Jensen of autocratic governments, while the freer English garden suggested democratic ideals.[14] Jensen was familiar with Olmsted's work in Chicago and particularly admired the meadow in Washington Park although he lamented the loss of the original wetland and prairie filled with purple phlox that had once graced the grounds of Jackson Park.[15]

ELEMENTS OF THE PRAIRIE STYLE

The Midwest possessed several peculiar qualities that helped give rise to the approach to design promoted by Simonds and Jensen. The generally flat or rolling landscape and the mosaic of prairies and woodlands provided inspiration for a style of design that emphasized broad horizontal lines; these lines were repeated in the buildings of the prairie architects as well as in the gardens of Simonds and Jensen (Fig. 6). The harsh

[14] J. Jensen, *Siftings*, Chicago, 1939, 28, 34–37.
[15] Ibid., 33–34.

climatic conditions limited the use of many evergreen and tender garden plants common in the East and spurred a greater interest in the native flora adapted to local conditions.

A major tenet of the Prairie Style, as practiced by Jensen and Simonds, was its emphasis on native flora of the region. As Miller emphasized, in his article, the Prairie Style gardens of the Midwest relied not on new forms or principles of composition, but rather on the native plants and landforms that produced "local color." As he wrote: "The laws of composition are the same in all the fine arts the world over. The Midwest cannot invent new principles such as the open lawn, the irregular borders of shrubbery, the avoidance of straight lines; it can only apply them to new material." Miller went on to encourage his readers to follow the example of Simonds and Jensen in planting more native species:

> Therefore we should be cosmopolitan as to design, and provincial as to material. We now plant 90 percent foreigners and 'horticulturals;' we should plant 90 per cent natives. For cosmopolitan material surely tends to kill all local color, and without that no good art can exist. There is no Western color in the purple-leaved plum, golden privet, variegated weigela, althea, or Crimson Rambler, which you see in every yard. There is plenty of Western color in the prairie rose, the crab apple of Iowa, the buckeyes, the buffalo berry, the Wisconsin willow, the green ash, and Minnesota honeysuckle.[16]

Both Simonds and Jensen spent much time in conscious study of the native landscape of the Midwest. Simonds credited his youth on a farm in Grand Rapids, Michigan, with providing inspiration for his designs and his attraction to the native landscape. He described the back part of his father's farm as "all the park I needed." On the steep bluffs and river valley, he would study the many plant and animal species found there and watch the beauty of the changing seasons:

> The opening of the flowers, the bursting into leaf of the various trees, the arrival of birds, the music of our feathered songsters, the sweet perfumes, the animal life, the summer growth, the various discoveries to be made, the fall coloring, the various nuts and fruits, made of the season a perpetual delight, and this delight was not limited by the arrival of snow.[17]

In his designs, Simonds accentuated the beauty of the garden in all seasons. While he did not restrict himself to native plants alone, they represented the predominant material of his gardens. He was particularly fond of using plants "once considered so common as to command little more respect than weeds." These included sumac, elderberry, hazelnut, goldenrod, and aster—all of which were given places of honor in his compositions.[18] Simonds noted that the work of landscape gardeners was to "create safe retreats"

[16] W. Miller, "How the Middle West Can Come into Its Own," *Country Life in America* 22, 10 (15 September 1912), 13.
[17] Simonds, "Landscape Design in Public Parks," 50.
[18] O. C. Simonds, *Landscape Gardening*, New York, 1920, 46.

for the native flora of the region, while using their skills to produce attractive pictures. Like the landscape painter, he argued the landscape gardener's richest inspiration could come only from the natural settings of the region.[19] Much of his own inspiration came from the native plants of his father's farm which he explored as a child. He wished that all children could share the same pleasures in native surroundings that he experienced as a child, a desire intensified by seeing the natural bluffs and woods of his youth converted to commercial truck gardens (Fig. 7).[20]

Jensen, too, credited his childhood experiences with shaping his attitudes toward the landscape. Like Simonds, he took great joy in exploring the fields and fence rows of his father's farm. The hedgerows found in his native Denmark were full of hawthorn and blackberry, sweetbriar rose, and many birds and wild animals. With his father, Jensen sought out the first flowers of spring, and an ancient bog and oak trees provided ties to the past. Studying at one of Denmark's famed folk high schools, where many of the classes were held out-of-doors and special efforts made to celebrate the changing seasons, Jensen further learned to appreciate the Danish landscape and its relation to the folk traditions of its people. Upon coming to the midwestern region of the United States, he readily adopted the landscape and strove to find ways to express its beauty in his work.[21]

During his early days in Chicago, Jensen spent considerable time exploring and studying in the wild lands:

> I obtained my love for native plants and my knowledge of their habits by spending my Sundays in search of them in the environments of Chicago, sometimes going as far as one hundred to one hundred fifty miles from this center. In that way I discovered for myself the dunes of Northern Indiana with their rich plant life, the bogs in northern Illinois and southern Wisconsin, the lime and sand stone canyons on the Illinois and Rock Rivers, the majestic cliffs and the extensive river bottoms on the Mississippi and what was left of the varied and beautiful flora. Each section with plant life typical to itself. How profitable these weekend trips became. Usually my wife and the children accompanied me.[22]

Photographs by Jensen from these trips show his careful study of individual plants as well as their general habitat. Many of his photographs were taken in pairs: a close-up of the plant, as well as a general photograph of the specimen in its surroundings (Fig. 8).

During his early years with Chicago's West Park District and the beginning years of his private practice, Jensen experimented with many horticultural species.[23] His plan for the St. Ann Hospital grounds in Chicago, which he published in *Park and Cemetery* in

[19] Simonds, "Landscape Design in Public Parks," 50; Simonds, *Landscape Gardening,* 3–8.
[20] Simonds, "Landscape Design in Public Parks," 50.
[21] Jensen, *Siftings,* 13–21.
[22] Jens Jensen to Camillo Schneider, 15 April 1939, personal files of Darrel Morrison.
[23] In 1900, Jensen wrote several articles for *Park and Cemetery,* extolling various horticultural plants: "Magnolia soulangiana," 10, 3 (May), 69; "Eleagnus angustifolia (Russian olive)," 10, 4 (June), 66; and "Azalea mollis and Ghent Varieties," 10, 5 (July), 103.

7. Illustration from Simonds's *Landscape Gardening* (1920) urging designers to study the natural arrangement of trees at the edge of a wood for inspiration

8. Photograph by Jensen of lupine habitat in the Indiana Dunes (photo: Art and Architecture Library, University of Michigan)

108

December 1901, called for as many non-native as indigenous plants.[24] Slowly, however, Jensen observed that these foreign plants "didn't take kindly to our Chicago soil." He noted:

> And after a while I began to think, "There's something wrong here. We are trying to force plants to grow where they don't want to grow." And then I took less and less pleasure in looking at these formal designs. They were always the same. There was no swaying of leaves in the wind, no mysterious play of light and shade. And a garden should give you more delight the more you look at it.[25]

His 1888 design for the American Garden in Union Park, which was a collection of native perennial wildflowers, became only one of a series of experiments with native plants in both the parks and private consulting work. By the time he created designs for the Rubens garden in Glencoe, Illinois, in 1903, and the Magnus garden in Winnetka, Illinois, in 1904, Jensen had clearly developed motifs in working with the native flora that would permeate the rest of his career. These gardens evidenced the early forms of his "prairie rivers" that Miller would celebrate as icons of the "prairie style" water garden[26] and that Jensen would use as central features in Humboldt Park in 1907 (Fig. 9) and Columbus Park in 1917 in Chicago.

While Jensen may have turned his emphasis to native plants somewhat later than Simonds, ultimately his development of the prairie landscape motif extended much further. Whereas Simonds wanted to create "safe retreats" for the native flora, he also "welcome[d] the plants of other countries and [gave] them fitting surroundings." Throughout his career, Norway maple, lilac, spiraea, mock-orange, and other common horticultural species would be liberally interspersed with the natives. Jensen gradually limited these non-natives to areas around buildings or formal gardens. In works such as the Lincoln Memorial Garden in Springfield, Illinois (1936), Jensen's entire palette comprised only native species, and plantings were grouped in ecological associations as they might be found in the wild.

Certain native species were used by both Simonds and Jensen as symbols of the midwestern landscape. They saw the horizontal branching habit of hawthorn and crabapple as particularly appropriate in echoing the broad prairie horizon and uniting woodland areas with meadows or sun openings in the woods. Many of the earlier designers in the Midwest, such as Olmsted and H. W. S. Cleveland, had described the landscape as flat and uninteresting.[27] The sites of Chicago's parks were depicted as a "monotonous

---

[24] J. Jensen, "Plan for Hospital Grounds," *Park and Cemetery* 11, 10 (December 1901), 185–86.

[25] Jensen and Eskil, "Natural Parks and Gardens," 18.

[26] W. Miller, "What is the Matter with Our Water Gardens," *Country Life in America* 22, 4 (15 June 1912), 23–26, 54.

[27] F. L. Olmsted and C. Vaux, "Chicago, Taming the Waterfront," (originally published in 1871 as "Report Accompanying Plan for Laying Out the South Park, Chicago South Park Commission), in F. L. Olmsted, *Civilizing American Cities: A Selection of Frederick Law Olmsted's Writings on City Landscapes*, ed. S. B. Sutton, Cambridge, Mass., 1971, 156–80; H. W. S. Cleveland to F. L. Olmsted, 8 November 1893, excerpted in K. Haglund, "Rural Tastes, Rectangular Ideas, and the Skirmishes of H. W. S. Cleveland," *Landscape Architecture* 66 (January 1976), 78.

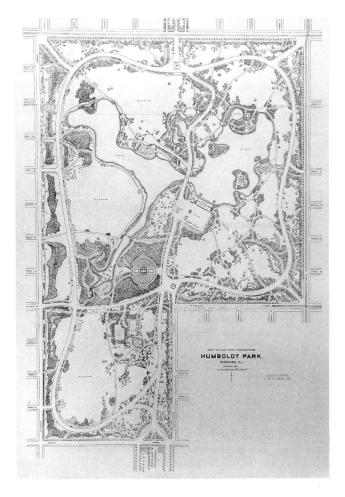

9. Plan of Humboldt Park by Jensen for the West Chicago
Park Commissioners, 1912 (photo: Art and Architecture Library, University of Michigan)

swampy barrenness" which lacked "the natural features of eminences, ledges, rippling
streams, lakelets, and stately forest growths."[28] In the prairie gardens of Simonds and
Jensen, on the other hand, the flat or gently rolling character of the landscape became a
central asset, enframed by hawthorn or crabapple trees. Miller noted that Simonds and
Jensen had "moved thousands upon thousands of hawthorns from farm pastures to the
estates of millionaires"[29] (Fig. 10).

Shrubs such as sumac, gray dogwood, hazelnut, elderberry, nannyberry viburnum,
and others were planted in large masses to suggest the clusters found in nature. A favorite "prairie" plant was the prairie rose, (*Rosa setigera*). The graceful American elm, so
common along the streams and low areas of the Midwest and easily transplanted in large

[28] C. Pullen, "The Parks and Parkways of Chicago," *Harper's Weekly* 35 (6 June 1891), 412.
[29] Miller, *Beautifying the Farm,* 9.

10. Hawthorn trees featured in Simonds's design for the Hibbard Estate, Dixon, Illinois (photo: from W. Miller, "A Series of Outdoor Salons," *Country Life in America* 25, 6 [April 1914], 40)

sizes, was frequently used by both Simonds and Jensen as a canopy tree. The white and red oak, sugar maple, and white ash also appeared frequently in their work. The grasses and forbs of the prairie were only occasionally restored in any great measure. Jensen's work for the ideal mile section of the Lincoln Highway, 1917–25, near Merrillville, Indiana, where he advocated the restoration of prairie species, is one such example. Usually, however, only a selected group of prairie forbs were used at the edge of clearings to provide a limited suggestion of the larger prairie context, the most frequent among them were various asters, goldenrod species, purple coneflower, black-eyed Susan, and phlox.[30]

Design Principles

Simonds and Jensen did not propose literal restorations of the prairie/forest landscape, nor was that their intention. Instead, both argued that their gardens were art, providing idealized images of the prairie. One of their greatest challenges was to create a sense of the expansive prairie on the smaller lots of private gardens and public parks. Miller noted two approaches utilized by Simonds and Jensen: the broad view and the long view. The broad view attempted to capture some of the openness and feeling of limitlessness that marked the original prairie landscape. The long view, in contrast, nar-

[30] For "Materials Used in the Prairie Style," see Miller, *Prairie Spirit*, 24–25.

11. "Long view" down meadow space at the A. G. Becker Estate in Highland Park, Illinois, 1926. Designed by Jensen (photo: Art and Architecture Library, University of Michigan)

rowed a view down a human-scaled corridor that ended in what Miller described as "a hazy ridge or misty piece of the woods"[31] (Fig. 11).

To create the broad view, Simonds and Jensen borrowed techniques from Olmsted, Downing, Repton, Pückler-Muscau, and other naturalistic designers. They used irregular masses of trees and shrubs to create an indefinite border that made the open space seem to extend beyond its actual boundaries. Roads and walkways were routed in broad curves around the edges of these openings, creating an ever-changing perspective as one drove or walked through the space. At times large islands of woody vegetation—open-grown trees and masses of shrubs—were introduced in the middle of these meadows to partially obscure the border and create a greater sense of mystery. In Jensen's design for Columbus Park in Chicago (1917), an island of trees partially interrupts the view of the large meadow space, a good example of this approach. Small trees such as the hawthorn or crabapple were often repeated down the length and around the border of these meadows to provide a transition from the lawn areas to the taller trees of the woods beyond. From any given perspective, the repetition of these trees, which become hazier and smaller in the distance, tended to increase the overall perception of depth (Fig. 12).

Not all of these broad views appeared on large properties. Miller's article "A Series of Outdoor Salons," (1914), for example, describes Simonds's design for the Hibbard garden in Winnetka, Illinois. Rather than create one large expansive view, Simonds cre-

[31] Ibid., 17–18.

112

12. Prairie meadow at the Magnus Estate in Winnetka, Illinois, 1904–5. Designed by Jensen. The house here is by Robert Spencer, who featured the hawthorn in the design for some of the stained glass in the house. This photograph was featured on the cover of Wilhelm Miller's *The "Illinois Way" of Beautifying the Farm* (photo: University of Illinois Agricultural Experiment Station, Circular 170, Urbana, Illinois, 1914)

ated a series of "sylvan living rooms," that guide the visitor through the expanding landscape. Larger trees were kept in the background, and beds of flowers or masses of shrubbery delineated the immediate walls of each room. On the ground plane, the lawn surface flowed from one room to the next around hawthorn and other small trees, inviting the visitor to move through the entire garden. Simonds used similar approaches in other gardens such as the Ives and Howell gardens in Dixon, Illinois, situated on bluffs overlooking the valley of the Rock River. In both of these relatively small gardens, he artfully used masses of shrubs and small trees to create a series of small rooms with borrowed views across the river valley. In small as well as larger gardens, Simonds adamantly preserved "open space to show sky, clouds, and sunshine" and urged designers to study the borders of woods for inspiration in creating an attractive skyline. In the Howell garden, which was described by Arthur Eldredge in "Making a Small Garden Look Large" in *Garden Magazine* (1924), Simonds included a small lily pond which echoed both the rock work and plants native to the river's edge[32] (Fig. 13).

Jensen also created small room-like spaces in his designs, often as an opening in the

[32] W. Miller, "A Series of Outdoor Salons," *Country Life in America* 25, 6 (April 1914), 39–40; Simonds, *Landscape Gardening,* 52–53, 142; A. G. Eldredge, "Making a Small Garden Look Large," *Garden Magazine* 28, 6 (February 1924), 332–34.

13. Network of outdoor spaces bordered with perennial plantings by Simonds at the Howell Estate in Dixon, Illinois (photo: from A. G. Eldredge, "Making a Small Garden Look Large," *Garden Magazine* 28, 6 [February 1924], 333)

woods, just off the larger meadow that might occupy the center of the park or residential garden. Perhaps one of the best examples of Jensen's small "room" gardens was the trail gardens area of Fair Lane, the Henry Ford Estate (1914). Here, Jensen created a series of outdoor sitting rooms bordered by the woodland border, shrub masses, and beds of phlox and asters. As with Simonds's gardens, the space flowed from one of these rooms to the next, drawing the viewer on to trace the entire circuit. In small alcoves scattered along the border, Jensen placed benches as quiet places to sit and enjoy the limited view. In other gardens, Jensen frequently furnished these small rooms with council rings, a low circular stone seat intended as a place for drama, dance, discussion, and other social activities.

The long view was used by both Simonds and Jensen to emphasize distant features or views. Perhaps more than most other landscape designers, they were particularly sensitive to the atmospheric qualities of the garden and the alternating bright and hazy sunlight of the Midwest. Like the painter, Simonds noted that the landscape gardener forms the composition of the garden against the sky and allows "generous open space on his canvas for nature to fill in with clouds and sunshine, with stars and moonlight."[33] Similarly, Jensen described the raw materials of the landscape gardener as "the contours of the earth, the vegetation that covers it, the changing seasons, the rays of the setting

[33] Simonds, *Landscape Gardening,* 6.

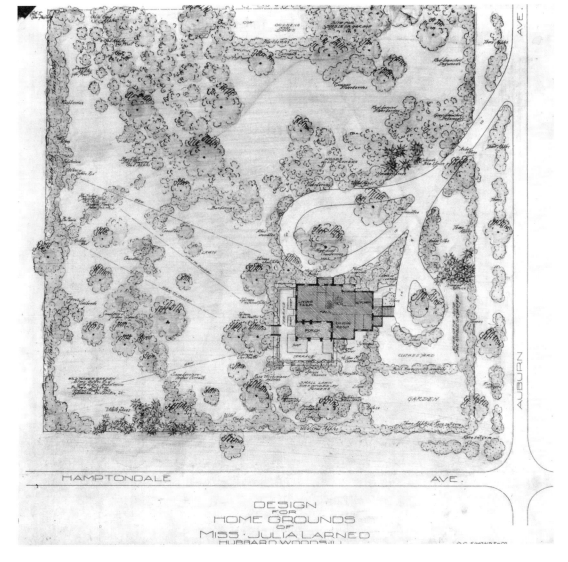

HAMPTONDALE

AVE.

AUBURN

AVE.

DESIGN
FOR
HOME GROUNDS
OF
MISS · JULIA LARNED
HUBBARD WOODS·ILL.

14. Simonds's plan for the Julia Larned home grounds in Hubbard Woods, Illinois, date unknown. Note the lines on the plan denoting that Simonds obviously thought were important. The views to the sunset end in masses of goldenrod and aster which would highlight the low-angled sun with their feathery seed heads

sun and the afterglow, and the light of the moon."[34] Both Simonds and Jensen would often lay out paths to view the sunrise and sunset in their gardens and use plants that highlighted the low-angled light at the beginning and end of the day. Goldenrod, for example, was planted at the end of a view to the setting sun where its feathery seed heads would be highlighted by the low-angled sun. Jensen delighted in planting plants with bright orange or red autumn color such as sumac and sugar maple where the warm light of the setting sun would set them ablaze (Fig. 14).

Jensen also deliberately punctuated his woodland plantings with openings to create an intricate pattern of sun and shadow throughout the garden. For him, a clearing repre-

[34] Jensen and Eskil, "Natural Parks and Gardens," 169.

15. Council ring by Jensen at Lincoln Memorial Garden, Springfield, Illinois, 1934–36. This council ring is set on the edge of a clearing where it is partly shaded by the surrounding woods and has views into the opening

sented a ray of hope in an oft-troubled world. Gardens were to convey a sense of peace and tranquility; as he noted, "I always have a clearing in every garden I design—a clearing that lets in the smiling and healing rays of the sun. A sunlit clearing invites hope"[35] (Fig. 15).

Unlike designers that saw gardens as static objects, both Simonds and Jensen nurtured an appreciation of time and seasonal change. Rather than fill their gardens with evergreen plants, they deliberately emphasized deciduous plants that would change dramatically with each passing season. Both Simonds's treatise *Landscape Gardening* and Jensen's memoirs *Siftings* contain numerous references to an appreciation of the garden in different types of weather and at different times of year. They also planned for the dynamic qualities of their parks and gardens and advocated the planting of long-lived trees as a legacy for future generations.[36] In later designs such as the Lincoln Memorial Garden, Jensen worked closely with natural plant succession whereby his design served merely as a framework for the mosaic of woodlands and openings that he knew would develop with time.[37]

[35] Ibid.

[36] Simonds, *Landscape Gardening*, 17, 47–50, 65–66; Jensen, *Siftings*, 39–61.

[37] R. E. Grese, "A Process for the interpretation and Management of a Designed Landscape: The Landscape Art of Jens Jensen at Lincoln Memorial Garden, Springfield, Illinois," Master's thesis, University of Wisconsin, 1989, 168–70.

PRAIRIE GARDENS OF SIMONDS AND JENSEN

Miller noted that repetition was an integral feature of Simonds's and Jensen's Prairie Style of design. The beauty of the midwestern landscape lay not in dramatic topography or showy plants, but in the repetition of quiet forms and lines. Miller described the experience of the Illinois landscape:

> You notice an absence of spectacular forms; there are no steep hills, pointed rocks, or spiry trees; all vertical lines are obscured. At first you are a little disappointed, because you are used to picturesque or romantic scenery, and here is something very different. Then your curiosity is aroused as to what can be the secret of the prairie's beauty. For the prairie is obviously beautiful, but its beauty is hard to define . . . . Then it gradually dawns upon you that the essence of the prairie's beauty lies in all these horizontal lines, no two of which are of the same length or at the same elevation, but all of which repeat in soft and gentle ways the great story of the horizon.[38]

The prairie's unique character also derived from repetition of certain dominant plants:

> Any botanist can demonstrate that the Middle West contains few plants of the first importance that are also not native to the East. Nevertheless, nature has emphasized certain things about the Middle West—bur oak, stratified haws and crabs, prairie rose and low rose, American bluebells, wild blue phlox, phlox divaricata, sunflowers, purple coneflower, gaillardia, compass plant, and others. The result is a landscape very different from one dominated by pine or palm. It is the frequent combination of a few species that makes 'local color.'[39]

Simonds and Jensen seemed to understand these principles and used repetition to create an intimate relationship between their gardens and the surrounding natural landscape. The horizontal lines of the ground plane were echoed in the plant massings, in trees with horizontal branching habits such as hawthorn and crabapple, and in rock work that repeated the characteristic horizontal bedding of the limestone bluffs found along many of the major rivers of the region. For both Simonds and Jensen, their gardens were intended not only as pleasant places for outdoor recreation, but also as places that preserved the quickly passing beauty of the native landscape. They hoped that their gardens would inspire people to maintain the remaining local wildlands. Conservation was both a logical outgrowth and reason for much of their work.

Using their skills as designers, they sought to awaken people to the beauty of the region. Simonds saw the profession of landscape gardening as teaching people "to see the beauty of nature, the beauty of this world, of which many are now as ignorant." Landscape gardening would teach people in cities "to respect the wooded bluffs and hillsides, the springs, streams, river banks, and lake shores within the city boundaries, and preserve them with loving care." While architects could help city dwellers appreciate

[38] Miller, *Prairie Spirit,* 19.
[39] Miller, "Prairie Style," 591.

good building art, the landscape gardener must inspire the public at large to appreciate first the beauty of parks and gardens and ultimately the beauty of the natural landscape.[40]

Jensen also saw a similar role for his gardens and felt that the garden should express the native landscape of its locale:

> It has become my creed that a garden, to be a work of art, must have the soul of the native landscape in it. You cannot put a French garden or an English garden or a German garden or an Italian garden in America and have it express America any more than you can put an American garden in Europe and have it express France or England or Germany or Italy. Nor can you transpose a Florida or Iowa garden to California and have it feel true, or a New England garden to Illinois, or an Illinois garden to Maine. Each type of landscape must have its individual expression.[41]

He saw the natural landscape as a sacred trust that the designer ought to protect and use for inspiration. Yet, his gardens were not meant to imitate nature. Jensen noted, "A landscape architect like a landscape painter, can't photograph; he must idealize the things he sees. In other words, he must try to portray its soul."[42]

For Jensen, there were inevitable links between a people and their environment. He firmly believed that, over time, people develop cultural traits as an outgrowth of their racial heritage and of living in a particular place. He pointed to the people of Europe as clear examples of this process. In the days before modern transportation, he suggested that "the people's work, especially in the arts, had a better chance to develop in accordance with environmental influences and native intellect."[43] Jensen's own training in the Danish Folk Schools was deliberately focused on the Danish people's cultural traditions and their associations with the land. The Danes were intent upon keeping their cultural traditions alive in the face of German occupation of their country. Subjects such as history and science were deliberately merged with direct study of nature and culture in an attempt to emphasize the connection of the Danish people to their landscape.[44] Jensen firmly believed that Americans needed a similar attachment to the land and wanted his gardens to help inspire such feelings. In the United States, Jensen noted that some re-

[40] Simonds, *Landscape Gardening*, 22–23.
[41] Jensen and Eskil, "Natural Parks and Gardens," 169.
[42] Ibid.
[43] Jensen, *Siftings*, 24–25.
[44] Grese, "Landscape Art of Jens Jensen," 4–5. Jensen clearly struggled with questions of race and environment. Like some other Northern Europeans of his period, Jensen felt that "northern" races were superior. In a letter to Henry Ford's general secretary, E. G. Liebold, Jensen expressed concern over the practice of importing workers from Southern Europe and from the southern portions of the United States. He suggested that a mixing of races would reduce "vitality and intellect" (27 July 1920, Ford Archives, Henry Ford Library, Dearborn, Mich.). He felt that southern climates destroy "the strong and hardy characteristics" of "northern people" (Jensen, *Siftings*, 26). With his disappointing experience of working on a celery plantation in Florida shortly after coming to the United States before moving to Chicago, Jensen may have felt that his personal experience justified these beliefs (L. K. Eaton, *Landscape Artist in America: The Life and Work of Jens Jensen*, Chicago, 1964, 12–13).

gionalization was already happening, even among people of similar origins distributed across different parts of the country. In *Siftings,* he points to the Californian who he says "is bound to the soil" because of the "forceful environments which are his state" and the amount of time spent in the out-of-doors. Likewise, Jensen points to the "great plains of Mid-America" as having a potential "power far greater than that of the mountains."[45] He clearly saw the Midwest as a region of artistic promise.

Conservation Principles

Often in a Simonds or Jensen landscape there was as much artistry in what they preserved of the existing site conditions as what they physically changed. In many of the estates on the North Shore of Chicago, they carefully fitted roads, houses, and garden features into the landscape of wooded ravines, preserving the native character as much as possible and down playing the visual impact of human intrusions. Occasionally the efforts were so successful that their clients felt that they did not get their money's worth. The Michigan State University campus was set in what was originally an oak opening. When Simonds was asked to locate several new buildings in 1906, he drew a line on the campus map designating a zone that should be kept forever open at the center of campus. He wrote,

> I would regard all the ground included within the area, marked by a dotted red line on the accompanying map, as a sacred space from which all buildings must be forever excluded. This area contains beautifully rolling land with a pleasing arrangement of groups of trees, many of which have developed into fine specimens. This area is, I am sure, that feature of the College which is most pleasantly and affectionately remembered by the students after they leave their Alma Mater, and I doubt if any instruction has a greater effect upon their lives.[46]

While campus officials respected the "sacred space" he suggested, they followed few of his other ideas and hired another designer shortly thereafter.

Both Simonds and Jensen saw conservation activities as a natural extension of their design careers. Both were members of the Special Park Commission of Chicago in 1904 that recommended the preservation of a wide band of forest preserves around the metropolitan region,[47] and each wrote widely about their conservation convictions. In his chapter on "Natural Features and Resources" in *Landscape Gardening* (1920), Simonds argued for a new land ethic that would preserve the beauty and ecological health of the landscape. In succeeding chapters on farms, public thoroughfares, railway stations, parks, school grounds, and city and regional planning, he argued for integrating conservation attitudes and a concern for beauty into all walks of American life. In "The Aesthetic Value of Wooded Areas in Michigan," Simonds noted both functional and spiritual reasons for

[45] Jensen, *Siftings,* 26–27.

[46] Simonds quoted in H. W. Lautner, *From an Oak Opening: A Record of the Development of the Campus Park of Michigan State University, 1855–1969,* vol. 1855–1945, East Lansing, Mich., 1969, 83–84.

[47] Perkins, *Metropolitan Park System.*

preserving the state's native beauty: "In order to live, we need something to eat, something to wear, something to keep warm, but we need something more than all of this—something to live for, and the beauty of the forest may be compared favorably with sculpture, painting, literature, music, and all the things that make life worth the while."[48]

Jensen took an even more active role in conservation activities. In many of his parks and gardens, Jensen included council rings and outdoor theaters, or "player's greens" as he called them, as places for pageantry, music, poetry, and drama to reinforce his belief in conservation as an extension of the arts (Fig. 16). A tireless crusader, he wrote countless letters to congressmen and newspaper editors and spoke widely on behalf of the American landscape. Through the efforts of the Prairie Club and the Friends of Our Native Landscape, two groups that he helped to form and led for many years, he fought to establish a state park system in Illinois and to save the Indiana Dunes and many other remnant wilds. For Jensen, the effort to establish a national park in the Indiana Dunes was particularly critical to the continued health and happiness of the people of the Midwest. In a paper supporting its protection, he wrote:

> It [the dunes] is the only landscape of its kind within reach of the millions that need its softening influence for the restoration of their souls and the balance of their minds. Of all the national parks and monuments donated by Congress to the American people, there is none more valuable and none more useful to the people of the Middle West than the dune country of northern Indiana. It is today the Mecca of the artist and the scientist. No one knows what the future has in store. Possibly the influence of these wild and romantic dunes may be the source from which America's greatest poets and artists get their inspiration. Who can tell?[49]

Jensen's *A Greater West Park System* (1920), a proposal never implemented, provides the clearest picture of his vision for integrating parks and gardens into the fabric of the city using a network of small and large parks and gardens connected by "prairie drives." Municipal farms and kitchen gardens were to return agricultural practices to the city and help city residents appreciate the source of their food. Along the Chicago River and its associated streams and drainage canal, a linear ribbon of parkland would be established. Throughout the finer fabric of the city, Jensen proposed a network of small parks and neighborhood centers to bring gardens and breathing space to every block of the city. A series of natural gardens would be developed on school sites to bring the children of the city in contact with the natural heritage of Illinois[50] (Fig. 17).

[48] O. C. Simonds, "The Aesthetic Value of Wooded Areas in Michigan," *Michigan Forestry: Some Questions Answered Connected with a Vital Subject*, Lansing, Mich., 1907.

[49] J. Jensen, "The Dunes of Northern Indiana," S. T. Mather, ed., *Report on the Proposed Sand Dunes National Park in Indiana*, Washington, D.C., 1917, 100.

[50] J. Jensen, *A Greater West Park System*, Chicago, 1920.

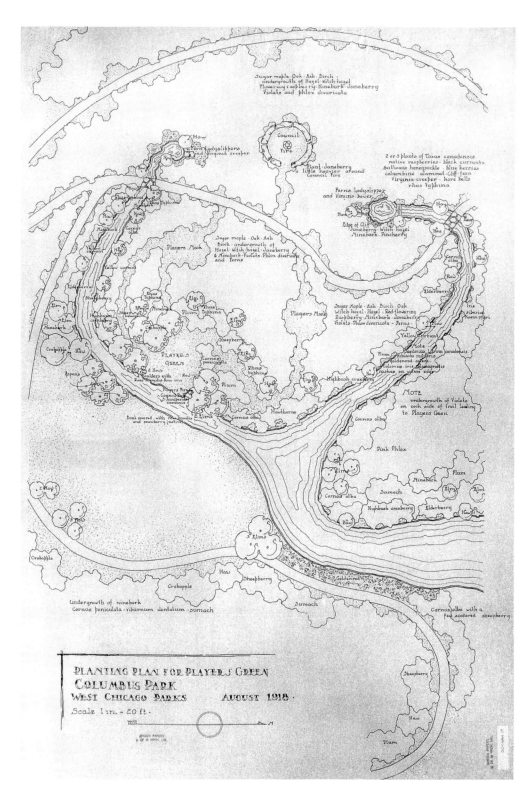

Sugar maple - Oak - Ash - Birch -
undergrowth of Hazel - Witch hazel
Flowering raspberry - Ninebark - Juneberry
Violets and phlox divaricata

Council
Fire

Haw

Ferns - ladyslippers
and Virginia creeper

Plant - Juneberry
a little heavier around
Council Fire

2 or 3 plants of Texas canadensis
native raspberries - black currants
Sullivans honeysuckle - blue berries
columbine - alumroot - Cliff fern
Virginia - creeper - hare bells
rhus typhina

Ferns - ladyslipper
and Virginia bower

Haw

Haw

Edge of Cliff
Juneberry - Witch hazel
Ninebark - Pincherry

Haw

Rhus Typhina

Players Mook

Sugar maple - Oak - Ash -
Birch - undergrowth of
Hazel - Witch hazel - Juneberry
& Ninebark - Violets - Phlox divaricata
and Ferns

Ninebark

Cornus

Yellow
current

Haw

Haw

Elderberry

Elderberry

Elm

Rhus
Typhina

Highbush
cranberry

Elm

Ninebark

Rhus
Typhina

Plum

Rhus
Typhina

Elgs

Players Mook

Sugar Maple - Ash - Birch - Oak
Witch hazel - Hazel - Red-flowering
Raspberry - Ninebark - Juneberry
Violets - Phlox divaricata - Ferns

Iris
siberica
Rosen otyiri

Yellow currant
Note
Wonderties Lilium canadensis
Goldenrod asters
Calamus - iris - Elymus
rushes on waters edge

Haw

Plum

Ferns

Crabapple

Haw

Players
Green

Kernia
paniculata

Rhus
Typhina

Highbush cranberry

Elm

NOTE
undergrowth of Violets
on each side of trail leading
to Players Green

Aspens

2 Hawks
Boulders with
Rosa Rugosa - fern - iris

Haw

Plum

Cornus alba

Council
Fire
Juniperus
communis

Hawthorne

Bank covered with rose canadis
and snowberry (native)

2 Elms

Cornus alba

Pink Phlox

Elms

Plum

Cornus alba

Sumach

Ninebark

Elms

Plum

Highbush cranberry

Elderberry

Haw

Haw

Elms

Haw

Haw

Crabapple

3 Elms

Crabapple

Haw

Sheepberry

Goldenrod

undergrowth of ninebark
Cornus paniculata - viburnum dentatum - sumach

Sumach

Cornus alba with a
few scattered sheepberry

Sheepberry

Haw

Plum

PLANTING PLAN FOR PLAYERS GREEN
COLUMBUS PARK
WEST CHICAGO PARKS   AUGUST 1918 -
Scale 1 in. = 20 ft -

JENSEN PAPERS
U OF M ARCH. LIB.

16. Jensen saw his gardens as providing spaces for outdoor celebrations and pageantry. Here in his design for Columbus Park (1918) in Chicago's West Parks, he included space for a Player's Green or outdoor theater as well as a council ring tucked into the nearby woods. The small streams shown here emanate from limestone "springs" built into the hillside and feed the large lagoon or "prairie river" in Columbus Park (photo: Art and Architecture Library, University of Michigan)

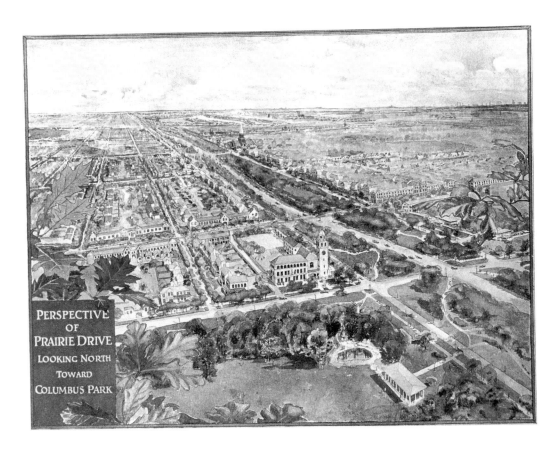

PERSPECTIVE
OF
PRAIRIE DRIVE
LOOKING NORTH
TOWARD
COLUMBUS PARK

17. Drawing by Lawrence Buck of Jensen's Prairie Drive (photo: West Chicago Park Commissioners, 1920)

THE PRAIRIE AS A REGIONAL STYLE

The prairie gardens of Simonds and Jensen provide a useful prototype for garden styles clearly based on the natural heritage of a region. They borrowed forms and techniques from naturalistic garden traditions that had no specific geographic focus, but these were combined with plants and patterns particularly appropriate to the landscape of the Midwest. While Miller was adamant that their work represented a unique style, Simonds was not so sure. In a letter to Miller reviewing the manuscript for *The Prairie Spirit in Landscape Gardening* (1915), Simonds argued that many of the features Miller found so distinctive were equally appropriate to other regions of the country. Simonds seemed to think of himself less as a midwestern designer per se, but more as a regional designer who responded to local conditions wherever he worked.[51] Jensen, on the other hand, was more flattered to think of his work as a distinctive prairie style; the mosaic of woodland, prairie, and wetland landscape of the Midwest, clearly remained his most fertile inspiration. While he occasionally created gardens outside of the Midwest, he al-

[51] O. C. Simonds to Wilhelm Miller, 20 July 1915, University Archives, University Library, University of Illinois, Urbana, Ill. Copy given to the author by Christopher Vernon.

ways approached such designs cautiously, trying to learn as much as possible about the local context before making any design decisions.

In this analysis of the prairie gardens of Simonds and Jensen, several dominant features support the characterization as a unique regional style of garden design. First and foremost, the emphasis on the native flora of the Midwest gave a distinctive flavor to their gardens. Both Simonds and Jensen spent years directly studying the flora of the prairie/forest border and idealized its patterns. They chose to emphasize the common over the exotic and idealized features such as the grassland flora of the prairie so difficult to recapture in the limited confines of their gardens. For spatial organization, they generally avoided formal geometry, borrowing instead from naturalistic traditions passed down through several generations of designers; they used the irregularly shaped lawns and masses of trees and shrubs to emphasize the expansiveness of the prairie landscape. Even in smaller gardens, they tried to convey a sense of a larger landscape and always highlighted the interaction of the sky with the garden. While others viewed the flatness of the prairie region as a serious drawback, Simonds and Jensen emphasized its horizontal character as an asset. Through the repetition of lines parallel to the horizon, in the branching patterns of trees and shrubs and in layers of rock-work, they created unified garden spaces that symbolically conveyed a sense of the larger prairie landscape. Rather than lament the lack of evergreens in the Midwest, they chose to accent the seasonal changes of their gardens, artfully playing with sunlight and atmospheric conditions. Finally, an underlying conservation theme pervaded nearly all their gardens; through their artistry, each design became a conscious effort to awaken people to the subtle beauty of the landscape of the Midwest and an effective plea for its preservation. The combination of these characteristics in the prairie gardens of Simonds and Jensen can indeed be considered a regionally appropriate style. A close examination of the principles they used and their approaches to landscape study can continue to serve as models for designers who want to evoke a spirit of the native landscape and create gardens steeped in the biological and cultural heritage of the Midwest.

Eighteenth-Century Virginia Plantation Gardens:
Translating an Ancient Idyll

C. ALLAN BROWN

And Judah and Israel dwelt safely, every man under his vine and under his fig tree . . . all the days of Solomon.[1]

1 Kings 4:25

Region, the shared concern of these collected essays, is an invention of mind. In a purely analytical sense, the mind surveys an area, recognizes distinctions, finds patterns, and suggests boundaries. But the mind may also impose imagery on the land, at times endowing a landscape with attributes that bear little relation to its physical character. At the beginning of the seventeenth century, when Virginia was the New World, when its actual landscape was still *terra incognita,* its idealized landscape became the new-found locus for an age-old myth. This paper considers real, physical regions on both sides of the Atlantic, but also addresses "region" as landscape conjured in the imagination. These mythical settings were "translated" from one cultural idiom into another and, in the archaic meaning of that word, were "carried across" the ocean from one hemisphere to another.[2]

Certain ideas developed in this paper owe much to concepts first suggested by Rhys Isaac in *The Transformation of Virginia, 1740–1790,* Chapel Hill, N.C., 1982, especially 34–42. Gratitude also is expressed to John Dixon Hunt, whose criticisms and insights directly benefited this research.

[1] Authorized (King James) Version of the Bible, 1611. Variations of the epigraph appear several places in the Old Testament: 1 Kings 4:25, 2 Kings 18:31, Isa. 36:16, and Mic. 4:3–4. The last citation is the celebrated passage:

> And he shall judge among many people, and rebuke strong nations afar off; and they shall beat their swords into plowshares, and their spears into pruning hooks: nation shall not lift up a sword against nation, neither shall they learn war any more. But they shall sit every man under his vine and under his fig tree; and none shall make *them* afraid: for the mouth of the LORD of hosts hath spoken *it.*

[2] On America as a landscape of the imagination, see R. Lawson-Peebles, *Landscape and Written Expression in Revolutionary America: The World Turned Upside Down,* Cambridge, 1988, especially 1–21, 44–46; L. Marx, *The Machine in the Garden: Technology and the Pastoral Ideal in America,* New York, 1964; R. Nash, *Wilderness and the American Mind,* rev. ed., New Haven, Conn., 1973; C. L. Sanford, *The Quest for Paradise: Europe and the American Moral Imagination,* Urbana, Ill., 1961; H. N. Smith, *Virgin Land: The American West as Symbol and Myth,* Cambridge, Mass., 1950.

In 1616, John Rolfe pleaded with the privy councillor, the earl of Pembroke, for further support of the fledgling colony at Jamestown, portraying Virginia as a land of "*Peace . . .* every man sitting under his *figtree* in safety, gathering and reaping the fruites of their labors with much joy and comfort."[3] Life in early-seventeenth-century Virginia was hardly peaceful and prosperous; gardens were for subsistence mostly, and orchards and vineyards were virtually nonexistent. Isolation and the unfamiliar environment, not to mention the anxious natives, threatened the colony's very survival.[4] Yet the Solomonic metaphor that Rolfe invoked persisted as a familiar refrain among Virginia planters well through the mid-nineteenth century. It would be a mistake to regard such usage of metaphorical language as merely rhetorical conceit; it will be shown that this idyll became an ideal which informed the life of the Virginia gentry and was expressed most tangibly in their gardens (Fig. 1).[5]

Virginia, the oldest colony, also became the wealthiest; John Rolfe is credited with having introduced to Virginia the chief means for achieving such affluence—the planting of tobacco. Extensive plantations of tobacco fostered the development of a rural society grown up from the rich alluvium of the coastal plain and dispersed along the navigable waterways leading to the sea. This "tidewater" culture spread throughout the Chesapeake Bay region of Virginia and Maryland and, in time, extended down the coastline to the Carolinas and Georgia. In the southern-most colonies, rice and indigo replaced tobacco, but plantation-based society there remained similar in many respects to that of the Chesapeake.[6]

One successful early planter on the Potomac River in Virginia, William Fitzhugh, assured prospective English colonists in a letter of 1687 that on a Virginia plantation "they may sit safely under their own Vines & fig trees."[7] The seeds of an American ideal of affluent, independent, rural, or quasi-rural living were first sown on the Virginia plantation, and its garden became the conspicuous emblem of this cultural paradigm. Today, the Virginia plantation garden is a familiar image to the American mind, a recognizable expression of regional culture in the United States (Fig. 2). The picture that is summoned is a symmetrical composition, aligned on axis with the house, and framed in

[3] J. Rolfe, *A True Relation of the State of Virginia lefte by Sir Thomas Dale Knight in May Last 1616*, New Haven, Conn., 1951, 35.

[4] W. M. Billings, ed., *The Old Dominion in the Seventeenth Century: A Documentary History of Virginia, 1606–1689*, Chapel Hill, N.C., 1975, especially 3–13, 288–98.

[5] On the significance of such biblical allusion within the context of millenarianism in early America, see R. Bloch, *Visionary Republic: Millennial Themes in American Thought, 1756–1800*, Cambridge, 1985, especially 112–13, 193–94. For an explanation as to why such bibilical allusion had lost much of its efficacy in America by the last quarter of the nineteenth century, see M. I. Lowance, Jr., *The Language of Canaan: Metaphor and Symbol in New England from the Puritans to the Transcendentalists*, Cambridge, Mass., 1980, ix, 115–23.

[6] Billings, *Old Dominion*, 3–13; T. H. Breen, *Tobacco Culture: The Mentality of the Great Tidewater Planters on the Eve of the Revolution*, Princeton, N.J., 1985; G. Main, *Tobacco Colony: Life in Early Maryland, 1650–1720*, Princeton, N.J., 1982; L. J. Cappon, B. B. Petchenik, and J. H. Long, eds., *Atlas of Early American History: The Revolutionary Era, 1760–1790*, Princeton, N.J., 1976, 22–23, 26–27, 64–65; for a contrasting interpretation (which I find unconvincing) see J. O'Mara, "The Riverine Myth in Interpretations of Eighteenth Century Virginia," *Southern Folklore Quarterly* 44 (1980), 165–77.

1. View of a plantation; anonymous, probably early nineteenth century, oil on wood panel (photo: Metropolitan Museum of Art, New York; gift of Edgar William and Bernice Chrysler Garbisch, 1963)

AN OLD VIRGINIA SETTING CREATED ON THE NORTH SHORE OF LONG ISLAND

2. Virginia regional garden transplanted to New York by Innocenti and Webel, landscape architects (photo: from *Architecture and Design,* 1937)

plantings. It probably has boxwood-bordered paths, brick walls, and turf terraces, but it is always envisioned with a sweep of lawn in front. Indeed, it may be that the modern American obsession with the residential grassed "yard" can be traced to the "bowling green" or "level green" of plantation gardens.

The garden at Westover, the Byrd family plantation on the north bank of the James River, was described in 1705 as "the finest in that Country," although little is known of its appearance except that it had "a Summer-House set round with the *Indian* Honey-Suckle." William Byrd I, who came from England to Virginia some time before 1670, built a house at Westover about 1690. A survey plan dated 1701 (Fig. 3) depicts the house as situated beside the river and surrounded by a modest area of grounds, which appear to be enclosed by a fence. Avenues of trees extended outward some distance from the house along the east-west axis and northward to a landing in a protected cove. Following William Byrd I's death in 1704, his son inherited the estate.[8]

William Byrd II had been born in Virginia in 1674 but spent most of his early life in England, obtaining an education and launching a career in the colonial government. Byrd, a protégé of Sir Robert Southwell, and a Fellow of the Royal Society, gained wide acquaintance among the English aristocracy. As did many English gentlemen of his era, Byrd cultivated an interest in gardens and appreciation of landscape. In 1701, he accompanied Sir John Percival on a long tour through England to Scotland, visiting a number of gardens along the way. William Byrd II's experiences in England and Virginia will be considered in some detail partly because more documentation of his garden interest exists than for any other early-eighteenth-century Virginia planter, but also because there is evidence that the garden at Westover was admired as an exemplar in the region through much of the century.[9]

After Byrd arrived in Virginia in 1705 to take up his inheritance, he spent the next decade establishing himself at Westover and in Virginia affairs. Very little is known of any garden improvements during this period, but Byrd noted in his diary in June 1712 that his houseguest, the visiting English naturalist Mark Catesby, "directed how I should mend my garden and put it into a better fashion than it is at present." In 1714, Byrd returned to England on business, and circumstances resulted in his remaining there for

[7] R. B. Davis, ed., *William Fitzhugh and His Chesapeake World, 1676–1701: The Fitzhugh Letters and Other Documents*, Chapel Hill, N.C., 1963, 203.

[8] R. Beverley, *The History and Present State of Virginia*, ed. L. B. Wright, Chapel Hill, N.C., 1947, 299; M. Tinling, ed., *The Correspondence of the Three William Byrds of Westover, Virginia, 1684–1776*, 1, Charlottesville, Va., 1977, 3–7.

[9] K. A. Lockridge, *The Diary, and Life, of William Byrd II of Virginia, 1674 1744*, Chapel Hill, N.C., 1987, 12–39; M. R. Wenger, ed., *The English Travels of Sir John Percival and William Byrd II: The Percival Diary of 1701*, Columbia, Mo., 1989. By 1738, Westover had the reputation as having "the best garden in Virginia," Peter Collinson to John Bartram, [1738], in W. Darlington, ed., *Memorials of John Bartram and Humphry Marshall*, Philadelphia, 1849, 113. As late as 1782, the marquis de Chastellux described Westover as surpassing all the other James River plantations "in the magnificence of the buildings, the beauty of its situation, and the pleasures of the society to be found there . . . [it] is still the most renowned and agreeable in the region," H. C. Rice, Jr., ed. and trans., *Travels in North America in the Years 1780, 1781, and 1782*, Chapel Hill, N.C., 1963, 430.

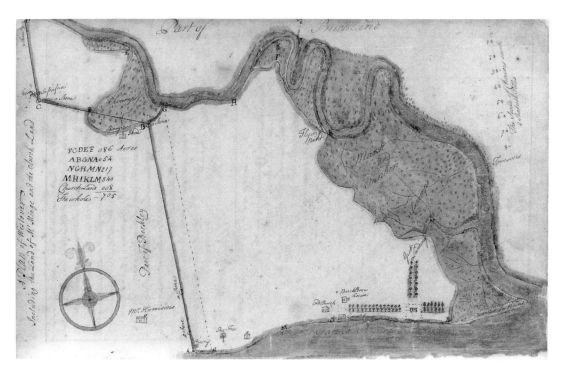

3. "A Plan of Westover," attributed to James Minge, 1701 (photo: William Byrd Title Book, Virginia Historical Society, Richmond, Virginia)

five years. During this period, as his diaries attest, Byrd often visited houses and gardens in the English countryside; among them were Cliveden (Fig. 4), the Thames-side, villa-like estate of the earl of Orkney, who was also the governor of Virginia from 1697 to 1737, and the duke of Marlborough's magnificent new house and garden at Blenheim. Back in Virginia during the years 1720 to 1721, Byrd began alterations to the garden at Westover, likely inspired by the scenes he had encountered on his frequent garden rambles. Working with his "old gardener Tom Cross," he hired bricklayers (probably to build garden walls), planned a "ditch" (possibly a ha-ha), positioned "seats" within the garden, and "began to turf the bowling green." Then, from 1721 to 1726, Byrd was once again in London.[10]

In the 1720s, the stretch of the Thames River beside the villages of Richmond and Twickenham, "where the silver Thames first rural grows," emerged as a highly fashionable retreat for genteel London society (Fig. 5); this region came to epitomize the eighteenth-century revival of the ancient ideal of "retired" life enjoyed away from the

[10] L. B. Wright and M. Tinling, eds., *The Secret Diary of William Byrd of Westover, 1709–1712*, Richmond, Va., 1941, 540; L. B. Wright and M. Tinling, eds., *William Byrd of Virginia: The London Diary (1717–1721) and Other Writings*, New York, 1958, 148, 150, 155, 378, 385–89, 394, 413, 492, 499, 507. John Evelyn compared Cliveden to "*Frascati*," see J. D. Hunt, *Garden and Grove: The Italian Renaissance Garden in the English Imagination, 1600–1750*, Princeton, N.J., 1986, 158.

4. Cliveden, Buckinghamshire; attributed to William Tompkins, ca. 1760 (photo: National Trust, Great Britain)

5. The Thames at Twickenham, with Pope's villa at left of center; painting by Pieter Tillemans, ca. 1730 (photo: British Rail Pension Fund Works of Art Collection)

cares of the city.[11] Over the course of the century, "Twit'nam" and Richmond, and particularly the view of the river from Richmond Hill, were widely celebrated in poetry, prose, and pictures by the likes of Pope, Thomson, Swift, Defoe, Reynolds, Wilson, Turner, and a host of lesser writers and artists.[12] Alexander Pope moved to Twickenham in 1719 where the Augustan poet conceived his life there as a rural retreat in the classical tradition as exemplified at Tusculum, the region near Rome where Cicero and other Romans built villas. Pope hired the architect James Gibbs to alter an existing riverside house, giving it a facade much like those of the villas along the Brenta River, near Venice, routinely seen by English gentlemen on the Grand Tour (Fig. 6).[13]

Similar to the development along the Brenta during the Renaissance, a villa culture inspired by classical precedent soon burgeoned in the Thames River valley. The English "villa" originated there as a relatively small, squarish, symmetrical suburban residence integrated with a modest garden; Roger North, in his treatise "Of Building" (ca. 1695) explained that a villa was "quasy a lodge, for the sake of a garden."[14] Often there was a portico, loggia, or balustraded terrace interposed between house and garden. Palladio, whose designs for villas of the Veneto became the principal models for the English villas, had written that gardens were the "chief recreation of a villa" and rehearsed the ancient idyll with these words: ". . . the antient sages commonly used to retire to such like places; where being oftentimes visited by their virtuous friends and relations, having houses, gardens, fountains, and such like pleasant places, and above all, their virtue, they could easily attain to as much happiness as can be attained here below."[15]

The Anglo-Palladian movement advanced by Richard Boyle, third earl of Burlington, produced a number of villas along the Thames River during the 1720s: prominent among them were Burlington's own villa at Chiswick, George II's White Lodge in

[11] J. Thomson, "Summer," 1727. Thomson's full poem, *The Seasons*, which began appearing in 1726 with "Winter," was first published in collected form in 1730. It was reissued throughout the century and became widely popular in America, as in England.

[12] M. Batey and D. Lambert, *The English Garden Tour: A View Into the Past*, London, 1990, 146–51; M. R. Brownell, "The Iconography of Pope's Villa: Images of Poetic Fame," in G. S. Rousseau and P. Rogers, eds., *The Enduring Legacy: Alexander Pope Tercentenary Essays*, Cambridge, 1988, 133–47; T. H. R. Cashmore, D. H. Simpson, and A. C. B. Urwin, *Alexander Pope's Twickenham: Eighteenth-Century Views of His "Classic Village,"* Borough of Twickenham Local History Society Occasional Paper 3, Twickenham, 1988; B. Gascoigne, *Images of Richmond*, Richmond, 1978, B. Gascoigne and J. Ditchburn, *Images of Twickenham*, Richmond, 1981; J. Bryant, *Finest Prospects: Three Historic Houses—A Study in London Topography*, London, 1986, 59–91.

[13] M. Mack, *The Garden and the City: Retirement and Politics in the Later Poetry of Pope, 1731–1743*, Toronto, 1969, 9–21, 65; J. D. Hunt, "Pope's Twickenham Revisited," in R. P. Maccubbin and P. Martin, eds., *British and American Gardens in the Eighteenth Century*, Williamsburg, Va., 1984, 26–35; P. Martin, *Pursuing Innocent Pleasures: The Gardening World of Alexander Pope*, Hamden, Conn., 1984, 19–22, 39–61; on Tusculum, see A. R. Littlewood, "Ancient Literary Evidence for the Pleasure Gardens of Roman Country Villas," in E. B. MacDougall, ed., *Ancient Roman Villa Gardens*, Dumbarton Oaks Colloquium on the History of Landscape Architecture 10, Washington, D.C., 1987, 11; J. Cornforth, "When the Thames was England's Brenta," *Country Life Annual* (1963), 73–75.

[14] J. Summerson, "The Classical Country House in Eighteenth-Century England," *Journal of the Royal Society of Arts* 107 (July 1959), 539–87; J. S. Ackerman, *The Villa: Form and Ideology of Country Houses*, Princeton, N.J., 1990, 150–51; H. Colvin and J. Newman, eds., *Of Building: Roger North's Writings on Architecture*, Oxford, 1981, 62.

[15] I. Ware, trans., *The Four Books of Andrea Palladio's Architecture*, London, 1738, 46.

Veduta del Palazzo del Sig.ʳ Bortoletti.
LIII

6. Plate LIII from Gianfrancesco Costa, *Delle delicie del fiume Brenta*, 1750 (photo: Dumbarton Oaks)

Richmond Park, and Henrietta Howard's Marble Hill at Twickenham. Sir John Summerson has called the idea of the villa "the essential innovation of the century" in English residential architecture and cited Marble Hill, in particular, as "an epoch-making model" (Fig. 7). It was built between 1724 and 1729 at the very center of the view from Richmond Hill and immediately hailed by Robert Morris in his *An Essay in Defence of Ancient Architecture* (1728) as a villa in the true ancient manner.[16] Its garden, too, might be considered as an early model landscape for Anglo-Palladian architecture. Charles Bridgeman and Alexander Pope collaborated on the landscape design in the mid-1720s.[17] The result, as it appears in the earliest mid-century depictions, was a simple setting composed of a modulated series of shallow turf terraces gently descending to the Thames and framed by

[16] Summerson, "Classical Country House," 552, 572–73; J. Summerson, *Architecture in Britain, 1530–1830*, Harmondsworth, 1979, 360; Bryant, *Finest Prospects*, 59–91.

[17] On this collaboration, see P. Willis, *Charles Bridgeman and the English Landscape Garden*, London, 1977, 77–78; Martin, *Pursuing Innocent Pleasures*, 130–31, 154–66. On Marble Hill as a model: ". . . the grounds at Marble Hill may also come to be studied as a 'textbook example'; but in a different sense in that they conveniently illustrate no existing definition, but rather invite further research into our understanding of the English Palladian garden," *Blest Retreats: A History of Private Gardens in Richmond Upon Thames*, Richmond, 1984, 36.

7. Marble Hill, Twickenham; view of the south front from the Thames. Engraving by James Mason, after Augustin Heckell, 1749

symmetrically-balanced files of trees staggered uniformly down the terraces, enhancing perspectives to and from the river. The design displayed an architectonic attitude toward landscape in contrast to the irregularity and increasing naturalism of the "landscape garden," which, from the mid-1730s, gradually emerged as the preferred setting for Anglo-Palladian architecture.[18]

Unfortunately no diary survives for Byrd's stay in London from 1721 to 1726, but it seems likely that he continued to visit the Richmond area as he had during the previous decade. Among Byrd's most frequent companions in England were several of "the progenitors—the first patrons and exponents—of Palladianism": Edward Southwell, son of Byrd's mentor Sir Robert; John Campbell, second duke of Argyll; and his brother, Archibald Campbell, earl of Islay. Colen Campbell cited Edward Southwell as an early patron in *Vitruvius Britannicus* in 1715. In the mid-1720s, James Gibbs produced designs for

[18] John Dixon Hunt has observed that "recent studies of the English landscape garden either turn their backs on 'the highly interesting period from . . . 1713 to 1733' because it cannot be read as a preliminary to 'the Reign of Nature,' or see the contribution of a gardenist like Alexander Pope almost solely in terms of later picturesque styles which he could not have known and therefore could not have anticipated," *Garden and Grove,* 181. Diana Balmori's recent article, "Architecture, Landscape, and the Intermediate Structure: Eighteenth-Century Experiments in Mediation" (*Journal of the Society of Architectural Historians* 50 [March 1991], 38–56), seems to reflect the latter approach when she describes Pope's garden as "composed of a number of classical elements arranged asymmetrically." John Serle's plan (1745) depicts a dominant linear space as the spine of Pope's layout, with "classical elements" (urns, statues, mounts, trees) symmetrically flanking the axis and an obelisk at the focal point, terminating the axis. Cf. the plans reproduced in Martin, *Pursuing Innocent Pleasures,* 48–49.

"*villas*" in the Thames valley for the Campbell brothers; moreover, these "Gardening Lords" were also friends of Alexander Pope and his circle. It has been suggested that Charles Bridgeman may have advised them on the designs of their gardens. Lord Islay was instrumental in the building of Marble Hill, serving as Mrs. Howard's agent throughout the construction; Byrd, himself, had become acquainted with her in the spring of 1719 and, reputedly, also with Pope.[19]

It was this villa-culture milieu that Byrd left when he returned permanently to Virginia in 1726, to the "solid pleasures of innocence, and retirement" at Westover. When Lieutenant-Governor Alexander Spotswood had first arrived in Virginia in 1710, he found the gentry enjoying "a perfect retir'd Country life; for here is not in the whole Colony a place that may be compar'd to a Brittish village; every one living disperst up & down at their Plantations. . . ."[20] The life of the villa, whether in Ancient Rome, Renaissance Italy, or Augustan England, was associated with the idea of "retirement" or withdrawal to the countryside; the "villa" was the setting to which one "retired." It was a common theme in the literature of each of these cultures. Roman writers such as Cicero, Virgil, and Horace had often portrayed the internal conflict between the excitements of a political, urban life and the simple delights of an independent, rural one.[21] This was the identification which Byrd made when he said that he was in "retirement" at Westover, away from the enticements of London. It is clear from Byrd's diaries and letters that he considered his life at Westover as "retired" from London (not Williamsburg, the mere village that was the colonial capital), as though the James were some far western tributary of the Thames; colonial Virginia was, in essence, only a particularly distant English province. As Byrd once asserted regarding his plantation: ". . . for God's sake, where's the difference between its lying in Virginia or in Berkshire as long as I receive the Profits of it in London?"[22]

Writing to Charles Boyle, fourth earl of Orrery, Byrd styled his life at Westover as "like one of the patriarchs, I have my flocks and my herds, my bond-men, and bond-women, and every soart of trade amongst my own servants, so that I live in a kind of independance on every one, but Providence. . . . we sit securely under our vines, and our fig-trees without any danger to our property. . . . Thus my Lord we are very happy

[19] Wright and Tinling, *London Diary*, passim; M. H. Woodfin and M. Tinling, eds. and trans., *Another Secret Diary of William Byrd of Westover, 1739–1741*, Richmond, Va., 1942, 310–11; Summerson, "Classical Country House," 549, 570; M. R. Brownell, *Alexander Pope and the Arts of Georgian England*, Oxford, 1978, 153–55, 158; Willis, *Charles Bridgeman*, 77–78; J. Bryant, *Marble Hill House, Twickenham*, London, 1988, 28–31.
[20] William Byrd II to Charles Boyle, earl of Orrery, 5 July 1726, in Tinling, *Correspondence*, 1, 356; Alexander Spotswood to John Spotswood, 17 August 1710, in L. J. Cappon, ed., "Correspondence of Alexander Spotswood with John Spotswood of Edinburgh," *Virginia Magazine of History and Biography* 60 (April 1952), 227.
[21] J. Pinto, "The Landscape of Allusion: Literary Themes in the Gardens of Classical Rome and Augustan England," *Smith College Studies in History* 48 (1980), 97–113; Summerson, "Classical Country House," 544; M. O'Loughlin, *The Garlands of Repose: The Literary Celebration of Civic and Retired Leisure*, Chicago, 1978; M. S. Røstvig, *The Happy Man: Studies in the Metamorphoses of a Classical Ideal*, rev. ed., Oslo, 1962.
[22] William Byrd II to Sabina, 28 March [1718], Woodfin and Tinling, *Another Secret Diary*, 337.

in our Canaan. . . ."[23] Byrd frequently employed both biblical and classical allusions in describing Virginia; it became commonplace to cast the New World as both Eden and Arcadia, the Promised Land and the Hesperides.[24] The manner of conflating biblical and classical myth in the imagination of the gentry may be illustrated by Byrd's custom, as his diaries detail, of beginning each day by reading in Hebrew, then in Greek or Latin (i.e., passages from the Old Testament followed by selections from classical texts). Among the Virginia gentry, the belief in the possible recovery in America of the archetypal garden was nowhere more literally manifest than in the plantation garden.

The Latin word *otium*, usually translated in the eighteenth century as "retirement," signified a complex of meanings—leisure, seclusion, and serenity coupled with sometimes rigorous mental and physical activity, all in a rural setting.[25] Its antithesis, "*negotium*" denoted "business," the affairs of the city. Plantations or gardens with names such as The Hermitage, The Retreat, The Recess, Solitude, Buen Retiro, Mon Repos, Sans Souci, Hors du Monde, Tusculum, or Sabine Hall, betray their shared mythopoeic origin.

Byrd admitted however, that there was some discontent in "Canaan" when he remembered the "onions, and flesh-pots of Egypt," acknowledging that the charms of English culture "always had I must own too strong an influence upon me."[26] Indeed, English tastes are directly reflected in the architecture of the house which he began about 1730 to replace his father's earlier one and in what is known of the layout of the garden (Fig. 8). Westover's large library included some dozen titles on architecture, including three editions of Palladio's *Quattro Libri,* and gardening books such as Stephen Switzer's *Ichnographia Rustica* (1718) and the ubiquitous Philip Miller's *The Gardeners Dictionary* (1731). Thomas Tileston Waterman demonstrated that a number of Westover's architectural details derive from *Palladio Londinensis; or the London Art of Building* (1734), and similarly, the features of its garden may be shown to reflect contemporary English practice. Westover serves as a clear reminder of the obvious relationship between prevailing English styles and their adaptation in colonial Virginia.[27]

[23] William Byrd II to Charles Boyle, earl of Orrery, 5 July 1726, in Tinling, *Correspondence,* 1, 355; Byrd used similar language to describe life at Westover in another letter five years later ("We live in all the innocence of the patriarchs, under our vines and our fig-trees, surrounded with our flocks and our herds. We enjoy our moderate possessions in great security. . . ."), William Byrd II to John Boyle, Baron Broghill, 15 June 1731, ibid., 444.

[24] See especially Byrd's "A Journey to the Land of Eden Anno 1733," in L. B. Wright, ed., *The Prose Works of William Byrd of Westover: Narratives of a Colonial Virginian,* Cambridge, Mass., 1966, 381–412; and the map of "Eden in Virginia," 1736, reproduced in J. W. Reps, *Tidewater Towns: City Planning in Colonial Virginia and Maryland,* Williamsburg, Va., 1972, 196–98. On the conflation of biblical and classical allusion in the American mythic image, see Marx, *Machine in the Garden,* especially 36–40, 73–88; and Lowance, *Language of Canaan,* chap. 9.

[25] D. R. Coffin, *The Villa in the Life of Renaissance Rome,* Princeton, 1979, 11–12; T. Comito, *The Idea of the Garden in the Renaissance,* New Brunswick, N.J., 1978, 69; Ackerman, *The Villa,* 37.

[26] Tinling, *Correspondence,* 1, 355–56.

[27] "A Catalogue of the Books in the Library at Westover Belonging to William Byrd, Esqr.," in J. S. Bassett, ed., *The Writings of Colonel William Byrd of Westover in Virginia, Esqr.,* New York, 1901, 413–43; T. T. Waterman, *The Mansions of Virginia, 1706–1776,* Chapel Hill, N.C., 1945, 150–53, 157; M. R. Wenger, "Westover: William Byrd's Mansion Reconsidered," Master's thesis, University of Virginia, 1981; D. D. Reiff, *Small Georgian Houses in England and Virginia: Origins and Development Through the 1750s,* London, 1986.

8. Westover, Virginia; view of the south front from the James, 1811 (photo: J. S. Glennie Journal, Andre deCoppet Collection, Princeton University Library)

In 1735 Byrd mentioned having had "a draught" made of "the gardens & cheif of the buildings" at Westover, yet it appears the drawing has not survived. John Bartram, the Philadelphia botanist, wrote after visiting Westover in 1738 that "Colonel Byrd is very prodigalle . . . [with] new Gates, gravel Walks, hedges, and cedars finely twined and a little green house with two or three orange trees . . . in short, he hath the finest seat in Virginia." Some indication of the design of the landscape at Westover is provided by a description and sketch plan which a visitor made in 1783 (Fig. 9). By that time William Byrd II had been dead for almost forty years, and it is unclear what changes, if any, his widow or son may have made to the estate layout. Regardless, the document provides a rare detailed account of the grounds of an eighteenth-century Virginia plantation.[28]

The grounds, as shown in the sketch plan, were disposed in a symmetrical fashion about the house in the center, with each feature on one side balanced by a corresponding one on the other. Extending outward from the principal facades of the house were trees arranged in precise arcs. To the west of the house was a "very large and exceedingly beautiful" garden whose walls apparently were torn down in the late nineteenth-century and rebuilt in the early twentieth, leaving us with an unclear picture of its original de-

[28] William Byrd II to Peter Beckford, 6 December 1735, in Tinling, *Correspondence*, 2, 464; John Bartram to Peter Collinson, 18 July 1740, Bartram Papers, Pennsylvania Historical Society; Thomas Lee Shippen to William Shippen, Jr., 30 December 1783, Shippen Family Papers, Library of Congress (the sketch and text of the letter were reproduced in A. G. B. Lockwood, ed., *Gardens of Colony and State: Gardens and Gardeners of the American Colonies and of the Republic Before 1840*, 2, New York, 1934, 97–101.)

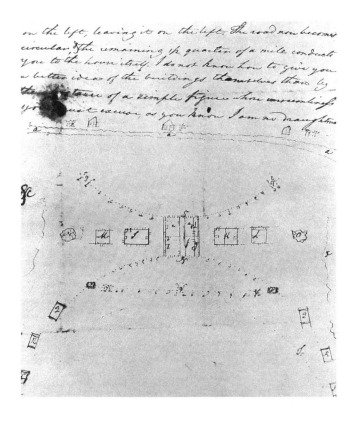

9. Sketch plan of the Westover grounds; Thomas Lee Shippen, 1783 (photo: Shippen Family Papers, Library of Congress)

sign.[29] Opposite the garden, to the east of the house, was "a pretty grove neatly kept"; to the cultivated eighteenth-century mind, "grove" carried classical connotations, ranging from the mystical sacred grove to the intellectual setting for Plato's academy.[30] Baron Ludwig Von Closen, who visited Westover at about the same period as when the sketch plan was made, described seeing along the riverside, perhaps in the grove, "very lovely statues, two ponds, and two little summer-houses, prettily arranged . . . art and natural beauty are delightfully combined there."[31] On one occasion Byrd succinctly summed up the delights of Westover: "a library, a garden, a grove, and a purling stream are the innocent scenes that divert our leizure."[32]

To the south of the house, beside the "purling stream" of the James was "a prettily falling grass plat variegated with pedestals of many different kinds, about 300 by 100 yards in extent [with] an extensive prospect of James River and of all the Country and

[29] Shippen letter, 1783; Lockwood, *Gardens,* 2, 95–96; M. N. Stanard, *Colonial Virginia: Its People and Customs,* Philadelphia, 1917, 70–71.

[30] Shippen letter, 1783; Hunt, *Garden and Grove,* especially 161–62.

[31] E. M. Acomb, ed. and trans., *The Revolutionary Journal of Baron Ludwig Von Closen, 1780–1783,* Chapel Hill, N.C., 1958, 188. The Englishman Thomas Anburey, who visited Westover in 1779, wrote that "the grounds around the house at Westover, are laid out in a most beautiful manner and with great taste, and from the river appear delightful," *Travels Through the Interior Parts of America; in a Series of Letters,* 2, London, 1789, 369–70.

[32] William Byrd II to "Mrs. Armiger," 25 June 1729, in Tinling, *Correspondence,* 1, 413.

10. Carter's Grove, Virginia; anonymous mid-nineteenth-century watercolor. Plantings on the terrace slopes are likely Victorian additions (photo: Colonial Williamsburg Foundation, Williamsburg, Virginia)

some Gentlemen's seats on the other side; the river is banked up by a wall of four feet high and about 300 yards in length, and above this wall there is as you may suppose the most enchanting walk in ye world."[33]

One of these "Gentlemen's seats on the other side" was David Meade's plantation at Maycox, whose garden, as the marquis de Chastellux described it in 1781, was "like the one at Westover, forms a terrace along the bank of the river"; another visitor described the terrace at Maycox as "land thrown into many artificial hollows or gentle swellings with the pleasing verdure of the turf."[34] This could also have been a description of a number of other gardens along the James from Carter's Grove (Fig. 10) and Kingsmill, near Williamsburg, to Berkeley and Shirley, near Richmond. As Baron Von Closen portrayed it: "For the most part, both banks of this river are embellished with plantations, one more beautiful than the other, and inhabited by the aristocracy of the country . . . Our journey along the James River seemed to us like a pleasant dream, or, to speak as a

[33] Shippen letter, 1783; perhaps these "pedestals of many different kinds," which once ornamented the river side of the garden were the "stone ornaments . . . of Italian origin, brought over for William Byrd the second," which, by the late nineteenth century, reportedly were "scattered about on the ground, some of them in pieces," and evidently later incorporated in the present fence along the north side of the house. See Lockwood, *Gardens,* 2, 97.

[34] Rice, *Travels,* 431; "A Topographical Description of the County of Prince George, in Virginia, 1793. By the Rev. John Jones Spooner . . . ," quoted in F. Kimball, "A Landscape Garden on the James in 1793," *Landscape Architecture* 14 (January 1924), 123.

young man, like the flight of a butterfly, who goes from one flower to another. . . ."[35]

This scene, of riverside gardens stepping down in green terraces to the James, which Chastellux dubbed "the garden of Virginia," inevitably evoked impressions of the villa gardens bordering the banks of the Thames. But these associations were not limited to the James; visitors along other rivers in eighteenth-century Virginia also transplanted the Thames River valley to the landscape before them. In 1732, the English gentleman, William Hugh Grove, perceived the elevated situation of Yorktown as "Like Black heath or Richmond Hill and Like that Overlooks a fine river Broader than the Thames at Those places"; and he found the Mattaponi River to be "Thick seated with gentry on its Banks with in a Mile or at most 2 mile from Each other . . . Most of These have pleasant Gardens and the Prospect of the River render them very pleasant [and] equall to the Thames from London to Richmond, supposing the Towns omitted."[36] Such remarks are a measure of the presence of the Thames villa "region" in the eighteenth-century English, and English colonial, imagination.

It would seem Byrd fully intended such a visualization when, in 1733, his surveying party laid out the foundations for a town, that he named Richmond, on property which he owned near the falls of the James some distance above Westover: "we did not build Castles only, but also Citys in the Air," he noted in his journal.[37] Likely he envisioned a villa society at Richmond on the James recalling that which he had enjoyed at Richmond Upon Thames (Fig. 11); a hundred years later, the Virginia Richmond was described as "a beautiful little city, built up of rich and tasteful villas, and embellished with all the varieties of town and country, scattered with a refined and exquisite skill." Byrd's son, William Byrd III, built a house overlooking the James at Richmond in the mid-eighteenth century. With its Italianate name, Belvidere was described as "an elegant villa" by an English traveler in 1779, and once again by another Englishman in 1784; furthermore, when English clergyman Andrew Burnaby visited Belvidere in 1759, he found it "as romantic and elegant as any thing I have ever seen." Late-eighteenth-century views of Belvidere hardly suggest literal comparison with the Anglo-Palladian villas along the Thames, but the English visitors' comments may exemplify their capacity to see beyond the actual to the signified. Summerson concluded that the term "villa" in eighteenth-century England "was never used with any *architectural* precision"; its significance lay more in the idea of the country life it suggested than in any specific architectural form.[38]

Benjamin Henry Latrobe, the English-born architect, visited Richmond, Virginia, shortly after arriving in America in 1796, and he, also, immediately sensed the association of this place (Fig. 12) with its namesake:

[35] Acomb, *Revolutionary Journal,* 187–88.

[36] Rice, *Travels,* 430; G. A. Stiverson and P. H. Butler III, eds., "Virginia in 1732: The Travel Journal of William Hugh Grove," *Virginia Magazine of History and Biography* 85 (January 1977), 18–44.

[37] Wright, *Prose Works,* 388; V. Dabney, *Richmond: The Story of a City,* Garden City, N.Y., 1976, 12–22; J. Seelye, *Prophetic Waters: The River in Early American Life and Literature,* New York, 1977, 385–88.

[38] [J. P. Kennedy], *Swallow Barn, or A Sojourn in the Old Dominion,* Philadelphia, 1832, 10; Anburey, *Travels,* 2, 369; J. F. D. Smyth, *A Tour in the United States of America,* 1, London, 1784, 57; A. Burnaby, *Travels Through the Middle Settlements in North America, in the Years 1759 and 1760,* London, 1775, 39; E. C. Carter II, J. C. Van Horne, and C. E. Brownell, eds., *Latrobe's View of America, 1795–1820: Selections from the Watercolors and Sketches,* New Haven, Conn., 1985, 120–21, 144–45; Summerson, "Classical Country House," 570–71.

11. Richmond, Surrey; aquatint by Joseph Farington in *An History of the River Thames*, 1794

The general landscapes from the two Richmond-hills are so similar in their great features, that at first sight the likeness is most striking. The detail of course must be extremely different. But the windings of James river have so much the same *cast* with those of the Thames, the amphitheatre of hills covered partly with wood partly with buildings, and the opposite shore with the town of Manchester in front, and fields and woods in the rear, are so like the range of hills on the south bank of the Thames, and the situation of Twickenham on the north backed by the neighbouring woody parks, that if a man could be imperceptibly and in an instant conveyed from the one side of the Atlantic to the other he might hesitate for some minutes before he could discover the difference.

The want of finish and neatness in the American landscape would first strike his eye, while his ear would be arrested by the roar of the falls of James river below him. He would miss the elegance of Richmond bridge, and find in its place the impatient torrent tumbling over huge masses of granite. . . . When however the whole country was in wood, I am convinced that it was the *general* similarity of the characters of the two situations that impressed upon this spot the name of Richmond.[39]

[39] Carter, Van Horne, and Brownell, *Latrobe's View of America*, 72–73.

12. Richmond, Virginia; watercolor by Benjamin Henry Latrobe, 1796 (photo: Maryland Historical Society)

With the establishment of the commonwealth, the capital was moved upriver to Richmond in 1780. Reinforcing the republican ambitions of this landscape was the new capitol, designed in 1785–86 by Thomas Jefferson and Charles-Louis Clérisseau as though it were an acropolis-cum-temple. Jefferson explained that they had based the building on the so-called *Maison Carrée* at Nîmes, "the best morsel of antient architecture now remaining. It has obtained the approbation of fifteen or sixteen centuries, and is therefore preferable to any design which might be newly contrived." That was a prescription he later advanced for the national capitol as well—"I should prefer the adoption of some one of the models of antiquity which have had the approbation of thousands of years."[40] These words suggest how strong was the appeal of ancient traditions of idea and form, the meshing of which in Virginia gave physical as well as conceptual shape to a specific region. As the supreme ceremonial symbol of the young commonwealth, the Virginia capitol reified the authority of antiquity that was celebrated in eighteenth-century gentry society.

John Dixon Hunt has demonstrated in *Garden and Grove: The Italian Renaissance Garden in the English Imagination, 1600–1750* that English gardens of this period, the same as that of the colonization of America, embodied Italianate garden ideas and forms. Should

[40] T. J. McCormick, *Charles-Louis Clerisseau and the Genesis of Neo-Classicism*, Cambridge, Mass., 1990, 191–99; Thomas Jefferson to James Madison, 1 September 1785, in J. Boyd, ed., *The Papers of Thomas Jefferson*, 8, Princeton, N.J., 1952– , 462; Thomas Jefferson to Pierre Charles L'Enfant, 10 April 1791, ibid., 20, 86.

C. ALLAN BROWN

it be any surprise that gardens designed in the English province of Virginia would reflect this same fascination with Italian traditions, albeit in more modest fashion? In each stage of the cultural translation, from Italy to England to America, the text was somewhat altered, so that in its final form, the original was sometimes almost unrecognizable.[41] Yet, there were indications in eighteenth-century Virginia plantation gardens to suggest their legacy. Terracing was the most characteristic formal element of the Italian Renaissance garden. In England in the seventeenth and early eighteenth centuries, terraces also became common in gardens; sometimes the terraces were only turf-covered, sloping embankments whose nevertheless precise edges and angles recalled the multileveled platforms and masonry retaining walls of their Italian models.[42] In eighteenth-century Virginia gardens, earthen terraces of this sort were commonly known as "falls" or "Falling gardens," as the terraced gardens of the Governor's Palace in Williamsburg were referred to in 1719.[43] "Falls" were the single most distinctive feature of tidewater gardens, from the steep inclines of Hampton, outside Baltimore, Maryland, to the more gradual undulations of Middleton Place, near Charleston, South Carolina.

In practical terms, "falls" provided level areas for placing structures, diverted drainage, and reduced soil erosion. In addition, the modulation of the slope gave improved access to the house, which was often approached from the water below. Books such as John James's *The Theory and Practice of Gardening* (1712), a translation of Dézallier d'Argenville's *La théorie et la pratique du jardinage* (1709), and Stephen Switzer's *Ichnographia Rustica* (1718) were available in colonial Virginia and provided instruction in forming such terracing (Fig. 13).[44] Of course these terraces also served an aesthetic function: as architectonic extensions of the house, as platforms for viewing the landscape, and as settings for ornament.

One of the best preserved terraced gardens in Virginia is at Sabine Hall, whose "falls" may date from as early as the 1730s. The garden is laid out as a series of six terraces falling gradually toward the Rappahannock River (Fig 14). From the "piazza" (the Italianate term commonly used in eighteenth-century Virginia for a covered walk-

[41] Barbara Wells Sarudy, whose seminal study of eighteenth-century gardens in Maryland documents geometrically regular gardens similar to those in Virginia, regards the influences on these gardens as more directly Italian than as mediated through the English: ". . . the more formal classical garden evolved from Roman and early Italian Renaissance designs. . . . In fact, the falling pleasure gardens of the colonial Chesapeake gentry were not copied from prevalent English garden styles of either the seventeenth or early eighteenth centuries, although a few English country house gardens of this period added classical terraces to their grounds," in "Eighteenth-Century Gardens of the Chesapeake," *Journal of Garden History* 9 (July–September 1989), 127.
[42] Hunt, *Garden and Grove*, especially 104–32, 139–92; R. Strong, *The Renaissance Garden in England*, London, 1979, 117, 144–46, 156–58, 161–63, 176–85.
[43] P. Martin, "'Promised Fruites of Well Ordered Towns'—Gardens in Early 18th-Century Williamsburg," *Journal of Garden History* 2 (October-December 1982), 309–24.
[44] J. James, *The Theory and Practice of Gardening*, London, 1712, 116–23; S. Switzer, *Ichnographia Rustica: or, The Nobleman, Gentleman, and Gardener's Recreation*, 2, London, 1718, 150–82. Advertisements for these books appeared in the Williamsburg *Virginia Gazette* as late as April 1771 for the former and December 1776 for the latter.

142

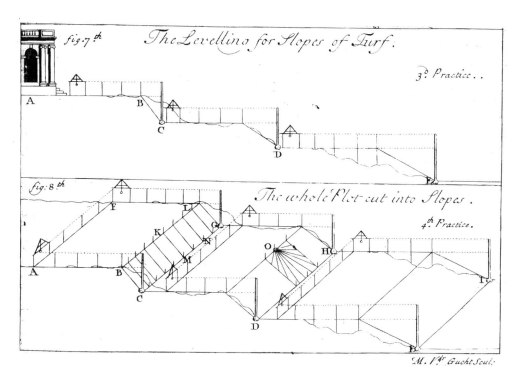

13. "The Levelling for Slopes of Turf"; detail of plate G (photo: from J. James, *The Theory and Practice of Gardening*, 1712)

14. Sabine Hall, Virginia; view south from the "piazza" toward the Rappahannock River

15. Mount Deposit, Maryland; chairback painting by Francis Guy, ca. 1805 (photo: Baltimore Museum of Art)

way), a central gravel walk, aligned axially with the house, descends the garden through turfed ramps rather than steps. The terrace just below the house still displays a gravel and grass plat design, composed in a reversed mirror-image geometrical pattern, which is thought to be a rare, perhaps unique, survival of its kind from the colonial period in Virginia. When Landon Carter, the wealthy planter who built Sabine Hall, resigned from the House of Burgesses in 1758, his fellow burgess Richard Bland wrote a poem exalting Carter "at Sabine Hall, retir'd from public praise." It was an American echo of an ancient paean, which Switzer had recited in *Ichnographia Rustica* as "'twas in their *Villas*, that the Antient *Greeks* and *Romans* pass'd away the happiest Part of their Times. How does *Horace* exult in his Sabine *Villa!*"[45]

Beyond their practical or aesthetic appeal, terraces were replete with Italian villa garden associations; and both in England and America, their introduction into a garden prompted waves of allusion among educated observers. By the late eighteenth century, the enormous popularity in America of the Lombardy Poplar (introduced ca. 1784) only further enhanced such associations (Figs. 8, 15). The columnar tree—"the most admired of all trees in the palmy days of old Virginia"—quickly became the American equivalent of the ancient Mediterranean poplar or Italian cypress.[46] An observer in 1816 remarked that the Lombardy Poplars about Virginia farm houses "recall to mind the sweet fables of yore . . . poplars on the banks of the Po. . . ."; and a visitor to Mount Vernon in 1790

[45] W. M. S. Rasmussen, "Sabine Hall, A Classical Villa in Virginia," *Journal of the Society of Architectural Historians* 39 (December 1980), 286–96; idem, "For Profit and Pleasure: The Art of Gardening in Colonial Virginia—A Study With Focus on Landon Carter's Extant Garden at Sabine Hall," *Arts in Virginia* 21 (Fall 1980), 18–27; J. P. Greene, *Landon Carter: An Inquiry into the Personal Values and Social Imperatives of the Eighteenth-Century Virginia Gentry*, Charlottesville, Va., 1967, 87; Switzer, *Ichnographia Rustica*, 3, xvi. Cf. the parterre designs reproduced in G. Masson, *Italian Gardens*, rev. ed., Woodbridge, Suffolk, 1987, 184.

[46] H. S. Randall, *The Life of Thomas Jefferson*, 2, New York, 1858, 359; U. P. Hedrick, *A History of Horticulture in America to 1860*, New York, 1950, 146, 191.

especially noted, among the variety of trees there, "the Lombardy poplar, or the poplar of the Po of which Ovid sang many hundred years ago. . . ."[47] In conjunction with garden terraces and pedimented houses, the associative response was "classical ground."

Other classical features such as grottoes, as well as terraces and groves, may have adorned a few Virginia gardens in the eighteenth century. As early as 1705, Robert Beverley remarked that Virginians sought relief from the sun in "Summer-Houses, Arbors and Grottos" in their gardens. In 1731, William Byrd's wife, Maria, requested that "a small barrel full" of shells ("Conk Shells Wilks & such Variety") be sent to her from Barbados, perhaps to ornament some type of grotto. Later in the century, Thomas Jefferson proposed an elaborate plan for a grotto at Monticello to surround "a sleeping figure reclined on a plain marble slab" that was to be inscribed with Alexander Pope's famous translation of some pseudo-classical verses that had been associated with villa grottoes since the Renaissance; and the floor and walls of Jefferson's grotto were to be spangled with "translucent pebbles from Hanovertown, and beautiful shells from the shore at Burwell's ferry."[48]

Perhaps even more significant than the various villa garden features present in eighteenth-century Virginia gardens was the overall geometric regularity of composition which they shared in common with Renaissance villas. The exacting geometry and proportionality of Renaissance villas established similar responses in house and garden design: i.e., regular gardens for regular architecture.[49] The geometric regularity or "formality" of eighteenth-century Virginia plantation gardens has often been dismissed as anachronism or American *retardataire* taste, resulting from a presumed culture lag in crossing the ocean, yet, there is scant evidence to support such a conclusion. To the contrary, there is substantial documentation of a vigorous and virtually immediate exchange between Virginia and England, at least until the time of the Revolution.[50] A more

[47] [J. K. Paulding], *Letters from the South, By a Northern Man*, New York, 1835, 104; William Blount to John Gray Blount, 1790, quoted in A. Henderson, *Washington's Southern Tour, 1791*, Boston, 1923, 6.

[48] Beverley, *History, and Present State*, 299; "Virginia Council Journals, 1726–1753," *Virginia Magazine of History and Biography* 32 (January 1924), 56; E. M. Betts, ed., *Thomas Jefferson's Garden Book, 1766–1824*, Philadelphia, 1944, 26–27. On Alexander Pope's grotto, see Mack, *Garden and the City*, 41–82; Hunt, "Pope's Twickenham," 29–32. William L. Beiswanger first noticed the relationship between Pope's grotto and Jefferson's plans in "The Temple in the Garden: Thomas Jefferson's Vision of the Monticello Landscape," in R. P. Maccubbin and P. Martin, eds., *British and American Gardens in the Eighteenth Century*, Williamsburg, Va., 1984, 170–88. Jefferson later visited Pope's grotto in April 1786, Boyd, *Papers*, 9, 369–70.

[49] C. Lazzaro, *The Italian Renaissance Garden*, New Haven, Conn., 1990, especially 69–108; L. Puppi, "The Villa Garden of the Veneto from the Fifteenth to the Eighteenth Century," in D. R. Coffin, ed., *The Italian Garden*, Dumbarton Oaks Colloquium on the History of Landscape Architecture 1, Washington, D.C., 1972, 81–114.

[50] For a succinct statement of the *retardataire* thesis, see N. T. Newton, *Design on the Land: The Development of Landscape Architecture*, Cambridge, Mass., 1971, 250. On the dynamic exchange between Virginia and England, see J. P. Greene and J. R. Pole, eds., *Colonial British America: Essays in the New History of the Early Modern Era*, Baltimore, 1984, especially 345–83. Recent research of gentry estates in England itself is revealing that geometric gardens remained a presence there, in certain regions at least, "well into the second half of the eighteenth century," see A. Taigel and T. Williamson, "Some Early Geometric Gardens in Norfolk," *Journal of Garden History* 11 (January-June 1991), 15–16.

sufficient explanation may be that the eighteenth-century Virginia plantation garden took as its model not so much the later landscape garden of the English country seat as the garden landscape of the early English villa. The scale of the English villas, which were often secondary residences of the aristocracy, matched the ambitions of Virginia squires more closely than did the sprawling country estates of the nobility.

Recall that the period when the first substantial plantation houses began appearing along the riverbanks of Virginia—the second quarter of the eighteenth century—was also the era when the idea of the villa emerged in the Thames River valley as distinct from the established concept of the "greater house" in the country. The Veneto villa garden, which no doubt influenced conceptions of the English villa garden, has been summarized as arranged "on an axis with the portico and loggia of the owner's house, [and] was centered, broadly speaking, on a short walkway leading away from the house, arbored or banked by hedges and flanked by ordered plantings of vineyards and fruit trees (the orchard), then leading to a wilder grove in which might be found a pavilion of bushes." As with the architecture of the house itself, it was the compact character of the early eighteenth-century English villa garden, perhaps more than anything else, that distinguished it from the more expansive gardens of the "greater house" tradition.[51]

Contemporary measured drawings of eighteenth-century Virginia gardens are rare. One unidentified drawing (Fig. 16), apparently for an eighteenth-century plantation garden, may provide some indication of the geometrical principles of their layout. The drawing depicts a symmetrical garden aligned axially on the facade of a house about 80 feet wide; the garden is "240 ft. broad" (three times the width of the house) and "450 feet long." In the plan, flaring steps descend to an area of grass plats edged with borders and twenty-foot wide gravel paths; the principal grass plat is semicircular and may have outlined a carriage turnaround. Beyond this is a central walk lined on each side by long borders (about 105 and 110 feet in each section), composed of "tall blooming Flowers & clipt Evergreens" (spaced about eight feet apart), and fronted by a "grass Verge" or margin of turf. Four large rectangular beds (the near ones about 50 × 100 feet, the far ones about 50 × 110 feet) flank the central walk. The beds are bordered on their inner three sides by a "Hedge 5 feet high," and on their outer sides by "Espaliers of Vines or fruit Trees." The garden is enclosed on its long sides by a "dwarf Wall supporting Pales 3 feet long & 2 inches wide each Pale & the pillars of Brick instead of Posts." Along the inside of the wall is "a border of flowers 4 feet wide," and the far end is terminated by a "Ha Ha Wall." Perhaps a park was intended beyond the ha-ha.[52]

---

[51] On the distinction between "villa" and "greater house," see Summerson, "Classical Country House," 551–52; Puppi, "Villa Garden of the Veneto," 91.

[52] The drawing, which has been at the Massachusetts Historical Society (MHS 339) since at least 1916 when it was catalogued by Fiske Kimball in *Thomas Jefferson, Architect* (K231n), is of uncertain origin. It may have been part of Thomas Jefferson's personal papers (although not drawn by him), or it may have been collected (in Virginia?) by its donor, Thomas Jefferson Coolidge. In recent years the plan has been attributed to Rosewell, the ca. 1726 Page family seat on the York River, see W. H. Adams, ed., *The Eye of Thomas Jefferson*, Charlottesville, Va., 1981, 318. (Unless quoted, the dimensions given in the text above were determined by using the graphic scale on the drawing.)

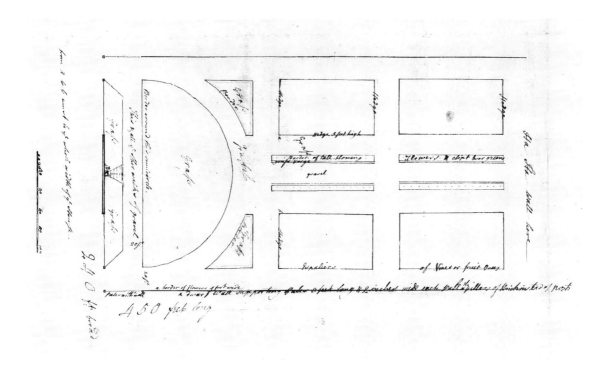

16. Unidentified garden plan, probably early to mid-eighteenth century (photo: Coolidge Collection, Massachusetts Historical Society)

The drawing records a garden design not unlike that which the English gardening authority Philip Miller described in *The Gardeners Dictionary*, a widely owned book in eighteenth-century Virginia: "As for the *Form*, a Square, or rather an Oblong, is most eligible when leading from the Middle of the House, with a Gravel-walk in the midst, having narrow Verges of Grass on each Side, and Rows of Variety of Winter-Greens on either Side of the Grass-Verges." Figure 17 depicts an English garden of this type about mid-century; the garden was situated on the Thames, very near the Chelsea Physic Garden, of which Miller was the superintendent from 1722 to 1770.[53]

In eighteenth-century garden design, an "Oblong or Long Square" was usually considered to be a double square, or some additional extension thereof, by even half-squares. As Miller recommended, it should "not be less than twice as long as it is broad; twice and a half is accounted a very good Proportion, and it is very rare that three times is exceeded." In Figure 16, the "parterre" or main body of the garden (i.e., the area within the peripheral border walks) is approximately a double square, about 200 × 400 feet. The width of the house in the drawing determined not only the proportional width of the garden but also fixed edges within it, as the note on the drawing dictates, "from a to b must be ye whole width of ye House." These conventions—square or "oblong" pro-

[53] P. Miller, *The Gardeners Dictionary*, London, 1731, s.v. "GARDENS"; H. Le Rougetel, *The Chelsea Gardener: Philip Miller, 1691–1771*, London, 1990, especially 67–68. On Gough House, see W. H. Godfrey, *The Parish of Chelsea . . . Being the Second Volume of the Survey of London*, London, 1909, 8–9.

17. Gough House, Chelsea; watercolor attributed to Elizabeth Galston, early nineteenth-century copy of an eighteenth-century original, now lost (photo: Chelsea Reference Library, Royal Borough of Kensington and Chelsea)

portions determined as multiples of the width of the house, central axis walk, tripartite division by crosswalks, and fourfold pattern of large rectangular beds (also oblong or square)—appear to have been recurring components of Virginia gardens of this era.[54]

At Gunston Hall, George Mason's plantation on the Potomac River (Fig. 18), the partially surviving mid-eighteenth-century garden design there displays features similar to those in Figure 16. The width of the garden at Gunston Hall, between the outer edges of the promontories of the "fall," is also about 240 feet (four times the width of the house),

[54] Miller, *Gardeners Dictionary*, s.v. "PARTERRE"; see also Switzer, *Ichnographia Rustica*, 2, 185–87, and James, *Theory and Practice*, 17, 32–35, 39–43. For the double-square proportions repeated in architecture and landscape at Sabine Hall, see Rasmussen, "Sabine Hall," 287–89, and idem, "For Profit and Pleasure," 27 (nn. 32, 34). Marcus Whiffen has demonstrated that the double-square proportion (advocated by Palladio and other theorists) was frequently used in architectural designs in eighteenth-century Virginia, see M. Whiffen, *The Eighteenth-Century Houses of Williamsburg: A Study of Architecture and Building in the Colonial Capital of Virginia*, rev. ed., Williamsburg, Va., 1984, 83–88. For related studies of geometrical proportional systems in eighteenth-century gardens in Maryland, see B. Paca-Steele, "The Mathematics of an Eighteenth-Century Wilderness Garden," *Journal of Garden History* 6 (October-December 1986), 299–320, and M. P. Leone and P. A. Shackel, "Plane and Solid Geometry in Colonial Gardens in Annapolis, Maryland," in W. M. Kelso and R. Most, eds., *Earth Patterns: Essays in Landscape Archaeology*, Charlottesville, Va., 1990, 153–67.

148

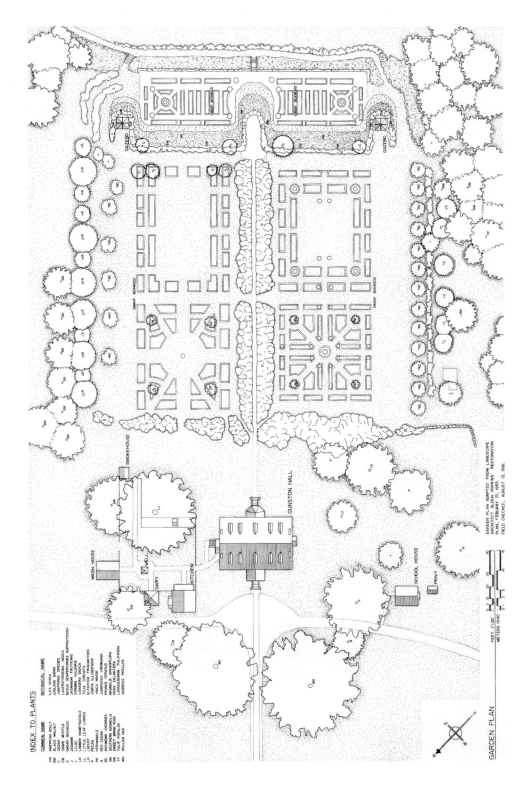

18. Gunston Hall, Virginia; Historic American Buildings Survey, 1981. Site plan adapted from Alden Hopkins's 1953 garden restoration plan (photo: Library of Congress)

149

but the length is only about 300 feet from the house to the brink of the "fall"; the garden in the drawing is one-half again longer, or 450 feet. The Gunston Hall garden, like that in the drawing, is organized along a central walk bordered by evergreens; but here, the boxwood, today over two centuries old, has grown together and across much of the central walk. The garden is also divided into three parts. The first section, nearest the house, is now a lawn and may have been a bowling green or arranged with grass plats and gravel paths, something like those shown in the unidentified plan. The remaining two sections (the "parterre") of the garden form roughly a 200-foot square. The crosswalk which separates these sections has remained evident over the years by the slight gap in the overgrown boxwood; the break in the boxwood at Gunston Hall occurs, like that shown in the plan, at about 100 to 110 feet. Although the rather elaborate compartmentalized beds seen today at Gunston Hall actually were designed in the twentieth century, their rectangular perimeters are believed to approximate those in the original layout.[55]

The geometry of regular gardens in the eighteenth-century often seems to have been intended to focus, channel, or clarify the experience of landscape, rather than merely to limit or contain it. Before the entrance facade at Gunston Hall were four long lines of trees converging, in exaggerated perspective, on the four columns of the portico and the four corresponding pilasters just inside the central hall. The dynamic extension of this axis continued through the house, down the middle of the garden to the deer park and directed the line of sight to the river on the horizon beyond. The result must have been, as Lionello Puppi characterized Palladio's own site designs, a setting charged "by a constant exchange between interior spaces and nature." The strong axial, symmetrical, and proportional relationship between house and garden in mid-eighteenth-century Virginia gardens evidently was lacking in seventeenth-century Virginia designs, as illustrated at Bacon's Castle (ca. 1665), where the large rectangular garden was placed off to one side of the house (Fig. 19). This new self-consciousness in the designed relationship between house and garden that first emerged in Virginia in the early eighteenth century may be linked to the influence of Anglo-Palladianism.[56]

Arguably the most architecturally sophisticated Anglo-palladian villa in colonial Virginia was Mount Airy, built on high ground above the broad bottomlands of the Rappahannock River in the 1750s by John Tayloe II (Fig. 20). It was the first villa in Virginia to achieve Palladio's expanded five-part plan, the "winged house" which Summerson calls a particular development of the "villa 'revival' of the '50's" in England. Its garden,

[55] P. S. Williamson, *The Restoration of the Garden at Gunston Hall*, n.p., 1969; D. H. Williams, *Historic Virginia Gardens: Preservations by the Garden Club of Virginia*, Charlottesville, Va., 1975, 99–113. It seems likely that once a fence was aligned with the outer edges of the promontories.

[56] H. H. Miller, *George Mason: Gentleman Revolutionary*, Chapel Hill, N.C., 1975, 58–59; Puppi, "Villa Garden of the Veneto," 99; N. Luccketti, "Archaeological Excavations at Bacon's Castle, Surry County, Virginia," in Kelso and Most, *Earth Patterns*, 23–42. On Palladianism in America, see M. Azzi Visentini, "Palladio in America, 1760–1820," in I. Jaffe, *The Italian Presence in American Art, 1760–1860*, New York, 1989, 231–47; and D. Lewis, "Il problema della villa e le plantations americane, 1760–1860," *Bollettino del Centro Internazionale di Studi di Architettura Andrea Palladio* 12 (1970), 231–50.

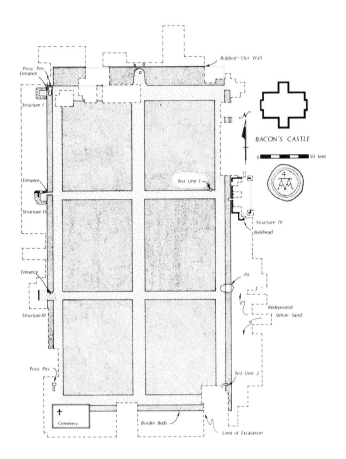

19. Bacon's Castle, Virginia; garden plan as revealed through the excavations directed by Nicholas Luccketti, archaeologist, 1986–87 (photo: courtesy of the Garden Club of Virginia and the Association for the Preservation of Virginia Antiquities)

too, was once one of the most elaborate in Virginia. A visitor in 1774 described it as "an elegant Seat! . . . [there is] a large well formed, beautiful Garden, as fine in every Respect as any I have seen in *Virginia*. In it stand four large beautiful Marble Statues." Another visitor, Anthony St. John Baker, British consul-general to the United States, sketched views of the Mount Airy landscape while a guest in 1827 and noted in his journal that he "took a long walk in the evening . . . into the park; thickly wooded and many fine deer. . . . The conservatory large, with orange and lemon trees put out on grass [Fig. 21]. An extensive garden, in squares and terraces, according to the fashion of that period. From back of house extensive view towards Rappahannock [Fig. 22]. . . . In front lawn planted and terrace, with flowers on pedestals." [57] The surviving outlines of the garden illustrate well the concept of geometrical integration of architecture with setting; the design is an intricate matrix of buildings, terraces, squares, and walks surrounding a broad bowling green (Fig. 23). (In eighteenth-century England, and also in Virginia, a

[57] W. M. S. Rasmussen, "Palladio in Tidewater Virginia: Mount Airy and Blandfield," in M. di Valmarana, ed., *Building by the Book*, Palladian Studies in America 1, Charlottesville, Va., 1984, 75–98; Summerson, "Classical Country House," 577–79; H. D. Farish, ed., *Journal and Letters of Philip Vickers Fithian, 1773–1774: A Plantation Tutor of the Old Dominion*, Williamsburg, Va., 1943, 126; [A. St. John Baker], *Memoires d'un voyageur qui se repose*, 4, London, 1850, 517–23; A Brooke, "A Colonial Mansion of Virginia," *Architectural Review* 6 (1899), 91–94.

20. Mount Airy, Virginia; northeast front, 1827. Watercolor by Anthony St. John Baker from *Mémoires d'un voyageur qui se repose,* London, 1850 (photo: Henry E. Huntington Library and Art Gallery, San Marino, California)

21. Mount Airy, Virginia; southwest front as viewed from the bowling green, 1827. The "conservatory" is visible at left of center. Watercolor by Anthony St. John Baker from *Mémoires d'un voyageur qui se repose,* London, 1850 (photo: Henry E. Huntington Library and Art Gallery, San Marino, California)

22. Mount Airy, Virginia; view near the Rappahannock, 1827. Watercolor by Anthony St. John Baker from *Mémoires d'un voyageur qui se repose,* London, 1850 (photo: Henry E. Huntington Library and Art Gallery, San Marino, California)

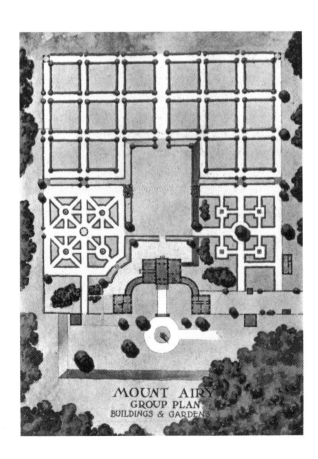

MOUNT AIRY
GROUP PLAN
BUILDINGS & GARDENS

23. Mount Airy, Virginia; garden plan (in part, conjectural) based on Arthur Brooke's 1899 survey of the site (photo: from E. T. Sale, ed., *Historic Gardens of Virginia,* Richmond, Virginia, 1923)

153

bowling green was a lawn, usually rectangular, sometimes slightly sunken, and often placed directly in front of the garden facade; it was a garden feature in its own right and not necessarily used, as its name suggests, for bowling.)[58]

Christian Norberg-Schulz has suggested that a significant difference between the architecture of the Old and New Worlds was that in America regularity of form, even in modest buildings, was the rule rather than the exception. This observation about the strong figural quality of eighteenth-century American architecture ("a hidden Classicism") may be extended to characterize the unified organization of Virginia plantation landscapes of the gentry.[59] Geometrical redimensioning of the landscape was a familiar activity to Virginia planters through their experiences in surveying. Their plantation versions of Arcadia no doubt were inspired by Euclid as much as by Theocritus and Virgil; the first six books of Euclid's *Elements* remained the standard mathematical text in schools in Virginia well into the nineteenth century. Planters routinely applied their school-boy knowledge of Euclid to surveying their own lands and laying out their grounds.[60] The challenge of coordinating the various individual components of a plantation landscape produced a variety of rationally-configured solutions in Virginia: among them, the double-square forecourt at Shirley; a sort of architectural quincunx ("a Square of which the Great-House is the Center" with outbuildings at the four corners) at Nomini Hall and Stratford Hall; the service "row" at Tuckahoe; and the circuit with service "row" arrangements of Mount Vernon and Monticello. In a sense, the plantation represented a form of "ideal" community which encouraged orderliness of living through designed order in the landscape.[61]

Upon the outbreak of the Revolution in 1776, George Mason of Gunston Hall wrote his neighbor George Washington, "May God grant us a return of those halcyon Days; when every Man may sit down at his Ease under the Shade of his own Vine, & his own fig-tree, & enjoy the Sweets of domestic life!" After resigning his command at the close of the war, Washington was immediately celebrated as the American "Cincinnatus," a model of rural virtue, who heard the call to public duty, performed ably and humbly,

[58] James, *Theory and Practice*, 61–64; D. Jacques and A. J. van der Horst, *The Gardens of William and Mary*, London, 1988, 126; J. Carson, *Colonial Virginians at Play*, Williamsburg, Va., 1965, 74–79.

[59] C. Norberg-Schulz, *New World Architecture*, New York, 1988, 12–17.

[60] S. S. Hughes, *Surveyors and Statesmen: Land Measuring in Colonial Virginia*, Richmond, Va., 1979; Thomas Jefferson commented in 1814 that "the first six books of Euclid" were part of the standard curriculum of even the "petty *academies*" of Virginia, see Thomas Jefferson to John Adams, 5 July 1814, in A. A. Lipscomb and A. E. Bergh, eds., *The Writings of Thomas Jefferson*, 14, Washington, D.C., 1905, 150–51. See also J. C. Greene, *American Science in the Age of Jefferson*, Ames, Iowa, 1984, 130; and S. A. Bedini, *Thomas Jefferson: Statesmen of Science*, New York, 1990, 21.

[61] On Shirley, see T. R. Reinhart, *The Archaeology of Shirley Plantation*, Charlottesville, Va., 1984; on Nomini Hall, see Farish, *Journal . . . Fithian*, 106–9; on Stratford Hall, see M. J. Williams, "The Restoration of Stratford," *Landscape Architecture* 23 (April 1933), 175–77; on Tuckahoe, see J. T. Krusen, *Tuckahoe Plantation*, Richmond, Va., 1975; on Mount Vernon, see E. K. de Forest, *The Gardens and Grounds at Mount Vernon: How George Washington Planned and Planted Them*, Mount Vernon, Va., 1982; on Monticello, see W. M. Kelso, "Landscape Archaeology at Thomas Jefferson's Monticello," in Kelso and Most, *Earth Patterns*, 7–22. It is surprising that no comparative analytical study of Virginia plantation layouts has been published.

then returned to plowing his fields. In truth, Washington was much interested in rural pursuits, including garden design. When he returned to Mount Vernon, his plantation on the Potomac, Washington repeatedly invoked the familiar "vine and fig tree" phrase in letters describing his retirement; for example, as in this letter written in 1784, encouraging the marquise de Lafayette to accompany her husband on a visit to America: "I am now enjoying domestic ease under the shadow of my own Vine and my own Fig tree; and in a small Villa, with the implements of Husbandry, and Lambkins around me. . . . You will see the plain manner in which we live; and meet the rustic civility, and you shall taste the simplicity of rural life." In this significant passage, Washington makes explicit the merging in the gentry mind of biblical traditions of the pastoral and the classical idea of the villa. In reality, it was "under the shadow" of the remarkable two-story "Piazza" of his "Villa" where Washington sat to view the "park" and the placid Potomac beyond (Fig. 24). An English visitor along the Potomac, in the same year as Washington's letter to the marquise was written, remarked that "to describe the most delightful and charming situations and villas on this majestic river would far exceed the bounds of a volume . . . ," but listed Mount Vernon and Gunston Hall among them.[62]

As early as 1759, at the age of twenty-seven, in the first year of his residence at Mount Vernon, Washington had begun assuming the pose of "retirement": "I am now I beleive fix'd at this Seat with an agreable Consort for Life and hope to find more happiness in retirement than I ever experienc'd amidst a wide and bustling World." The Mount Vernon landscape, through much of the century, was strictly rectilinear in configuration, approached by a straight road directly on axis to the house, and flanked by rectangular gardens (Fig. 25). By the mid-1780s, Washington had effected a thoroughly new curvilinear design by linking the house to its flankers with semicircular colonnades, removing the straight entrance road and replacing it with a broad bowling green bordered by serpentine drives, and extending the rectangular garden walls in curves to complement the overall rounded lines of the new scheme (Fig. 26). The result was the first notable essay in naturalistic garden design (the so-called "landscape garden") that is known to have been implemented on a Virginia plantation; however, it is significant that the outlines of the plan remained rigidly symmetrical.[63]

---

[62] George Mason to George Washington, 2 April 1776, in R. A. Rutland, ed., *The Papers of George Mason, 1725–1792*, 1, Chapel Hill, N.C., 1970, 267; G. Wills, *Cincinnatus: George Washington and the Enlightenment*, New York, 1984; George Washington to the marquise de Lafayette, 4 April 1784, in J. C. Fitzpatrick, ed., *The Writings of George Washington*, 27, Washington, D.C., 1931, 385; for other retirement letters employing the "vine and fig tree" phrase, see ibid., vol. 27, pp. 312, 314, 317; vol. 35, pp. 432, 447, 452, 471, 473, 475, 476, 480, 488, 493; vol. 36, pp. 4, 41, 292, 343, 364. Smyth, *A Tour*, 1, 146.

[63] George Washington to Richard Washington, 20 September 1759, in W. W. Abbot, ed., *The Papers of George Washington: Colonial Series*, 6, Charlottesville, Va., 1988, 359; de Forest, *Gardens and Grounds*, 11–21; archaeological evidence indicates that diagonal alignments of dependencies predated the construction in 1775 of the present flankers, see M. J. Williams, "Washington's Changes at Mount Vernon Plantation," *Landscape Architecture* 28 (January 1938), 66. Evidently a number of contemporary Virginia plantation gardens included a "park" or naturalistic areas within their extended grounds (e.g., Westover, Nomini Hall, Gunston Hall, Mount Airy, and early Monticello), but unlike Mount Vernon these naturalistic areas appear to have been distinct from the geometrically regular garden immediately adjacent to the house. Separate park-like areas were components of some Italian villa gardens, see Lazzaro, *Italian Renaissance Garden*, 109–30.

24. Mount Vernon, Virginia; Washington family gathered on the "Piazza" of the "Villa." Watercolor by Benjamin Henry Latrobe, 1796. Private Collection

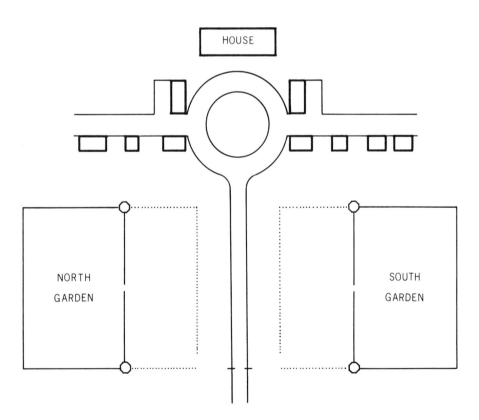

25. Mount Vernon, Virginia; diagram of the site arrangement, ca. 1776, based on historical documentation and surviving features. Drawing by the author, after Morley J. Williams

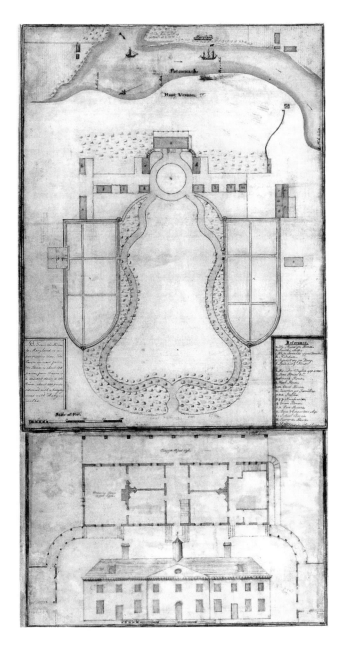

26. Mount Vernon, Virginia; site plan drawn by Samuel Vaughan for George Washington, 1787 (photo: Mount Vernon Ladies Association of the Union)

The most informed attempt to evoke the classical villa on a Virginia plantation was manifest in Thomas Jefferson's early designs for Monticello (Fig. 27). The classical scholar Karl Lehmann was the first to recognize that Jefferson consciously attempted "to revive the idea of the ancient villa" at Monticello. In *Thomas Jefferson: American Humanist* (1947), Lehmann observed that "exactly those features [of Monticello] not to be found in Palladio, and equally novel in the Virginia of his time, are typical of the Roman villas described by ancient authors." In particular, Lehmann noted the hippodrome shape of the early terrace plan (perhaps inspired by Jefferson's copy of Robert Castell's extrapolations of Pliny's villas in *The Villas of the Ancients Illustrated*, published in 1728), the *diaetae-*

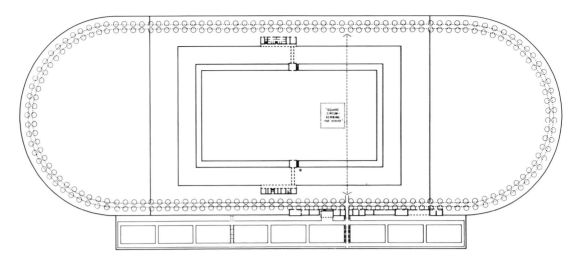

27. Monticello, Virginia; composite diagram of Thomas Jefferson's site plan proposals, ca. 1768–72. Drawing by the author

like character of the outlying pavilions, and the remarkable *cryptoporticus*-like form of the submerged service wings. To fully cast this spell, Jefferson proposed in 1771 to inscribe the Horatian anthem (*"Beatus ille qui procul negotiis, Ut prisca gens mortalium, Paterna rura bobus exercet suis, solutus omni foenore. . . ."*) "on stone, or a metal plate fastened to a tree" near the spring at Monticello, in a grove of aspen and beech.[64]

Jefferson, who has been called "the most learned and dedicated classicist" of the Revolutionary generation in America, was probably never any happier than when, in the spring of 1787, he was touring "the remains of Roman grandeur" in southern France: "I am immersed in antiquities from morning to night. For me the city of Rome is actually existing in all the splendor of it's empire." It is clear that for Jefferson, as for his contemporaries among the gentry, life in Virginia also was redolent of ancient associations—a time-distant outpost of Rome or Athens or Jerusalem or even Babylon. To borrow a phrase which Jefferson employed to explain his admiration of the grid plan of Philadelphia (i.e., that it was "the old Babylon, revived in Philadelphia and exemplified"), eighteenth-century Virginian society, in the imagination of the gentry, seemed almost to have been ancient culture "revived . . . and exemplified."[65]

[64] K. Lehmann, *Thomas Jefferson: American Humanist*, New York, 1947, 52–53, 177–85. For further endorsements of Lehman's interpretation, see W. H. Pierson, Jr., *American Buildings and Their Architects: The Colonial and Neoclassical Styles*, New York, 1970, 310–16; Ackerman, *The Villa*, 185–211. For the full inscription, see Betts, *Garden Book*, 26.

[65] M. Reinhold, "The Classical World," in M. D. Peterson, ed., *Thomas Jefferson: A Reference Biography*, New York, 1986, 155; Thomas Jefferson to Madame de Tessé, 20 March 1787, in Boyd, *Papers*, 11, 226–28; Thomas Jefferson to George Washington, 10 April 1791, in Boyd, *Papers*, 20, 88. See also R. M. Gummere, *The American Colonial Mind and the Classical Tradition*, Cambridge, Mass., 1963; and L. B. Wright, "The Classical Tradition in Colonial Virginia," *Papers of the Bibliographical Society of America* 33 (1939), 85–97.

28. Monticello, Virginia; study drawing of the northeast front by Thomas Jefferson, early 1770s (photo: Coolidge Collection, Massachusetts Historical Society)

In some real ways for Virginia planters, their vision of their world was as a Virgilian Virginia. Landon Carter's diary is sprinkled with phrases such as, ". . . I was ever thinking of Virgil . . . ," "I often think of the old Roman . . . ," or ". . . from the days of Virgil to this time"; moreover, he claimed that a local bridge was built in 1770 according to "my own [plan] taken from Vitruvius's bridge over the Rhine in Julius Caesar's days." Classical writings on agriculture continued to be consulted, either directly or in compilations such as Richard Bradley's *A Survey of the Ancient Husbandry and Gardening* (1725) and Adam Dickson's *The Husbandry of the Ancients* (1788). Jefferson once boasted that "ours [i.e., America's] are the only farmers who can read Homer." Jefferson's brother-in-law, Henry Skipwith, wrote a young fellow planter in 1813, offering him landscape design advice, and admonished, "Virgil's Georgics would have given you a full idea of his Quincunx, which is nothing more than a square with a tree at each corner and one in the center and thus continued throughout an orchard."[66]

The early designs for Monticello, from the 1760s and 1770s (Figs. 27, 28), exhibit a more distinct villa character than does Jefferson's remodeling of house and grounds

[66] J. P. Greene, ed., *The Diary of Colonel Landon Carter of Sabine Hall, 1752–1778*, Charlottesville, Va., 1965, 457, 755, 976, 1051; Thomas Jefferson to St. John de Crèvecoeur, 15 January 1787, in Boyd, *Papers*,

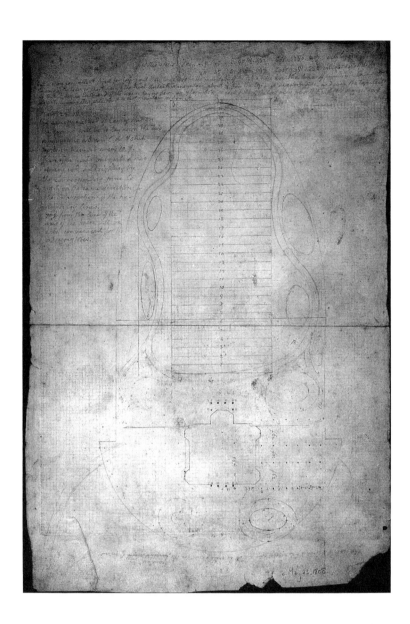

29. Monticello, Virginia; site plan of the summit, drawn by Thomas Jefferson. Probably begun in the early 1790s, with amendments to 1808 (photo: Coolidge Collection, Massachusetts Historical Society)

which occurred following his return to Virginia in 1789, after living five years in France. The pure symmetrical geometry of his original Monticello site plan, with its elaborate tiers of terraces, gradually gave way to the influence of naturalism as was fashionable in Europe. Yet, as in Washington's 1780s redesign of the Mount Vernon landscape, geometrical rigor was maintained at Monticello even while laying out the asymmetry of serpentine paths (Fig. 29). Jefferson, like Washington, had adopted the pose of "retirement" from an early age. In 1775, the year before he drafted the Declaration of Independence, and with a long public career yet ahead that would keep him away from home for lengthy

11, 44; Henry Skipwith to John Hartwell Cocke, 19 March 1813, Cocke Family Papers, Alderman Library, University of Virginia; D. L. Wilson, "The American *Agricola:* Jefferson's Agrarianism and the Classical Tradition," *South Atlantic Quarterly* 80 (Summer 1981), 339–54. See also, G. E. Fussell, *The Classical Tradition in West European Farming*, Cranbury, N.J., 1972, especially chap. 6.

30. Monticello, Virginia; watercolor of the southwest front by Jane Braddick Peticolas, 1825 (photo: Thomas Jefferson Memorial Foundation)

periods during the next three decades, Jefferson wrote then that he was considering retirement, at the age of thirty-two, from active involvement in political affairs: ". . . I may withdraw myself totally from the public stage and pass the rest of my days in domestic ease and tranquillity, banishing every desire of afterwards even hearing what passes in the world." A lasting retirement finally found Jefferson, at the end of his political career in 1809: "I am retired to Monticello, where, in the bosom of my family, and surrounded by my books, I enjoy a repose to which I have been long a stranger" (Fig. 30).[67]

During that summer of 1809, Margaret Bayard Smith, a friend from Washington, visited the former president at Monticello and afterward related the following to her journal: "as we walked [about the grounds], he explained his future designs. 'My long absence from this place, has left a wilderness around me.' 'But you have returned,' said I, 'and the wilderness shall blossom . . . and you, I hope, will long sit beneath your own vine and your own fig-tree.'"[68] A quarter century after Jefferson's death, Fredrika Bremer, the Swedish writer whose observations of America were recorded in *The Homes of the New World*, and who was a close friend of the prominent nineteenth-century American landscape gardener Andrew Jackson Downing, visited the "elegant villas" of Virginia, as she termed them, and declared after "wandering in the park" at Monticello that "no-

[67] Thomas Jefferson to John Randolph, 25 August 1775 in Boyd, *Papers*, 1, 241; Thomas Jefferson to Thaddeus Kosciusko, 26 February 1810, in Lipscomb and Bergh, *Writings*, 12, 369. On the Monticello landscape, see W. H. Adams, *Jefferson's Monticello*, New York, 1983, 145–89.

[68] G. Hunt, ed., *The First Forty Years of Washington Society, in the Family Letters of Margaret Bayard Smith*, New York, 1906, 69.

where so much as here does the prophecy seem to be fulfilled, of every man sitting under his own vine or fig-tree, and no one making him afraid." [69]

After traveling widely in the young republic, Congressman Richard Bland Lee, of Sully plantation in northern Virginia, had asserted in 1794 that "every man is safe under his own vine and fig tree, and there is none to make him afraid. To produce this effect was the intent of the Constitution, and it has succeeded." [70] Thus, the ancient idyll was translated to the American strand, and its promise, into a new covenant for a new nation. The dream of peaceful, prosperous, freeholder living early entered the American consciousness on the Virginia plantation and was symbolized in its garden. [71]

[69] F. Bremer, *The Homes of the New World; Impressions of America,* 2, New York, 1854, 514–15.

[70] Quoted in M. Kammen, *A Machine That Would Go of Itself: The Constitution in American Culture,* New York, 1986, 15, 41. I am grateful to Pamela Scott for drawing this quote to my attention.

[71] Of course, it was a tragic irony that this idyll was sustained on the plantations through the enslavement of others. For the contributions of black culture to Virginia plantation society, see M. Sobel, *The World They Made Together: Black and White Values in Eighteenth-Century Virginia,* Princeton, N.J., 1987.

Roots of a Regional Garden Tradition:
The Drawings of the New Orleans Notarial Archives

SUZANNE TURNER

The beginnings of any American regional garden tradition lie in early settlement patterns and in the gardens of the first generations of residents. For many regions, documents that describe these early gardens are uncommon. Written descriptions often survive, but pictorial evidence is rare, particularly for urban gardens. When a graphic depiction does survive, it may only give a perspective view of the front layers of a garden, making it difficult to discover the garden's backbone—its plan. Moreover, most pictorial evidence involves a great deal of artistic license, since the landscape or a specific garden is rarely the subject but rather the backdrop for important people or events.

The city of New Orleans is blessed with a collection of measured drawings and plans of over 5,500 properties dating from the nineteenth century—the drawings of the Notarial Archives. This paper will present the collection as primary documents for a landscape history of New Orleans neighborhoods; these documents provide insight and a point of departure for describing the gardens that typified the region surrounding New Orleans—roughly the Mississippi River corridor from Natchez downriver and the Gulf Coast east to Pensacola.

THE VERNACULAR AND REGIONALISM

Many of the drawings from the Archives depict vernacular gardens, and to consider them as sources for later-designed gardens one must examine the relationship between vernacular garden traditions and regional garden design. Contemporary garden designs often owe a great debt to the vernacular traditions of the locale, and this is certainly the case in New Orleans, where the great majority of nineteenth-century gardens were created by nondesigners.

The vernacular process is intuitive and often subconscious; the builder responds to the unique qualities of a place: climate, indigenous or available building materials and vegetation, topography, soil, and hydrology. The motivation for design is utility and economy. The vernacular evolves slowly over time. Several generations of vernacular landscape layers in a given locale produce a vernacular tradition, which can be described in terms of typical motifs, ordering principles, and patterns; this vernacular tradition encodes cultural values.

A regional garden design, on the other hand, implies a deliberate form-giving exercise; a designer takes into account the region in which he or she is working, and, through the act of design, attempts to capture the spirit of the place, the material and symbolic qualities that define its natural and cultural character. The sources for these designs often are vernacular gardens, since in these gardens one finds the most direct and uncluttered expression of place and people.

Regionalism has become a much-discussed design issue over the last ten or so years. Disenchantment with the International Style in architecture, increased mobility and uprootedness, and the pace of change in our technological society have all contributed to interest in the concept because it places value on cultural continuity. A recent renaissance in the development of regional gardens can be seen in the work of Terry Harkness, whose designs are based on the patterns of the agricultural landscape of the Midwest,[1] and that of Warren Byrd, who celebrates the tidewater Virginia landscape,[2] to name two. Regional landscape history is beginning to be explored, documented, and published; for example, David Streatfield's work on California, Catherine Howett's on Georgia, and Kenneth Helphand's on Colorado.[3]

DESCRIPTION OF STUDY AREA

The gardens of New Orleans are the starting point for the exploration of regional garden forms in the Louisiana-Mississippi Gulf Coast region. Although New Orleans was the fourth largest American city in 1840,[4] it by no means represented mainstream America. Remote from other major urban centers, situated in landscape more tropical than temperate, New Orleans appeared exotic to Europeans and Americans alike. Annexed to the nation by the Louisiana Purchase in 1803, the city, and particularly its

All figures are watercolor on paper and are located in the New Orleans Notarial Archives, New Orleans, Louisiana. The name of the civil engineer, when known, is listed first.

[1] See T. Harkness, "Garden from Region," in M. Francis and R. T. Hester, Jr., eds., *The Meaning of Gardens*, Cambridge, Mass., 1990, 110–19.

[2] W. T. Byrd, Jr., "Tidal Garden: Eastern Shore of Virginia," in *Transforming the American Garden: 12 New Landscape Designs*, exhibition catalogue, Cambridge, Mass., 1986, 30–33.

[3] See a series of articles on the evolution of the California landscape by D. Streatfield, "The Evolution of the Southern California Landscape: 1. Settling into Arcadia," *Landscape Architecture* 66 (January 1976), 39–46, 78; idem, "The Evolution of the California Landscape: 2. Arcadia Compromised," *Landscape Architecture* 66 (March 1976), 117–26, 170; idem, "The Evolution of the California Landscape: 3. The Great Promotions," *Landscape Architecture* 67 (May 1977), 229–39, 272; idem, "The Evolution of the California Landscape: 4. Suburbia at the Zenith," *Landscape Architecture* 67 (September 1977), 417–24. See also C. Howett, "Crying 'Taste' in the Wilderness: The Disciples of Andrew Jackson Downing in Georgia," *Landscape Journal* 1 (Spring 1982), 15–22, and idem, *Land of Our Own: 250 Years of Landscape and Gardening Tradition in Georgia, 1733–1983*, exhibition catalogue, Atlanta, 1983. Also, K. I. Helphand, *Colorado: Visions of an American Landscape*, ed. E. Manchester, Niwot, Colo., 1991.

[4] S. F. Starr, *Southern Comfort: The Garden District of New Orleans, 1800–1900*, Cambridge, Mass., 1989, 5.

French population, maintained European cultural ties more tenaciously than eastern seaboarders intent on developing a design tradition and a way of life uniquely American.

New Orleans was an international city from its very inception, a port through which people from all over the world passed. These early "tourists" viewed and wrote about not only the city's rich architectural collection—with its French, Spanish, West Indian, and American overlays—but more significantly, the landscape and the gardens that punctuated the urban fabric. These written accounts are evocative and in many cases quite specific in landscape description; the garden drawings of the Notarial Archives offer the opportunity to actually visualize what some of these nineteenth-century landscapes looked like.

The gardens illustrated in the Notarial Archives range from vernacular to high style. This study will be limited to two areas of the city: the French Quarter, the original core settled primarily by Europeans of French and Spanish descent beginning in the eighteenth century; and the Garden District, an early suburban neighborhood settled by Americans in the first half of the nineteenth century. These two areas were selected because they represent the two most distinctive neighborhoods in terms of tourism, and each can be characterized in terms of its distinct landscape. One does not talk about the French Quarter without the courtyard; St. Charles Avenue in the center of the Garden District is itself a tourist attraction because of the district's gardens and trees.

By first examining the Notarial Drawings of both neighborhoods, we can identify nineteenth-century antecedents and then compare them to contemporary expressions, both in New Orleans and in the broader region influenced by the city's economic and social dominance. What was the outfall of these early experiments in garden design and is there a continuity of ideas and forms?

THE DRAWINGS OF THE NOTARIAL ARCHIVES

The Notarial Archives drawings are a pivotal tool for the exploration of the evolution of a regional tradition in southern garden design. This collection of large format, measured watercolors depicts over 5,500 lots, houses, and tracts of land, executed by surveyors and engineers, from 1802 to 1903. The great majority of the drawings date from 1840 to 1866. Drawn at a scale of approximately one inch equals twenty-five feet, the average size of the sheets is approximately 2 x 4 feet. The drawings were used as official advertisements for judicially-ordered sales, such as successions and bankruptcies, and as official surveys of streets and public squares during the nineteenth century. They were executed and signed by civil engineers, many of whom had substantial artistic ability. Because these drawings were legal documents used to record features contributing to property value, the entire site was drawn both in plan and elevation (Fig. 1), with considerable attention devoted to the depiction of the arrangement and appearance of the outbuildings, planting beds, and other landscape features, such as cisterns, wells, fountains, arbors, trellises, and paved areas.

Although this study only focuses on two small parts of New Orleans, the collection includes all sections of the nineteenth-century city, as well as outlying plantations; some

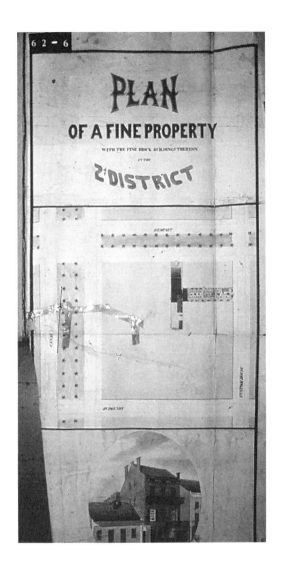

1. C. A. de Armas, Plan Book 62, fol. 8, 1853 (photo: courtesy of the New Orleans Notarial Archives)

views of the plantations provide three-dimensional glimpses of places that are very rarely treated pictorially, and never in such an accurate format. As a collection, these watercolors provide the most thorough graphic documentation of nineteenth-century properties and their gardens for any American city. They are important benchmarks and serve as datum points against which to compare landscape and garden designs that came later.

THE FRENCH QUARTER

Few people in the urbanized world, and fewer garden enthusiasts, do not have at least a cursory exposure to the Vieux Carré.[5] The Vieux Carré has been a mainstay of

[5] The Vieux Carré or French Quarter was the second neighborhood in the United States (after Charleston) to have its historic integrity protected by a local historic district zoning ordinance.

166

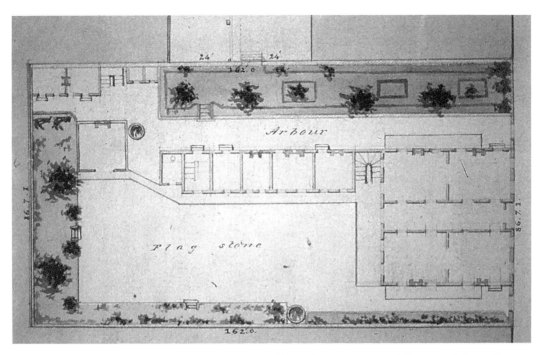

2. Leone J. Fremaux, Plan Book 44A, fol. 79, no date (photo: courtesy of the New Orleans Notarial Archives)

the city's economy from its inception, first as a major shipping and commercial center, and more recently as a major tourist attraction. The city was settled in 1718 and was to be France's gateway to its mid-continental empire in the New World. The Vieux Carré reached its capacity for development in the mid-nineteenth century, and urban growth forced the establishment of newer sections of the city open for American in-migration, new districts that included the Garden District. French culture predominated in the Vieux Carré, even during a period of Spanish rule. Like most early cities, the French Quarter was and still is a mixed-use area of primarily residential and commercial structures. It is dense, with most buildings fronting directly on the sidewalk; open space is scarce, with Jackson Square as the most significant public open space in the Quarter.

Analysis of French Quarter Drawings

The Notarial Archives includes one hundred eight drawings related to properties in the French Quarter. Of these, fifty-six were selected for analysis based upon the information they contained about either garden layout, plant materials, the arrangement of outbuildings, or details of landscape features, such as fencing.

Typical Property in Plan

The typical lot size was approximately 34 × 128 feet; the typical plan shows the main dwelling located at or near the front property line, with little or no "front yard." Behind the house are dependencies in the form of an ell attached to one side of the house (Fig. 2), or freestanding outbuildings housing the kitchen, dry goods storage, coal room, iron-

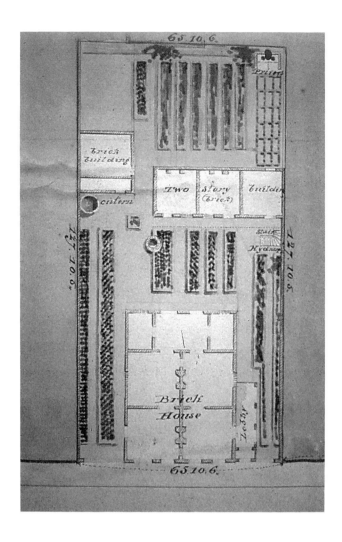

3. C. A. de Armas, Plan Book 44, fol.
41, 1856 (photo: courtesy of the
New Orleans Notarial Archives)

ing room, servants' rooms, and animal shelters (Fig. 3). The most common outbuildings
found in the drawings are privies which occur on all but six plans.

Of greatest interest in these plans is the configuration of the open space surrounding
the buildings; typically these are paved, although rarely is the material specified. One
drawing bears the label "Bricked Yard" (Fig. 4), another "Flag stone" (Fig. 2). Today,
these paved spaces behind and to the side of French Quarter buildings are commonly
termed "courtyards" or "patios." By far the most predominant features occurring in the
open spaces are those that relate to water—wells, cisterns, pumps, hydrants; and in some
cases the open spaces seem to exist only to provide a site for utilitarian water features.
While the contemporary courtyard derived from these early models typically includes a
fountain, or other ornamental water element, no clear depiction of such a feature appears in any of the drawings.

Spatial Zoning

Most plans indicate only one outdoor space that would have served as both the sole
private outdoor space for the family and servants and as a utility court for various house-

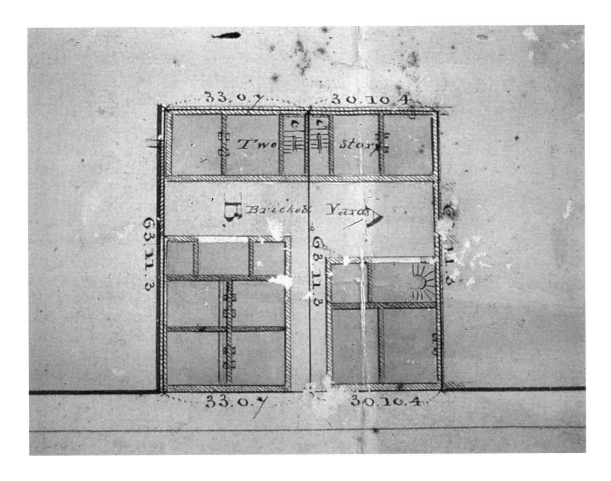

4. Arthur de Armas, Plan Book 5, fol. 5, 1871 (photo: courtesy of the New Orleans Notarial Archives)

hold activities such as keeping chickens, slaughtering animals, cleaning fish, drying clothes, and splitting wood. Several plans indicate skillful division of larger lots into smaller sub-spaces, allowing one area to be more visually ornamental and available for entertainment or privacy than another. In two of the larger properties (Fig. 5), some of the service and utility functions are relegated to lots set perpendicular to the main site with access to side streets, leaving the area overlooked by the houses and galleries free for more ornamental development. In another drawing (Fig. 6), the pattern is reversed, and the perpendicular lot is used as the site for the garden. Other properties exhibit spatial zoning by the use of outbuildings (Figs. 3, 7), walls (Fig. 8), fences or hedges (Fig. 9) as visual barriers.

    Evidence of Gardening

    Of the fifty-six drawings, eleven depict strictly commercial sites and include no indication of planting. Twenty-six of the drawings illustrate planting of some kind. One of the confusing issues in discussing vegetation in all of the Notarial Archives plans is terminology—whether planted areas should be described as gardens (as the rare example shown in Figure 10 does) or parterres. For the purposes of this paper, garden will be

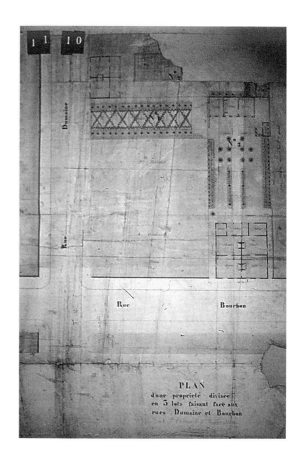

5. Dourgerol, Plan Book 11, fol. 10, 1839 (photo: courtesy of the New Orleans Notarial Archives)

6. C. A. de Armas, Plan Book 62, fol. 8, 1853 (photo: courtesy of the New Orleans Notarial Archives)

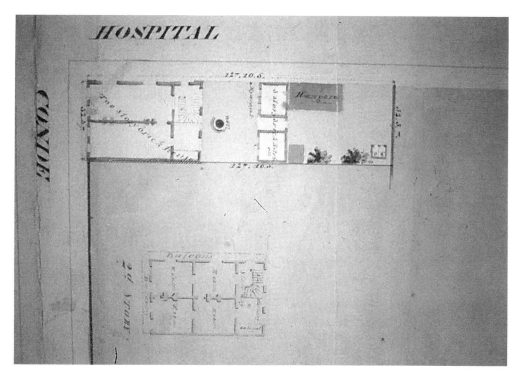

7. C. A. de Armas, Plan Book 6, fol. 42, 1856 (photo: courtesy of the New Orleans Notarial Archives)

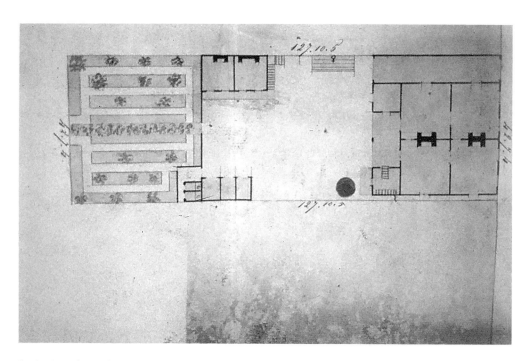

8. A. Castaing, Plan Book 87, fol. 28, 1859 (photo: courtesy of the New Orleans Notarial Archives)

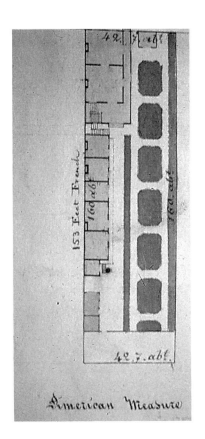

9. Adolphe Knell, Plan Book 95,
fol. 31, 1853 (photo: courtesy
of the New Orleans Notarial
Archives)

10. Leone J. Fremaux, Plan Book 44A, fol. 79, no date (photo: courtesy of the New Orleans Notarial Archives)

used as a general term to describe any planted space; parterre will describe a garden type characterized by the use of patterns on the ground that exhibit a degree of geometric complexity and a concern for composition; and planting beds will refer to areas that have been designated for planting but for which an overall composition is not evident. "Parterre" links the landscape to a high-style form vocabulary, while "planting bed" indicates a vernacular, often naive, layout. Of the twenty-five drawings with vegetation, nine have parterres, five having planting beds, and the remaining twelve have individual trees planted on the lot.

One 1832 plan (Figs. 11, 12) includes a written advertisement stating that the property has "un joli parterre sur le devant" (a pretty parterre in front). This plan is an anomaly in many ways: it is one of only three that have gardens in front of the house; a circle in the middle of the composition might possibly be an ornamental water feature. This is the only drawing from the French Quarter where the parterre is labeled as such.

Garden Form in the French Quarter

What were the guiding principles that dictated the form and arrangement of elements within these small garden spaces? In the case of the vernacular gardens, the placement and the form of planting areas seem to be direct results of the need for pedestrian circulation (Fig. 13). Planting beds were placed along walls and in the spots remaining after the major paths from house to outbuildings had been determined. Function and a spatial economy seem to be the overriding concerns, and the resultant forms are often awkward and naive.

With only nine gardens linked to a high-style vocabulary, one cannot make universal conclusions about the currents of garden style and how they drifted to New Orleans from France and England and down the eastern seaboard. This small sample does, however, suggest two different approaches to spatial conception and garden design.

The Urban Court   The concept of the urban court is one of the earliest forms of outdoor space and is associated with Mediterranean cultures. Usually a contained space, protected from the surrounding environment by tall walls, the New Orleans version (Fig. 2) begins with a central paved open space as the organizing element of the composition and uses planting to surround and define the space. A simple rectilinear geometry typically determines its form. The paved central space creates the sense of an outdoor room, and the walls separate the space from the chaos and activity of the surrounding streets.

In this simple plan (Fig. 2), similar to many courtyards which survive today, the flagstone court is surrounded by narrow planted areas, but the floor of the court, and not a single focal point, organizes the composition. Such a space provides the flexibility to accommodate a variety of purposes, from entertaining to executing household chores. The more elaborate scheme depicted in Figure 5, on the other hand, divides a court into numerous planting beds. When vegetation occurs within the floor of the court, the planted areas seem to have been lifted out after the floor was laid rather than having been a part of the initial spatial conception. Although the geometric composition of these

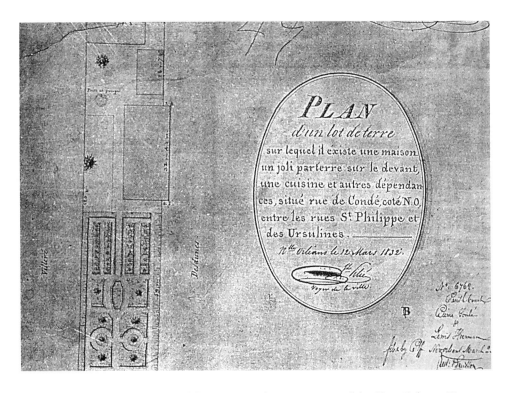

11. Joseph Pilié, Plan Book 15, fol. 22, 1832 (photo: courtesy of the New Orleans Notarial Archives)

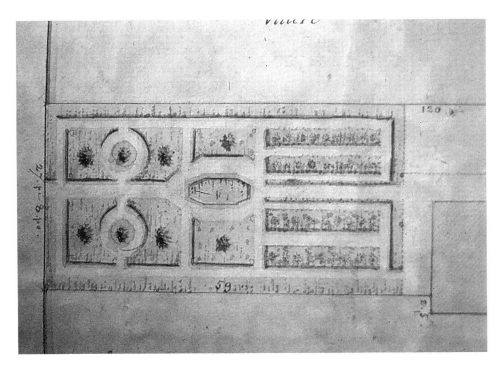

12. Joseph Pilié, Plan Book 15, fol. 22, 1832 (photo: courtesy of the New Orleans Notarial Archives)

174

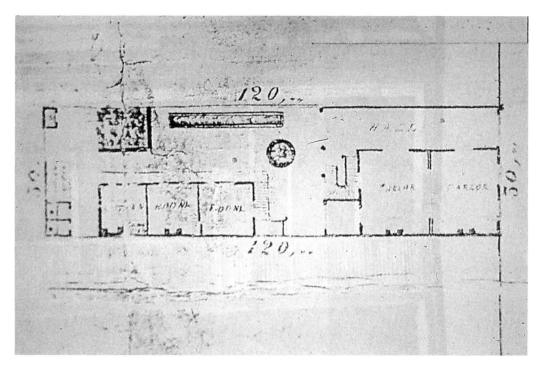

13. G. Stehler, Plan Book 2, fol. 5, 1872 (photo: courtesy of the New Orleans Notarial Archives)

plantings of small trees seems to have been an important part of the design's evolution, they still remain as secondary features within a large open space.

The Urban Parterre The second approach is derived from the French parterre tradition in which patterns bordered with pedestrian paths were created on the ground plane, with legibility from the second floor as a principal intention. Unlike earlier parterres intended for an expansive, palatially-scaled rural setting, this concept has been adapted, greatly compromised, and squeezed into much smaller, contained spaces in the French Quarter. The two-dimensional pattern on the ground is the starting point for the design, dividing the space into smaller units using linear geometry as the organizing vocabulary (Fig. 9). The geometry is at times complex, combining curved forms with rectilinear ones (Fig. 12). Spatially, the court reads more like a sequential journey through small spaces than a step into one large room.

Although several examples of this approach are shown in plan, only in one of these (Figs. 14, 15) is an idea of the three-dimensional character of the space suggested; the remainder of the properties are illustrated only in plan or not depicted behind the screening street wall. The lone elevation (Fig. 15) shows the front wall that encloses the garden from the street with trees of considerable size (fifteen or so feet) visible above the wall. This view indicates that although the plan appears as two-dimensional on the ground, with neither trees nor specimen plantings (Fig. 14), the spatial quality of the parterre must, in fact, be one of enclosure created by the canopies of the trees planted in at least some of the beds. This quality removes the court even further from

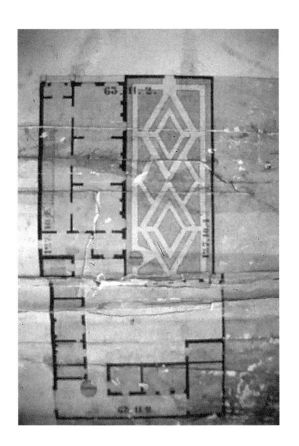

14. Attributed to C. A. Hedin, Plan Book
24, fol. 13, ca. 1852–55 (photo: courtesy
of the New Orleans Notarial Archives)

15. Attributed to C. A. Hedin, Plan Book 24, fol. 13, ca. 1852–55 (photo: courtesy of the New Orleans Notarial Archives)

its European roots, where beds were kept at almost ground level and the spatial flow left uninterrupted by the pattern.

Another clue that the court is read as a series of smaller intimate spaces rather than a large flat parterre is the curious placement of the cistern in the back corner of the garden. Not only does this critical utility intrude quite awkwardly into the garden's lay-out, but the sidewalk pattern has been laid out to accommodate it. If the garden is, in fact, defined by the canopy of trees, then the prominence of the cistern in plan would be greatly reduced in elevation and screened from view by foreground trees. Contrary to the twentieth-century romanticization of many of these courtyards through the addition of an ornamental fountain, this formal garden's sole water feature is a cistern.

In summary, the courtyards of the French Quarter were multipurpose spaces whose ambience exuded a sense of containment and the creation of a world apart. They provided security and relief from harsh public urban conditions—gutters that served as sewers, streets rendered impassable during the rainy season, noises of street vendors, and animals wandering freely. Their gesture toward the street was one of privacy, almost secrecy. Although several of the drawings include formal elements such as arbors and a central axis or planting bed, the overall expression is informal, responding in part to the irregular geometry resulting from the asymmetrical placement of outbuildings and utilities. Perhaps it is this inherent flexibility of the plans, as well as the informal character of most spaces, that has assured the survival of so many courtyards into the twentieth century. Although lifestyle and technology have radically altered the functional aspects of these spaces, they have been adapted over time to accommodate a new set of needs and pressures.

GARDEN DISTRICT

The Garden District is situated two miles upriver or uptown from the Vieux Carré and a half mile north of the Mississippi River, with St. Charles Avenue as its northern boundary and Magazine on the south. With the Louisiana Purchase, American traders and manufacturers flocked to the city in great numbers. After the economic crash of 1837, the economy of the city was revived by entrepreneurs whose wealth came from either cotton and credit, wholesaling, or allied fields such as shipping and insurance.[6] There was no love lost between the Creoles and the newcomers, and so the Americans settled in newer sections of the city upriver. These new magnates sought a healthy out-post shielded from the crowded, filthy, and crime-ridden older parts of the city. The neighborhood "was laid out in the 1830s and settled in the 1840s, approximately 120 years after New Orleans was founded but only three decades after Louisiana came under American rule."[7] In contrast to the French Quarter, the Garden District was settled pri-marily by Americans from the eastern seaboard, and, unlike the French Quarter, most of

[6] Starr, *Southern Comfort,* 45.
[7] Ibid., 17.

the drawings record the properties in their original form, or at most, with one generation of adaptation.

Because the Americans living in the Garden District had been treated as outsiders, they rejected the influences of the Creoles and staunchly clung to the traditions of the Northeast. As Frederick Starr has written,

> Instead of interior service courtyards and portes cocheres they favored narrow, airless alleys. . . .
>
> Only in the face of absolute necessity did the Anglo-Saxons adopt local practices. Kitchens, which in the Greek Revival houses of lower Manhattan were in the basement, were shifted to the wing extending to the rear. Servants' rooms, which throughout the Northeast were under the rooftop eaves, were also moved to the rear extension.[8]

The streetcar which ran along St. Charles Avenue served as a strong impetus for development uptown. Although the suburb was laid out on a rigid grid, lots were larger and open space more commodious. The invention of the lawnmower in England in the 1830s allowed even the bourgeoisie to have large expanses of lawn.[9]

Cultural differences produced different house plans. For the Creoles, once within the family compound, privacy was not a high priority. In response, many houses in the French Quarter lacked hallways, with principal rooms opening directly onto galleries. The Yankees, who came from a world in which privacy was important, were not comfortable with this lack of privacy.[10] So in many ways, the buildings in this suburb came to resemble designs in Philadelphia or Manhattan rather than those linked to the New Orleans region.

Analysis of Garden District Drawings

Thirty-six properties in the Garden District were selected for analysis.

Typical Property in Plan

The average lot size in the suburb was 30 × 120 feet, similar to the average dimensions in the French Quarter, but many of the drawings show single ownership of several contiguous lots, creating properties of the same lot depth (120 feet) but two or three times as wide (Fig. 16). In great contrast to the French Quarter, the majority of the houses (twenty-two properties) were set back from the front property line forming a landscaped space in front with no ornamental development behind the main house. In twelve of the properties, substantial landscape development occurs to the side of the house, often occupying an adjacent lot (Figs. 17, 18, 19). These extensive side gardens are often found in combination with a very shallow front garden or none at all. In any case, these layouts reveal a radical shift in cultural attitude, with the emphasis placed on the public face of

[8] Ibid., 17–19.
[9] Starr, *Southern Comfort*, 64.
[10] Ibid., 73.

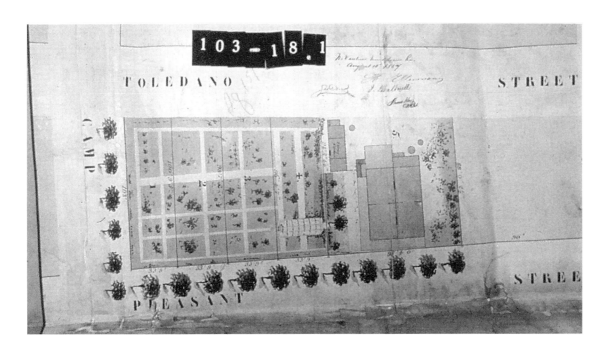

16. L. Reizenstein, Plan Book 103, fol. 18, 1867 (photo: courtesy of the New Orleans Notarial Archives)

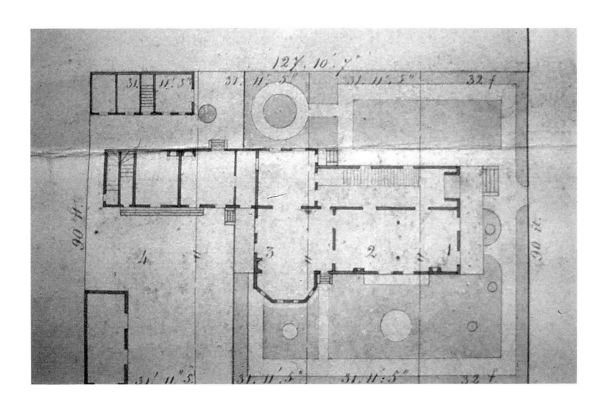

17. J. A. Celles, Plan Book 97, fol. 19, 1870 (photo: courtesy of the New Orleans Notarial Archives)

18. J. A. Celles, Plan Book 97, fol. 19, 1870 (photo: courtesy of the New Orleans Notarial Archives)

19. de L'isle, Plan Book 24, fol. 23, 1858 (photo: courtesy of the New Orleans Notarial Archives)

the property. Visually permeable fences replaced the tall walls used in the French Quarter. Although privacy was highly valued on the interior of the house, for these newcomers to the city their wealth and taste could be seen through their gardens.

Unlike the ornamental plantings, patterns for the treatment of utilitarian features such as outbuildings and service wings resembled forms found in the French Quarter. The type of outbuildings began to change; a service ell off the back of the house replaced detached kitchens and servants quarters (Figs. 17, 18). More space separated the house and the outbuildings, and more properties devoted space to stabling and the housing of carriages.

Cisterns appear on almost all sites, but only three wells are marked. Wells were not common after the early nineteenth century because of the high water table and the difficulty of preventing contamination by leaching from privies. A new graphic convention appears in these drawings more frequently than in the Vieux Carré, that is, the use of different tones to distinguish paving and sidewalks from the rest of the ground plane which might suggest either lawn or planting (Fig. 17).

In *Southern Comfort,* an important addition to the small amount of scholarship on the Garden District, Frederick Starr examines the social and economic milieu of the neighborhood by means of an architectural survey. He notes that a new attitude of "collective display" and a "sense of neighborhood" was apparent in the "absence of fences between lots," and that the traditional high board fence gave way to "low cedar rails, or, later, to cast-iron fencing."[11] Neither mid-century bird's-eye photos of the suburb, nor period engravings, nor the overwhelming majority of the drawings confirm this, but instead they show fences, typically wooden and quite high, albeit somewhat transparent, along the street (Fig. 20). The few drawings that do not show fences have been drawn from a point inside the front property to avoid having the fence conceal the front garden (Figs. 21, 22). Cast-iron fences were the exception rather than the rule.

Evidence of Gardening

Since the Garden District was entirely a residential neighborhood, all the properties but two show some form of landscape development. The drawings as a group indicate that a great deal of space and energy was dedicated to the cultivation of plants, and that garden design was an important aspect of the community from its inception. Of the thirty-four properties indicating gardening activity, six are classified as "parterres" (Figs. 23, 24) and two as "gardens in the romantic mode" (after Downing, although as in the French Quarter adaptation of the parterre, they were miniaturized and bastardized from the original concept) (Figs. 25, 26). Seven plans show simple planting beds, and nineteen show only individual trees. A great majority of these properties do not indicate the layout of planting beds on the plan. The elevational drawings, however, clearly depict some degree of gardening on the site, usually between the street fence and the front of the house.

[11] Ibid., 64.

20. C. A. Hedin, Plan Book 59, fol. 12, 1853 (photo: courtesy of the New Orleans Notarial Archives)

21. J. N. B. DePouilly, Plan Book 49A, fol. 60, 1866 (photo: courtesy of the New Orleans Notarial Archives)

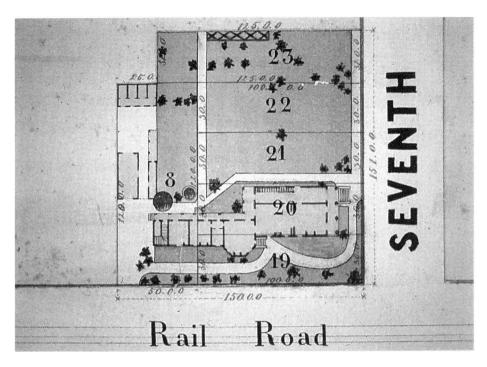

22. J. N. B. DePouilly, Plan Book 49A, fol. 60, 1866 (photo: courtesy of the New Orleans Notarial Archives)

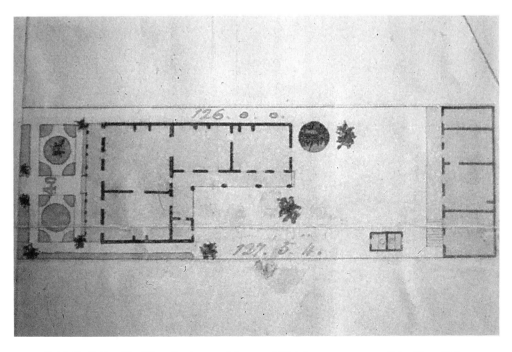

23. J. N. B. DePouilly, Plan Book 101, fol. 15, 1866 (photo: courtesy of the New Orleans Notarial Archives)

24. J. N. B. DePouilly, Plan Book 101, fol. 15, 1866 (photo: courtesy of the New Orleans Notarial Archives)

25. Louis Pilié, Plan Book 64, fol. 45, 1860 (photo: courtesy of the New Orleans Notarial Archives)

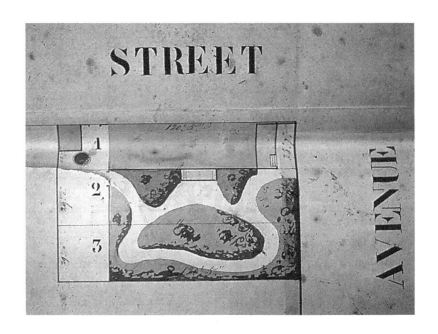

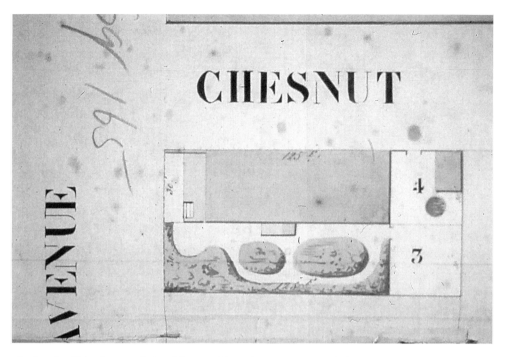

26. Louis Pilié, Plan Book 64, fol. 44, 1860 (photo: courtesy of the New Orleans Notarial Archives)

As a whole, the plans show a high degree of sophistication in the making of gardens. Most gardens rely on the conventions of formal geometry typical of parterres in the French Quarter, but the scale is larger and the effect bolder. Although all of the properties were surely built after 1840—Downing's *Treatise on the Theory and Practice of Landscape Gardening* was published in 1841—it is surprising that only two (Figs. 25, 26) suggest the influence of this important book which brought the ideas of the English Romantic Landscape Movement to thousands of American homeowners intent on escaping urbanity for a more rural existence. These two depart from rectilinear geometry; rather than straight lines, curved lines separate planting beds from lawn. Perhaps the weak presence of Downing's influence is a result of the conservative character of the city or a nod toward the Creole presence; or perhaps it simply represents the sensitive acknowledgment that these suburban properties were still quite small compared to the size and expanse of rural estates, and more space would be necessary to fully exploit the concepts of romantic naturalism.

A survey of the plans reveals a collection of suburban properties whose architecture and landscape plans would feel at home virtually anywhere on the eastern seaboard. Study of the elevations (Figs. 27, 28), however, reveals a hint of what distinguishes this neighborhood today, and what distinguished it from its Yankee neighbors in the last half of the nineteenth century. These qualities, which have developed over the last century and a half, produced a distinct, recognizable garden style that is truly regional and "of the place," inextricably bound to a specific set of physical and cultural circumstances.

27. C. A. Hedin, Plan Book 59, fol. 11, 1853 (photo: courtesy of the New Orleans Notarial Archives)

28. L. Reizenstein, Plan Book 97, fol. 6, 1858 (photo: courtesy of the New Orleans Notarial Archives)

A REGIONAL GARDEN TRADITION

The French Quarter and Garden District stand in high contrast to each other; each has gardens of different sizes based on separate cultural patterns, opposing postures toward the street, and varied antecedents. Like their sources, the gardens that have developed from these landscapes into the late twentieth century are still quite distinct from one another. In spite of these differences, the processes that prompted their evolution from the nineteenth century—when they were recorded—to the forms that they have today are very much the same.

Determinants of a Regional Ambience

Since settlement, the natural situation of the city has been a major issue. A great controversy accompanied the choice of the city's location because of its low elevation (near sea level), the frequency of flooding, the stifling summer heat, and the vulnerability to the Gulf and its weather fronts. Despite the negative products of all these conditions—muddy streets, devastating epidemics of yellow fever, annual floods, and hurricanes and tornadoes—the city and its gardens have acquired a certain ambience, an ephemeral quality so powerful that writers have not only commented upon it but have celebrated it since the city began.

The most obvious result of the semitropical climate and abundance of moisture is that vegetation in wide variety flourishes, reaching generous proportions in a relatively short period. Unlike coastal cities like Pensacola, where sea breezes mitigate the high humidity and seasonal change is less distinct, in New Orleans, the humidity persists without relief for months on end. The humidity produces mold, mildew, moss, scum—an organic patina, as it were—which in a garden setting suggest noble age and maturity rather than decay and unkemptness. The abundance of water and the warm temperatures produce hardwood trees of enormous scale and breadth, most notably the live oak and the Southern magnolia.

A direct result of the size and speed of vegetative growth is that most New Orleans gardens are shaded. The plant palette thus relies to a great extent upon shade-loving evergreen plants, particularly ground covers and shrubs. Related to this reliance upon evergreens and the scale of the vegetation is the quality of light filtered through the branches of mature trees. A remarkable chiaroscuro effect dances across the ground plane producing a vast range of greens that are subtle and refined. And even more ephemeral than the light is the fragrance. The atmospheric quality intensifies the sense of smell when the air is nearly palpable, especially when filled with the aroma of floral blossoms. Early travelers' accounts remark on the effect of the orange blossoms and jasmine perfuming the streets, and fragrant semitropical and night-blooming species are still favorites in New Orleans gardens.

Metamorphosis over Time

A recent piece in *Elle Decor* entitled "Secret New Orleans: Courtyards and Balconies Offer Green Sanctuary" tempts the reader in describing the French Quarter:

You can make out an ancient fountain, cool cast-iron furniture, marble statuary, and abundantly glossy plant life. There might be balconies, trellises, ironwork—or the four walls surrounding the garden might be simply stretched with vines. You breathe in tropical scents, hear the steady, calming noise of trickling water, and so apprehend the carefully preserved civility that has always been at the heart of life in New Orleans.[12]

"These outdoor sanctuaries speak strongly of Spanish and Caribbean influences," the author continues, "and yet the climate and vegetation are such that flowers and vines are never entirely civilized."[13]

In an April 1990 *New York Times* article on the Garden District by Starr he begins with,

> . . . One encounters serene streets tunneled through shaded alleys of oak and crape myrtle trees. Yards burst with camellia, cape jasmine, palms, and even a few fig, lemon, and pomegranate trees. . . . Wherever you wander you will notice deep drainage ditches—virtually canals—along the narrow streets. . . . These channels were built to drain the ubiquitous puddles of tropical rainwater in which yellow-fever-bearing mosquitoes bred.[14]

And most importantly for my purposes, Starr feels the heavy air:

> For block after block you can sense the dreams that gave rise to this early suburb, and gaze at the comfortable homes and gardens that crystallized the dream. No less important, you can absorb the gentle light and limpid air that defined the pace of life a century ago and still influences it today.[15]

Certainly not all gardens existing in this climate are regional in character, but regardless of the original forms of the gardens and the intent of their makers, it is only a matter of time before the gardens reach a point of natural stasis and become predominantly shady, and by extension, evergreen.

French Quarter Courtyard Today

The courtyards of the Quarter changed gradually over time. Small ornamental trees were planted for seasonal interest, and species considered "small" anywhere else grew to gargantuan proportions, buckling paving stones and shading the ground below. More often, volunteer seeds were allowed to develop, resulting in unplanned and over-scaled shade trees.

Changes in the courtyard mirrored shifts in social and economic patterns. With Abolition and Reconstruction, large outbuildings built for servants' quarters were no longer

---

[12] M. Read, "Secret New Orleans, Courtyards and Balconies Offer Green Sanctuary," *Elle Decor* 1 (February 1991), 68.

[13] Ibid.

[14] S. R. Starr, "Green Haven in New Orleans," *New York Times,* 8 April 1990.

[15] Ibid., 8.

required and were converted to rental property. As kitchens and plumbing facilities moved indoors, other outbuildings were also converted to accommodate new uses or demolished. And spaces that in the past had functioned for a variety of daily household tasks became more solidly geared toward leisure and entertainment.

The wave of preservation and restoration that followed the passage of the Historic District ordinance in 1937 produced the courtyards that typify today's French Quarter. Whereas only very few fountains can be traced to the antebellum period and none are conclusively illustrated in the Notarial Archives, they are the predominant feature in courtyards today. Often a fountain was simply placed over the circular remains of a property's original well, usually located in a central spot.

The Garden District Garden Today

The impact of tropical heat and humidity similarly transformed the Garden District. Evergreen shrubs and medium-scale trees form the gardens' structures and typify these gardens today. The plant palette, more than any other single element, gives these gardens their signatures. Magnolia, crape myrtles, sweet olives, cherry laurel, camellias, sasanquas, azaleas, pittosporum, and sago palms are the most common species, and the result is a composition of dark, glossy greens beneath the shade of very large trees, mostly live oaks.

Because most of the original builders in the district never intended to stay permanently, ownership changed relatively soon and often. New owners brought new ideas about garden design, and as American taste changed, so did the Garden District. Today, masses of planting define the edges of the properties and the perimeters of the houses; the luxuriant growth makes the plans imperceptible. Many of these gardens are not very different from the beds illustrated in the Notarial Archives drawings. The contemporary version is thicker and denser from over a century of prolific growth.

In plan, these gardens do not significantly differ from others in cities outside the region. The difference is the heat and humidity, the fragrance produced by the tropical vegetation, the scale and power of the trees, and the quality of the light. Although these may seem quite insignificant in relation to the larger issues of garden design, when one considers the perception of place, they are everything.

CONCLUSION

An analysis of the Notarial Archives drawings for these two neighborhoods shows garden plans that might be at home in many world cities. The gardens of Venice, for example, share elements with the gardens of the Vieux Carré; and early suburban estates in Boston, Philadelphia, and New York used approaches similar to those of the Garden District. But when the Louisiana gardens are viewed in three dimensions, even in the first half of the nineteenth century, the effects of the climate and the specter of water are clearly perceptible. The century and a half of growth since these drawings were made has only dramatized the power that begins to be hinted at in the drawings.

These early New Orleans gardens have left vivid imprints on the minds of designers in the region, and many gardens of nearby cities are modeled on the French Quarter

Courtyard, as well as gardens reminiscent of the Garden District suburban estate. Hybrids have begun to appear, using the Garden District model to present the public face and the courtyard for intimacy closer to the residence. Is there a line of continuity that weaves together these new Southern gardens with those pictured in the Notarial Archives? Similarities in plant palette, arrangement of major elements, and scale relationships are evident. And in some cases, the Notarial Archives drawings have been direct purveyors of the tradition; they have been used widely for architectural restoration, but less often for the restoration of gardens. As preservation has been firmly entrenched in the city for over fifty years, these drawings have played a major role in the formulation of a regional aesthetic.

And yet the reasons behind most of the earlier gardens were quite different from the motivations directing designers to work in regional idioms today. New Orleans garden designers of the nineteenth century attempted to create places that either resembled their homelands or symbolized wealth and status. They sought to alter and remove the look of the indigenous and hostile Louisiana landscape to conjure the feeling of a more civilized homeland or region of origin. And yet, over time the natural processes of the New Orleans environment transformed these imported ideas into living, growing gardens directly related to this wet and lush landscape.

And so this city near the mouth of one of the world's most powerful rivers has fostered the development of two very distinct versions of the Southern garden—the French Quarter Courtyard and the Garden District suburban estate. Both types have been emulated and reproduced within the region for generations. The drawings of the Notarial Archives provide a window through which to view the roots of these gardens; and, when overlaid with the humidity, the grandeur of the live oaks, the filter of light and shadow, and the fragrance of moist earth and tropical blooms, the lineage that connects the two becomes clear.

On Public Landscape Design Before
the Civil War, 1830–1860

JAMES S. ACKERMAN

My subject is the landscape design of public spaces before the Civil War; it relates in two ways to the regional theme we are considering. The relevant works are predominantly on the North Atlantic seaboard, and the design models were European and especially British, so that American practice could be seen as a regional variant of the general phenomenon of the picturesque style.

The public landscape design of the Northeast seaboard began as a provincial version of British design, as it was transmitted in books. But the key to distinctiveness of American design was to be found not primarily in the British forms used but rather in its ideological roots. American cemeteries and parks were promoted and given shape by an elite composed partly of old federalist families and newly successful manufacturers and merchants—a class in the process of simultaneous dissolution and formation—which sought to protect itself from the effects of mobility and disorder in American life, the perceived threat of which was intensified by the victory of Jacksonian democracy. It was the stated strategy of this class to provide for all classes at least a short-term escape from the oppressive conditions of urban life and to elevate the cultural level and tame the wildness and instability of the masses. The achievements tended to benefit the privileged members of society rather than poor, but they were seen to be socially conscious and philanthropic. The urban and public character of these enterprises distinguish them from achievements in the southern states, such as Virginia, which are treated in the article by C. Allan Brown in this volume.

The population of major cities in Europe and America exploded dramatically in the early nineteenth century causing conditions of overcrowding and poor sanitation that, while affecting the poor most intensely, also had an impact on the affluent. This was particularly true of Americans in the northeast, since so many of all classes had started life on a farm and had not yet developed an urban mentality, whereas in the walled towns of Europe dense settlement without open spaces had been normal since the Middle Ages. But already in the eighteenth century, in England and on the continent, urban density had been relieved by the preservation of open green space, available at first only to the privileged, like Regent's Park in London, but gradually being opened to public access (though most often located in areas inaccessible to slum dwellers). The ambition to create a *rus in urbe* followed closely on the earliest theory and practice of picturesque landscape design.[1] At first, such enterprises were spurred primarily by a taste for the informal and ultimately for the picturesque, but with the blight, bad air, and plagues of the industrial age, considerations of health and relaxation from burdensome labor reinforced the taste and altered its character. The provision of open public spaces of greenery initially proved easier in Europe than in America because amenities like the Tiergarten in Berlin, Parc Monceau in Paris, and Hyde Park in London, which already had existed as parks and hunting grounds of royalty and the aristocracy, had only to be made accessible to all. In this country efforts by northern city governments to rescue even small plots in major centers from development on the free market typically became bogged down in the political process or, having passed through city councils, failed to be implemented. Almost every significant public landscape project of the pre-Civil War period had to be initiated by private societies and corporations. These were composed primarily of members of an elite merchant and industrial class, primarily Federalist and conservative in their politics (and in Massachusetts, Unitarian in religious affiliation), who were unseated from political power and influence initially with the presidency of Jefferson and definitively in the era of Jacksonian democracy, but who held firmly to the control of existing cultural and educational institutions and formed new ones to extend their power.[2] Their sense of an urgent need to maintain control over the minds and tastes of Americans was strong enough to overcome the mutual suspicion aroused by the rivalries of a fiercely competitive marketplace and explains the passion with which they gathered together in support of scientific and civic enterprises. Their fear of mob rule after the election of Andrew Jackson in 1828 also gave impetus to their support of public parks as a civilizing influence, a way of releasing workers from the pressures of the slum and promoting family activities so that female influence could prevail over the appeal of the saloon.

That the first major undertaking in American landscape design in the modern informal style should have involved the planning of a cemetery is due primarily to the ominous health hazard created by the overcrowded burial grounds in the center of Boston where, as in Europe, bodies were left to decompose in open graves, and bones were removed to charnel houses to make way for more, offending every level of sensibility.

Before 1980 most of the projects I shall discuss—Mt. Auburn Cemetery in Cambridge, the Mall in Washington, and the squares of New York City—were little known; the fact that the date coincides with the initiation of *The Journal of Garden History* may be partly a sign of the evolution of a young field of study, but it is also a measure of what John Dixon Hunt's leadership has achieved. What has occurred is not simply an increment in our knowledge of this aspect of the past, but a substantially increased sophistication of interpretation, so that we can now perceive the landscape design of this period in the context of the intellectual, social, and economic life of our country at a moment of radical change. The work of John Archer, Charles Beveridge, Therese O'Malley, Blanche Linden-Ward, and David Schuyler deserve special mention.

[1] See J. Archer, "Rus in Urbe: Classical Ideals of Country and City in British Town Planning," *Studies in Eighteenth-Century Culture* 12 (1983), 159–86.

[2] My interpretation is indebted to that of P. D. Hall, *The Organization of American Culture, 1700–1900: Private Institution, Elites and the Origins of American Nationality,* New York, 1982.

Efforts were made by the city government throughout the 1820s to find additional space for burial in undeveloped land on the periphery but were frustrated by political and commercial interests. Ultimately a solution was found by private citizens who chose not to emulate New Haven's new but characterless burial plot on the edge of town, but to create a truly rural environment adapted to improvement by a modest intervention of sympathetic landscaping which, in contrast to earlier American burial places, would charm and instruct the living while commemorating the dead. This was Mt. Auburn Cemetery, located several miles from Boston between Camridge and Watertown, Massachusetts, which functioned as the first American public park in the British picturesque style (Figs. 1, 2).

Mt. Auburn's history has been meticulously published by Blanche Linden-Ward.[3] The inability of the Boston city administration to find open spaces for burial prompted Dr. Jacob Bigelow, a professor of medicine at Harvard and the author of four volumes on horticulture, to call together a group of leading Boston citizens in 1825 to discuss the establishment of such a cemetery and to seek suitable property outside Boston. The initiative stalled temporarily, but in 1830, George Brimmer, another member of the Boston establishment, agreed to sell the seventy-two acres he had purchased in 1825 as the site for his home to the Massachusetts Horticultural Society, which had been founded just a year before. The intention was to combine the functions of an experimental garden with those of a cemetery with the expectation that the income from the sale of burial plots would cover the costs of the educational and experimental plantings.

The site already constituted a picturesque landscape; its rolling terrain rose to a single hillock from which one could see Boston to the east and Fresh Pond to the north. There were a couple of small bodies of water that could be converted easily into ornamental ponds, and fine stands of evergreen and deciduous trees, some planted by Brimmer. The name "Mt. Auburn," proposed by Bigelow, was adapted from "Sweet Auburn," which Harvard students had taken, early in the century, from Oliver Goldsmith's poem, *The Deserted Village*, which is an incunabulum of picturesque sensibility. The original intention was to leave the property as much as possible in its original wild condition, modified only by a serpentine vehicular road and footpaths and to avoid any monumental space or structure. Responsibility for the design was assigned to a committee composed of the cofounder and first President of the Horticultural Society, General Henry Dearborn, Bigelow, and Brimmer, with Dearborn taking the major part of the responsibility and spending, during the first three years, all of his time away from his duties as a congressman, even laboring with a pick and hoe. The partnership between the cemetery and the Horticultural Society, however, was short lived, either because there was not

[3] B. Linden-Ward, *Silent City on a Hill: Landscapes of Memory and Boston's Mount Auburn Cemetery*, Columbus, 1989. On the role of the rural cemetery in American culture, see D. Schuyler, "The Evolution of the Anglo-American Rural Cemetery: Landscape Architecture as Social and Cultural History," *Journal of Garden History* 4 (1984), 291–304; N. Harris, *The Artist in American Society: The Formative Years, 1790–1860*, New York, 1966, 200–208; T. Bender, *Toward an Urban Vision: Ideas and Institutions in Nineteenth-Century America*, Lexington, Ky., 1975, 80 ff.

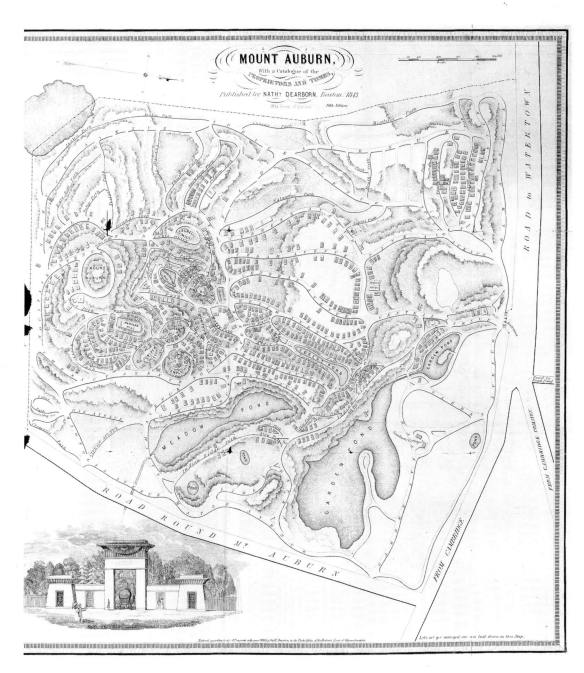

1. Plan of Mt. Auburn Cemetery, Cambridge, Massachusetts (photo: from *A Concise History of and Guide Through Mount Auburn*, Boston, 1843; courtesy of Harvard College Library)

2. View of Forest Pond, Mt. Auburn Cemetery, Cambridge, Massachusetts (photo: from *Mt. Auburn Illustrated in a Series of Views from Drawings by James Smillie,* New York, 1847; courtesy of Harvard College Library)

enough surplus to finance an experimental garden, or because the egos of Dearborn and Bigelow were too big to coexist on seventy-two acres.

Dearborn's design followed the contours of the land (Fig. 1); in laying out the paths and drives he intended, he wrote, "to run them as nearly level as possible by winding gradually and gracefully through the valley and obliquely over hills, without any unnecessary or unavoidable bend, and especially to avoid all sinuosities." He had written a two-volume *Treatise on Grecian Architecture* and was inspired by Greek moldings and vase profiles which, he claimed, are derived from conic sections and "are either parabolical, elliptical or hyperbolical." He had sent abroad for prints and books relating to landscape design, and his elliptical and kidney-shaped enclosures resemble slightly the beds for private gardens proposed by Loudon in his *Encyclopaedia of Gardening* (London, 1835). But, making allowances for the special function of accommodating burial plots, which explains the provision in some areas of roughly parallel paths, I would call the design generic and undistinguished informal English-Continental.

In England, a comparable adaptation of the picturesque style to cemeteries occurred at the same time as Mt. Auburn at London's Kensall Green cemetery. But in Paris, the Père Lachaise cemetery had been founded in 1804 and was widely known to American visitors (Fig. 3).[4]

[4] Linden-Ward, *Silent City,* 65 ff.

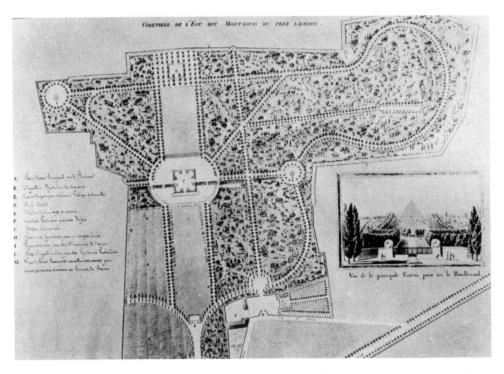

3. Plan of the Pére Lachaise cemetery, Paris, by Alexandre-Théodore Brongniart, ca. 1812
(photo: from B. Linden-Ward, *Silent City on a Hill*, Columbus, Ohio, 1989)

Although the Père Lachaise design reveals the impact of earlier British landscape style, there is a monumental quasi-classical central approach culminating in a grand monument. It was well outside the city at the time and perched on a hill with views comparable to those of Mt. Auburn, and it also served as a park retreat for the public. But it was fundamentally different in conception, first in being generated by the government, and second in its ambition to become a place to celebrate great individuals; the focus was more on the grand monument than on nature, and the educational ideology was directed more to national history than to horticulture. The topography precluded bodies of water. By the time Mt. Auburn was opened, monuments had almost overcome plantings at the Père Lachaise.

The model of Mt. Auburn was adopted rapidly by other major Northeast Atlantic cities. In Philadelphia, most of the public squares mandated by William Penn's original plan had been built over or left undeveloped:[5] in 1854, the Pennsylvania legislature had to demand an "adequate" number.[6] Here, the initiation of Laurel Hill cemetery was again

[5] In the 1794 map of Philadelphia, the surveyor had eliminated the squares of the 1682 plan (one was labeled "Potter's field grave yard"), but they were reestablished in ordinances of the next century and appear in a map of 1855. (See J. Reps, *The Making of Urban America*, Princeton, 1965, 167.)
[6] D. Schuyler, *The New Urban Landscape: The Redefinition of City Form in Nineteenth-Century America*, Baltimore, 1986, 103.

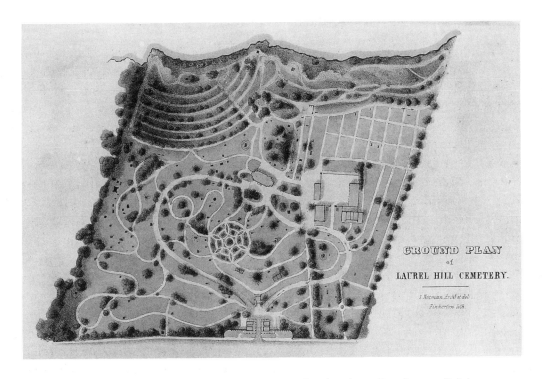

4. Plan of Laurel Hill Cemetery, Philadelphia, Pennsylvania (photo: Dumbarton Oaks)

the enterprise of influential citizens brought together by an amateur horticulturist, who announced a competition for its design in 1835. The architect, John Notman, who had not previously been engaged in landscape design, was awarded the commision on the basis of a more Loudonesque plan than that of Mt. Auburn, with a formal central element (Fig. 4).[7] In the course of the 1830s and 1840s, Loudon himself moved sharply away from the picturesque style toward more formal design in his writings on cemeteries. The first of the New York cemeteries was Green-Wood in Brooklyn, founded in 1838, again by a private corporation. Green-Wood, while difficult to get to even from Brooklyn, was a great public succcss as a recreational refuge, though most of its burial plots had been taken by a small number of wealthy families.[8] In the original prospective the proposed designation "Necropolis" was rejected because of its urban connotations.

When Andrew Jackson Downing submitted his project for the Mall in Washington, he wrote that it "would exercise as much influence in the public taste as Mount Auburn Cemetery . . . has done."[9] The design of the Mall was destined to be the most important and visible landscape commission of the antebellum period.[10]

[7] K. N. Morgan, "The Emergence of the American Landscape Professional: John Notman and the Design of Rural Cemeteries," *Journal of Garden History* 4 (1984), 269–89.
[8] D. Simon, "Green-Wood Cemetery and the American Park Movement," in I. Yellowitz, ed., *Essays in the History of New York City: A Memorial to Sidney Pomeranz*, Fort Washington, 1978, 61–77.
[9] Letter of 15 November 1841, from Downing to John Jay Smith, the motive force behind Laurel Hill Cemetery in Philadelphia, in J. K. Major, "The Downing Letters," *Landscape Architecture* 76 (January-February 1986), 52.
[10] Great progress has been made in research on the Mall in the last five years, notably by D. Schuyler,

By the fifth decade of the century, nothing had been done to implement the formal proposal of L'Enfant, which was not unlike the present-day solution. Congress had shown no interest in appropriating funds at a time when questions were still being raised about the viability of Washington as a capital, and the destiny of the Mall came to be intertwined with that of the National Institute for the Promotion of Science and its successor, the Smithsonian Institution.

In February of 1841 the Secretary of War, and of the Institute, Joel Poinsett, commissioned Robert Mills to design a building on the opposite side of the Mall from its present position and a botanical garden for whichever institute would be first chartered.[11] Mills responded with drawings that included, besides those requested, a proposal for the entire Mall in the picturesque style as well as alternative designs for the botanical garden: one picturesque and one in the mode of a medieval medicinal garden (Figs. 5, 6). Here again, educational aims came to the fore.

Mills, in his letter to Poinsett of 16 Feb., explains his intention "to provide locations for subjects allied to agriculture, the propagation of useful and ornamental trees, native and foreign, the provisions of sites for the erection of suitable buildings to accomodate the various subjects to be lectured on and taught in the Institute" (he lists the sciences, history, literature and fine arts, and the mechanical arts). And he adds, explaining his design principles, "By means of groups and vistas of trees, picturesque views may be obtained of the various buildings and such other objects as may be of a monumental character and thus there would be an attraction produced which would draw many of our citizens and strangers to partake of the pleasures of promenading there." A horticultural interest was again the motivating cause for the design, but Mills and probably his sponsor Joel Poinsett envisioned a wider educational mission not far from that of the later land-grant colleges.

The Mills landscape design is not distinguished, though it is a radical departure from the treatment of his contemporary work in Boston, the Bunker Hill Monument; its isolated spots of shrubbery and trees has affinities with Loudon's "gardenesque" style—where else, at this moment, would an architect suddenly turned landscape designer have turned but to Loudon's *Encyclopaedia*? The plan is divided into several segments by the cross streets; the portion around the Monument, like that of the triangular shapes left by the canal and the gardens at the base of Capitol Hill, are formed by webs of wandering

"The Washington Park and Downing's Legacy to Public Landscape Design," *Prophet with Honor: The Career of Andrew Jackson Downing, 1815–1852*, in G. B. Tatum and E. B. MacDougall, eds., Dumbarton Oaks Colloquium on the History of Landscape Architecture 11, Washington, D.C., 1989, 291–312; T. O'Malley, *Art and Science in American Landscape Architecture: The National Mall, Washington D.C., 1791–1852*, Ph.D. diss., University of Pennsylvania, 1989 (I want to thank Dr. O'Malley for graciously loaning me a copy of the typescript to assist this study); R. Longstreth, ed., *The Mall in Washington, 1791–1991*, National Gallery of Art, Studies in the History of Art 30, Hanover-London, 1991, chapters by Pamela Scott on the Mills plan and by Therese O'Malley on Downing.

[11] P. Scott, "'This Vast Empire': The Iconography of the Mall, 1791–1848," *The Mall in Washington*, 37–60; P. Scott, ed., *The Papers of Robert Mills, 1781–1855*, The Scholarly Resources Microfilm Edition, Wilmington, 1990, especially I, 2179. See also Scott's study of the Washington Monument in "Robert Mills and American Monuments," J. M. Boyan, ed., *Robert Mills, Architect*, Washington, D.C., 1989, chap. 5.

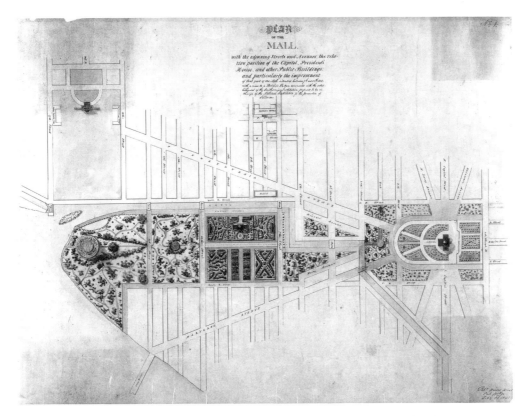

5. Robert Mills, "Plan of the Mall," Washington, D.C., 1841 (photo: National Archives, RG 77, Records of the Office of Engineers, Cartographic Records)

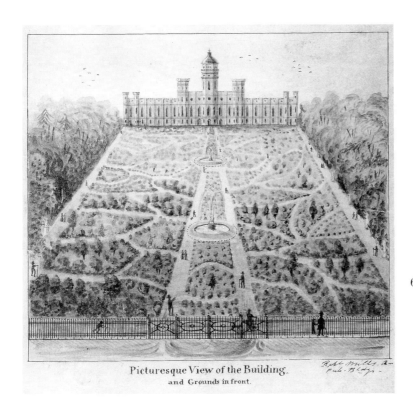

Picturesque View of the Building,
and Grounds in front.

6. Robert Mills, "Picturesque View of the Building (Smithsonian Institution) and Grounds in Front," Washington, D.C., 1841 (photo: National Archives, RG 77, Records of the Office of Engineers, Cartographic Records)

199

paths with the trees and shrubs artlessly set into the intervening areas. The entire block between seventh and twelfth Streets, assigned to the gardens of the Smithsonian Institution, is more densely planted in the style of Loudon's private gardens (three versions of this portion appear in the surviving renderings: besides Figures 5 and 6, a plan of the grounds alone). Nothing came of the Mills project because no funds were assigned to realize it, and a decade went by before the idea of instituting a respectable Mall was revived.

In 1850 a group of citizens from the class that promoted other public landscape projects in the northern states approached President Fillmore to get approval to initiate a Mall design, as did the Commissioner of Building, Ignatius Mudd, and the following year the building committee of the Smithsonian recommended the commissioning of a new design for the whole Mall, coordinated with the botanical garden of the Institution. At this date, Andrew Jackson Downing, whose design of 1841 for a 22-acre public garden in Boston remained unexecuted,[12] was the acknowledged American authority on landscape design and effectively the only professional practitioner.[13]

In February 1851, Downing submitted his design to the building committee of the Smithsonian, whose plan it had been to treat the entire area as an informal garden and arboretum. In a letter to the president of March 1851, Downing characterized his proposal for what he properly called the "Public Grounds" rather than the Mall as an example of "the natural style of landscape gardening which may have an influence on the taste of the country" and "a public school of Instruction in everything that relates to the tasteful arrangement of parks and grounds, and the growth and culture of trees."[14]

The scheme (Fig. 7) was to be composed of six distinct areas: the President's Park or Parade behind the President's house—a large, presumably paved open public space for gatherings and parades, surrounded by a broad carriage drive. This was to have been entered from Pennsylvania Avenue through a Roman triumphal arch, which probably was Downing's unique classical monument. The park around Mills's monument was to be planted exclusively with American trees. Also, there was a 16-acre garden of some one hundred thirty native and foreign evergreen shrubs and trees. The Smithsonian Park was to have the rarest trees and shrubs, arranged in the "national style." A Fountain Park would be created at the foot of Capitol Hill with a lake fed by a fountain. Finally, Downing writes that the Botanic garden (that on the slope of Capitol Hill?) already had been planned and that he was showing how his circuit drive would pass through it.

Downing died in a steamboat disaster in 1852, while en route from his home on the Hudson to Washington, and very little of his scheme was carried out before being killed by Congressional apathy.

[12] Letter cited in n. 9.

[13] Downing's career has been well documented in recent years, though more with respect to his impact on architecture than on landscape design; new contributions and references to the earlier literature may be found in *Prophet with Honor*. See also my chapter on Downing in *The Villa: Form and Ideology of Country Houses*, London-Princeton, 1990, chap. 10.

[14] Downing's letter on his Mall project was published by J. W. Reps, "Romantic Planning in a Baroque City: Downing and the Washington Mall," *Landscape* 16, 3 (1967), 6–11.

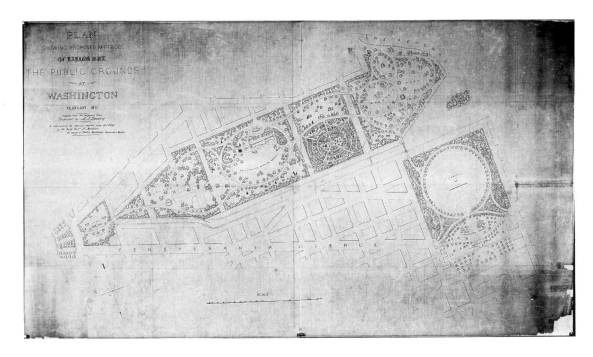

7. After Andrew Jackson Downing, landscape project for the "Public Grounds at Washington, 1851," Washington, D.C., 1867 (photo: National Archives, RG 77, Records of the Office of Engineers, Cartographic Records)

Downing's mission from the start of his career had been to civilize and educate Americans and to inculcate good taste; his Mall program was his greatest opportunity to realize those aims. The conception of the Mall as a horticultural museum best explains the radically unconventional decision to subdivide it into several semi-independent areas each having its own function of display, somewhat like the habitat groups in natural history museums (Downing also described his project as "a public museum of living trees and shrubs"). In L'Enfant's and in the Mall designs preceding this one, the attainment of visual unity was always a goal, and one cannot conceive of a public landscape project of major national symbolic import in Europe that would not be formal and axial. Yet Downing, the most effective spokesman for the picturesque in garden design and architecture, turned, on this one occasion, as Therese O'Malley has pointed out,[15] to the gentle contours and smooth undulations of the Beautiful. Like his colleague Alexander Jackson Davis, Downing thought of the picturesque as a private, individual style, to be accomodated to the character of the client and of the site and not suited to the expression of the ideals of republican government. Davis, the pioneer architect of the picturesque villa, designed state capitols and federal buildings in the classical style.

The education Downing hoped to effect as a landscape designer did not extend, like that of Mills in his letter to the building committee, to all the sciences and liberal and mechanical arts; it was specifically horticultural. This, as well as his marriage into a

[15] T. O'Malley, "*A Public Museum of Trees*': Mid-Nineteenth Century Plans for the Mall," *The Mall in Washington*, 67.

branch of the Adams family, allied him to the urban elites on the North Atlantic seaboard, among which horticulture had become a consuming passion and the principal avocation.

Study, conservation, and experimentation in this field was formalized in horticultural societies in the major cities, which remained as exclusive in their membership as private clubs, and similarly excluded women.[16] The one in Boston was referred to by Dearborn as "An association of men of taste, of influence and industry."[17] It was seen as a civilizing force, a demonstration of sensibility among the members of a materialistic establishment, and a stabilizing influence in a restless and mobile society. Dearborn called horticulture "the most distinguished of the fine arts."[18] It played a major role in the consolidation of the upper middle class. The societies were oriented not primarily to the betterment of agriculture but rather to an esoteric pursuit of ingenuity in collecting and breeding species reminiscent of the Dutch tulipomania of the previous century: three hundred ten varieties of pear were shown in the Massachusetts Horticultural Society's exhibition of 1852. The pursuit of what was called "cultivation" had a special meaning for the Jacksonian period because it carried implications both in the sphere of husbandry and of manners; while "cultivation" evoked the rural roots of the republic, it signaled on one hand a distancing from the rough behavior of the pioneer, and on the other an avoidance of what was seen as European oversophistication and depravity. It provided a middle ground, a symbol by which to overcome the sense of inferiority surviving from a colonial era.[19]

The story of city squares in this period has not yet been systematically studied, and it bears on the relationship to British practice. The case of Gramercy Park in New York is interesting because it closely followed the model of London squares (Fig. 8).[20] There, as exemplified by the relatively generous apportionment of open space in the part of Bloomsbury centered on Russell square, the motivation for the sacrifice of such large areas of potential building lots is explained by London's particular patterns of Georgian land development (Fig. 9).[21] Land was not sold but leased for long periods by hereditary and institutional landholders (Bloomsbury was in the estate of the Duke of Bedford); these landholders gave out to contractors the right to design and build leasable properties according to their specifications. Commonly, the landholder would require the type of amenity that would attract high-class (meaning rich) tenants, which also would benefit the contractor.

---

[16] The role of horticulture in American culture of the time is intriguingly presented by T. Thornton, *Cultivating Gentlemen: The Meaning of Country Life among the Boston Elite, 1785–1860,* New Haven, 1989, 147–73, 207–12. The author's earlier version of the chapter on horticultural societies was published as "The Moral Dimensions of Horticulture in Antebellum America," *New England Quarterly* 62 (1984), 3–24.

[17] Quoted by Linden-Ward, *Silent City,* 175, from a paper by Henry Dearborn in *New England Farmer,* citation not given.

[18] Quoted in Linden-Ward, *Silent City,* 175, from Dearborn's first anniversary address to the Massachusetts Horticultural Society, from the Society's *Transactions, 1829–1838,* Boston, 1847, 1, 5.

[19] P. Miller, "Nature and the National Ego," in *Errand into the Wilderness,* New York, 1964.

[20] S. Garmey, *Gramercy Park,* New York, 1984; C. Klein, *Gramercy Park,* Boston, 1987, is less informative.

[21] D. Olsen, *Town Planning in London: The Eighteenth and Nineteenth Centuries,* New Haven, 1964, 15 ff; on Bloomsbury, 51 ff.

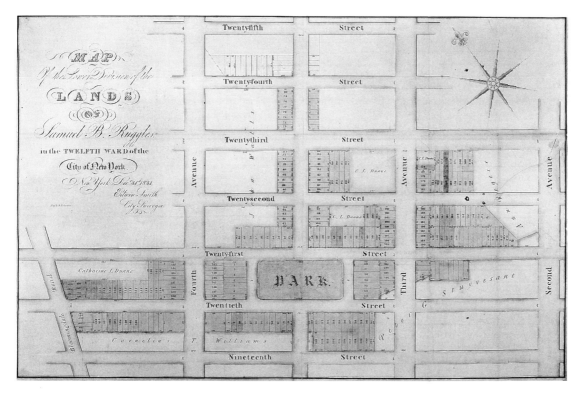

8. Plan of Gramercy Park and environs, City of New York, as developed by Samuel B. Ruggles, 1831 (photo: New York Public Library)

On the Northeast seaboard, however, the open land on the edge of cities was initially public, but cities could sell directly to developers. In the case of New York the original planners had no truck with issues of aesthetics or breathing space. The master plan of 1811, which proposed an uninterrupted grid of streets up to 155th Street, dismissed the need of parks in these words:

> "It may, to many, be a matter of surprise that too few vacant places have been left, and those so small, for the benefit of fresh air, and consequent preservation of health. Certainly if the City of New York were destined to stand on the side of a small stream, such as the Seine or the Thames, a great number of ample places might be needful, but those large arms of the sea which embrace Manhattan Island, render its situation particularly felicitous." [22]

Clearly, any open space in Manhattan would have to be provided by private enterprise.

In November 1831, Samuel Ruggles, a wealthy businessman, petitioned the city for a tax exemption for the development of a square with bordering dwellings on former farmland somewhat to the north of the then limits of New York, without mentioning that he intended it to be kept private as the property of the abutting homeowners. The city

---

[22] D. Schuyler, *New Urban Landscape*, 5.

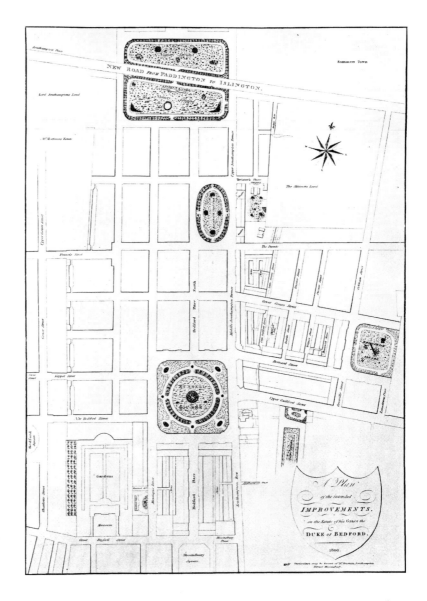

9. Plan of Russel Square and vicinity, London, 1800 (photo: from J. Olsen,
Town Planning in London, 2nd ed., New Haven, 1964)

granted the petition, with the provision that it remain an "ornamental" park, and Ruggles proceeded to provide a handsome fenced-in square to be offered as an inducement to buyers (Fig. 8). Initially the project floundered; the park was too far from the center, but a decade later, Gramercy Park was among the most desirable addresses in Manhattan. It was not the first of its kind: St. John's Square had been laid out in 1803 by Trinity Church, at a time when its Britishness caused the public to shun it. By 1827, when houses were beginning to be built around it, the church sold out and deeded the square to neighbors. The next year it was fenced in, and before its decline after the Civil War, shares in the park were worth $13,000. These are vestiges of the quasi-aristocratic mentality of the early years of the century. New York's Washington Square, by contrast, was democratic, but it was only moderately ornamental; it had remained undeveloped because it was a burial ground, and in 1828 it was redeveloped as a parade ground.[23] These instances are at the opposite pole from the ideals of the elite educators of Mt. Auburn and the Mall in Washington, D.C.

In Philadelphia, the first effort to provide a large public park was launched in 1844 when the city decided to purchase Lemon Hill by the Schuylkill River.[24] A resolution on the "appointment of a Special Committee . . . to consider the expedience of leasing the grounds of the Lemon Hill property to a company of gentlemen for enclosure and improvement as a Public Promenade" was postponed and, after the issue was revived in 1855, a competition for the design of Fairmount Park was postponed another four years. Though the execution was to be left in the hands of the same elite group as those we have examined, it was primarily a public enterprise, as the landscaping of the Fairmount waterworks in 1815 had been.

The city councils, however, were reluctant to provide the funding; a special property tax was proposed for the purpose, but I have not determined whether it was levied. In the meanwhile, a group of private citizens acquired and donated to the city a neighboring estate. The aim of the park was described as "allied . . . to the comfort, the health and the lives of our citizens. Nay, the manners, the moral and the political stability of our institution in large cities, have efficient aids in the general intercourse afforded to the people by these places in the harmonizing effects of nature, and in those social habits engendered by them which break down the curse of caste among us, resulting most frequently from habits of isolation." This enterprise, which preceded Central Park in New York in concept if not in execution, also anticipated the goals of Olmsted in placing the health and physical welfare of the whole public ahead of uplift and education; indeed, an application in 1844 by the Horticultural Society to establish a botanical garden there was ignored.[25] The only pre-War design for the park was that of Sidney and Adams, who won the initial competition, but the area at the time was so small that it looked more like a garden than a park, and little was done to develop it. Ultimately, thanks to extensive contributions of the State, Fairmount grew to over 2,600 acres.

The new parks of Britain at this time were also promoted by national and city governments, sometimes, as in the case of Manchester, with support of funds solicited from the public at large.[26] But they differed from the American examples in being much more integrated with the city and in providing spaces explicitly designed for athletic activity, an accommodation explicitly barred by Olmsted. The precedent of Regent's Park led to ringing the landscaped area of Victoria Park in London, of 1845, and others in the

[23] T. Bender, in M. Cantor, ed., *Around the Square, 1830–1890,* New York, 1982, 30 ff.

[24] *Lemon Hill and Fairmount Park: The Papers of Charles S. Keyser and Thomas Cochran Relative to a Public Park for Philadelphia,* 2nd ed., Philadelphia, 1886, 4–29. D. Schuyler, *New Urban Landscape,* 101 f. See pp. 101–108 for the following references to Fairmount Park.

[25] T. O'Malley, "Landscape Gardening in the Early National Period," in E. J. Nygren, ed., *Views and Visions: American Landscape Before 1830,* Washington, D.C., 1986, 133–59.

[26] See H. Conway, "The Manchester/Salford Parks: Their Design and Development," *Journal of Garden History* 5 (July-September 1985), 234.

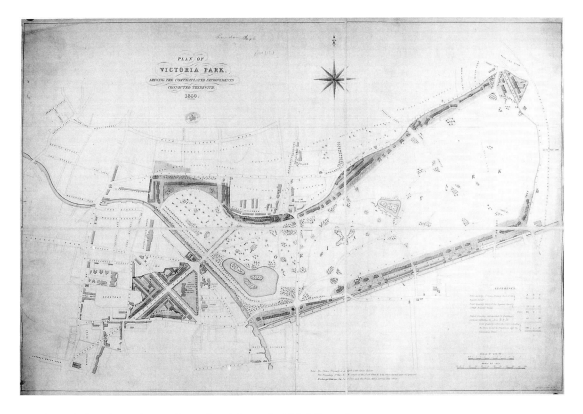

10. Plan of Victoria Park, London, 1850 (photo: British Library)

poorer suburbs with residential terraces that provided income for the acquisition and maintenance of the amenity (Fig. 10).[27]

While the English and Americans had in common the conviction that open green space was essential to the health and mental well-being of city dwellers, English park planning was more an extension of social welfare than an effort on the part of the establishment to educate and uplift the masses; in consequence the new parks were often more accessible to the slums.

As the Civil War neared and as the country was suffering a major depression, the aims of public park design shifted toward the democratic and ceased to be defined exclusively by an elite. Olmsted, in designing Central Park and its immediate successors, did not set out to educate visitors through horticultural exhibits, but simply to provide "the most agreeable contrast to the confinement, bustle and monotonous street-division of the city."[28] His parks also represented a final break with the principles of the gar-

[27] G. F. Chadwick, *The Park and the Town: Public Landscapes in the Nineteenth and Twentieth Centuries,* New York, 1966, 121–31. Contrasts between British and American practice in the planning of suburbs (in particular, Llewellyn Park) are perceptively explored in J. Archer, "Country and City in the American Romantic Suburb," *Journal of the Society of Architectural Historians* 42 (May 1983), 139–56.

[28] F. L. Olmsted, "Description of the Central Park," (January 1859) *The Papers of Frederick Law Olmsted,* III, Creating Central Park, 1857–1861, Baltimore, 1983, 212. For a valuable discussion of Olmsted's landscape theories, see T. Bender, *Toward an Urban Vision,* 161–87.

denesque, and in general of Repton and Loudon, and finally of Downing, in subordinating individual elements to a central purpose, a coherent effect. While Olmsted was a Jeffersonian with respect to his democratic convictions, he broke with that tradition in affirming the positive value of the city. The pastoral landscape he aimed to create was conceived as a way of making the city livable, of augmenting its benefits. Charles Beveridge also shows that Olmsted's highest goal was the realization of a community in which citizens take responsibility and are mutually supportive; the innovation in the design and in the social vision were interactive, and conformed to a vision quite distinct from that of the preceding generation. Though that vision was initially confined to the Northeast seaboard, it eventually appealed to planners in larger cities across the nation. It was in harmony with what the historian John Higham, in an essay of 1969 called "From Boundlessness to Consolidation" characterized as "a great turning point in our history,"[29] when the fear of disintegration and chaos, the bombastic and undisciplined individualism, gave way to "a stronger and more disciplined culture." The new "communitiveness," as Olmsted called it, characterized the Age of Lincoln—a leader who was more intent on preserving the integrity of the Union than on the abolition of slavery—in contrast to the Age of Jackson and Downing.

[29] J. Higham, *From Boundlessness to Consolidation: The Transformation of American Culture: 1848–1860*, Ann Arbor, 1969.

Regionalism in Frederick Law Olmsted's Social Thought and Landscape Design Practice

CHARLES E. BEVERIDGE

Regionalism played a significant role in Frederick Law Olmsted's thought in two different ways. One is the marked influence of regional traditions on the development of his social ideas. This influence was at work during the whole period prior to 1865 in which he received his formal education and pursued careers as a farmer, administrator, publisher, travel-writer, and social commentator. His experiences in these years helped him to define the social purpose that would underly his work as an artist. During his thirty years of practice after the Civil War, moreover, he was greatly interested in the problem of developing a distinctive style of landscape architecture for the semiarid regions of the United States. The issue of regionalism in landscape design, he believed, provided his profession with one of its greatest challenges.

A strong consciousness of the identity of his native region of New England is evident in Olmsted's social and political thought from an early period. So is an awareness of sectional antagonism between the North and the South, the East and the West. He came of age in the mid-1840s, when renewed slavery expansionism and abrogation of the Missouri Compromise of 1820 created new tensions between North and South. As he declared to a friend in the midst of the Mexican War, "You've no sort of sectional feeling—I have the strongest in the world."[1]

Even Olmsted's sectional sense, however, was based on New England values. The most comprehensive expression of that sectionalism is to be found in the books that he wrote in the late 1850s recounting his travels in the American South. His primary concern was the effect of slavery on all elements of southern society, and he concluded that all suffered from it. But his analysis clearly reflected his sectional bias. In effect, he judged the South with the values of his native New England. Degradation of free labor by slavery, he thought, caused the poor quality of work he found among slave and white workers alike—a far cry from the careful craftsmanship and conscientious working habits he at-

---

[1] Frederick Law Olmsted to Frederick J. Kingsbury, 23 September 1847, Frederick Law Olmsted Papers, Manuscript Division, Library of Congress, Washington, D.C., in C. C. McLaughlin and C. E. Beveridge, eds., *The Formative Years, 1822–1852*, The Papers of Frederick Law Olmsted 1, Baltimore, 1977, 304.

tributed to the labor force of his own region. In regard to other standards for civilized society, the South was equally bereft. Even slaveholders, he found, were seriously lacking in domestic amenities. They had to endure the lack of skill of their slave house-servants, while the pressure to invest all available capital in slaves severely limited their ability to acquire objects of art and culture. As he summarized his experience:

> From the banks of the Mississippi to the banks of the James, I did not (that I remember) see, except perhaps in one or two towns, a thermometer, nor a book of Shakespeare, nor a piano-forte or sheet of music; nor the light of a carcel or other good center-table reading-lamp, nor an engraving, or a copy of any kind, of a work of art of the slightest merit.
>
> Most of the houses, were, I should say, the mansions of "planters," "slave owners," "cotton lords" of the "southern aristocracy."[2]

Equally important for Olmsted was the existence of community. He particularly valued the physical community found in the New England town, which facilitated the exchange of services and knowledge that was a crucial element of the good society. Slavery, he concluded, caused the leaders of southern society to live in isolation and discouraged the development of towns. This in turn weakened effective demand for public education and the building of a system of roads that would facilitate commerce and the diffusion of knowledge. Whereas the Connecticut River towns including his native Hartford had long nurtured these values, areas of the South settled even earlier showed fewer signs of permanent settlement and so of civilization. As he declared in his last volume of writings on the South, "in Virginia itself, an essentially frontier condition of society prevails to this day. Beasts and birds of prey, forests and marshes are increasing; bridges, schools, churches and shops diminishing in number, where slavery has existed longest. The habits of the people correspond."[3]

Thus, slavery perpetuated in the South a "frontier condition of society" by scattering settlement and fostering agricultural practices that forced farmers constantly to seek new land. Olmsted's analysis expressed a concern about the disintegrating social effect of westward emigration: for generations, this had been a frequent theme of sermons and editorials in his native Connecticut.[4] Having examined the southern slavery frontier and found it wanting, Olmsted prescribed for it the social institutions of New England.

To a significant degree, Olmsted's work as a landscape architect represented this same desire to extend to other parts of the country the New England values that he had absorbed and embraced. His career is part of that "Greater New-Englandism" by which Yankee settlers carried their institutions of town, church congregation, and school with them across the northern tier of states from the Hudson to the Mississippi and beyond,

[2] F. L. Olmsted, *A Journey in the Back Country,* New York, 1860, 395.

[3] Ibid., 292.

[4] R. J. Purcell, *Connecticut in Transition: 1775–1818,* Middletown, Conn., 1963, 100–101; J. M. Morse, *A Neglected Period in Connecticut's History, 1818–1850,* New Haven, Conn., 1933, 20–22; H. Bushnell, *Barbarism the First Danger: A Discourse for Home Missions,* New York, 1847.

and to metropolitan centers of the Middle Atlantic states as well.[5] Olmsted himself moved from Connecticut to the New York City area at the age of twenty-six to practice scientific farming and agricultural reform. Soon he was joined by his childhood friend, Charles Loring Brace, who remained in New York City the rest of his life directing the institution he created, the Childrens' Aid Society. The Society provided living quarters and employment for street children in the city and moved many others to a supposedly more virtuous and healthful situation with farmers in the country. In this way the children secured the advantages of community and domesticity instead of the barbaric anarchy of the streets—or so Brace and his supporters believed.[6]

In his search for stable social institutions, Olmsted hoped to counteract the social forces, including individualism and materialism, that threatened the realization of his vision for America. What he found in New York City during his residence in the area between 1848 and 1861 was one part of that "triple frontier" of the South, the West, and the Metropolis with which he concerned himself in various ways prior to his final commitment to landscape architecture at the end of the Civil War.

The period of Olmsted's involvement with the South lasted from December 1852, when he began his first journey there, until the publication of his third volume, *A Journey in the Back Country*, in the summer of 1860. In the seventy-five newspaper articles he wrote on the South, and the numerous books he then published, Olmsted provided a detailed critique of the society of that region, and set forth a program of reform. He also became actively involved in opposing the expansion of slavery, securing support for antislavery Germans in Texas, and purchasing weapons for the defense of free soil settlers in Kansas.

The same process occurred in his encounter with frontier society in California. From 1863 to 1865 he was general manager of the Mariposa Estate, a 44,000-acre gold mining enterprise in the foothills of the Sierra Nevada. He was distressed by the same pattern of poor working habits and lack of community and domesticity that he had earlier encountered in the slaveholding South. The frequency with which men changed occupations and residence appalled him. As he observed to his friend Henry W. Bellows, "In this part of the State I do not know a man, woman or child, except such as are essentially savage in their habits and intentions, who intends, or is intended, to be permanently settled on the ground or among the people or under the local institutions, with which they are now associated."[7] He was dismayed by the "squatterations" that passed for settlements and set about to create a new village as a center for settlement—and civilization.

[5] See L. K. M. Rosenberry, *The Expansion of New England: The Spread of New England Settlement and Institutions to the Mississippi River, 1620–1865*, Boston, 1909.

[6] E. Brace, ed., *The Life of Charles Loring Brace Chiefly Told in His Own Letters*, New York, 1894, 153–221; R. H. Bremner, *The Public Good: Philanthropy & Welfare in the Civil War Era*, New York, 1980, 31; T. Bender, *Toward an Urban Vision: Ideas and Institutions in Nineteenth-Century America*, Lexington, Ky., 1975, 143–47.

[7] Frederick Law Olmsted to Henry W. Bellows, 28 April 1864, Henry Whitney Bellows Papers, Massachusetts Historical Society, Boston, in V. P. Ranney, G. Rauluk, and C. F. Hoffman, eds., *The California Frontier, 1863–1865*, The Papers of Frederick Law Olmsted 5, Baltimore, 1990, 227.

However disorganized the slaveholding and gold-mining frontiers might be, Olmsted eventually concluded that the great cities of the East, swarming with newcomers from both the countryside and the Old World, constituted the frontier area that presented the greatest challenge. As he observed:

> We are too apt to regard the great towns in which so many newcomers are held as old towns—old settled towns, but we have nowhere on the western frontier a population newer to its locality and so little socially rooted or in which it is possible for a man to live so isolatedly from humanizing influences and with such constant practice of heart-hardening and taste smothering habits as that to be found in our great Eastern cities.[8]

Olmsted developed a program as a landscape architect to solve this problem and pursued it for thirty years following the Civil War. He sought to build a sense of community in the cities of the East by creating public parks and recreational areas that all elements of society could share. At the same time, he designed residential areas in the suburbs that provided both physical community and a setting for domesticity. In the grounds that he designed for residences he sought to make the family home a permanent, taste-enhancing center of daily life. His decision to pursue a career in landscape design meant that he would implement his social and civilizing values through that art. At the same time, those values would play a role in shaping and sustaining his basic principles of design.

The two most fundamental tenets of Olmsted's design theory were the power of the "unconscious" action of scenery on the human psyche and the importance of creating a unified experience of landscape by separation of different kinds of spaces from each other. Drawing from his own experience and from extensive reading of works on aesthetics, philosophy, psychology, theology, and medicine, he concluded that scenery acted most powerfully when experienced in a contemplative, musing state by a process that operated below the level of conscious thought. In his earliest description of this process, relating his response to the scenery of the Isle of Wight during a walking tour of the British Isles in 1850, he wrote: "Gradually and silently the charm comes over us; we know not exactly where or how."[9] His great parks were the primary spaces that provided what he termed "*unconscious, or indirect recreation.*"[10] Their purpose was to produce "an effect on the human organism by an action of what it presents to view, which action, like that of music, is of a kind that goes back of thought, and cannot be fully given the form of words."[11]

The key to designing scenery that would act powerfully on the observer by an unconscious process was to design so that no individual elements of the scene distracted the

[8] [F. L. Olmsted], manuscript fragment, Frederick Law Olmsted Papers.
[9] [F. L. Olmsted], *Walks & Talks of an American Farmer in England*, 2, New York, 1852, 155.
[10] F. L. Olmsted, "Trees in Streets and in Parks," *The Sanitarian* 10 (1882), 518.
[11] City of Boston, Park Department [F. L. Olmsted], *Notes on the Plan of Franklin Park and Related Matters*, Boston, 1886, 107.

viewer by calling for particular attention and examination. Thus, the total subordination of all elements of a design to its central purpose, to the creation of a single, coherent effect, was the leading characteristic of Olmsted's park planning. No other landscape designer of his time adhered so consistently to this practice, or emphasized its importance so strongly. And this would not have been the case had not this part of his design theory concurred so closely with his deeply held social beliefs. The subordination of elements in a landscape was the aesthetic equivalent of the idea of community in his social thought—the subordination of individuals to the purpose of the whole community.

There was a further element to the concept of community in the Puritan social thought from which Olmsted drew; this was the belief that one of the most important purposes of life on earth was to serve others. The transcendent purpose of community was to facilitate that exchange of service.[12] The apparent lack of this tradition in the society of the slaveholding South had distressed Olmsted, and his experience in California reinforced its importance for him. As he examined his own concept of civilization while living in the mining camp of Bear Valley, he concluded that the highest point on his scale of civilization could be met only by a person who possessed what he termed "communitiveness." This was a combination of qualities that enabled one "to serve others and to be served by others in the most intimate, complete and extend[ed] degree imaginable."[13]

The concept was an old one, but for Olmsted it had a modern version. In his view, the division of labor was the most advanced form of exchange of service, with each member of the community perfecting a particular skill for the benefit of all.[14] This concept was the societal version of another basic element of his design theory, the principle of separation. He separated different kinds of landscape effects in order to avoid an "incongruous mixture of styles" that would weaken the psychological effect of each, and he separated different activities so that each could have a space carefully prepared to meet its special requirements. The separation of landscape styles was fundamental to his designing of parks, while the separation of activities was the basic principal of his park systems. And, as with the subordination of elements in a design, the separation of functions in his parks and park systems reflected a parallel principle in his social thought— in this case the importance of division of labor.

While the traditions of his native New England played an important role in shaping Olmsted's ideas, he was far from being a regionalist, or even a self-conscious nationalist, in his concept of what an American art of landscape should be. He did not feel that such an art should be based on "local-color" or be in any way provincial in character. He felt himself to be a part of the culture of Europe and intended to make a significant contribu-

[12] P. Miller, *The New England Mind: From Colony to Province*, Cambridge, Mass., 1953, 40–42; P. Miller, *Errand Into the Wilderness*, Cambridge, Mass., 1956, 142–43.

[13] F. L. Olmsted, "The Pioneer Condition and the Drift of Civilization in America," in Ranney, Rauluk, and Hoffman, *California Frontier*, 659; F. L. Olmsted, *Public Parks and the Enlargement of Towns*, Cambridge, Mass., 1870, 6–7.

[14] Olmsted, "Pioneer Condition," 660–67.

tion to its art. While American thinkers like Horace Bushnell, Ralph Waldo Emerson, and Andrew Jackson Downing strongly influenced his ideas, he drew even more heavily from British writers. Even as a youth he had immersed himself in the writings of English landscape and gardening theorists, and Thomas Carlyle, John Stuart Mill, and John Ruskin were of paramount importance to the development of his philosophical, economic, and aesthetic beliefs.

Olmsted, then, believed that his art should be international, not simply American. Even more important, he wanted his art to be universal. What he sought was not simply European precedents—historical styles and examples that would justify his work. Rather, he spent his career in a painstaking and arduous search for the fundamental psychological principles that underlay human response to scenery. As he described his quest to Charles Eliot Norton:

> Now & then I do meet a man who says: "I know what you think and I think—" with me or otherwise as may happen, but always with the assumption that I have original and peculiar ideas and am not what I only want to be, the expounder, vindicator and applyer of views which are—not views at all but well established science.[15]

In his search, Olmsted drew from the writings of a number of philosophers, from the teachings of English landscape theorists, and from his own experience. In the end, all three sources sanctified what Edmund Burke had defined as the Beautiful, and what Olmsted called the Pastoral, landscape style. That kind of scenery, Olmsted concluded, conferred great psychological benefits. It provided a specific antidote to the confinement and artificiality of city life. An expanse of gently rolling greensward, constantly opening new vistas as one moved through it, with indefinite edges and the promise of limitless space beyond, made possible the release and relaxation that all people in a large city needed (Fig. 1). The "range" of such landscape produced the "unbending of faculties" that was the most restorative experience for those living in close-packed cities.[16] Olmsted was convinced of the beneficial effect of such scenery, and he made it the central feature of his great parks. Even on the rugged and rocky site of lower Central Park in New York he created the Sheep Meadow, at great expense, so that those coming to the park would have such scenery within easy walking distance of the entrances at Fifty-ninth Street.

As he sought to understand the process by which the healing effect of pastoral scenery took place, Olmsted found both a psychological basis for it and a historical one. In his most comprehensive discussion of the question, he analyzed the way that pastoral scenery appealed to "the common & elementary impulses of all classes of mankind." The process of park design, then, was to

---

[15] Frederick Law Olmsted to Charles Eliot Norton, 19 October 1881, Charles Eliot Norton Papers, Houghton Library, Harvard University, Cambridge, Mass.

[16] Olmsted, Vaux & Company, "Report of the Landscape Architects," 24 January 1866, in Brooklyn. Park Commissioners, *Annual Reports of the Brooklyn Park Commissioners, 1861–1873*, Brooklyn, N.Y., 1873, 93–97.

1. The Long Meadow, Prospect Park, Brooklyn, New York (photo: National Park Service, Frederick Law Olmsted National Historic Site, Brookline, Massachusetts)

study to secure a combination of elements which shall invite and stimulate the simplest purest and most primeval action of the poetic element of human nature, and thus tend to remove those who are affected by it to the greatest possible distance from the highly elaborate, sophistical and artificial condition of their ordinary civilized life.[17]

To illustrate this concept, Olmsted described his experience while crossing the plains of Texas on horseback with his brother in 1853. They camped near streams for wood and water, and on high ground within protecting groves of trees whereby they had both shelter and prospect for espying marauding border ruffians and Indian bands. Such landscape, Olmsted mused, had offered a welcome home for the human race since tribes first spread onto open savannahs at the dawn of herding culture. He concluded that human beings had a special affinity for pastoral landscape that stemmed from the experience of thousands of years.

Olmsted believed, therefore, that he was drawing from a source far more profound than the taste of the British aristocracy when he created pastoral landscapes in public parks. Even so, the challenge of producing the effect he desired outside the climate of England was a daunting one. A rich, green turf was essential to that effect, and depended

[17] Frederick Law Olmsted, address to the Prospect Park Scientific Association, 1868, National Park Service, Frederick Law Olmsted National Historic Site, Brookline, Mass.

on a cool and rainy climate. As he expressed the problem to his protégé and partner Henry Sargent Codman while traveling in England near the end of his career:

> ... such is the advantage of temperate & moist climate, there is nothing in America to be compared with the pastoral or with the picturesque beauty that is common property in England. I cannot go out without being delighted. The view before me as I write, veiled by the rain, is just enchanting. Sometimes the question comes to me, whether, even in the Atlantic slopes, we are not so far removed in climatic conditions from those on which this pastoral beauty depends that it is futile to contend with our difficulties. But when I ask what is the alternative, I always conclude that we must be only the more fertile in expedients to make the most of our opportunities.[18]

Even so, Olmsted became convinced that broad areas of greensward could not be sustained south of Pennsylvania or west of Missouri except at prohibitive cost for watering. He concluded his exposition to Codman by declaring, "The absurdity of seeking for good pastoral beauty in the far West is more & more manifest." As we shall see, it was primarily through his work in the semiarid American West that Olmsted came to develop a comprehensive and imaginative series of design principles to deal with the challenge posed by limited rainfall in regions of the South and West. It was the regions of the United States that could not sustain greensward that created the need for a distinctive new style of landscape design.

The extent to which affordable greensward was the dominant issue in Olmsted's concept of regional landscape design can be seen in his approach to design commissions for New England and the Midwest. He often used the particular "genius of the place" in those areas to find the key for his designs, but his concern in those instances was the individual site rather than the general character of the region. Olmsted's willingness to design broad expanses of greensward is evident in his plan for Franklin Park in Boston, his largest New England park (Figs. 2, 3). It is true that in Massachusetts he made extensive use of "the stones of the place" (as Robert Frost called them in his poem with that title). Working with Henry Hobson Richardson in particular, Olmsted planned rough fieldstone bridges for the Back Bay Fens and structures of similar character in Franklin Park. For the town of North Easton, the site of several collaborations with Richardson, he created a massive stone memorial cairn as the central feature of the public space in front of the town hall (Fig. 4).[19] Elsewhere, at his own home and on the estates of J. C. Phillips in North Beverly (Fig. 5), Robert Treat Paine in Waltham and Charles Storrow in Brookline, he created fieldstone terraces and arches that emphasized the rocky character of those sites.[20] But he did not describe this stonework as an element of a distinctive

[18] Frederick Law Olmsted to Henry Sargent Codman, 30 July 1892, Frederick Law Olmsted Papers.

[19] C. Zaitzevsky, *Frederick Law Olmsted and the Boston Park System*, Cambridge, Mass., 1982, 164–79; Frederick Law Olmsted to Oakes Ames, 10 April 1882, Frederick Law Olmsted Papers.

[20] Frederick Law Olmsted to Robert Treat Paine, letterpress book A1, 244–46, Olmsted Associates Records, Manuscript Division, Library of Congress, Washington, D.C.

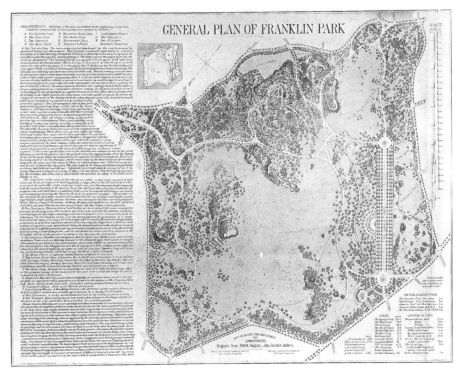

2. Frederick Law Olmsted, "General Plan of Franklin Park," Boston, Massachusetts, 1885. Lithograph (photo: National Park Service, Frederick Law Olmsted National Historic Site, Brookline, Massachusetts)

3. Pastoral landscape, Franklin Park, Boston, Massachusetts, 1904 (photo: National Park Service, Frederick Law Olmsted National Historic Site, Brookline, Massachusetts)

217

4. Memorial cairn, North Easton, Massachusetts (photo: National Park Service, Frederick Law Olmsted National Historic Site, Brookline, Massachusetts)

5. Rockwork arch, with summer house by Peabody & Stearns, J. C. Phillips Estate, North Beverly, Massachusetts (photo: private collection)

regional landscape style. In any case, he had begun the use of rough rockwork with bridges in Central Park before the Civil War.[21]

Olmsted carried out several significant commissions in the Midwest, but none were outside the area that he judged suitable for creating pastoral scenery. In the Chicago region, where his work was most extensive, he took the principal landscape features of the area, prairie and lakeshore, for his theme. The plan that he and Calvert Vaux prepared for the city's South Park in 1871 contained these two kinds of landscape (Fig. 6). In the section that later became known as Washington Park, a flat, inland site, the two partners used the theme of prairie for a pastoral park of nearly five hundred acres. The section that became Jackson Park, consisting of beach-front and marsh, they proposed to transform into a "water-park," with sinuous, protected waterways, and numerous islands for picnicking and raising waterfowl.

Still, Olmsted did not seek to create a distinctly midwestern landscape style by his design projects in that region. The two landscape themes he chose for Washington and Jackson parks, for instance, were the universal styles in which he usually chose to work, the pastoral and the picturesque. It was not a prairie that he sought to create in Washington Park but rather a piece of pastoral scenery such as he had already constructed in the upper meadow and Sheep Meadow of Central Park and the Long Meadow of Prospect Park in Brooklyn (Fig. 7). Nor did he seek to create a "prairie river" in the lagoons of Jackson Park, however similar his work was to later designs bearing that name by Jens Jensen and O. C. Simonds. Instead, he envisioned a rich and profusely planted passage of picturesque scenery whose inspiration was the lush vegetation of the Panama rainforest and the semitropical coast of the Isle of Wight. The chief qualities of such scenery, which Olmsted sought to evoke in his designs, were the "profuse careless utterance of Nature" as evinced in a rich variety of vegetation, and its mystery, as evoked by brilliantly sunlit foliage and dark shadows.[22] The tropical inspiration for Olmsted's lagoon plantings had been evident in the original 1871 report on the Chicago South Park, which observed:

> You certainly cannot set the madrepore or the mangrove at work on the banks of Lake Michigan, you cannot naturalize bamboo or papyrus, aspiring palm or waving parasites, but you *can* set firm barriers to the violence of winds and waves, and make shores as intricate, as arborescent and as densely overhung with foliage as any. You can have placid and limpid water within these shores that will mirror and double all above it as truly as any, and thus, if you cannot reproduce the tropical forest in all its mysterious depths of shade and visionary reflections of light, you can secure a combination of the fresh and healthy nature of the North with the restful, dreamy nature of the South that would in our judgment be admirably fitted to the general purposes of any park, not only on account of the present

---

[21] See C. E. Beveridge and D. Schuyler, eds., *Creating Central Park, 1857–1861*, The Papers of Frederick Law Olmsted 3, Baltimore, 1983, 32–33.

[22] Frederick Law Olmsted to Mary Perkins Olmsted, 25 September 1863, Frederick Law Olmsted Papers, in Ranney, Rauluk, and Hoffman, *California Frontier*, 80, 83; Frederick Law Olmsted to Ignaz Pilat, 26 September 1863, in Ranney, Rauluk, and Hoffman, *California Frontier*, 85.

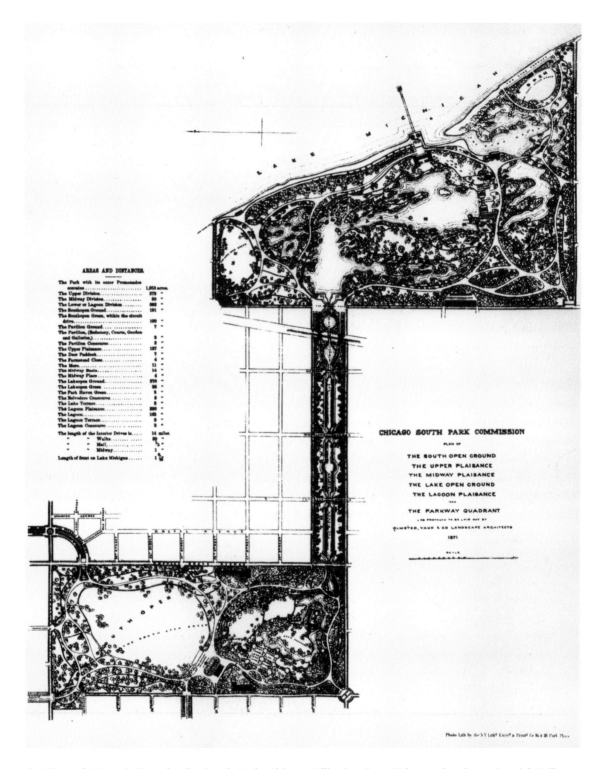

6. Olmsted, Vaux & Co., plan for South Park, Chicago, Illinois, 1871. Lithograph (photo: Special Collections, Chicago Park District)

7. Pastoral scenery of "Southopen Ground," Washington Park, Chicago, Illinois (photo: Chicago Historical Society)

intensely wide-awake character of its people, but because of the special quality of the scenery about Chicago in which flat and treeless prairie and limitless expanse of lake are such prominent characteristics.[23]

When he came to plan the lagoon of the World's Columbian Exposition (Fig. 8), Olmsted offered a similar conception:

> The thing is to make it appear that we *found* this body of water and its shores and have done nothing to them except at the landings and bridges. They were rich, rank, luxurious, crowded with vegetation, like the banks of some tropical rivers that I have seen on Louisiana bayous. The vegetation must appear spontaneous and thoroughly wild (to all unlearned visitors).[24]

Olmsted used great numbers of plants gathered near Chicago in his planting of the lagoon, but he was not attempting to recreate the natural scenery of the site, for as he observed, "The natural condition of the locality is a swamp. Chicago has grown out of a swamp, and as far as I know a swamp without beauty. Let us try to show the possible beauty of a swamp, even without trees."[25] This beauty depended on density and lushness

[23] Olmsted, Vaux & Company, *Report Accompanying Plan for Laying Out the South Park*, Chicago, 1871, 6.

[24] Frederick Law Olmsted to Rudolph Ulrich, 24 March 1891, letterpress book A13, 185, Olmsted Associates Records.

[25] Ibid., 186–87.

8. Section of lagoon, World's Columbian Exposition, Chicago, Illinois, 1893 (photo: Library of Congress)

of vegetation, creating a greater sense of profusion, richness and mystery than could be found in the natural scenery of the region. But while the experience transcended what nature could achieve unassisted, most of the plants were local. On the shores of the lagoon were planted over one million plants, including one hundred thousand small willows, seventy-five large railroad flatcar-loads of aquatic plants taken from the wild, one hundred forty thousand other aquatic plants (mostly irises), and two hundred eighty-five thousand ferns and other perennial herbaceous plants.[26] Only occasionally in the screen of foliage did Olmsted propose to use plants from other climatic regions, as an enrichment of his palette. And even these, he directed, should merge into the landscape composition and not stand out as specimens or exotics:

> While the greater number of plants to be used will be such as are indigenous
> to the river banks and swamps of Northern Illinois, and therefore hardy, in order

[26] F. L. Olmsted, "Report upon the Landscape Architecture of the Columbian Exposition to the American Institute of Architects," *American Architect and Building News* (9 September 1893), 153.

to increase intricacy and richness of general effect, many are to be scattered among them that a botanist looking closely, would know could not have grown in the locality naturally. The work is thus to be in some degree of the character of a theatrical scene, to occupy the Exposition stage for a single Summer. But it is not intended that the slightly exotic forms of verdure to be thus used shall call, any more than the flowers, for individual notice. Rather, seen as they will generally be, at some distance, they will merge indistinguishably with other forms of verdure, and not suggest a question as to what they are, or how they have come to be where they are.[27]

Unlike New England and the Midwest, Olmsted viewed the American South as a problematic region for creating and maintaining greensward, and so an important area in which to develop a distinctive regional style of landscape design that provided an alternative to broad expanses of turf. However, he seems to have accomplished little in this regard in the dozen projects he undertook south of the Mason-Dixon Line. The fact that several of these were in border states and Washington, D.C. may account for his lack of innovation. One of his commissions was the U.S. Capitol grounds. The massive terrace he designed for the newly expanded building was the most striking element of his plan, but in both the eastern and western sections of the grounds he created areas of turf and scattered trees in order to provide a feeling of cool shade, expanse, and repose (Fig. 9). Likewise, considerable portions of his campus plans for Gallaudet University and The American University in the District of Columbia consisted of parklike settings of greensward and trees. His two principal designs in the Baltimore area were the four small rectangles of ground adjoining the Washington Monument in Mount Vernon Square and the suburban residential community of Sudbrook. There was no room for expanse of greensward on the Mount Vernon Square site, and he proposed that each panel of ground receive a design emblematic and evocative of one of the four seasons.[28] The open common ground, "Cliveden Green," that he included in the Sudbrook plan contained only eight and one-half acres, but it was the largest public space that he had proposed for a residential community since the plan for Riverside, Illinois, in 1869, twenty years earlier.[29]

Olmsted's approach to the park system of Louisville, Kentucky, beginning in 1891, shows no obvious or clearly enunciated attempt to find alternatives to greensward for large public parks. It is true that the plan for 300-acre Cherokee Park contained no single open area that even approached in size the broad meadows in his large northern parks, although he planned numerous open glades among the groves of trees on the hilly site

[27] Frederick Law Olmsted, "Memorandum as to What Is to Be Aimed at in the Planting of the Lagoon District of the Chicago Exposition, as Proposed March, 1891," letterpress book A13, 174–75, Olmsted Associates Records.

[28] Frederick Law Olmsted to J. M. Lanahan, 23 December 1876, Frederick Law Olmsted Papers.

[29] F. L. Olmsted and Company, *General Plan for Sudbrook, the Property of the Sudbrook Co. of Baltimore Co. Maryland*, Boston, 1889.

9. Frederick Law Olmsted, "General Plan for the Improvement of the U.S. Capitol Grounds," Washington, D.C., 1875. Lithograph (photo: National Park Service, Frederick Law Olmsted National Historic Site, Brookline, Massachusetts)

224

(Fig. 10).[30] The terrain of the park, steeper and more convoluted than that of any of his other large pastoral spaces, may have been the determining consideration for this aspect of the design. The most distinctly regional element of the Cherokee Park plan was Olmsted's proposal to include a collection of the woody plants of Kentucky, consisting of three hundred species in forty-three families.[31] However, his willingness to create a large area of greensward in the Louisville climate is evident in his plan for Shawnee Park on flat tableland along the Ohio River in the western section of the city. The central feature of the plan (Fig. 11) was a 35-acre area that was to serve as a public common, providing the city with "broad and tranquil meadowy spaces, with, by and by, the shadows of great spreading trees slanting across them, and offering at once areas of turf to be inexpensively kept in a suitable condition for lawn games."[32]

The public grounds that Olmsted included in his plan for the residential neighborhood of Druid Hills in northern Atlanta, Georgia, were each small in size and had limited areas of greensward (Fig. 12). In that project, he began to experiment with the use of ground cover and other alternatives to turf. He arranged for creation of a nursery of plant materials that included thirty kinds of ground cover.[33] But the actual selection of plant materials and planting program took place during the second stage of planning the community, several years after his retirement.[34]

Olmsted's most ambitious attempt to select plant materials for use in the South came in 1889 with his commission to plan the grounds of George W. Vanderbilt's vast estate, "Biltmore," near Asheville, North Carolina. Biltmore was Olmsted's last major project in the South. He rejected Vanderbilt's proposal to create a great park as a setting for Richard Morris Hunt's grandiose version of a French chateau. Instead, he reserved for landscape treatment only a strip on each side of the three-mile approach road and a series of

---

[30] F. L. and J. C. Olmsted, *General Plan for Cherokee Park*, 1 December 1897, Frederick Law Olmsted National Historic Site.

[31] Olmsted, Olmsted & Eliot to John B. Castleman, 4 January 1895, letterpress book A39, 840–41, Olmsted Associates Records; F. L. and J. C. Olmsted, "List of Plants Desired by Park Commission of Louisville, Ky. to Complete a Collection of Woody Plants of the State at Cherokee Park," 22 September 1897, letterpress book A54, 392, Olmsted Associates Records: F. L. and J. C. Olmsted, "Cherokee Park. Collection of Woody Plants of Kentucky," 20 December 1897, letterpress book A55, 543, Olmsted Associates Records.

[32] Frederick Law Olmsted to Thomas H. Sherley, 26 August 1891, letterpress book A16, 590, Olmsted Associates Records, in "Report of F. L. Olmsted & Co., Landscape Architects," in Board of Park Commissioners of the City of Louisville, *First Annual Report*, Louisville, Ky., 1891, 663.

[33] [Olmsted, Olmsted & Eliot], "Kirkwood Land Company. A List of Plants Recommended a Nursery," 5 February 1894, letterpress book A32, 294–95, Olmsted Associates Records. Ground cover plants were to include: *Arctostaphylos uva-ursi* (common bearberry), *Daphne cneorum* (garland flower), *Euonymus radicans*, *Euonymus radicans* 'Carierri,' *Rubus hispidus* (swamp blackberry), *Lycium barbarum* (matrimony vine), *Cotoneaster microphylla*, *Cotoneaster congesta*, *Cytisus purpureus*, *Rubus fruticosus* ("English bramble"), *Polygala chamaebuxus*, *Hypericum calycinum* (Rose-of-Sharon), *Vinca minor* (periwinkle), all of which were to be purchased for the nursery, as well as the following, which were to be collected in the South: *Gaylussacia brachycera*, *Leiophyllum buxifolium* (sand myrtle), *Yucca smalliana* (bear grass), *Xanthorhiza apiifolia* (shrub yellow-root), *Euonymus americana* 'Obovatus' (bursting-heart), *Veronica officinalis* (gypsy weed), and *Lonicera japonica* 'Flexuosa.'

[34] See E. A. Lyon, "Frederick Law Olmsted and Joel Hurt: Planning for Atlanta," in D. F. White and V. A. Kramer, eds., *Olmsted South: Old South Critic/New South Planner*, Westport, Conn., 1979, 165–82.

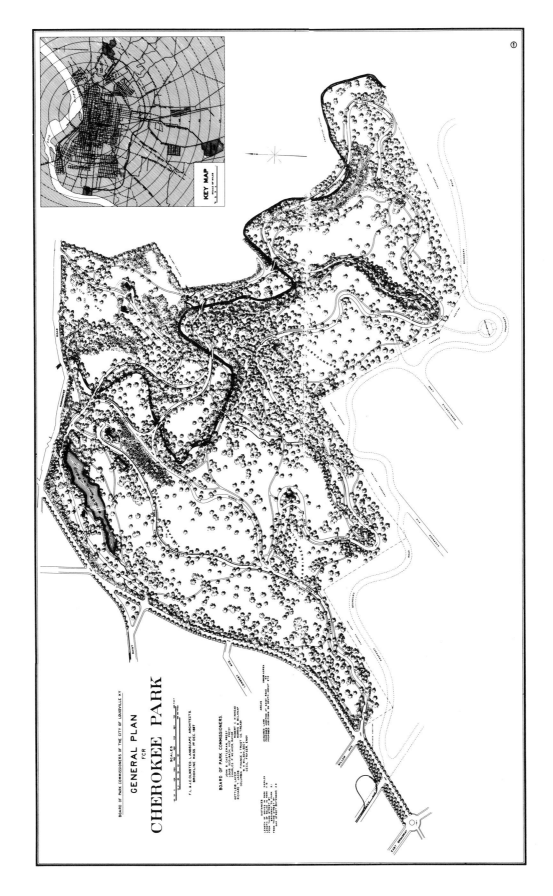

10. F. L. & J. C. Olmsted, "General Plan for Cherokee Park," Louisville, Kentucky, 1897. Lithograph (photo: National Park Service, Frederick Law Olmsted National Historic Site, Brookline, Massachusetts)

226

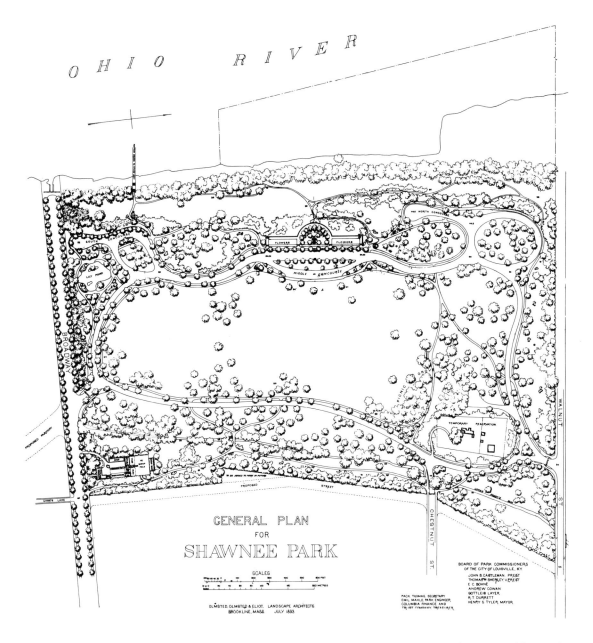

11. Olmsted, Olmsted & Eliot, "General Plan for Shawnee Park," Louisville, Kentucky, 1893. Lithograph (photo: National Park Service, Frederick Law Olmsted National Historic Site, Brookline, Massachusetts)

enclosed spaces near the mansion. Of these, only a narrow "Esplanade" and hillside facing the east front of the mansion was planted as lawn (Figs. 13, 14). Several acres of hillside below the mansion, in the direction of the French Broad river and the principal view from the site, were also kept as an open "deer park." On the remaining thousands of acres of the estate, Olmsted convinced Vanderbilt to carry out the first extensive American experiment in scientific forestry.

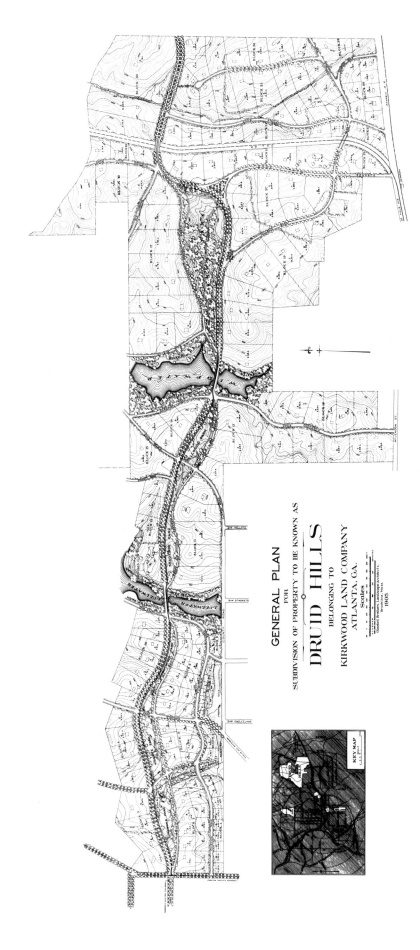

12. Olmsted Brothers, "General Plan for Subdivision of Property to be Known as Druid Hills Belonging to Kirkwood Land Company," Atlanta, Georgia, 1905. Lithograph (photo: National Park Service, Frederick Law Olmsted National Historic Site, Brookline, Massachusetts)

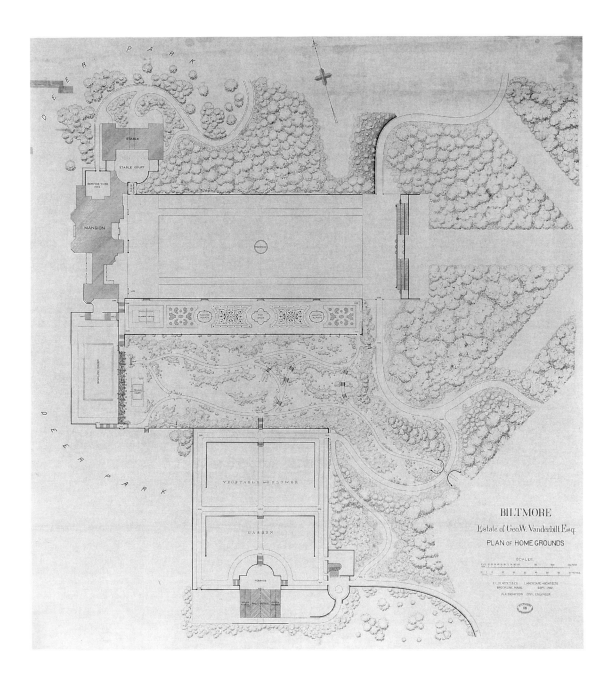

13. F. L. Olmsted & Co., "Biltmore, Estate of Geo. W. Vanderbilt, Esq., Plan of Home Grounds," near
    Asheville, North Carolina, ca. 1892. Lithograph (photo: Biltmore Company, Asheville, North Carolina)

14. View of "Home Grounds," Biltmore Estate, near Asheville, North Carolina, ca. 1895 (photo: National Park Service, Frederick Law Olmsted National Historic Site, Brookline, Massachusetts)

The most important aspect of the Biltmore project for Olmsted, however, was the great arboretum that he began to create there. In it he proposed to display and test for hardiness all the plant materials that could be expected to thrive in that region. He intended to display most species of trees as individual specimens and in a landscape setting. Thus the arboretum would both establish the range of palette of vegetation available to landscape designers in the South, and display to the public the appearance of many trees and shrubs.[35] The Biltmore arboretum was one of his most ambitious projects and his last, a sign of the importance he attached to devising a distinctive kind of landscape architecture for the South. The climate of the Blue Ridge at Asheville was more severe than that of the urbanized areas further south and at lower altitude, however, so that the Biltmore arboretum, as Olmsted observed, was to serve primarily as a demonstration ground for plant materials for "the middle region of the Southern States."[36] Even had it been completed, the Biltmore arboretum could have provided only a general and incomplete guide to dealing with the problems of landscape architecture in much of the South.

The region where Olmsted felt it was most important to develop a new and original landscape style was the semiarid American West. As he described the problem to his son in Colorado during the last weeks of his own practice:

> I need not say that the great puzzle of our profession for the future, for your period, is going to be how to deal satisfactorily with the difficulties of the more arid parts of our continent. . . . It is not improbable that the principle [sic] field for originality in our profession for what may be called a new school of L.A., will be found in the future, just where you are.[37]

In his own attempts to solve the problem, Olmsted looked to the practices of the Mediterranean region. He drew from his memory of Italy in 1856, before he began his landscape career, and his observations during a two-week return visit in 1878. In addition, he sent his protégés Charles Eliot and Henry Sargent Codman to that region to find examples to emulate. He also examined photographs of Spanish gardens but found no contemporary examples that provided useful suggestions. "There is no landscape work," he lamented, "no agreeable foreground (domestic) landscape, and the decorative gardening work seemed to me either forlorn or puerile & frittering."[38]

The set of principles for creating landscape designs in semiarid regions that Olmsted developed during his career was four-fold:

[35] Frederick Law Olmsted to Frederick J. Kingsbury, 20 January 1891, Frederick Law Olmsted Papers; F. L. Olmsted, "George W. Vanderbilt's Nursery," *The Lyceum* (Asheville, N.C.), December 1891, 5–7; Frederick Law Olmsted to Charles S. Sargent, 25 April 1895, letterpress book H2, 94, Olmsted Associates Records; Frederick Law Olmsted to "Dear Partners," 25 May 1895, Frederick Law Olmsted Papers.

[36] Frederick Law Olmsted to James McNamee, 6 October 1894, letterpress book A36, 286, Olmsted Associates Records.

[37] Frederick Law Olmsted to Frederick Law Olmsted, Jr., 1 August 1895, Frederick Law Olmsted Papers.

[38] Frederick Law Olmsted to Henry Sargent Codman, 30 July 1892, Frederick Law Olmsted Papers.

First, to leave little bare ground, such as would be covered with turf in more humid climates, exposed to view close to the point of outlook.

Second, to arrange heavily used areas and the foregrounds of buildings in such fashion that it would be "comparatively easy to so apply water to them that they may be kept clean, fresh and in nice order."

Third, to arrange the foregrounds of views, through raised and dense planting, so that the dry middle distance would be obscured and the features in view would be sufficiently far away that they would not appear dry and dusty.

Fourth, to plant so that buildings, terraces, and other architectural elements would be covered with vines and crowded about with plants needing little water, thus achieving "a picturesquely intimate association of natural and artificial objects."[39]

Olmsted's final enunciation of these principles resulted from his work on two projects in Colorado in the early 1890s. One of these was a village for the Denver and Lookout Mountain Resort Company, and the other was a summer colony in Perry Park, near Larkspur, thirty miles south of Denver. However, even his earliest projects in the semiarid West, beginning in the San Francisco Bay area in 1864, contained the basic elements of his approach to the problem.

Numerous features of Olmsted's plans for the campus of the College of California at Berkeley and for a system of pleasure grounds for the city of San Francisco illustrate what he intended to achieve by following these concepts. He realized that much of the college campus and adjoining residential areas of the "Berkeley Neighborhood" that he designed in 1865 would not be built on for a long time, and so he proposed dense plantings along the roads running through the property that would screen out the "harsh brown surface" of the nearby land. For the residences he hoped to have constructed near the college buildings, Olmsted developed one of his most important ideas—the concept that the rich, green foregrounds of the houses would serve two purposes. First, they would block out the dusty middle distance and heighten the visual impact of distant water and hills by the "perspective effect" thus achieved; and second, those densely planted areas would provide a pleasing, verdant foreground for residences behind them. Succinctly put, a situation would then be created where one person's foreground was another person's middle distance, and much of the unpleasant visual effect of aridity in the dry season would be ameliorated. Nonetheless, Olmsted believed that some expanse of turf was necessary in any community and so made provisions for a 27-acre area of greensward in a dell near Strawberry Creek in the lower part of the property.

In his proposal for a system of pleasure grounds in San Francisco, drawn up in 1865–66, Olmsted applied the ideas of limiting the area to be watered and restricting views of the middle distance in a different way. He rejected the idea of creating a pastoral park in the city and proposed instead a series of public spaces linked by a sunken "Promenade" for pedestrians, carriages, and equestrians, twenty feet or more deep and fifty yards wide running from the harbor to a point four miles inland (Fig. 15). The steep

[39] See Frederick Law Olmsted to A. E. Fisk, 21 April 1890, letterpress book A7, 3, Olmsted Associates Records.

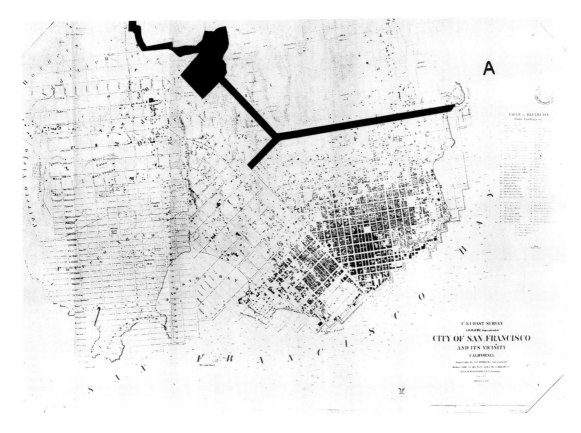

15. Map of San Francisco with outline of Olmsted's proposed Public Pleasure Grounds superimposed. Lithograph with pen and ink (photo: from Olmsted, Vaux & Co., *Preliminary Report in Regard to a Plan of Public Pleasure Grounds for the City of San Francisco*, New York, 1866; courtesy of the Frances Loeb Library, Graduate School of Design, Harvard University)

sides of the promenade would be planted heavily with drought-tolerant shrubs and could be watered when needed from hydrants set along its top edge (Fig. 16).[40] The slope would be kept adequately green, while the sinking of the promenade below street level would hide from view the dusty undeveloped lots nearby. At the inland end of the promenade would be a small parklike area containing the irreducible minimum of turf that Olmsted felt the city's residents should have available for their refreshment. Since broad landscape treatment was not possible in the narrow promenade area, Olmsted did not feel constrained to subordinate all elements of the design to creation of a single, unified experience, as was the case in his large urban parks in the East. Instead, he proposed a number of horticultural and zoological displays to add interest and variety. Sections of the promenade, he suggested, could be devoted to different kinds of horticultural displays:

[40] The plant materials that Olmsted proposed to use on side slopes of the San Francisco Promenade included "smooth-leaved evergreen shrubs and vines" with which to create a "Winter Garden" effect, as well as numerous common shrubs and small trees that he proposed to have gathered from the canyons of the coast range; see Ranney, Rauluk, and Hoffman, *California Frontier*, 540–41.

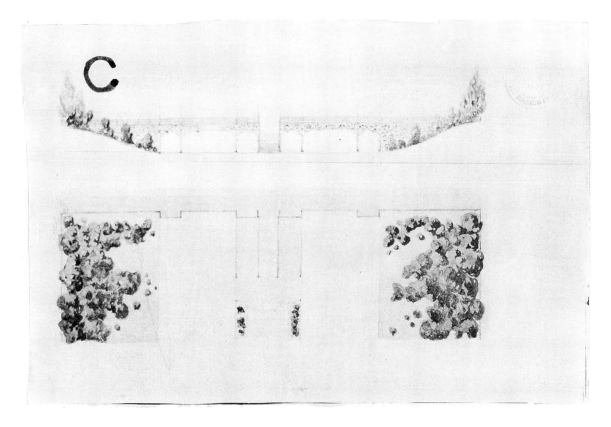

16. Plan of a section of the San Francisco "Promenade," shown in elevation and bird's-eye view. Pen and ink drawing (photo: from Olmsted, Vaux & Co., *Preliminary Report in Regard to a Plan of Public Pleasure Grounds for the City of San Francisco*, New York, 1866; courtesy of the Frances Loeb Library, Graduate School of Design, Harvard University)

. . . at some point, the border may be decorated with vases elevated on pedestals, baskets of flowers, yuccas, aloes, orange trees, or other exotic plants in tubs. . . . Another section of the mall should be planted with fastigiate trees and shrubs, another with cactuses, another with standard roses, another with a particular class of flowering shrubs, another with creeping plants pegged down, another with a vegetable embroidery upon fine turf, another with beds of tulips, of violets, or of callas, etc.[41]

In addition to this horticultural display, he suggested other exhibits of educational and entertainment value, including "fountains, statues, cages of birds, dove cotes, rabbit hutches, small paddocks of gazelles or antelopes, tanks of aquatic plants, globes of fish, or such suitable objects of art or curiosity, as may from time to time be acquired by the city, either as gifts or by purchase."[42] So far from his usual concept of what was appropriate in a park was Olmsted willing to depart under the peculiar climatic conditions of California.

[41] F. L. Olmsted, *Preliminary Report in Regard to a Plan of Public Pleasure Grounds for the City of San Francisco*, New York, 1866, in Ranney, Rauluk, and Hoffman, *California Frontier*, 540.

[42] Ranney, Rauluk, and Hoffman, *California Frontier*, 540.

However, by the time Olmsted completed his report and plans in the spring of 1866, the opportunity to carry out his conception had been lost. The subsequent story of park-planning for San Francisco illustrates the continuing difficulty he encountered in weaning Californians from the landscaping practices of the eastern states. When William Hammond Hall, newly appointed engineer and superintendent of Golden Gate Park, requested Olmsted's comments on his plan to create a park that closely resembled Central Park in New York in both shape and expanse of turf, it was difficult to frame a diplomatic response. (Hall proposed to devote some two hundred of the park's thousand acres to parklike greensward and groves and picnic areas.)[43] The project was an enigma for Olmsted from the start, since he felt that no large parklike public space could appropriately be built in San Francisco. Several times between 1871 and 1886 he offered comments on the progress of the park, always obliquely suggesting that his San Francisco pleasure grounds report of 1866 be consulted and its precepts followed. The argument that heavy irrigation was prohibitively expensive could have little influence in this case, since a large natural reservoir of fresh water had been discovered beneath the park. But the issue of cost was by no means Olmsted's sole concern. He firmly believed that the climate of California had created a unique set of natural conditions that should be dealt with by experimentation and originality. Only by consulting the "genius of the place" could the full possibilities and promise of the Golden Gate Park undertaking be realized. As he urged in one of his last statements on the issue:

> Cutting yourself completely clear of the traditions of Europe and the East, and shaping your course in details by no rigorously predetermined design, but as you find from year to year that nature is leading you on, you will, I feel sure, be able to give San Francisco a pleasure ground adapted to the peculiar wants of her people, with a scenery as unusual in parks as the conditions social, climatic, and of the soil, to which your design is required to be accommodated.[44]

The desire for copious use of water and its effects persisted in San Francisco, however, and Olmsted's suggestions had little influence on the development of Golden Gate Park.

Olmsted's last opportunity to see his ideas realized in California came in the mid-1880s with the creation of Stanford University. He devoted considerable energy to planning the Stanford campus, and proposed to employ there the full set of principles for semiarid landscape design that he had developed over two decades. The interior of the main Quad was to be paved and so would be easy to sweep and keep clean. The colonnaded walk around the Quad provided shelter from sun and rain, while the eight densely planted circles within it produced a lush concentration of vegetation that required watering only a small part of the whole space (Fig. 17). Leland Stanford refused to site the university on the Palo Alto hills as Olmsted proposed, which would have secured distant

[43] R. H. Clary, *The Making of Golden Gate Park, The Early Years: 1865–1906*, San Francisco, 1980, 15–27.
[44] Frederick Law Olmsted to William Hammond Hall, 1874, in "Extracts from Letters Found of Record in the Files of the Board of Park Commissioners," in San Francisco. Board of Park Commissioners, *The Development of Golden Gate Park and Particularly the Management and Thinning of Its Forest Trees . . .*, San Francisco, 1886, 31–32.

17. F. L. & J. C. Olmsted, "The Le-
land Stanford Junior Univer-
sity, Plan of Central Premises,
1888," Palo Alto, California.
Lithograph (photo: National
Park Service, Frederick Law
Olmsted National Historic Site,
Brookline, Massachusetts)

views and a layered series of planted foregrounds and middle distances. But in at least
one part of the site, Olmsted was able to demonstrate his approach to that issue. For the
whole width of the area in front of the central Quad he created a sunken area with two
wide walks in the form of an oval leading to the central entry-arch of the Quad (Fig. 18).
This area was to be planted with shrubs requiring little water, creating a dense foreground of foliage over which the eye could range eastward toward lower San Francisco
Bay, enhancing the distant view. Should turf be used instead, he warned Stanford, the
whole area would be "unsuitable, dreary and forlorn" in the dry season unless watered
at unjustifiable expense.[45] However, as construction progressed the Olmsted firm had
less and less influence on the form of the Stanford campus. When the university opened

[45] Frederick Law Olmsted to Leland Stanford, 27 November 1886, Frederick Law Olmsted Papers.

236

18. Shepley, Rutan & Coolidge, and F. L. and J. C. Olmsted, "The Leland Stanford Jr. University," Palo Alto, California. Lithograph (photo: National Park Service, Frederick Law Olmsted National Historic Site, Brookline, Massachusetts)

in 1891, Olmsted sent Stanford a stiff, formal note of congratulation, having learned of the event in the newspapers.[46] He had long since lost influence over the development of the campus to whose early stages he had devoted much time and thought.

At the time that Stanford University opened so disappointingly for him, Olmsted was engaged in Colorado on his last projects in the semiarid West. The best documented of these was the summer colony of "Lake Wauconda" at Perry Park (Fig. 19). The colony was to be sited around a lake created by damming the creek in the valley. The narrow ribbon of lots around the lake would front on a road along the shore, with a sidewalk on the side nearest the lake. The area between the sidewalk and the lake, commonly owned and maintained, would be densely planted with masses of trees and low-growing shrubs. Olmsted insisted on small lots with narrow, fifty-foot fronts, thus making it economical to construct various improvements including sewer and water systems, paving, gutters, and retaining walls. "Our entire plan," he declared "is based on the conviction that . . . the settlement will, in the end, be a great deal more attractive if it produces very distinctly the impression of a *community*. . . ."[47] The "belt of peculiarly luxuriant trees, vines and creepers" in the front yards of the houses and along the lake shore would produce a model of domestic landscape in a dry climate (Fig. 20). To achieve this effect, Olmsted expected to use hydrants connected to the village's water system to secure adequate watering of the front yards with their "little garden plots and terraces, leafy arbors, verandas and balconies."[48] He specifically warned, however, against the introduction of any decorative gardening or the planting of turf. He proposed to employ the same means of

[46] Frederick Law Olmsted to Leland Stanford, 28 October 1891, letterpress book A17, 348, Olmsted Associates Records.

[47] Frederick Law Olmsted to C. A. Roberts, 9 December 1890, letterpress book A11, 277–78, Olmsted Associates Records.

[48] [Frederick Law Olmsted], typescript, folder B1091, Olmsted Associates Records.

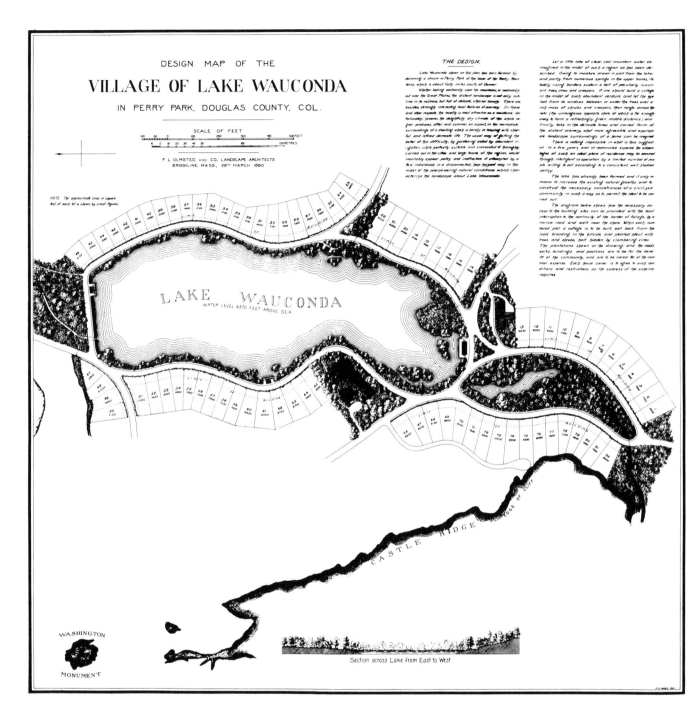

19. F. L. Olmsted & Co., "Design Map of the Village of Lake Wauconda in Perry Park, Douglas County, Col.," 1890. Lithograph (photo: National Park Service, Frederick Law Olmsted National Historic Site, Brookline, Massachusetts)

238

20. Sketch of houses and lakeshore plantings, Lake Wauconda, Colorado, 1890. Lithograph (photo: National Park Service, Frederick Law Olmsted National Historic Site, Brookline, Massachusetts)

providing a green foreground and middle distance for each house and a "perspective effect" for distant views that he had first conceived for the Berkeley neighborhood in 1865–66:

> If one should build a cottage in the midst of such abundant verdure and let the eye look from its windows between or under the trees over a rich mass of shrubs and creepers, then range across the lake (the umbrageous opposite shore of which is far enough away to form a refreshingly green middle distance) and finally take in the delicate tones and varied form of the distant scenery, what more agreeable and appropriate landscape surroundings of a home can be imagined.[49]

Unfortunately, little more than construction of the dam and grading of the road around the lake were accomplished before the Panic of 1893 brought investment in the

[49] F. L. & J. C. Olmsted, *Design Map for Lake Wauconda, Village of Perry Park, Douglas County, Colorado,* 28 March 1890, Frederick Law Olmsted National Historic Site. Olmsted proposed that the belt of planting around the lake consist of masses of trees such as cottonwoods, willows, birches, and alders, with occasional openings for views. For the dense cover of low-growing plants, he proposed to use *Ampelopsis quinquefolia* (Virginia creeper), *Berberis repens* (Barberry), *Ceanothus americanus* (red root), *Ceanothus velutinus, Clematis ligustifolia* (virgin's bower), *Ribes aureum* (Missouri currant), *Ribes oxycanthoides* (hawthorn-leaved gooseberry), *Ribes glandulosum* (fetid currant), *Rhus glabra* (smooth sumac), *Symphoricarpos albus* (snowberry), *Symphoricarpos occidentalis* (wolfberry), *Rosa blanda* (wild rose), *Rosa arkansana, Rubius idaeus* 'Strigosus' (wild raspberry), *Negundo aceroides* (box elder), *Alnus incana* (hoary alder), *Alnus viridis* (European green alder), *Sambucus racemosa* (red-berried elder), *Rhamnus alnifolia* (alder-leaved buckthorn), *Vitis riparia* (river-bank grape), *Acer glabrum* (Rocky Mountain maple), *Amorpha fruticosa* (false indigo), *Amorpha nana, Amorpha canescens* (lead plant), *Lonicera involucrata* (twinberry), *Arctostaphylos uva-ursi* (common bearberry), *Celtis occidentalis* (hackberry), and *Juniperus communis* 'Alpina.'

project to a halt. This was most disappointing, because as Olmsted observed, Lake Wauconda was "the only work we have done, except at Palo Alto, in which we have attempted to wrestle at all with the class of conditions in question" in the semiarid West. At one point he had had high hopes for another Colorado project, a resort village on Lookout Mountain fifteen miles west of Denver. The most substantial result of this commission seems to have been Olmsted's last and clearest formulation of landscape design principles for semiarid areas, as set forth in his letter to A. E. Fisk of 21 April 1890 (see page 232). The Olmsted firm drew up a preliminary plan for the Lookout Mountain village, and began to create a nursery for native plant materials to be used on the site.[50] But correspondence relating to the project lagged thereafter and ended by mid-1891.

As his career came to a close, Olmsted regretted how little he had been able to accomplish in dealing with the challenge of the semiarid American West. "I have had no opportunity of working out anything in practice," he lamented, "nor has anything been done honestly on my advice. Those whom I have attempted to guide have bolted. The general result is that I have never seen anything on a large scale in landscape work in the parts of our country where permanent greensward is not natural, that was at all satisfactory."[51]

Still, Olmsted had been prescient in his recognition of the importance of finding original solutions to the problems of landscape architecture in the West. The extent to which his views have been vindicated in California in recent years shows the relevance of his design principles to present-day landscape practice in the region. But his advice fell on deaf ears in his own time. It would take another generation, different patterns of population and growing problems of water supply before the concerns he voiced would receive serious attention.

For Olmsted, the chief reason for developing a distinctive regional style of landscape was to provide an alternative, where necessary, to the extensive use of greensward that was such an essential element of his landscape designing wherever the climate permitted. During his four decades of practice, however, he could do no more than begin to develop design principles for the areas south of the Mason-Dixon Line and in the semiarid West where it was impossible to grow presentable turf at reasonable cost. Even his efforts to

[50] F. L. Olmsted & Co. to A. E. Fisk, 29 May 1890, letterpress book A8, 880–85, Olmsted Associates Records.

In the sole surviving memorandum concerning plants to be included in the nursery (which did not include foreign plants that could be used), the Olmsted firm listed eight plants to be purchased from nurseries, all of which appear on the March 1890 list of plants for use at Lake Wauconda. The memorandum also listed twenty-eight plants to be gathered in the mountains or grown from seeds and cuttings, of which the following had not been proposed for Lake Wauconda: *Clematis ligusticifolia*, *Ptelea angustifolia* (hop tree), *Ptelea trifoliata* (stinking ash), *Prunus Americana* (wild plum), *Prunus chicasa* (Chickasaw plum), *Rosa blanda*, *Sorbus sambucifolia*, *Viburnum pauciflorum* (mooseberry), *Shepherdia argentea* (buffalo berry), and *Juniperus virginiana* (red cedar) (F. L. Olmsted & Co. to A. E. Fisk, 29 May 1890, letterpress book A8, 652–57, Olmsted Associates Records).

[51] Frederick Law Olmsted to Frederick Law Olmsted, Jr., 1 August 1894, Frederick Law Olmsted Papers; [Frederick Law Olmsted, Jr.], "Report on Perry Park, Douglass Co., Colorado," 8 September 1894, Frederick Law Olmsted Papers.

begin experimentation with plant materials by creating major arboreta at Stanford University and the Biltmore Estate were unsuccessful. Instead, his principal success was the adaptation to the American landscape and American conditions of universal landscape styles that, he believed, evoked a universal human response. Originating in the design traditions and climatic conditions of the British Isles, the pastoral style, in particular, was essential to his parks, residential subdivisions, institutions, and grounds of private residences. But the pastoral spaces that Olmsted designed from Louisville to Montreal and from Washington, D.C. to Chicago were not examples of regional design: rather, they were an extension to the North American continent of universal forms of landscape art. Olmsted's efforts to develop regional styles of landscape design were limited to the areas of America where those universal forms could not be appropriately or economically employed. The challenge was a serious one in his view, but one whose solution he was obliged to leave to succeeding generations of landscape architects.

Regionalism and the Practice of Hanna/Olin, Ltd.

LAURIE OLIN

This essay will examine the issue of regionalism and the degree to which it informs and affects the work of a contemporary landscape architectural design practice, and when it does, what forms and expressions do such considerations take? To answer this question, the following must be considered: what is generally meant by the term regionalism, ecologically and culturally? What is meant by the term regionalism in design? Definitions and examples are given, first for architecture, and then for landscape architecture. With these criteria and definitions established, one can then turn to the body of work executed by the firm of Hanna/Olin, Ltd., in the fifteen-year span from 1976 to 1991, to determine to what degree these projects exhibit an interest in or understanding of their regional situation, and which strategies are employed to make them regional or not. Of further interest, and possibly more importantly, to what purpose is this done? Several examples of deeply regional, highly particularized schemes are given, along with examples of more universal, generalist (potentially "placeless") schemes and those with elements that merely refer to their regional situation. This leads to an examination of the strategies employed in those deemed more regional. These include elements that are both biological and cultural. Among the latter are references to the history of the region and place, formal and stylistic traditions, notions and theories of predecessors, earlier designers, heroes, myths, and cultural norms. Finally, what conclusions are reached by a practitioner after such self-examination and critical reflection? What is (or was) the purpose of the intention to invest work with regional properties? Should it have been attempted and why? The conclusion for the moment is both cautionary and optimistic.

ON REGIONALISM

What is a region? Generally, *region* is a term used to connote a geographic area of considerable extent, indefinite in size and shape, that despite considerable diversity within its parts exhibits some overall commonality or possesses a set of shared properties that render it distinct from other areas and their general properties which are in some way(s) different. An example of the ambiguity and specificity of such a term may be found in one of the opening paragraphs of Victor Shelford's landmark work, *The Ecology of North America,* where he writes:

> The temperate deciduous forest, or the *oak-deer-maple-biome,* occupies North America from the center of the Great Lakes region south to the Gulf of Mexico. It covers the northern two-thirds of the Florida Peninsula and extends west beyond the Mississippi River to the Ozark Mountains. The chief characteristic of the temperate deciduous forest is the predominance of trees with broad leaves that are shed every autumn. An understory of small trees and shrubs is usually also deciduous. The shedding of the leaves brings a striking change in light conditions and shelter for animals. The forest floor is covered with a dense layer of leaves in various stages of decay. The extreme southern part of the forest also contains evergreen species. The white oak, white-tailed deer and turkey are very important throughout practically all of the biome.[1]

He then goes on for the next seventy-one pages to explain the constituent elements that make up this forest biome, its variety and consistency, identifying three large subdivisions or regions: a) Northern and upland forests, b) Southern and lowland forests, and c) Stream-skirting forests.[2] Each of these he further subdivides. For instance, the Northern and Upland Regions usually have beech and sugar maple in climax stands and wapiti and deer as permanent dominant animals. There are five regions: the tulip-oak region, oak-chestnut region, maple-basswood-birch region, maple-beech-hemlock region, and maple-basswood region. Each of these has its particular soils, climate, animals, and plant community.

Of particular interest is the concept that each region grades off into the next and is a constellation of various factors having to do with dynamic communities within a physiographic setting. Shelford's work is a masterpiece of observation, data gathering, description, and synthesis. Similar works by cultural anthropologists and ethnographers have attempted to do the same for human settlements, community, and ecology. Here, however, several differences creep in. Henry Glassie in his early work, *Pattern in the Material Folk Culture of the Eastern United States* observes that:

> In general, folk material exhibits major variation over space and minor variation through time, while the projects of popular or academic culture exhibit minor variation over space and major variation through time. The natural divisions of popular material are temporal; that is, a search for patterns in folk material yields regions, where a search for patterns in popular material yields periods.[3]

Glassie asserts that folk or vernacular artifacts are different in kind and purpose from those of popular culture, and he places works of art, those products that are in-

[1] V. E. Shelford, *The Ecology of North America,* Urbana, Ill., 1963, 17.
[2] Ibid., 18.
[3] H. Glassie, *Pattern in the Material Folk Culture of the Eastern United States,* Philadelphia, 1968, 33.

tended to please aesthetically, together with popular products of the dominant culture in a regionless, placeless continuum. Interestingly enough, this is consonant with the prevailing use of the terms "regional" and "regionalism." These terms have been used to characterize and enfold a wide array of work that has been generally considered in some way separate or counter to the mainstream of contemporary culture. "Regional" development in broader movements often was (and still is) motivated by the desire of some local group to express their own identity and to resist being overrun by the personality or expression of others or from distant centers of power of influence, Los Angeles and New York, for example. The geographic isolation and contiguity of each region, likewise, gives it its identity. A further connotation implied in Glassie's study and listed as a specific characteristic of folk culture is that it be conservative, backward-looking, and resistant to change. The dilemma that modernity has posed to those involved in regional movements has been discussed at length by several authors. (See for example, the essays by Freidrich Achleitner, Alena Kabova and Guy Ballange, and Francois Burkhardt in *Joze Plecnik, Architect: 1872–1957*, ed. Burkhardt, Eveno, and Podrecca.) Put simply, regionalism in the arts connotes some sort of localized tradition that is inevitably in conflict with many forces of change, especially those of international modernism.

If regions in natural science are characterized by physical and geographic characteristics, cultural regions are also spatially defined. They may, however, cross or subdivide physiographic boundaries (e.g., German and French development of the Rhine River Valley or the Athabascan Indians and later European settlers on the Pacific Coast who colonized both the Pacific Littoral with its distinctive physiography, climate, and biota, and the eastern area between the Coast Range and the Rocky Mountains). In this second case, not so surprisingly, the people, their settlements, art, and politics turned out to be quite different on each side of the mountains after several centuries. In all of this one must be careful about notions of causality and determinism. The chance results of human variability and individual personality have been easily as powerful as the natural environment. Think of Joseph Smith and his Mormons, of Fremont's expedition, Sutter's Mill, or of Chief Joseph and Chief Seattle, or why the Pacific Northwest is neither a Russian nor Spanish speaking country or colony such as Mexico.

The differences in physiographic regions, therefore, are most pronounced in terms of geology (land form) and plant and animal ecology which have to do with soil and climate as well. The differences in cultural regions have largely to do with language, land development practices—primarily agricultural and the habits of property division, inheritance, and management—the religious beliefs and ethical system that underpin the economy and development pattern, and the art and architecture created by and for the group. Often this kind of art and architecture has evolved in direct response to the opportunities and constraints posed by the physical environment.

WHAT IS REGIONALISM IN ARCHITECTURE?

Regionalist work inevitably looks in two directions simultaneously: back to a past tradition and to aspects of the vernacular and folk culture on the one hand; and forward to new forces, ideas, and styles emanating from elsewhere that must be dealt with lest they overwhelm whatever traditions and regional character may remain on the other. Central to the concept of regionalism is the notion of giving a particular version, a "regional" variation to some thing, force, or activity that is widespread. Thus, regional schools of painting and writing are known for the particular flavor or distinctive stylistic characteristics that their otherwise ordinary, ubiquitous work might have especially in relation to that which is seen to be more central, original, or dominant. For example, Siennese painting in the cinquecento is a regionalist school compared to that of Rome or Florence (they were the norm and presumed dominant standard of Italian Renaissance painting at the time). In architecture the characteristics of regionalism most noticeably include the conscious use and adaptation of aspects of vernacular building characteristics, especially those related to climate and indigenous building materials, combined with more general and accepted methods of design and composition common to broader national or international practice.

Good examples of this in architecture range from the remarkably flat and prismatic buildings built in England in the early seventeenth century to those of the American prairie school or pueblo-deco buildings of this century. Among the first of these examples are Kirby Hall and Montacute House, clearly renaissance buildings of sophistication that despite having all of the compositional elements of similar buildings in Italy of the same and previous generation, look nothing like them. So too, one would have to say that the buildings of Frank Lloyd Wright built between 1900 and 1910 in Oak Park, Illinois—which launched an entire stylistic movement and are touchstones of modernism in both America and abroad—exhibit many of the characteristic elements, materials, and concerns of the contemporary arts and crafts movement and of late Victorian/Edwardian building elsewhere such as the work of Greene and Greene or Gustave Stickley, none of which look the same at all. As is often the case, Wright's work was the combined product of his conscious selection of elements and motifs found around him in the Midwest and of his unconscious handwriting and compositional traits. His later work in California and the Arizona Desert show further evolution and experiment with highly regionalist notions.

Even more pointedly one can consider the Kimo Theater in Albuquerque, New Mexico, the Ahwahnee Hotel in Yosemite Park, California, or Union Station in Los Angeles, and conclude that they are very cunning and self-conscious attempts to transform particular generic building types of their era (theater, hotel, train station) into particular and localized civic and public monuments.[4] Careful effort is employed to "ground" them in time and space so as to take banal, universal building programs and make them "local heroes" architecturally. The attempt is both to create a regional imag-

---

[4] For discussions of the Ahwahnee Hotel and Kimo Theater, see C. Breeze, *Pueblo Deco*, New York, 1990. For a discussion of the Ahwahnee Hotel in considering the career of Stanley Underwood who designed it, see J. Zaitlen, *Gilbert Stanley Underwood*, Malibu, Calif., 1989. See B. Bradley, *The Last of the Great Train Stations*, Burbank, Calif., 1989, for a discussion of Union Station in Los Angeles.

ery, not unrelated to myth making, and to personalize an impersonal program, a highly poetic activity.

To summarize, the difference between the merely vernacular and the regional is one of intent, expression, and self-consciousness. Regionalist works are self-conscious in the face of alternatives and resistant to the pressure to conform to someone else's aesthetic, proffering instead a counter-cultural artifice that combines carefully selected elements that are intended to relate a building to regional traditions in some way. The motive can be aesthetic or political, and often is both. Phoebe Cutler has written on this aspect of regionalism concerning Harold Ickes and Franklin D. Roosevelt: she discusses their agenda regarding American public life, the land, and the regionalist images employed by their designers across the country from 1934–44 in the parks and structures of the Interior Department and Works Progress Administration.[5]

Strategies of Regionalism in Architecture

Using the Kimo (means King of its Kind) Theater as a regional work of high degree, what are the strategies employed that convey its regionality? These may be summarized as comprising: overall form or shape; fabric, that is, the material and technique employed for its structure and materials; and details and ornament which include those that are merely applied rather than integral; and finally narrative devices that convey messages. In this case, the overall form is derived from the profile and general shape of Taos pueblo. In terms of the fabric, here the adobe and timber infill themes derive from the mission churches of Las Trampas and, particularly, San Estaban at Acoma pueblo. The fabric, thick walls, small openings, beam ends, flat roof, stucco finish, texture, and color are particularly consonant with the first image, that of a pueblo. Third, the details are all subjected to the theme of Indian religious devices and are selected/invented to evoke this world. Indian shields, ceremonial staffs, and beam ends with carved ornaments are all applied to surface. Finally, representative narrative paintings are added which firmly place the building within the tradition of these earlier vernacular buildings. The similarity of this device to the paintings of Antonio Tempesta in the Villa Lante and of Paolo Veronese at the Villa Barbero is striking. At the same time the arrangement of elements, the design and pattern for the windows, and the choice of decorative motifs and materials are very much in the Art Deco mode, an international movement within the design fields between the two world wars concerning compositional strategies, formal structure, the relationship between flat surface and decoration, particularly shallow relief and patterning.

The magnificent railroad station in Los Angeles designed by Donald and John Parkinson with W. E. Markas as chief draftsman between 1937 and 1939 is a similar distillation and adaptation of the Spanish Colonial Mission Churches with their simple Basilica Halls, campanile, and cloisters. Again, southwest Indian motifs are used here in the pav-

---

[5] P. Cutler, *The Public Landscape of the New Deal*, New Haven, 1985. The entire book advances this argument, see particularly pp. 64–82.

ing, and mission derived ornament is used throughout the fabric mixed with those of Spanish baroque and Deco ornament.

What is Regionalism in Landscape Architecture?

Regionalism in landscape architecture is the very same thing described above in architecture; however, as is common when discussing the two fields, it must be said that the means are somewhat different, and the results often unrecognizably different. (The medium leads to different concerns and perspective.) The first implication of difference is that of physiographic determinants of location; secondarily one considers cultural traditions. The medium (the physical material of the landscape) and especially the living palette of plants does indeed offer an opportunity to declare a particularity not afforded to architecture. On the other hand plants alone rarely constitute the full complement of design elements in a landscape, nor can they fulfill all of the cultural and social needs or responses in a human landscape. As in the architecture of buildings, designed, self-conscious landscapes can and often are intended to derive strength and instrumental devices from the vernacular, in this case the landscapes, indigenous settlement patterns, and agriculture as well as natural physiographic and ecological conditions of particular regions.

Also, as in architecture, the twin poles of design, ideas, and technique come into play: values (religious, ethical, and commercial) on the one hand, and working practices (artistic and technological) on the other. Furthermore, the central purpose of regionalism, that of resistance to homogenizing and leveling tendencies coming from distant or dominant groups, if anything, is stronger in landscape design. For centuries the precept, "consult the genius of the place" to use Pope's phrase, has been a central tenet of landscape design. Although most commonly considered in the context of immediate sites, this principle of ascertaining the underlying order and processes of larger areas that at times do have a genuine regional nature and of shaping one's plans and design so that they do indeed respect, preserve, and enhance these preexisting qualities is fundamental to the concept of regionalism.

This was an underlying belief propelling Ian L. McHarg's *Design with Nature*. Certainly at the gross planning level presented in his book, the rhetoric and studies present an attempt to orchestrate a modernist regionalism in landscape planning.[6] In a quasi-scientific manner, the studies in this work authored by McHarg, Juneja, and others, as in the architectural examples given above, look backward and forward simultaneously: backward to land unspoiled by human settlement and a set of interrelated physiographic and ecological phenomena, and forward to a landscape of development and change. One of the principle criticisms of this work has been its scale of operations and the lack of demonstration of its methods at smaller, site-specific scales. The desire for rational, non-

---

[6] I. L. McHarg, *Design with Nature*, New York, 1969, see especially "A Response to Values," 79–93, and "The Naturalists," 177 ff.

nostalgic methods to use in the production of critically regional work at a more normal project scale has not been met, not only by McHarg, but also not by anyone else in the field.

Nevertheless, despite the lack of theoretical texts, there is a body of work that one can point to in the field that is truly regional. Bernard Maybeck, Horace W. S. Cleveland, Jens Jensen, and Thomas Church and their work are exemplars of regionalism. To these one could also add Roberto Burle Marx, Luis Barragan, Dimitrius Pikionis, Florence Yoch, and Richard Haag,[7] each of whom found their own way to relate to the broad forces of modernism and, in some ways, was a proponent of it while simultaneously producing work that was quintessentially regional and personal. Two of these designers, Burle Marx and Haag, are deeply knowledgeable about plants, their work largely grounded in native flora. Two others, Barragan and Pikionis, were both architects who managed to produce remarkable and deeply regional landscape spaces and ensembles with a minimum of plants. Their work, while considered exclusively modern, was also tied to the vernacular in terms of building, forms, technics, and materials. Florence Yoch, conversely, mastered the eclectic palette of exotic, imported plants and Mediterranean revival architectural elements that have come to be so characteristic of Southern California.

Strategies in the Production of Regional Landscapes

Highly pragmatic and heavily constrained developments over long periods of time in agriculture and diet have played a significant role in shaping the cultural regions of the world. So much so, in fact, that much of modern industrialization in agriculture has had to do with questions of how to produce more of the traditional produce faster and cheaper and not to changing what might be produced. At the same time this practice has led to a universalization or homogenization of what is produced and, as a side effect, an increasing standardization and loss of regional differences of the lands affected. Historically farms have been our largest cultural artifact and have been the predominant formal structures in our landscapes, giving each region its particular character. One has only to consider the different character of landscapes such as that of southwest Britain, the Isle-de France, Holland, or the American Midwest to acknowledge this.

While I have argued elsewhere that one of the greatest sources of form and ideas for landscape designers has been nature and its processes, it also can be argued that agriculture has also been one of the other great sources of material for the design of parks, gardens, and public space. One obvious example of this is the pastoral parks of

---

[7] See P. M. Bardi, *The Tropical Gardens of Burle Marx*, New York, 1964, and forthcoming exhibition catalogue by William Howard Adams for the Museum of Modern Art, New York, May 1991; E. Ambasz, *The Architecture of Luis Barragan*, New York, 1976; H. Binet, "Landscaping the Athens Acropolis," in *Dimitrius Pikionis, Architect 1887–1968, A Sentimental Topography*, London, 1990, 70–97; L. Kreisman, *The Bloedell Reserve, Gardens in the Forest*, Bainbridge Island, Wash., 1988, for discussion of Church's work, 49–70, and for that of Haag, 63–75.

the eighteenth and nineteenth centuries, based directly upon the pasturage of livestock in Greece and Italy and subsequent associations with classical life, literature, and late renaissance art, which in themselves became emblematic pastoral icons for western society. Another is the Moorish and Hispanic use of Mediterranean orchards, groves, and small market gardens for the basic structure, materials, and details (primarily irrigation and water conservation devices) for their famous, highly poetic gardens. Le Nôtre's great parks, adaptations of Italian gardens and parks to the flat, poorly drained sites of the Isle-de-France, are more redolent of the agricultural boundaries, hedgerows, and windrows along roads, canals and rivers, and of forest plantations for timber (one of the oldest of Mediterranean harvest crops) than they are of the small country estates and gardens in the hills surrounding Rome. The most common and obvious strategy used in such work has been to seize upon one or two key elements without which the countryside or agricultural type would not be recognizable, or to isolate and refine it, presenting it, as on a platter, to the viewer or user of the new design for their pleasure and contemplation. In the case of Moorish gardens, the key elements are the runnel of water (the jube of Middle Eastern agriculture) and the tank or well, a bosquet (the grove of fruit trees— oranges, dates, etc.), and an assortment of potted plants (the fruit, herbs, and flowers of every farm, nursery, and souk from Spain to India). Taken out of context, burnished and re-presented, these elements fill our senses and imaginations. Entering the Alhambra or The Madrid Botanic Garden, one is overwhelmed by a presentation of the familiar that is as reductive as it is generous. Like recombinant DNA, new aesthetic organisms have been fashioned from ordinary bits that have existed for ages in the everyday, working world.

Thus it is that Barragan's work seems so fresh and new, so old yet familiar. It partakes equally of the vernacular painted adobe of Mexican haciendas and villages and of the modernism descending from de Stijl, Adolf Loos, and The Bauhaus. The jazzy counterpoint of his colored volumes is both forward and backward looking, referring to high and low art. The walls and windows, horse troughs, and exercise yards are literally agricultural elements as old as the work of the Roman agronomists Columella, Cato, and Varro. Their form and color are rooted in Latin American culture and its traditions from before as well as after the arrival of Europeans. Other examples abound: Olmsted's hacienda/mission cum botanic garden for Leland Stanford and Rich Haag's Garden of Stumps on Bainbridge Island. The list can be expanded to great length.

Another common strategy is to identify key natural forms and processes (in addition to vegetation) and, as in regionalist architecture, isolate their form and structural properties. In such cases, vegetation is used as an ornamental addition to reinforce the forms and give more specificity. Probably the most obvious example of this strategy has been the work of Lawrence Halprin done in the American West during the late 1960s and throughout the 1970s.[8] The waterfall and plaza structures, choice of material, color and

[8] The best presentation of these works to date are "Portland and Open Space Sequence," and "Seattle Freeway Park," in *Lawrence Halprin, Process: Architecture 4*, Tokyo, 1978, 159–84, 227–37, respectively.

texture, local forms, and planting of the projects executed in Portland, Oregon; Seattle, Washington; and Denver, Colorado all demonstrate these ideas at work.

As in the production of regionalist architecture, one can summarize that those elements or operations that offer the most toward attempts to create regional work are: the structure and overall form; the fabric of this structure; the elements and technics of the structure; and the details and ornament, whether integral to the form and structure or applied. This last issue, ornament and structure, poses a particular and unresolved problem in all modern work. Are the patterns of a tree's branching or a bridge truss ornament or merely structure? Another structure would have a different pattern. Is ornament only an applied and extraneous phenomenon as Adolf Loos asserted, or can it be integral with form and elements of the fabric and "deep structure" as Louis Sullivan, Christopher Alexander, and Thomas Beebe propose?[9] Finally there is narrative. Of all of these, narrative has been the least attempted and exploited in twentieth-century landscape design until very recently. (See the work of Ian Hamilton Findlay, Bernard Lassus, and Pamela Burton for recent developments in this area. Their work does not necessarily promote regional attitudes, with the exception of Lassus. Exceptions such as Carol Johnson's Chelsea Market Square and SWA's Plaza at Los Colinas in Dallas come to mind as examples that have, however.)

EXAMPLES OF REGIONAL ELEMENTS OR STRATEGIES IN HANNA/OLIN'S WORK

Few elements so immediately connote place and regionality as do key indicator species of plants. As mentioned earlier, this is one of the most common and important aspects of ecological description and analysis. One has only to conjure up the pines of Rome, the maples of Japan, the rows of poplars lining canals and plane trees along the country roads of France, or the lindens of Berlin and the chestnuts of the parks in Paris to realize that cultural landscapes, even the most urban places, have such particular possibilities. Two of America's most characteristic species, the chestnut and elm, have vanished from our cities in this century, leaving them poignantly barren and bereft of what had been one of their essential regional place-making elements. Nevertheless, many other specific plants and humble vernacular elements can be drawn upon in the different regions of America. In our work, plants and materials have often played an important role in the establishment of place and region. One such example is the use of paper birches, white pines, kinikinik and herbaceous material such as wigelia, Solomons seal, and duetzia associated with traditional domestic gardens, and a very Yankee wood fence of white dowels and urns upon a granite base that unmistakably locate one project in Maine. Another example is the Codex Corporation Headquarters, Canton, Massachusetts (Fig. 1). Here brilliant Sugar Maples, dry-laid fieldstone walls, mill ponds, and a granite-

[9] See L. Sullivan, "Plastic and Color Description of the Auditorium," "Ornament in Architecture," and "The Tall Office Building Artistically Considered," in R. Twombly, ed., *The Public Papers*, Chicago, 1988, 73–79, 79–85, 103–13, respectively; C. Alexander et al., *A Pattern Language*, Oxford, 1977, x–xix, lays out the premise; and T. Beebe, "The Grammar of Ornament/Ornament as Grammar," *Via* III (1977), 10–29.

1. View across the pond, Codex Corporation Headquarters, Canton, Massachusetts (photo: Hanna/Olin, Ltd.)

trimmed knot garden of herbs with painted trellis and lattice place this project also in New England, but further south. Even the winter garden with its small lawn, baby's tears, palms, and small tank of water plants evokes a memory of Isabella Stewart Gardener's fantasy in the Back Bay Fens of Boston and a yearning after warmer climes on the part of this frequently ice bound population.

Robert Frost's remark that good fences make good neighbors was literally followed by us on a small rocky hill at Pitney Bowes Headquarters, Stamford, Connecticut (Fig. 2). Covered with a scrap of native second-growth woodland that we took great pains to edit—removing invasive non-native material, nursing the forest back into health—this hill became the centerpiece for the entire composition. Once we had restored the basic structure, we were able to add numerous native understory plants and reinforce the edges. This project was as much a meditation upon the stony outcrops, ledges and generations of shifting them about by settlers as it is about planting or shaping of spaces.

The Playa Vista project in Los Angeles, California, is in many ways a more ambitious project. We are re-creating wetland and a riparian habitat complete with two hundred forty acres of estuary with native plants, fluvial processes, and animal habitat restoration, along with two miles of stream bed and plant and animal habitats (Fig. 3). It also includes miles of streets with street trees, some native and many naturalized exotics, albeit linked to the cultural history of city and region, for example, the palms, pines, and flowering

2. View of sodded terraces, Pitney Bowes Headquarters, Stamford, Connecticut, 1985 (photo: Hanna/Olin, Ltd.)

trees of Beverly Hills, Santa Monica, Santa Barbara, Pasadena, and numerous other small towns of the region (Fig. 4). The identity of this American coastal community is linked to Mediterranean and tropical vegetation in countless images from orange crates to motion pictures. Today part of the genius of the Los Angeles region lies in this profusion of lush imported vegetation.

The projects referred to above display a marked absence or low volume of rhetoric with little or no persuasion beyond that of "being there." Whatever argument they contain, it is not so much about regionalism (their place in a particular region is assumed), these projects are more concerned about the relationships between public and private realms and the creation of socially useful and aesthetically rewarding spaces. As these examples may indicate, it is hard to limit landscape design to matters of planting indigenous, or even native, species. To understand and operate effectively, regardless of point of view, one must also consider purely cultural elements. Certainly as one shifts the focus of consideration and work from rural, suburban and small town settings to more urban ones, the cultural, built artifacts become more strident and dominant than vegetation. (This is not to say that vegetation is no longer important, in some senses it becomes even more so, for all of its scarcity.) In the context of cities, the devices that give particularity, place, and regional character range from the general urban structure, streets, squares,

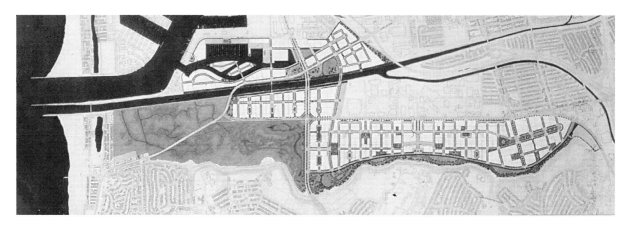

3. Plan, Playa Vista, Los Angeles, California, 1992 (photo: Hanna/Olin, Ltd.)

4. Sketch of the view down the avenue, Playa Vista, Los Angeles, California (photo: Hanna/Olin, Ltd.)

and building types, with the particular dimensions, scale, and grain of the parcels and block sizes (200' × 200' in Portland, Oregon to the 300' × 600' east-west oriented blocks of Midtown Manhattan) to the habits of public infrastructure, street furnishings, selection of building materials, and architectural styles that predominated when particular districts and significant public institutions were built. These many separate and interrelated variables combine to form urban ensembles that are unique and memorable. One has

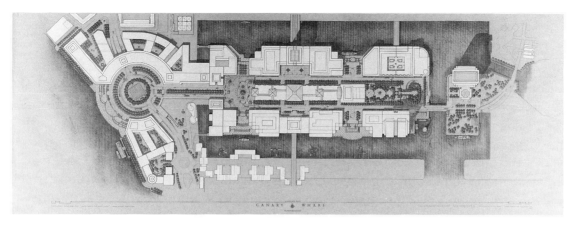

5. Plan, Canary Wharf, London (photo: Hanna/Olin, Ltd.)

only to think of the French Quarter in New Orleans, or Midtown Manhattan, the nineteenth-century expansion district of Barcelona, the West End and Mayfair in London, or Hausmann's Paris to realize how clear and distinct these collective works can be. Rasmusson's study, *London, The Unique City*, Olson's recent book, *The City as a Work of Art*, and Carl Schorske's study of Vienna all elaborate this theme.[10]

In our practice, therefore, we have consciously pursued what we perceived to be the "genius of the place" in urban works, employing several of the strategies listed earlier. For projects in New York, London, and Los Angeles, we have consciously perused the ordinary properties of streets, buildings, and open spaces and proposed either extending or creating new districts in the spirit of the patterns that we observed. In no case, however, were these direct copies or literal extensions, but rather exercises done in the manner of what we perceived. None of the blocks in Battery Park City are really the same or typical of each other or the adjacent city, although they are perceived as such. The principal square at Canary Wharf in London, although surrounded by enormous buildings that are quite different from those around the well-known squares of Westminster, is bathed in light due to the proportions and strategies used regarding cornice heights, arcades, and materials (Fig. 5). The fabric of Playa Vista, although possessing no single-family detached houses, will join other districts of the city as a familiar and attractive set of streets and buildings with a decided ambience of Los Angeles not seen elsewhere. Urban structure, the proportion and length of streets and blocks and the very pattern of the city not just the detail, is one of the key elements in the creation of urban regionalism. The ignorance and open disregard for such knowledge and values lies at the heart of the suburban sprawl so ubiquitous today, with the result being the placelessness and regional devastation so often commented upon, but so rarely confronted or countered with the alternative just discussed.[11] (There are rural equivalents popularized by Tony

[10] S. E. Rasmussen, *London, The Unique City*, London, 1934; D. J. Olsen, *The City as a Work of Art*, New Haven, 1986; C. E. Schorske, *Fin-de-Siècle Vienna: Politics and Culture*, New York, 1980.
[11] See E. Relph, *Place and Placelessness*, London, 1976.

Hiss in his book, *The Experience of Place,* which is one of the most accessible examples.) The short term financial gains and greed that are often cited as the root cause are only possible once one dispenses with a sense of value in the existing structure, landscape, and ecology, which often can be demonstrated to generate more and longer term profits for developers, that is, ignorance of net long term value drives these short term goals.

At the other extreme, street furnishings are among the most common, often banal, and yet conclusive indicators of place. One has only to consider the elements of a street in Paris or London to see how they reveal the results of evolution of particular elements through industry, governance, use, and an aesthetic (that can be every bit as idiosyncratic as it may also represent any gestalt). The result of such processes can be a highly particular set of ordinary details that eloquently bespeak of "place." At Battery Park City, therefore, we chose to forgo the pleasures of invention and instead dipped into the array of furnishings developed for public spaces in New York City, selecting and modifying several that we felt had become part of the anonymous background to life in the city. It was our belief that these furnishings would give familiarity and continuity to this enormous project that was to be created almost overnight and would help to weave it into the existing fabric of the city, adding—as it were—a new link to the chain of parks and open spaces begun in the nineteenth century by Olmsted and expanded so dramatically by Robert Moses, New York City Park Commissioner for three decades ending in the 1960s (Fig. 6). We have been publicly attacked by our peers and elders for doing this. Paul Friedburg at a Harvard symposium and Richard Haag in comments made while on an American Society of Landscape Architects design award jury have seen our decision not to make these elements new and personal as a failure of artistic vision. Our counter view is that this is precisely the best use of modern machine tool production, and that like automobiles, light bulbs, and ready-to-wear clothing, there are valid and important uses for off-the-shelf manufactured goods in the creation of places. The point of the public spaces at Battery Park City was to open the city out to the river and to provide places to walk, sit, and stand wherein to partake of the broader context and social intercourse. It was our intent to produce an environment that would not call attention to itself, but rather one that would direct one's consideration elsewhere. We hoped to produce an environment so quintessentially "New York" that it would unconsciously become part of peoples' lives as well as an armature for works of art and future developments by others. All of which have happened. In an interesting reversal, the hexagonal asphalt paving, B-pole lamp from Central Park, Belgian blocks, standard New York Parks railings, and ready-made benches are now as much identified in the public's mind with Battery Park City as they are with our sources of inspiration (Fig. 7).

A different approach to such key details is to make of the most humble elements, something radically new, self-conscious, and imbued with meaning. In two projects, the Sixteenth Street Transitway Mall in Denver (Fig. 8), and in Westlake Park, Seattle (Fig. 9), we chose to reexamine paving, the most common element in terms of its geographic area, extent, and normal expectations regarding its material properties, and used it as the principal design intervention. In both cases, we transformed the ground surface, ordinarily made of moderately durable, albeit cheap and not particularly attractive mate-

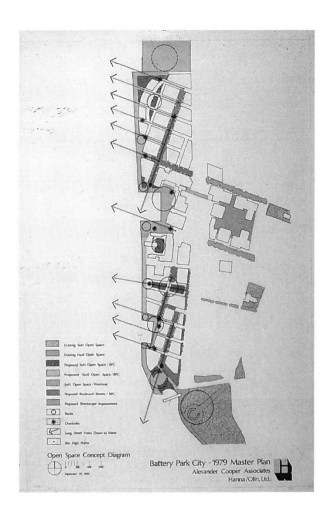

Open Space Concept Diagram

Battery Park City · 1979 Master Plan
Alexander Cooper Associates
Hanna/Olin, Ltd.

6. Master plan, Battery Park City,
   New York, 1979 (photo: Hanna/
   Olin, Ltd.)

7. View of benches along the esplanade, Battery Park City, New York (photo: Hanna/
   Olin, Ltd.)

8. Aerial view of polychrome granite pavement, Sixteenth Street Transitway Mall, Denver, Colorado (photo: Hanna/Olin, Ltd.)

9. Aerial view of pedestrians on rain-soaked granite pavement, Westlake Park, Seattle, Washington (photo: Hanna/Olin, Ltd.)

10. Salish Indian basket showing pattern that inspired polychrome granite pavement at Westlake Park (photo: Hanna/Olin, Ltd.)

258

rials such as concrete or asphalt, into extensive polychrome stone carpets. Although there were numerous reasons for doing so, especially to achieve our particular social or artistic goals (maximize the apparent size and extent of the spaces, unify disparate, episodic, or far flung spatial portions, create a statement of social importance and assertion of civic worth and pride, create a unique sense of location and place within the labyrinth of the city, etc.) from the perspective of this discussion, it should be noted which patterns we chose to use and their affect upon the appearance, success, and potential meaning of each project.

During the design stages of both Denver and Seattle, numerous options for pattern, color, and material were considered. In Denver, because the public space under design was eighty feet wide and twelve blocks long, analogies to a carpet runner came to mind almost immediately. At one point I discovered that both Harry Cobb, the partner of I. M. Pei who was leading the project, and myself were studying nineteenth-century Navaho Indian blankets. The pattern finally developed with a progression from large, separate, geometric figures in the center to continuously linked ones in the bus lanes to a diffusion at the edges, each responding to a particular zone of movement, refuge, or commercial activity. The pattern is strongest under the trees, less dense in the busway, and of less force and insistence as one moves toward the shop windows, where the eye should be redirected from this public show of generosity and spirit to that of the private entrepreneur. I will also confess to thinking of the pattern of rattlesnake skins, which were being sold as belts and souvenirs at a shop at one end of the street on my initial site visit. Whether the citizens of Denver and tourists to the mall realize these sources of form, or not, I do not know. I only know we would not, and could not, have come up with such a pattern somewhere else. To me it is deeply regional and particular to its place and condition.

At Westlake Park in Seattle, after a series of pattern studies, my partner, Robert Hanna, and I determined that we could not utilize a bounded figure with variable density and directionality as at Denver, but needed instead an all over field of uniform density. What pattern to use? Again, after considerable study and trial and error, Bob began experimenting with a particular pattern of an obscure Salish Indian basket that we found in a book I had bought on the subject of Northwest Indian basketry (Fig. 10). This particular geometric structure, although containing elements common to Athabascan design from the desert southwest to Alaska, turned out to work remarkably well with the proportions and shape of the triangular piece of land designated for the park. In our final design this pattern has been greatly enlarged. The change of scale has freed the pattern from its original material, grass, bark, and roots and allowed each twist of fiber to be transformed into a large paving block. No longer evocative of these soft baskets, despite some recall of weaving and blankets, the patterned stone surface becomes a remarkable "ground" for both public events and ordinary business and respite. It at once declares a unique condition in the city. The main ornament of the space is the very surface of the space itself. Its pattern comes from the oldest known people of the region. It has not been applied or added to a structure, but rather is the structure and base for everything that can take place there, providing a ground for trees, pavilions, sculpture, and people.

Although there are other elements such as a fountain made of large sheets of water, a speaker's platform and arch, benches, and trees, it is this lithic surface that dominates. There are embellishments that in their literal representation comment upon and enhance this surface. These consist of planting pots and carved capitals employing references to the Art Deco buildings that surround the square, whose ornament itself refers to the vegetation and marine life of the region.

Even in projects of ours that have been labeled avant-garde, deconstructionist, and post modern, we have pursued both local and regional properties, seeking to imbue our work with a considered and deep sense of place. Over the last ten years, we have collaborated on nine projects with Peter Eisenman, a well-known and controversial architectural theorist. To date, Peter and I have only managed to get one of our collaborations built, the Wexner Center for the Visual Arts in Columbus, Ohio. We have produced a work that could be in no other place. It is a highly personal work on the part of both of us. It is also rooted in place through an open appeal to memory, specifically the demolition of an old Armory building that once stood on the site and is evoked in our scheme by fragments of architecture and several landscape features; that is, a small garden contained within a partial recreation of fragments of its structure, and the outline of the former building traced in the ground. Regional issues are raised in the overall site strategy and by the landscape structure, fabric, detail, and metaphor. Again, without presenting the whole project, the logic of its artistic gestures regarding the campus context, town, and gown, the dilemmas of an architectural stance of uncertainty versus that of classical revival, modern attitudes toward spatial organization, and tendencies toward hierarchy and centrality in western architectural tradition which this project deliberately questions and confronts, let me present two aspects that relate to the topic of regionalism. If anything, the other issues raised by this project only reinforce my earlier assertion that regionalist concerns are strategies employed in confronting broad international or universalist design practices and theories.

In 1967, I executed a number of illustrations for Sybil Moholy Nagy's book, *Matrix of Man,* an extended discussion about environmental design. One of these depicted the Jeffersonian survey grid as applied to the eastern portion of the state of Ohio in the first decades of the nineteenth century. When Peter and I decided to extend the building program throughout the entire site offered by the university and to intertwine the building and landscape so as to make each become portions of the other, it was this Cartesian, abstract, and placeless grid—that oddly enough has come to characterize the settlement pattern, agriculture, and towns, the very look and feel of the Midwest and great plains—that became our first organizing device. At the same time, I became obsessed with the notion of growing prairie grasses and flowers over, across, and through this grid and buildings. Despite long opposition from the university who wanted instead the conventional ground covers and shrubs that are found in commercial nurseries (another industry partially responsible for the loss of place and the homogenization of America's regions and cities), I persevered and finally persuaded a new generation of physical plant administrators to let me use a selection of ornamental grasses and flowers (Fig. 11). The effect is very much a suggestion and abstraction of prairie fragments without replicating or

11. View of planting, Wexner Center for the Visual Arts, Ohio State University, Columbus, Ohio
(photo: Hanna/Olin, Ltd.)

pretending to be one. The restlessness of the tilted and heaved planes of earth and grass
is in stark and seemingly violent contrast to the marked flatness of the site and entire
surrounding region (Fig. 12). One result is that everyone becomes acutely aware of the
surface of the earth, its color, texture, and seasonal change. As in Seattle, it looks like
nothing else around, could not be called contextual, does not come from some immediate or even distant design tradition (except perhaps the Ohio River mound builders of
Pre-Columbian times), yet like the Kimo Theater, it is in my view deeply regional in its
purpose and essence. Like Westlake Park in Seattle, it appears to have developed a strong
popular appeal to those who experience it and seems to be well on the way to being
taken up as a local landmark of meaning and significance.

Failure and Success in Courting the Regional

Working with I. M. Pei & Partners on a project for a particularly dramatic hilltop in
Westchester County, north of New York City, I became particularly interested in producing a landscape that would provide a regional setting for a series of quintessentially modern buildings. The buildings were to be a series of highly abstract white prisms, loosely
grouped about on the mountain top, connected by tenuous covered walks and surrounded by large areas of parking. My attempts to get Pei's office to group the buildings
more closely together, similar to a village or college, was rebuffed. No buildings could be

261

12. Sketch of the raised plantings, Wexner Center for the Visual Arts, Ohio State University, Columbus, Ohio (photo: Hanna/Olin, Ltd.)

less regional, except from the point of view that they were very much in an American 1980s high-tech corporate office style, metal panels, continuous ribbon windows, pyramidal atriums with angled shapes jutting out toward various points of the compass. As one moves about the country and sees the dissemination of these forms, materials, and building topologies, one can only speculate that a new industrial vernacular has emerged, on the one hand placeless and mechanical, on the other deeply American and of the moment.

I decided that I would attempt to create a quintessential Upstate New York landscape to bind these buildings to the site and yoke them together into a more cohesive and tempered whole. To do so I proposed filling the entire set of open spaces between the buildings with apple orchards. Then I planned to reach out to the north and south with two large meadows, similar to the old fields one sees in farms throughout the region, fragments of which existed on the site before we began. Along the sides of these meadows, I proposed planting alleys of deciduous trees similar to old farm lanes. Finally I began layering each parking lot with brushy hedgerows of native species, through which the employees must pass on arriving and leaving each day. The allees of trees were to serve as lanes for employees to walk or jog on their breaks, at lunch, or after work, as well as to aid the many deer on the site to move up to the orchards to feed and return to the woods without having to move across clearings. Detention basins needed to control storm water runoff and for fire fighting were to be made of puddled clay similar to farm ponds. The decision on my part to focus upon and create this evocative and fulsome middle ground landscape was partly informed by the surrounding forests, mountains, farms, and villages that formed a background and by the client's expressed intent to eschew the foreground. For reasons of economy, project politics, and aesthetic consistency, there were to be virtually no fine details or site furnishings around or near the

262

buildings. They were in the country, not the suburbs, and the imagery was rural, not suburban. The inspiration and subject matter of the landscape design was that of the declining agricultural landscape of the Hudson River Valley. I was as aware of nineteenth-century American landscape painting as I was of the current state of affairs, having an affection for both and finding strong cultural support for my intent in both.

In my opinion, this approach was never fully appreciated by the architects or the owner and client and was badly mangled in the construction process. Simple and clear as the concept appeared at the time, it now seems to me that it was too pure and remote from the expectations and techniques of the owner, contractors, and architects.[12] It is my greatest and saddest defeat in professional practice to date, for it seemed to be among the most spiritual and fundamental of all our projects in terms of a landscape concept that was as timeless as it was regional and particular, as ecological as it was cultural, as economical in means as it was generous in spirit.

Are such attempts to reach directly into the structure of a region and to use primary elements to give character and order to modern endeavors inevitably doomed? I do not think so, but I do think that the methods to achieve such goals cannot be those of modern fast-track, large-scale construction but rather must proceed at slower pace and with more care. On the other hand, it does not require pre-industrial handcraft methods either, merely people who have a sympathy and understanding for this sort of construction, something we have recently found on a project in central Ohio.

Kitzmiller Residence; New Albany, Ohio

Again working in a lovely agricultural region, this time the Midwest, I turned once more to agricultural traditions for clues and materials with which to fashion several private estates. This time sympathetic owners and superb contractors have understood the spirit of our proposals. Although it is still under construction, the orchards, meadows,

---

[12] Many designers have had their work mangled or destroyed by the process of construction. I am currently working on an article concerning Riverside Drive and Park designed by Olmsted, Vaux, and John Bogart. An account of its terrible history is outlined by "The New York Riverside Drive" (*Engineering News* 6, 1 [4 January 1879], 3–5), wherein the author writes: "Without ever having had, so far as known, a single day's experience in the designing or construction of park or road-work, they have changed at will the width, location and arrangements of roads, walks and drives, and the plans of walls and other structures; they have permitted nearly every tree on the drive and many in the park to be cut down, and have leveled off the natural knolls, making a barren waste out of what should be a picturesque scene, and, worse than all, they have permitted the construction of work to be done in a negligent and faulty manner, and have paid the contractor some $7,000 for material taken from the park outside of the lines of the avenue, endangering the validity of the assessment which should be laid upon the adjacent property . . . The present Park Commission, in placing in incompetent hands the power of mutilating the work of art designed by Olmsted & Bogart, should be judged by the same standard that we would apply to a person who, having ordered a landscape from Kensett, should turn it over, when half finished, to be completed by a journeyman house-painter." The Olmsted correspondence in the National Archives sheds further light on the subsequent saga of despoliation and transmogrification as monuments are added that destroyed both the form and meaning of the design. See the letters between Florence Kellogg and Olmsted in July 1885, Olmsted's response of 6 August 1885, as well as John Haven's letter to him of 12 August 1885. The results of this and twentieth-century encroachments are there for everyone to see.

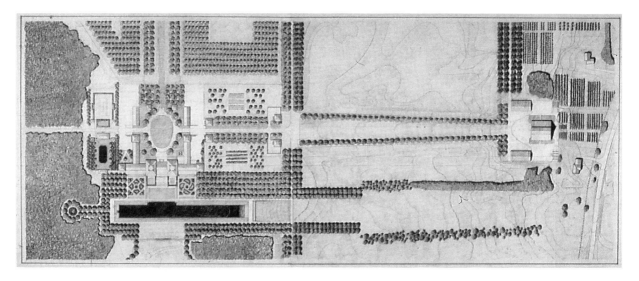

13. Plan, Kitzmiller Residence, New Albany, Ohio, 1992 (photo: Hanna/Olin, Ltd.)

hedgerows, ponds, canals, lakes, roads, hills, gardens, and architectural elements are deeply American (Fig. 13). It remains to be seen whether it will also end up truly regional as discussed above.

If asked why, despite some of its quite derivative European inspired elements, I think this project is American in feeling, not English or French, I would start out by saying "because it was built here, and we cannot help thinking and building in an American way." From the brick architecture—a reverie on tidewater Georgian, that particular moment of American palladianism that has had a deep imprint upon our nation's public and private institutions and country retreats—to the white wooden fences, whether horse fences or those of the dependencies and gardens, the flood of memories that they evoke of blue grass pastures, New England villages, Tom Sawyer, and every midwestern town is so strong as to clearly position this work in the American heartland. Interestingly enough, the particular combination of elements employed also rules out New England and the South, either of which might possess some, but not all, of these elements, commonly found together between the Appalachians and the Mississippi. There is a subtlety in the use and inflection of these materials akin to local accents in language that probably only an American would perceive or care about.

As in many of the works of Lancelot Brown in England, the entire ensemble can be taken as an emblematic construction, not as one of symbolism or prone to iconography. It is what it purports to be: a country estate that demonstrates its owner's and designer's awareness of the tradition of country estates at home and abroad. The Kitzmiller estate, now known locally as Abigail House, exhibits a series of architectural and landscape elements that possess a rambling order and loosely formal set of relationships to each other, to the site and surrounding landscape. Each part—roads, gatehouse, drive, barn, main house and dependencies, tennis and pool pavilions, paddocks, pastures, lakes, canals, basins, stable, riding ring, guest pavilion (a rotunda with gardens), the rides and allees, meadows, orchards, kennels, gardens, and woods—demonstrates that the designers and client are historically informed and working within a tradition. Despite a modicum of atavism, both in buildings and landscape, the ensemble also seems to succeed in reaching a degree of regionalism not found today in the bulk of the design work executed by major commercial landscape architecture design firms, or the estate work done by prominent society garden designers.

CONCLUSION

Several issues have been raised by the forgoing that should be considered directly:

Given the roles of the owner, builder, and designer and the nature of practice and the landscape industry today, what effect do these have upon regionalism, if any?

Having worked in urban, suburban, and rural situations, can one draw any conclusions from this? Are there differences that result from the nature of place, clients, or projects? Do any lend themselves to considerations of regionalism more or less, etc.?

What is the degree of influence exerted by earlier designers and their work? Does it help or hinder?

Despite a generally accepted belief that there are several different and distinct regions in the United States, could one see the whole of America as a region in much the same way that France and England have come to be. What is the relationship between regionalism and nationalism?

Despite my attempt to discuss our work in terms of the conference theme regionalism, are not many of the things that have been presented more properly local and place specific as much or more so than they are truly regional?

Finally, one should consider Henry James' three questions: What was the author trying to do? How well did he succeed? Was it worth it?

To start with the first issue, what are the effects upon regional expression due to the changing nature of practice and clients? As the Westchester corporate example suggests, many modern clients are international in nature and go to great lengths to create a recognizable image for their facilities that is openly opposed to regionally responsive design solutions. Fast food franchises and corporations are not alone in behaving this way. Government agencies, sophisticated developers, private individuals, and all kinds of people and institutions are "worldly" and chary of what they consider "provincial." Contractors and builders, whom one would expect to be locally or regionally based, frequently are when small or medium scale in their operations. However, many of the construction management firms that we work with in Los Angeles, we also work with in New York and Philadelphia. The firm that built the Codex Corporation Headquarters in Canton, Massachusetts, is also working on two of our Los Angeles projects in addition to having produced two of our works in Philadelphia earlier. A construction firm that we are now working with in Barcelona and London also executed worked for us in New York. Small subcontractors may still be local, but stone which is quarried in Africa, Spain, or India is shipped to Italy for cutting before being sent to Ohio, London, or New York for our projects. The trees we are planting at Canary Wharf in London are coming from a nursery in Hamburg, Germany, which grew them up from lining out stock supplied from Oregon.

At a certain scale of operation, the construction industry today is one of the most international of all our businesses. Methods are becoming so standardized and schedules so compressed that designers concerned with craft are tearing out their hair. The small, private garden is, of course, a haven from this, which partly accounts for its current appeal to designers of all sorts. Firms like ours that attempt to use native plants, concern themselves with ecology, and look for local materials and methods are swimming upstream. At Ohio State University, when I decided to use native red sandstone for the walls of the sliced planes of the grass terraces, I discovered that all of the local quarries in Indiana and Ohio were played out. Only rubble was available. Recent restorations of nineteenth-century American red sandstone buildings had to import it from England, Germany, or India. Thus we used German sandstone in Columbus to achieve the "sense" of a native stone. This does not bother me since artifice lies at the heart of all design. The pressures to conform and make everything the same does, however, bother me.

Are rural settings more resistant to this deadening homogeneity and sameness of expression than urban ones? I do not think so. The pressures on modern farming to become one vast business network with a reduced number of common products, the continuing adoption of horrendous and deadening highway standards throughout the country, the ubiquitous foundation planting, lawns, and limited palette of commercially produced trees has rendered our countryside and highway corridors in rural settings remarkably similar and placeless. The urban scene is equally banal in large part. Nonetheless, most cities still have a flavor that is unique. So do most truly rural areas. The suburban areas in between are the most intractable. Certainly the work we have done in the suburbs—because it has been primarily corporate (Johnson & Johnson, IBM, Pitney Bowes, Nestlé, AT&T, INA, etc.)—has been most commonly in what could be called American Pastoralism and is regional to the degree that America may be considered a region (as opposed to Europe). Despite our attempts to "ground" them, locally they are, in general, fairly consistent and uniform in both their ideas and handling.

In my memory, I cannot remember any client or owner ever saying to us that they were interested in regional expression. Local character or "appropriateness" are ideas they have mentioned. Leslie Wexner and Jack Kessler in Columbus have talked to us and to their builders and contractors at considerable length about their desire to "build a house in the country" and that the estates and other structures we are creating for them should be "country," not suburban. The form such instincts takes is usually to question our ability to know local flora, for most people still think that landscape architects merely plant things. Horticulturalists, on the other hand, think that as a group we are fairly ignorant about plants. One client after another has wondered why or how a landscape architect from another region can solve their problems and has challenged us on the subject. Sometimes we satisfy their insecurity on the subject by associating with a local landscape architect who purportedly will know more about the local soils, climate, plants, and the nursery business, which in fact they often do. In the process, we have made many close friendships and learned a lot from these other professionals. At times, clients have worried that we would bring inappropriate cultural (and thereby inappropriate formal) attitudes to their situation. The most skeptical critics of our working in other regions have been European civil servants and journalists, both of which groups are extremely chauvinistic and resentful of what they perceive to be American imperialism. Since I have not presented our European work to any extent, I will not dwell on the point. They, too, remain skeptical of our understanding their particular ecological conditions. My only comment here would be that as outsiders we have probably been far more sensitive to the cultural traditions and ecology than most of the professionals we have met who are practicing there.

As we have seen in the case of H. W. S. Cleveland and Olmsted, the cultural agenda of a designer can be one of the strongest influences upon his form and material expression. The committee that awarded us the commission for Westlake Park in Seattle expressed concern that we might be too formal and stiff in our response to their needs and character. In the repartee of the interview, it became clear to us that they had visions of themselves as relaxed, fun-loving folks and considered us a bit too serious. They also expressed a desire for quintessentially suburban elements—lawns, flowers, and "informal" spaces, for example, biomorphic, curving, or asymmetrical forms. In many other commissions we have found clients who have believed and hoped that the "landscape," which to them is trees and bushes, would be used to "soften" or "humanize" the urban quality of some project. They intended our work to counteract some basically unwelcome characteristics of the architecture that they were commissioning.

The continuing American anti-urban bias that began as an agrarian, political, and economic stance has been transformed into a suburban, consumer stance. Americans did not like and trust cities when most people did not live in them, and now that most people do, they still do not like them. This may have a lot to do with the absence of "sense of place" in our urban scene, but should not necessarily be so. In fact, it could as easily lead to highly or pseudo-rustic expressions. Instead, however, a dreadful suburban homogenization has spread in both directions to country and city. This in fact is what much of the regional and situational strategies that have been employed by us and others have been intended to counteract.

The question of whether regional cultural differences can survive current universalizing forces is a question with no clear answer. Biophysical differences will certainly persist. To the degree that society ignores them, there will be problems, at times of great consequence, such as those of water shortage, pollution, and famine. In many cases, however, such problems will not occur nor be so severe. What, therefore, is the motive to seek and produce a regional character in a work of landscape architecture, especially at a moment when travel, contact, dialogue, and interchange—commercial, social, intellectual, scientific, and artistic—is taking place throughout the world? The answer must be that this movement of goods, ideas, and images which began as an outgrowth of the centuries-old quest for more personal freedom and self-realization—a struggle for economic and religious opportunity as well—has not been seen as necessarily leading to better societies. The same forces that are so beguiling to Third World countries urgently seeking to improve their quality of life and to join the prosperous nations of the world are also the same that are leading to a pronounced loss of self and place there and in the most industrialized regions. The ubiquitous homogenization of culture and environment, the rapacious consumption of the products of art and heritage, the proliferation and rapid debasing of the accumulation of works of architecture and art through mass industry, marketing, and consumption, and the substitution of images and simulacra for real objects or places of historic achievement that are ideologically or aesthetically laden with meaning for particular societies has led to a revulsion for such facile and exploitive devices on the part of many practitioners and academics in design. As a counter strategy to mainstream, post-modern architectural design which has largely been co-opted by the most banal and rapacious aspects of international commerce and development, at least three different strategies have emerged.

One, following architects of the early decades of this century, such as the Vesnin brothers and El Lissitzky, proposes a radical agenda that asks architecture to refer only to itself, to transcend or eschew function, even construction (building), and to propose designs that critique the institutions that call them into being.[13] This approach asks for architecture that resists any attempt to pin it down, except as being architecture. It dreams of permanent and continual revolution in its break with the past and tradition. Needless to say, this strategy to resist mainstream materialism and conformity is incompatible with the procedures of regionalism outlined above.

A second, related strategy also attempts to return to portions of early modernism, picking up certain dropped threads, but not others. This approach pursues its resistance and meaning through techniques borrowed from twentieth-century art, literature, criticism, and scientific theory. Equally distrustful of the mechanisms of the marketplace and programmatic determinism, it rejects Hegelian and Kantian progressive theories and notions of historic continuity and formal evolution.[14] Using devices of fragmentation, dislocation, and collage, and borrowing metaphors and theory from structuralism and surrealism, this work is dependent upon the conventional and historic world of signs and images for the raw material of its productions. This strategy can and has produced significant designs and built works that have had a marked effect upon mainstream practice, but have also, at the same time, largely succeeded in their resistance to co-option, retaining much of their potency. It is not a strategy generally thought of as conducive to regionalist concerns, (think of George Hargreaves's Harliquin Plaza in Denver, for ex-

---

[13] See K. Frampton, "The Millenialistic Impulse in European Art and Architecture: Russia and Holland 1913–1922," in *Modern Architecture 1851–1945*, New York, 1983, especially 306–16; and the recent collection of essays by Bernard Tschumi, *Questions of Space*, London, 1990, especially "Episodes of Geometry and Lust," 38–59, "Architecture and Its Double," 62–77, and "The Architecture of Dissidence," 80–85.

[14] See P. Eisenman, "The End of the Classical: The End of the Beginning, The End of the End," *Perspecta* 21 (1984), 155–72, and idem, "The Futility of Objects: Decomposition and the Process of Difference," *Harvard Architectural Review* 3 (Winter 1984), 64–81; A. Colquhon, *Modernity and the Classical Tradition*, Cambridge, Mass., 1989, especially "Regionalism and Technology," 207–11.

ample), although I would assert that Peter Eisenman and I have in fact shown that the two are not necessarily exclusive in the Ohio State University Wexner Center project.

The third strategy, that which has come to be called "Critical Regionalism" by Kenneth Frampton and Jurgen Habermas, has also been around since the turn of the century and has been used by several designers responsible for works considered to be masterpieces of the modern movement, as well as by others, who, until recently, have been ignored by history and criticism. Examples include work by the following: Frank Lloyd Wright, Greene and Greene, Dimitrius Pikionis, Sigurd Leveritz, Joze Plecnik, Alvar Aalto, Ralph Cornell, Thomas Church, A. E. Bye, and Richard Haag.[15] This strategy opposes co-option by a rapacious and image hungry market through the production of works that are so grounded in a particular time and place that neither their image nor their particular formal organization can be copied or repeated elsewhere with success. Although this is also a goal of the two previous strategies, their methods are intended to be used wherever one finds oneself; that is, the strategies are conceived as somewhat universalist, while the product is intended to be unique. In the so-called "critical-regionalist" strategy, it is possible to vary the technique from place to place while striving for results that are more familiar and tied to tradition.

Our practice, Hanna/Olin, Ltd., has never been interested in the first of these strategies: that of endless revolution, the rejection of history, and a hermetic discourse of architectural theory *sans* object. We have a strong urge to build and would rather make mistakes and produce flawed experiments than merely talk about things. Thus, we have on several occasions participated in schemes of the second sort, but we have succeeded in getting very few built because of client or public resistance to their unorthodox appearance and organization. To date I have collaborated on nine projects with Peter Eisenman, every one of which has had elements as particular to their geographic location as the Wexner Center at Ohio State University, but have succeeded in getting only one built. Other such projects done on our own or with others for London, Florida, and California have also foundered and remain unbuilt. Apparently, therefore, there is a strong normative ethos expected by the viewer (owner, client) in works that contain regional devices. For this reason most of the work that we have executed that could be termed regional or regionalist has been highly conventional or "ordinary" in many or most of its properties. Our motive to create these works stems from the fact that we are deeply troubled by the loss of identity, the despoliation of land and cities by late twentieth-century commerce, and the exploitive use of imagery and heritage by widely divergent sectors of our economy ranging from perfume and clothing manufacturers to real estate and entertainment organizations—all of which blend together in our urban centers and our daily lives. Many of our clients have been part of this spectrum of modern commerce and institu-

[15] See J. Habermas, "Modernity, an Unfinished Project," in H. Foster, ed., *The Anti-Aesthetic, Essays on Post Modern Culture*, Port Townsend, Wash., 1983, 3–15, and K. Frampton, "Towards a Critical Regionalism: Six Points for an Architecture of Resistance," in H. Foster, ed., *The Anti-Aesthetic, Essays on Post Modern Culture*, Port Townsend, Wash., 1983, 16–30, and K. Frampton, *Modern Architecture and the Critical Present*, London, 1982.

tions. They have sought us out (not the other way around), presumably for our skills in fulfilling programmatic needs while bringing other contributions to the situation. What these seem to be are both an ability to understand this Orwellian pressure to wield imagery laden with secondary, desirable meanings to their advantage (i.e., to lend them legitimacy, pedigree, quality, and concern for traditional social and landscape values) and an intuition that we will in some way resist this, producing something of worth on its own terms that remains aloof from their goals and manipulations, that speaks directly to the region and setting that surrounds them spatially that precedes and succeeds them in time. Although we have been attacked from the left and accused of manipulating and exploiting images of traditional landscapes for the benefit of a capitalist consumer apparatus that parasitically feeds on the people, places, and history it co-opts and destroys, it is my view that the devices, concerns, and strategies I have presented above are part of a conscious effort on our part, while working within the mainstream of modern (contemporary) practice, frequently for large and powerful developers, corporations, and institutions, to resist their unconscious (and conscious) desires to co-opt, dominate, and destroy the various local and regional societies and landscape they engage. I often feel that the people who hire us silently count on our knowledge and sensibility to do this for them. Our quiet lobbying and scheming to accommodate and contribute to the experience and life of the common man, their employees, passersby, as well as to the board and executives who pay our bills, is something that they more than tolerate, but hope for and count on. Concerning issues of regionalism, here too, our clients expect their designers to solve them, to know what is appropriate and what will work, and to contribute positively to their property and society. How we choose to work it out really is our problem, no one else's, and there is no clear path to follow. In fact, outside of particular courses in a small handful of universities such issues are rarely discussed. It is with great pleasure and curiosity, therefore, that I share these thoughts on a subject that has played such a central role in our work.

Appendix

Wilhelm Miller and *The Prairie Spirit in Landscape Gardening*

CHRISTOPHER VERNON

The Prairie Spirit in Landscape Gardening was originally published by the University of Illinois in 1915 as its Agricultural Experiment Station circular, number 184. Its author, Wilhelm Miller, then a professor of "landscape horticulture" and Head of the University's Division of Landscape Extension, is remembered today almost exclusively for this single document. In turn, this document has been regarded primarily as a "regionalist" manifesto and consequently of provincial interest only. In contrast to these more recent perceptions, however, Miller was already widely read and had distinguished himself nationally in the fields of horticulture and landscape gardening prior to its publication. Furthermore, *The Prairie Spirit in Landscape Gardening* marked the culmination of his fifteen year quest for a national, "American" landscape design aesthetic.

Born on the 14th of November 1869, Wilhelm Tyler Miller was raised in Detroit, Michigan.[1] Upon graduation from the University of Michigan in 1892, Miller pursued graduate studies at Cornell University. Interest in nature and plants brought him in contact with Cornell's celebrated horticulturalist and social philosopher, Liberty Hyde Bailey (1858–1954). Miller, working under Bailey's direction, eventually received both an A.M. (1897) and Ph.D. (1899) from Cornell.

Wilhelm Miller's decision to attend Cornell initiated what would prove to be a life-long friendship and association with Liberty Hyde Bailey. While still a student, Miller first was hired as Bailey's assistant at Cornell's agricultural experiment station in 1896. Bailey, evidently impressed by Miller's literary ability, employed him three years later as associate editor of and contributor to his monumental and now classic publication, the *Cyclopedia of American Horticulture*.[2] In conjunction with his work for Bailey, Miller surveyed American landscape gardening for the *Cyclopedia*. This survey was not only instrumental in expanding Miller's interest from horticulture to embrace landscape gardening,

---

[1] For a chronological outline of Miller's career, see L. B. Bailey, ed., *R[ural]. U[plook]. S[ervice].*, Ithaca, New York, 1918.

[2] L. H. Bailey, ed., and W. Miller, assoc. ed., *Cyclopedia of American Horticulture*, New York, 1900–1902.

but also apparently stimulated his consideration of what constituted an American "style"; something that he believed America lacked. This idea would come to dominate Miller's writings for the remainder of is career.

Bailey became the editor of Doubleday, Page, and Company's new magazine, *Country Life in America* (New York), in 1901. Apparently at Bailey's suggestion, Wilhelm Miller was retained as the periodical's horticultural editor. Miller, as he had for the *Cyclopedia*, soon began writing feature articles for the magazine in addition to editing its horticultural contributions. These essays continued to promote the establishment of an American landscape design aesthetic as the title of Miller's initial feature article, "An American Idea in Landscape Art," suggests.[3]

Due to his abilities, and perhaps to his growing popularity with his readers within professional horticultural circles, Miller was retained as the founding editor of the *Garden Magazine* (New York) in 1905. His articles for this periodical also reflected an expansion from horticulture to landscape design, more specifically to a quest for "Americanism." Miller's attempt to discover "the causes of English garden excellence" and to discern "methods by which the most satisfying English effects might be produced in America with American materials" led him to England in 1908.[4] Three years later, the results of Miller's English garden studies were published as a book, *What England Can Teach Us About Gardening*.[5] In this, Miller contended that "the noblest lesson English gardens can teach us is this: Let every country use chiefly its own native trees, shrubs, and vines and other permanent material, and let the style of gardening grow naturally out of the necessity, the soil, and the new conditions. When we stop imitating and do this, America will soon find herself."[6] These ideas were to become the foundation of Miller's later Prairie School ideals.

Prior to the publication of this book, Miller primarily illustrated Atlantic Seaboard garden exemplars, perhaps in part a response to the largely eastern readership of *Country Life in America*. In September 1911, however, an indication that Miller's journalistic crusade for "Americanism" would find regional expression appeared in print: Miller published the first of a series of *Country Life in America* articles that included a promotion of the work of Chicago landscape architect, Jens Jensen (1860–1951).[7] Jensen's work, Miller reported, was inspired by and derived from Illinois prairie landscape and not from an English landscape park or an Italian renaissance garden. This indigenous inspiration, for Miller, not only distinguished Jensen's work from his previously published examples,

[3] W. Miller, "An American Idea in Landscape Art," *Country Life in America* 4 (1903), 349–50. Here Miller discusses, using Chicago's Graceland Cemetery as his example, the landscape cemetery as an "American institution." Miller's discussion focuses on Graceland's design by Ossian C. Simonds.

[4] "What England Can Teach Us about Gardening" [book review], *Country Life in America* 22 (1912), 10–12.

[5] W. Miller, *What England Can Teach Us about Gardening*, New York, 1911.

[6] Ibid., v.

[7] W. Miller, "Successful American Gardens VIII," *Country Life in America* 20 (1911), 35–38.

but also as "American." Miller increasingly focused upon both the Midwest and Jensen's work in subsequent articles.

The Midwest—an environment Miller perceived to be less laden with European landscape gardening traditions than the East—would prove to be a place more in sympathy with his aesthetic ideal. Apparently due to his national visibility, Cornell education, and association with the highly-respected Bailey, Miller was offered a faculty position at the University of Illinois in 1912. Perhaps seeking the opportunity to participate more actively in the development of a regional aesthetic, Miller accepted and became an Assistant Professor of Landscape Horticulture. Although he could no longer serve as editor, Miller did continue to publish articles in both *Country Life* and the *Garden Magazine* while employed by the university. As a faculty member, Miller's primary responsibility was to further the university's "Country Beautiful" programs via publications and public lectures, illustrated with lantern-slides.

Following the passage of the Smith-Lever Act (which funded extension programs at Land Grant universities), Wilhelm Miller was appointed Head of the University's newly-created Division of Landscape Extension in 1914. It was under these auspices that Miller wrote *The Prairie Spirit in Landscape Gardening* the following year.

Here Miller for the first time defined the "prairie style" as:

> a new mode of design and planting, which aims to fit the peculiar scenery, climate, soil, labor and other conditions of the prairies, instead of copying literally the manners and materials of other regions. . . . [The prairie style is] based upon the practical needs of the middle western people and characterized by preservation of typical western scenery, by restoration of local color, and by repetition of the horizontal line of land or sky which is the strongest feature of prairie scenery.[8]

Miller cited the work of Ossian Cole Simonds (1851–1931), Jensen, and Walter Burley Griffin (1876–1937) as being inspired by the "prairie spirit" and expressed in the "prairie style." Of these three designers, the majority of Miller's text was devoted to the work of his by now personal friend Jensen.[9] Jensen at the time manifested Miller's "prairie spirit" primarily through the then-novel ecological use of plants in naturalistic compositions. The most symbolically evocative of these "prairie style" landscapes were those spatially emulative of the actual and remembered grove and prairie checkerboard of the native landscape of the Midwest. Many of the devices promoted by Miller as a means to express the "prairie spirit," such as "stratified" trees and shrubs (i.e., those with horizontal branching habits) and striated rock work, were, in fact, design features adopted directly from Jensen.

[8] W. Miller, *The Prairie Spirit in Landscape Gardening,* University of Illinois Agricultural Experiment Station, Circular 184, Urbana, Ill., 1915, 1, 5.
[9] Miller illustrated twenty-four examples of Jensen's work and ten of Simonds's; Griffin's work was not illustrated. Beyond illustrations of his work, Jensen is quoted—in some instances without attribution—throughout the text.

Miller's "prairie style" was distinguished essentially by its horticultural program. The "prairie spirit" was to be expressed fundamentally through the use of plants indigenous to the prairie landscape. Beyond this, Miller's application of plant ecology to landscape design also distinguished the "prairie spirit." Possibly at the suggestion of Jensen, Miller urged his readers to compose native plant groupings in ecologically appropriate "plant societies" or associations.[10]

Miller presupposed that the native plants would be grouped in essentially naturalistic compositions. Although he did offer a one-sentence palliative that "the prairie style can be executed in the formal manner," the "prairie *style*" was implicitly derived from English picturesque naturalism—as interpreted by American sources such as A. J. Downing (1815–52).[11] Miller, for example, characterized Griffin as a "landscape architect who has been greatly influenced by the prairie"; however, strangely absent from this profusely illustrated publication are photographs of Griffin's typically formal, architectonic gardens. Miller apparently included Griffin's work primarily because "as early as 1906 he was using a high percentage of plants native to Illinois."[12] "To summarize it all," Miller concluded, "people generally pass in their appreciation from the temporary to the permanent, from the spectacular to the restful, from the showy to the quiet, from the artificial to the natural, from rare to common, from foreign to native."[13]

Ultimately, Miller's synthesis of plant ecology and landscape gardening was the most characteristic expression of the "prairie spirit." This idea was an outgrowth of Miller's ecologically-informed effort to make more psychologically comprehensible the sweep of

[10] Jensen first (and later Miller) gained knowledge of ecology from Henry Chandler Cowles (1869–1939), the pioneering plant ecologist of the University of Chicago. Both Cowles and Miller were charter members of The Friends of Our Native Landscape, a conservation organization founded by Jensen in 1913. Miller included Cowles's publication, *The Plant Societies of Chicago and Vicinity* (Chicago, 1901), in his "Literature of the Prairie Style of Landscape Gardening," bibliography (*Prairie Spirit*, 27).

[11] Miller, *Prairie Spirit*, 4. Miller included this palliative in his caption for an illustration of Jensen's formal rose garden in Chicago's Humboldt Park (fig. 8). Although primarily remembered today for his advocacy and design of naturalistic landscapes (as well as for his self-professed "hatred" of formal gardens), Jensen did in fact design formal gardens (in some instances at his client's insistence)—albeit with less frequency through the remainder of his career. Perhaps attributable to his growing bias against formal gardens, Jensen in describing this one—which he had designed eight years earlier in 1907—somewhat apologetically qualified that he had "lowered the garden two feet in order to get the flowers well below the level of the eye as they are on the prairie in the spring." As Robert E. Grese has noted, Jensen later dismissed this garden as a "folly" of his youth (*Jens Jensen: A Maker of Natural Parks and Gardens*, Baltimore and London, 1992, 180). The rose garden's larger setting, Humboldt Park, itself also had been redesigned in a naturalistic manner by Jensen in 1907–17.

[12] Miller, *Prairie Spirit*, 3. Griffin's "prairie style" architecture (and the fact that he had graduated from the University of Illinois) also may have suggested his inclusion. Furthermore, all of the residences that Miller illustrated as examples of "prairie architecture" or "the Prairie Style of Architecture" (see Miller's figs. 1, 5, 17, 76, and the cover), were depicted set amidst naturalistic landscapes. If this in fact were not the actual setting, as in the case of the architect William Drummond's house (fig. 17), only a detail photograph or a "creatively" cropped one apparently was used. In contrast, these houses more frequently were given a formal garden setting. In fact, Jensen himself was responsible for the naturalistic landscape designs for the August Magnus (1904; Winnetka, Illinois) (cover) and Babson (1909–17; Riverside, Illinois) (fig. 1) residences.

[13] Miller, *Prairie Spirit*, 32.

prairie landscape through the identification of its "Romantic Scenery," or of its landscape typology when characteristic of Illinois (and, similarly, throughout the region). The ecological use of plants was to complement Miller's effort to ascertain authentic landscape elements (again probably informed by Jensen's selections), for example, the horizontal land and striated limestone rock work, peculiar to the region. In addition to "conserving" or "restoring" these features, often lost through pioneer action, Miller's "prairie spirit" dictated that they be "intensified" through landscape design "instead of importing foreign beauty."[14] This sentiment leads to another aspect of the "prairie style": the nationalist, democratic character embodied in the principle of the "prairie spirit."

Although now often obscured by its regional associations, Miller intended the principle of the "prairie spirit" to be applied beyond Illinois. He elaborated:

> The prairie style ought not to be copied by people who live among the mountains or in the arid regions, simply because their friends in Illinois may have something beautiful in that style. The essence of landscape gardening is the accentuation of native scenery, and the strong feature in mountainous countries is the vertical line, which mountaineers should repeat by planting their own aspiring evergreens, such as white spruce, hemlock, and balsam.[15]

Through the intensification of the native landscape, whether prairie, mountain, bog, or sand dune, Miller envisioned the emergence of a genuine, convincing "American style." For Miller, regionalism was the path to nationalism.

Miller's urgent manifesto proved to be a premature swan song. Due to dramatically reduced funding, the university disbanded its Division of Landscape Extension in the summer of 1916; Miller's contract was not renewed. He then attempted to establish a landscape architectural practice in Chicago. Unsuccessful at that, he returned to his hometown of Detroit with the same goal in 1918. By then, however, World War I had eliminated the demand for new commissions. In response to anti-German sentiments engendered by the war, Miller changed his first name from "Wilhelm" to "William" in 1919. Shortly thereafter, he retired to southern California and later died there in obscurity on 16 March 1938. Although at the time of his death Miller's publications numbered in the hundreds, neither *Country Life in America* nor the *Garden Magazine* published an obituary.

[14] Ibid., 23.
[15] Ibid.

Circular 184 ❧ ILLINOIS AGRICULTURAL EXPERIMENT STATION ❧ November, 1915

The Prairie Spirit in Landscape Gardening

WHAT THE PEOPLE OF ILLINOIS HAVE DONE AND CAN DO TOWARD DESIGNING
AND PLANTING PUBLIC AND PRIVATE GROUNDS FOR EFFICIENCY AND BEAUTY

By WILHELM MILLER

Department of Horticulture, Division of Landscape Extension

A forerunner of a prairie type of permanent farm home surrounded by permanent vegetation native to Illinois

UNIVERSITY OF ILLINOIS
COLLEGE OF AGRICULTURE
URBANA

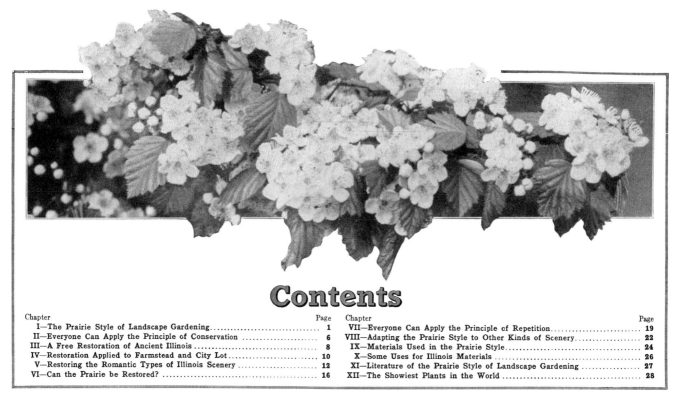

Contents

"DONE IN ILLINOIS"

The above words, accompanied by a bur-oak leaf, have been inserted inconspicuously in the lower corners of many photographs as a guarantee that the pictures were really taken in Illinois and not in other states and represent cultivation rather than wild nature. All such pictures are examples of the "Illinois way of planting," since they contain a high percentage of trees and shrubs native to Illinois. Many of these landscape effects have been consciously designed in the prairie style of landscape gardening. Collectively these pictures offer convincing evidence that Illinois is creating a new and appropriate type of beauty.

"Conservation" is the First Principle of the Prairie Style of Landscape Gardening

Has your community destroyed its oldest trees or has it saved its scenery, like Riverside? These trees line a river bank, which is not treated as a dump-heap, while the elders and sumacs show that the lot owners save and encourage in their back yards the luxuriant, native vegetation.

I---The Prairie Style of
Landscape Gardening

A New Mode of Designing and Planting, Which Aims to Fit the Peculiar Scenery, Climate, Soil, Labor, and Other Conditions of the Prairies, Instead of Copying Literally the Manners and Materials of Other Regions

THE Middle West is just beginning to evolve a new style of architecture, interior decoration, and landscape gardening, in an effort to create the perfect home amid the prairie states. This movement is founded on the fact that one of the greatest assets which any country or natural part of it can have, is a strong national or regional character, especially in the homes of the common people. Its westernism grows out of the most striking peculiarity of middle-western scenery, which is the prairie, i. e., flat or gently rolling land that was treeless when the white man came to Illinois. Some of the progress that has been made toward a prairie style of architecture is incidentally illustrated in these pages. (See front cover, and Figs. 1, 5, 17, and 76.)

The progress in landscape gardening is typified by the following statement from one member of the new "middle-western school of artists: "When I was landscape gardener for the West Side parks in Chicago I directed the expenditure of nearly $4,000,000 on projects inspired by the prairie. Some of the money went for salaries and maintenance, but there was a bond issue of $3,000,000 for new construction. This was chiefly spent on such designs as the Prairie River in Humboldt Park (Fig. 2), the Prairie Rose-garden (Fig. 8), and the Conservatories in Garfield Park (Figs. 25-34). Of course, the primary motive was to give recreation and pleasure to the people, but the secondary motive was to inspire them with the vanishing beauty of the prairie. Therefore, I used many symbols of the prairie, i. e., plants with strongly horizontal branches or flower clusters that repeat

in obvious or subtle ways the horizontal line of land and sky which is the most impressive phenomenon on the boundless plains. Also, I aimed to re-create the atmosphere of the prairie by restoring as high a proportion as possible of the trees, shrubs, and flowers native to Illinois."

The principles of design on which the "prairie men" lay most stress are conservation, restoration, and repetition, as illustrated on the contents page and by Figs. 2 and 3.

A great field for applying these principles is offered by our parks. Of course, literal restoration of prairie scenery is impractical in places that are visited by thousands of people daily. But the spirit of truth can be restored to every large city park in the Middle West, witness the Prairie River and its adjacent meadow (Fig. 2). Each city can produce a different picture by restoring its local color, or characteristic vegetation. There are three ways of doing this, for the prairie spirit can be idealized, conventionalized, or symbolized. For example, it is idealized in the Conservatories (Figs. 25-34) by suggesting the appearance of Illinois in geological periods before the coming of man. It is conventionalized in the Rose-garden (Fig. 8) so much so that there are no prairie flowers in it, and in Humboldt boulevard (Fig. 59). It is symbolized at the playground at Douglas Park (Figs. 55-56) by means of plants with horizontal branches and flower clusters.

The same principles and methods have been used on many private estates, which offer a larger canvas for pure restorations than the average farmstead or city lot. However, every home can express the new idea in proportion to its means. The farmer may idealize his farm view by fram-

1. The Prairie Style of Landscape Gardening Married to the Prairie Style of Architecture

"The environment is woodland," says the landscape architect, "but the newly planted crab apples are designed to frame the view of the house and give an invitation to the prairie which is not far away." (Home of Henry Babson, River Forest; Louis H. Sullivan, architect.)

2. "Restoration" Is the Second Principle in the Prairie Style

The aim is to re-create the spirit of disappearing types of American scenery by restoring as much as possible of the "local color" or peculiar character impressed upon each scenic unit by nature thru ages of experiment. The famous "Prairie River" in Humboldt Park, Chicago. (Jens Jensen, landscape architect.)

ing it with haws as in Fig. 12. The city dweller may conventionalize the prairie in his garden, as in Fig. 13. The humblest renter may symbolize the prairie by putting a prairie rose beside the door, as in Fig. 14. Amid the most artificial surroundings it is possible to hint at the bountiful prairie which surrounds every city and is the source of its prosperity. Even among the tenements, a single brown-eyed daisy in a window box may keep alive the hope of freedom, prosperity, and a life amid more beautiful surroundings. Thus every home in Illinois can connect itself with the greatest source of inspiration

in middle-western scenery, by preserving, restoring, or repeating some phase of the prairie.

The origin of the "middle-western movement" in landscape gardening, if it may be so called, can be traced back to 1878 when Mr. Bryan Lathrop "discovered" Mr. O. C. Simonds and persuaded him to become a landscape gardener. The latter then began to lay out the new part of Graceland Cemetery, which, during the next quarter of a century, was perhaps the most famous example of landscape gardening designed by a western man. It is more than a mere cemetery, for it is full of spiritual suggestion, and its wonderful effects produced by trees and shrubs native to Illinois have profoundly influenced the planting of home grounds. In 1880 Mr. Simonds began to transplant from the wilds the common Illinois species of oak, maple, ash, hornbeam, pepperidge, thorn apple, witch hazel, panicled dogwood, sheepberry,

elder, and the like. Many of these plants have achieved great size and beauty. All the species named are nowadays called "stratified plants," but there was no talk then of "repetition," or even of "restoration." The guiding spirit was that respect for the quieter beauties of native vegetation which comes to every cultured person after he has lived a few years among the showiest plants from all foreign lands as assembled in ordinary nurseries and in the front yards of beginners. Graceland was to be a place of rest and peace, not a museum or a gaudy show. Should not the same ideal prevail in our home grounds?

The first piece of work done by Mr. Simonds that suggests what is now called "restoration," was begun in 1895 at Quincy, Illinois, when its famous park system overlooking the Mississippi was projected under the leadership of the late Edward J. Parker. One glance at the plans shows that Mr. Simonds had drunk deep of the spirit of Downing and the elder Olmsted, who taught that preservation of the natural landscape is usually more beautiful and less costly than leveling every hill and filling every ravine. Some of the best-known work of Mr. Simonds is in Lincoln Park, Chicago, but the whole "North Shore" shows his influence in home grounds.

Probably the first designer who consciously took the prairie as a leading motive is Mr. Jens Jensen, who was trained in Denmark and came to America in 1883. In 1885 he settled in Chicago and was at once impressed by the surrounding prairie, which was then a sea of grasses and flowers. Acres of phlox and

3. "Repetition" is the Third Principle in the Prairie Style of Landscape Gardening.

The branches or flowers of hawthorns repeat many times on a small scale the horizontal line of land or sky, which is often the strongest feature of middle-western scenery. Every flat flower cluster is a symbol of the prairie. Graceland Cemetery, Chicago, has greatly influenced home planting in Illinois. (O. C. Simonds, landscape gardener.)

4-5. Can We Make out of Simple Scenery and Common Plants a Prairie Style of Architecture and Landscape Gardening?

Beside the barbed-wire or occasional rail fences of Illinois, the farmer sometimes leaves a relic of "the glory that was," some "repeater of the prairie," i. e., a harmless shrub with flat flower clusters, like elder, dogwood, or viburnum.

"I purposely repeated the prairie line in the roofs," says the architect, William Drummond. "The elder in the back yard echoes the same note. It suggests that this house would look more homelike with foundation planting."

blazing star and thousands of compass plants were a familiar sight. The first design in which prairie flowers were used in a large, impressive way, was made in 1901 for Mr. Chalmers at Lake Geneva. Here were planted hundreds of the wild Phlox paniculata, parent of more than 400 garden varieties; hundreds of purple flags (Iris versicolor) collected from the banks of the Desplaines river, and hundreds of swamp rose mallows which glorify the rivers of Illinois in August with their pink flowers five inches in diameter. The first attempt to epitomize the beauty of Illinois rivers was made in 1901 for Mr. Harry Rubens at Glencoe, where there are a miniature spring, brook, waterfall, and lake (Figs. 47-48). Practically all the surrounding trees, shrubs, and flowers were planted, and more than ninety-five percent of the species grow wild within a mile of the spot. From 1905 to 1907 he designed and planted the Prairie River and Prairie Rose-garden in Humboldt Park, and the Conservatories in Garfield Park.

A third landscape architect who has been greatly influenced by the prairie is Walter Burley Griffin. He received his training in landscape gardening at the University of Illinois, and supplemented it by work in the offices of several

architects of the western school. He planned many houses in the prairie style. His chief American work in landscape architecture has been done at DeKalb, Decatur, Oak Park, Hubbard's Woods, Edwardsville, and Veedersburg, Indiana. The planting list for DeKalb shows that as early as 1906 he was using a high percentage of plants native to Illinois—especially the stratified materials. In 1912 he won a world-competition for a city plan for Canberra, the new capital of Australia. Mr. Griffin must be regarded as a middle-western landscape architect, since he maintains an office in Illinois and undertakes new work in the Middle West.

There are many other good landscape gardeners now practicing in the Middle West. Those who acknowledge the prairie as a leading motive in their work, are, however, not numerous at the time this paper is prepared. There are several young men whose work is promising, but not mature or extensive enough to show their feeling for the prairie style. One of the older men has submitted an itemized list of his work in the prairie style done in Illinois and nearby states since 1901 which makes the respectable total of $6,000,000.

Whether the work here described and illustrated consti-

6. A Farm View without a Frame of Trees

Altho corn is considered one of the most beautiful crops, people often complain that Illinois scenery is tame and monotonous. The wild prairie, with its varied flowers, has gone forever. How can men restore flowers and poetic suggestion to a land nearly ninety percent of which is tilled?

7. A Farm View Framed by Hawthorns in Bloom

The farmer can increase the natural beauty of his pasture or cornfields by planting trees near his front door, beside the dining-room window, along the road, or wherever he can frame a good view. Especially suitable are stratified trees, like haws, crabs, honey locust, and flowering dogwood.

8. The Prairie Style can be Executed in the Formal Manner

This rose garden in Humboldt Park is so conventionalized that it contains no prairie flowers. "But," says the designer, "I put hawthorns at the entrance to suggest the meeting of woods and prairie. Also I lowered the garden two feet in order to get the flowers well below the level of the eye as they are on the prairie in the spring. I gave the people the obvious beauty of roses and I hope a subtle charm also."

them as the formal and informal manners. For example, the prairie style has been executed in the formal manner, as in the Rose-garden (Fig. 8), tho it is generally executed in the informal manner. Authoritative books commonly speak of the 'gardenesque style,' which is typified by canna beds in the middle of the lawn. Surely all the middle-western work is better than that, and even the most conservative examples are colored more or less by middle-western materials. For these reasons I am willing to accept 'the prairie style of landscape gardening' (a phrase which I did not propose) until a better name for this new thing is discovered and agreed upon."

The settlement of this amicable difference of opinion we leave to our readers. Whether the new work is good or bad, time alone can tell. Perhaps the publication of this circular should have been postponed a century

tutes a new style or not is an interesting and important question. One of the conservative group among the middle-western landscape gardeners says, "I doubt if there is any western style of art. Good design must always grow out of the necessities peculiar to each case—not out of pet theories. I am not conscious of any new principles of design." As to motives, of course, the creator of an artwork is the final authority, but as to results the general public is entitled to an opinion. The popular belief is that the man just quoted has a style of his own, and that his work also possesses an indefinable quality that may be called middle-western. He generally uses a rather large proportion of western plants—more than most eastern landscape gardeners who have done important work in Illinois.

When the same question was put to one of the progressive or prairie group he replied: "Undoubtedly there is a middle-western style of landscape gardening. All good design that meets western conditions counts toward a western style. Style, according to Webster, is a characteristic or peculiar mode of developing an idea or accomplishing a result. The conservatives unconsciously use, to some extent, conservation, restoration, and repetition. The middle-western work is not a 'style' in the same sense that people speak of the 'formal and informal styles.' It would be more accurate to speak of

or two. On the other hand, the average person has a strange disinclination to wait a hundred years for the news. The people of Illinois actually seem glad to know about a new thing before it is too late for them to benefit by it. And they are generally willing to assume full responsibility for their own opinions. We do not advise any one style of architecture or landscape gardening for all conditions, nor have we any quarrel with those who prefer older styles of architecture and gardening. All we ask is that every reader see some of the new work for himself, with a mind free from prejudice.

Symbol of the Illinois Way—Illinois or Prairie Rose.

Definition of the "Illinois Way"

The Illinois way of planting is not a new system of design. The original definition says, "The Illinois way is to meet all the outdoor needs of the family by having ninety percent of the planting composed of trees and shrubs that grow wild in Illinois." However, in the most exacting and artificial conditions, like downtown parks, formal gardens, and the smallest city yard, only ten to twenty percent of Illinois plants may be consistent with good design.

9-10. Before and After Restoring the Native Flora to a Man-Made Watercourse in Humboldt Park

"This bank had been denuded of its original vegetation," says the designer. "The margin did not look as bad as this, because it was grassed, but it was not redeemed by a single tree, shrub, or flower. The location is identified by a good old cottonwood in the park and an exclamatory Lombardy poplar, which I spared in a moment of weakness. I shall be glad when the poplar dies, for it cuts like a knife thru the billowy masses of western woodland."

Around the foundations of the ordinary house, forty to fifty percent may be suitable, while the borders may contain sixty to ninety percent of Illinois species with general satisfaction. Therefore, the following revised definition is proposed: "The Illinois way of planting is to use as high a proportion of plants native to Illinois as is consistent with practical requirements and the principles of design." In this sense, our neighboring states may have an Iowa or Indiana way, using the same plants that we do, for there is no plant of importance native to Illinois that is not also native to other prairie states. And, by the same method, every state in the Union can develop a beauty of its own, even if no state is a scenic unit.

Definition of the "Prairie Style"

The prairie style of landscape gardening, however, is a genuine style in the opinion of several critics, for it is based on a geographic, climatic, and scenic unit, and it employs three accepted principles of design—conservation of native scenery, restoration of local vegetation, and repetition of a dominant line. However, it is not a system of rules and there never can be anything of the sort in any fine art, tho people crave it forever. In good design there are only principles. Nor is the prairie style a mere collection of novel features, such as campfires, players' greens, council hills, prairie gardens, and Illinois borders. Features never make a style. Sundials, pergolas, and blue spruces may fit certain conditions to perfection, but a man who uses them in every plan is open to the suspicion of being an inferior designer. Therefore, until something better can be had, the following definition is proposed: The prairie style of landscape gardening is an American mode of design based upon the practical needs of the middle-western people and characterized by preservation of typical western scenery, by restoration of local color, and by repetition of the horizontal line of land or sky which is the strongest feature of prairie scenery.

To those who are in danger of being carried away by new fashions, may we give a word of caution? The best gardens cannot be had simply for paying money and copying or imitating. One must patiently study fundamental principles. There is nothing new about the principles used in the prairie style; only their applications are new. Some even declare that the only new thing in the world is undying zeal for hard, persistent work in adapting old principles to new conditions. Surely there is no other way to produce that thing which is infinitely more precious than the universal, endless imitation of the past—a living national art which grows out of the heart of the people and which the humblest mortal can understand and enjoy, as every Greek did in the thrilling new days when temples and

Symbol of the Prairie Style—A Stratified Hawthorn.

statues were growing out of the rock at Athens!

In the great work of fitting homes to the prairie country every one of us may have a part, for everyone may strive towards a permanent home surrounded by permanent native plants. Let us do all we can to help realize an Illinois type of farmhouse married to an Illinois type of interior decoration and landscape gardening.

11. The Minnesota Model Farmhouse

Plans secured (1913) by Minnesota State Art Society, published by University of Minnesota, St. Paul, in Extension Bulletin 52. Who will help Illinois develop an Illinois type of farmhouse set in a farmstead designed for efficiency and beauty?

Note on Chapter Endings

To meet the ever-recurring question, "What shall we do?" we have put, at the ends of certain chapters, summaries in the form of practical suggestions headed by the phrase "I will" or "We will." The former is a motto of Chicago; the latter has been suggested as a new, informal motto for Illinois. Is your family united on any of the projects named below? If not, the "We will" suggestions may help you agree on what you wish to do. Again, to realize one's ideal it is often helpful to record one's aim. If you wish to record an individual determination or family agreement you may make a cross in the appropriate square. Such action commits nobody to any expense or publicity. It is merely a private memorandum.

WE WILL

☐ See some of the chief works of the western landscape gardeners.

☐ Have a landscape gardener make a comprehensive design for our home grounds.

☐ Draw to scale a plan for our farmstead or city lot and get the best advice we can.

☐ Connect with the "Illinois way" by putting in our front yard at least one mass of shrubs native to Illinois.

☐ Study some of the best "prairie houses," indoors and out, with a mind free from prejudice.

☐ Build a farmhouse or country home in prairie style.

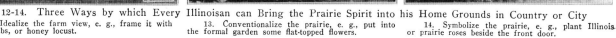

12-14. Three Ways by which Every Illinoisan can Bring the Prairie Spirit into his Home Grounds in Country or City

12. Idealize the farm view, e. g., frame it with haws, crabs, or honey locust.

13. Conventionalize the prairie, e. g., put into the formal garden some flat-topped flowers.

14. Symbolize the prairie, e. g., plant Illinois or prairie roses beside the front door.

15-16. Is your Community Butchering its Trees, or is it Saving them as Urbana Does?

The elms at the right and all other street trees in Urbana are being saved by a public-spirited citizen, who serves as "tree warden" without pay. No one can cut down, prune, or plant a tree without his permission. Cannot your community have a city forester or shade-tree commission?

II—Everyone Can Apply the Principle of Conservation

I T WILL do little good to bewail the beauty that has been destroyed in Illinois. Let us save the beauty that is left. Here is a simple program that may help every reader decide what he can do for this great cause.

1. Save the trees on your home grounds. Have a tree surgeon examine them and estimate the cost of putting them in perfect condition. Locate the new house so as to save trees (see Figs. 17 and 76). Let every farmer save a few trees for shade and beauty, even if they do harm crops a little. For example, save some trees along the roadside, around the farmstead, near the barns, and at least one tree in the permanent pasture. See Figs. 19-20.

2. Help save the street trees. Take the trees out of politics and put them in charge of a public-spirited citizen serving without pay—a city forester, or tree warden (see Figs. 15-16). He can stop tree butchery caused by telegraph and telephone companies.

3. Help save roadside trees and shrubs. See your township supervisor or county superintendent of highways. Show him Figs. 21 to 24 and 51 to 54.

4. Help save the watercourses. Get the authorities to forbid their use as dumping grounds (see contents page).

5. Help save the historic features of your community and give them a proper setting. See Fig. 18.

6. Help save the state's scenery. Join an organization that works for state reservations, like White Pine Grove, Cahokia Mounds, and the proposed addition to Starved Rock.

Organizations Devoted to Conservation

O N LOCAL propositions it is generally best to work thru the Chamber of Commerce or the Woman's Club.

The National Conservation Association, of which Gifford Pinchot is president, is devoted to saving our natural resources, especially the forests, waterways, and minerals. The secretary is Harry A. Slattery, Colorado building, Washington, D. C.

The American Civic Association, of which J. Horace McFarland is president, is devoted largely to city planning, including housing. It has issued important publications on smoke, billboards, saving Niagara, and other subjects. The secretary is Richard Watrous, 913 Union Trust building, Washington, D. C.

The Friends of Our Native Landscape, of which Jens Jensen is president, aim to save all types of native scenery by means of national, state, and local reservations. The secretary is Sherman M. Booth, Borland building, Chicago.

The General Federation of Woman's Clubs has a Conservation Department with committees on forestry (including street trees, waterways, birds, and Lincoln Highway). The chairman of the Conservation Department is Mrs. John Dickinson Sherman, Hyde Park Hotel, Chicago.

The Illinois Federation of Woman's Clubs has a Conservation Department, the chairman of which is Mrs. Charles W. Irion, Ottawa, Illinois.

I WILL

☐ Write to national, state, and local organizations interested in conservation, study their literature, and help them all I can.

☐ Work and vote for the extension of the state park system to include all types of Illinois scenery.

☐ Ask the county highway superintendent to save trees, shrubs, and flowers on state and country roadsides.

☐ Work and vote to help our community extend its system of local parks and reservations, and to save the street trees.

☐ Give the people some piece of scenery to enjoy forever.

☐ Save the permanent native vegetation on my farm or home grounds, as far as possible.

17. Let us Save the Trees on our Home Grounds

"Because I love trees I bought this lot and snuggled my house among them, so that three big trees are growing thru the front porch. I cut a hole in the eaves to make room for one."—William Drummond, River Forest.

18. Save Every Historic Feature and Give It a Proper Setting!

"Lincoln often slept in this century-old cabin—the first built in Piatt county. We moved it to an environment like the original. Many old settlers' cabins are now preserved in parks and more should be."—William F. Lodge, Monticello.

19-20. Have you sent your Woodlot to the Sawmill, or have you Saved it?

"Here is the sawmill with which I cut up my neighbors' trees, but not my own. If they insist on selling their birthright, I might as well have some of the pottage. But before I accept a job I remind my neighbor that for three generations my family has never cut a tree on our farm, just because they are beautiful. And the fourth generation promises to do the same. At the right are some of our trees."—L. D. Seass, Arthur, Illinois.

21-22. Have you Saved the "Brush" along the Roadside?

Farmers, will you reduce your daily drive to this condition or do you want something in your life besides dollars? You can save beauty that would cost you $500 to $1,500 a mile to replace by conference with your highway superintendent or county supervisor. The Illinois law does not compel the cutting of brush, only of *noxious weeds*. These sumacs have been saved by Wisconsin people along a famous drive into Madison.

23-24. Have you Saved the Trees along the Roadside for Shade and Beauty?

These ash trees at the left were cut down for the usual reason, "they harmed ten rows of corn." The trees at the right have been preserved near Sidell by getting every supervisor to agree not to cut them down. Trees in the middle of a road have great educational value because they compel attention.

III—A Free Restoration of Ancient Illinois

A SERIES OF LANDSCAPES UNDER GLASS, SUGGESTING THE BEAUTY OF VANISHED AND DISAPPEARING TYPES OF SCENERY

PARK design is an important part of landscape gardening, and a popular feature in every large park system is a range of greenhouses. The famous Conservatories in Garfield Park, Chicago, have attracted hundreds of thousands of visitors and have been pronounced the "best of the kind in the world." Prior to 1906 the West Side had three small, old-fashioned greenhouses in separate parks. These buildings were visited by few persons and could hardly be said to adorn the scenery. The new landscape gardener proposed to destroy them in favor of one great new structure in which Chicagoans could take real pride. At first the project was resisted, for no locality likes to lose any permanent improvement, but when the plans were explained, the people became enthusiastic.

Instead of the customary potted plants on high benches we are surprised to find these nature-like gardens. The most intelligent visitors are deeply moved by these exquisite scenes and feel that they convey an idea too deep for words. This intuition is correct, for the designer's motive is restoration. His pictures do not pretend to furnish a literal, scientific restoration of any particular geological epoch, such as a museum might have. The idea is poetical—to suggest the tropical beauty of prairie-land before the coming of man. And the reason for this is that we need to see our surroundings from a fresh point of view. We need to realize that modern Illinois contains equally beautiful scenery that we thoughtlessly destroy, but ought to save or restore.

Few communities in Illinois can afford greenhouses large enough for such landscapes under glass, but they all have a great opportunity out-of-doors. Every large park can preserve or re-create one epitome of the scenery and vegetation of Illinois.

Can you not apply the principle of restoration to your own home grounds? These pictures should stimulate your imagination. If you have room for only one bush to symbolize the vanished scenery, may we suggest the prairie rose? See also pages 24, 25.

25. The First Spring in Prairie-Land
This man-made rockwork is so successful that visitors commonly believe that it is a natural spring, around which the greenhouse was built.

26. First Cascade in First Prairie River
Perhaps it stepped down then as now, with giant ferns, like the golden polypody arching over the cliffs like falling water.

26a. A Man-Made Cascade in Kentucky
One of the many ways in which the restoration spirit expresses itself out-of-doors. This is forty-two inches high and cost about $40.

27. When Chicago was a Jungle
The first greenhouse contains a long vista like a tunnel lined with palms and ferns. At the end is this fountain, which alternately leaps and disappears.

28. The First Hint of Stratification, or Repetition of the Prairie Line
Tropical evergreens, like Norfolk Island pines or araucarias, may have sounded the note now echoed by white pines beside Lake Michigan and hawthorns on the prairie. The rocks of this primitive watercourse are horizontally stratified like the St. Peter sandstone of some prairie rivers of today.

29. Some Ancient River Bluff or Rolling Prairie

When the forest may have been composed of tree ferns and fringed with Venus' hair, forerunner of our matchless hardy maidenhair. Let us restore to woodlots and river banks the overhanging bushes and ferns that form the most picturesque and romantic element in middle-western scenery!

30. Nature's First Dream of Prairie-Land

This open, central lawn (one of the fundamental conceptions of landscape gardening out-of-doors) is not composed of vertical grass blades. To give the prairie feeling the designer used a moss-like plant with stratified foliage—Selaginella denticulata. In Fig. 25 he used the moisture-loving S. Martensii.

31. The Original Woodland Border

Not like the stark southern pine forests where there is no undergrowth to soften the abrupt descent from tall trees to flat meadow. The transition from forest to prairie made by haws and crabs should be the motive of our hardy borders.

32. The Primitive Glade in a Middle-Western Forest

Half close the eyes, and the hard brick walk becomes the winding trail that leads to woodland mysteries, hinting of primeval campfires, council rocks, and players' greens. Forest and prairie subtly connected by stratified maidenhair.

33. The Beginning of a Prairie Bog

Here are water hyacinth, cardamon, umbrella plant, and the palm-like curculigo. In modern bogs grow orchids, pitcher plants, and fringed gentian. Shall we save no moist spot near each community where future generations may enjoy the unique flowers of bog gardens?

34. The Margin of some Ancient "Lake Illinois"

When tropical plants arched over the bank, as do these tree ferns, cardamon, and Nephrolepis. Let us put this grace into hardy water gardens by planting the Cornus stolonifera, Typha angustifolia, and Calamagrostis of the prairie rivers.

35-36. The Kind of Restoration that costs the Farmer not one Cent—only the Labor of Collecting and Planting Waterside Flowers

The cattle must have a place to drink, but why not restore to some creeks the original margin of shrubs and perennials? The first picture typifies the "early goose pond" style of treating water in city parks. The second shows a restoration in an Illinois city park. (Pickerel weed and calamus.)

IV—Restoration Applied to Farmstead and City Lot

EVEN WHEN LITTLE MONEY AND SPACE ARE AVAILABLE,
EVERYONE CAN APPLY THE PRINCIPLE OF RESTORATION

THE aim of restoration is to re-create as much of the local scenery or vegetation as is practical. Like every other great idea, restoration can be expressed in some way by everyone. No matter how humble the individual or how crude the expression, the effort is worth while because it is one's own experience and not another's. On one square foot of ground a child expresses his love of country in a map of sand, epitomizing the whole United States by using pebbles for mountains, maple seedlings for forests, and a little real water for the Great Lakes and the Mississippi. This effort means more to the child than a better map made or bought for him by others. So, too, every "grown-up" in Illinois can apply the principles of landscape gardening. The popular notion that landscape gardening is only for city parks and the wealthy few is a great mistake. Of course, the grandest public examples involve much space and cost, but so far as self-expression goes, landscape gardening offers as great an opportunity to every living soul as music does, or any other fine art. The one principle that everyone can apply is restoration.

For example, take the two extreme cases of the people who have no money and those who have no land. The farm laborer goes to the woods, digs up an unknown bush or vine and plants it beside his tenant cottage. To him it may suggest the fatherland from which he has just come, or the child on whose birthday it was planted, or the place he likes to go on Sunday afternoons. It is a crude expression of the manifold charms of Illinois woodland, but to this immigrant it is a step toward naturalization, perhaps even the beginning of wisdom. Moreover, real beauty is there for everyone to see and enjoy. The country folk pause and think: "Life is not all corn and hogs—to him."

On the other hand, the city merchant may have plenty of money, but not one foot of earth in front of his store. Let us assume that he is tired of the artificial surroundings and goes to the country for a day's rest and change. And, while there, an idea comes to him—he will have something more permanent and natural than window boxes. He will have vines—the kind he used to like as a boy on the farm, the narrow-leaved "woodbine," a

variety of Virginia creeper so common in Illinois that, for purposes of sentiment, we may call it the "Illinois creeper." He has two holes cut in the concrete sidewalk, and plants his souvenirs of Illinois. To him they may recall the parents that are gone, or they may remind him of "the day" when he is to shut up shop for good and retire to a country home. The passers-by know nothing of all this, but they are glad to see some sign of country beauty in the city. They say, "Life is not all dollars to that man."

Can such simple plantings be called "restorations" in any important sense? Certainly, if they honestly express the individual's love of the local scenery, combined with his love of home, and town, and state. Restoration is fundamentally an act of the spirit; the scale of operations is incidental. If there is space or money available only for a pair of Illinois roses beside the front door, anything more is pretense. The essential thing is to plant some permanent reminder of the native beauty, and the cost should always be well within one's means. A person may

37-38. Scene of a Woodlot Restoration in Vermilion County, where the Aim is Typified by these Illinois Bluebells

"Like many other farmers, I must plead guilty to harming the beauty of woodlots by cutting out shrubs and letting animals destroy the flowers. But I am now restocking this grove. This process costs a good deal more than saving the original ground-cover. Since I have no business but farming and live on the farm the year round, I feel that my family is entitled to some of the enjoyments that can be had only in the country."—Harvey J. Sconce, Sidell, Illinois.

prefer to have foreign plants in his garden but he must care enough about the native kinds to plant some of them in the public part of his property. For restoration means more than mere gardening—more than the planting of double roses and lilacs, the beauty of which everyone can see. The "restorer" must prove that he wants to be surrounded by common, native things, rather than by rare and costly foreigners.

Is such restoration of any value to the public? Undoubtedly. Even if the results were wholly subjective and individual they would be worth while because everyone is better for making some harmless expression of an unselfish ideal. But the results are evident to all! The Illinois rose beside the door is beautiful in itself and every year it will come to mean more to every passer-by because it will suggest pleasant thoughts of Illinois. Everyone will know that it is put there not to display wealth, but in the pure spirit of restoration. Everyone will know that it is not intended to deceive, for no bush can imitate the prairie, and no person can ever mistake a tree for a forest. But, every year, more people accept the stratified bush or flat-topped flower as a symbol of the prairie and therefore of peace, freedom, and plenty. Every year more people accept the prairie rose as a symbol of the "Prairie State" of Illinois. When people see that rose in your yard, their eyes brighten and their manner says, "It is for Illinois. You have restored something of her native beauty."

What the Average Farmer Can Restore

THE ordinary farmer has little time, labor, or knowledge of design and ornamental plants, but he has two immense advantages— plenty of room (often 160 acres), and a chance to collect wild shrubs and flowers. Starting with no cash outlay and a day's work in the fall, he can accomplish eventually ten things.

1. *Foundation planting.* He can make the house look like a home by moving some shrubs from the woods.

2. *Screens.* He can hide part of the barnyard and out-buildings, at least from his windows.

3. *Views.* He can frame the view of his house from the road and the best view of his farm from the house by transplanting a pair of red haws. See Fig. 7.

4. *The border.* He can enclose the farmstead with an irregular border of shrubbery that will give more year-round beauty than a hedge, trimmed or untrimmed.

5. *The farmstead.* He can plant the whole farmstead to meet the above-named needs of the family, as well as shade, playground, laundry yard, etc.

6. *The creek.* He can restore some of the marginal vegetation. See Figs. 35, 36.

7. *The woodlot.* He can restore many wild flowers simply by fencing a piece of woods. See Figs. 37, 38.

8. *Edges of fields.* He can attract the song birds that are friendly to his crops by planting at the edges or corners of one or more fields some native shrubs, especially the kinds that do not breed pests or rob the soil too much.

9. *Roadside.* He can plant beside the public road a few trees and some harmless shrubs and flowers, and he can often persuade the commissioner not to cut them down. See Figs. 51, 52.

10. *The whole farm.* By "planting the waste land to scenery" he can create a private park—not as showy as the millionaire's, but beautiful and appropriate.

Mr. Farmer, can you not take all or most of these steps in about five years? It may cost a good deal, but it will be worth while. You cannot transplant everything from the wild without expense. Surely you can see the wisdom of buying your Illinois species whenever nursery stock is better or cheaper than collected stock. You should also see the wisdom of getting the best advice and designs that you can afford—especially at the outset. All or most of these plantings may be acts of restoration, instead of copy work. If you use only foreign and artificial varieties your place will make a gaudy contrast with the country scenery. If you restore a high percentage of Illinois trees and shrubs your home will fit the landscape.

What the City Lot Owner Can Restore

THE renter in a city cannot afford to make costly permanent improvements, but the average owner of a city lot is justified in doing so. His great trouble is not about money (for we are assuming that everyone keeps within his means and takes his time to do these things), but he has less space than the farmer. On the other hand, he can give more time per year to ornamental gardening than the farmer, because he needs outdoor exercise after his day's work. Starting with no knowledge of horticulture, and with whatever leisure the gardening members of the family may have, the average lot owner can accomplish eventually about seven things.

1. *Foundation planting.* He can restore something of the Illinois vegetation, even in this exacting location, for example, by viburnum (Fig. 40), fragrant sumac, or prairie rose (Fig. 39).

2. *Screens.* He can hide some of the unsightly surroundings, such as high fence or

outhouse, by wild grape, trumpet creeper, common sumac, elder, and other Illinois plants that are sometimes considered rather coarse for the front of the house. See contents page and Figs. 4, 5.

3. *Views.* He can frame the view of his home, for example, by a pair of elms, haws, or prairie crab apples, or if he considers his house ugly, he can transform it by hiding much of it with vines.

4. *Boundaries.* He can enclose the back yard with an irregular border of native shrubs in variety, instead of with an artificial and monotonous privet hedge.

5. *Front yard.* He can help tie the whole street into a park by persuading the neighbors to plant "connecting shrubbery" from the front of one house to another.

6. *Parking.* He can restore old trees to good health thru tree surgeons; he can combine with his neighbors to get a uniform street tree at uniform distances, or plant low shrubbery. See back cover.

7. *Entire lot.* He can have a plan made for the whole property, arranging in good order all features. He can restore the birds, with the aid of shrubbery, especially the Illinois dogwoods and viburnums.

Every one of these acts can, and usually should be, an act of restoration in some degree. Every list of the most efficient plants may include some Illinois materials—a low percentage near the house, and a higher one at the boundaries.

There is little danger of carrying restoration too far in cities. The great danger is that all front yards will look too gaudy, because beginners tend to buy the showiest varieties, like blue Colorado spruce and golden elder. Consequently they often plant 90 to 100 percent of foreign varieties. The same percentage of native plants would be more restful. We do not ask anyone to deny himself any flower he likes—only to move to the back yard the things that rarely fit the front yard, for example, cutleaved, weeping, variegated, and tropical plants. Everyone has a place of unquestioned privilege in the back yard, provided it is shut off from the public gaze, but the front yard is public. And the real question is, "Shall we have 90 to 100 percent foreigners, or shall we have a clear suggestion of Illinois such as a majority of native plants may give?"

WE WILL

☐ Restore native scenery or vegetation to our farm at some of the ten places mentioned above.

☐ Restore native vegetation to our city lot, at some of the seven places mentioned above.

39. Every Illinoisan can Restore some Prairie Roses

Literal restoration of scenery is, of course, impossible amid cramped and artificial surroundings, but each year more people accept the prairie rose as a symbol of the Prairie State.

40. Every Illinoisan can Restore some Illinois Viburnums

Each year more people accept the stratified bush or flat-topped flower as a symbol of the prairie. This is Viburnum pubescens. One of the best for foundation planting is Viburnum dentatum.

41-42. Before and after Restoring a Typical Creek and Ravine in Northeastern Illinois

This picture was taken only a few feet away from the next and shows that the ravine was nearly dry, as are most of the ravines along Lake Michigan, owing, as some assert, to drainage caused by dense population. Also the wild flowers had been destroyed by picnic parties.

The owners have restored canoeing for about 1,000 feet, using city water from three three-quarter-inch pipes. A dam retains the water, which does not evaporate rapidly, owing to the shade. They have planted many nursery-grown wild flowers. Home of Mr. and Mrs. Julius Rosenwald, Ravinia, Illinois.

V—Restoring the Romantic Types of Illinois Scenery

EIGHT TYPES OF PICTURESQUE SCENERY DIFFERENT FROM
THE PRAIRIE, WITH EXAMPLES OF THEIR RESTORATION

ALL varieties of Illinois scenery can, for practical purposes, be resolved into nine types, of which the prairie is most important, since it probably affects the greatest number of homes. The eight other types may be regarded as foils to the prairie. They are the lake bluffs, ravines, river-banks, ponds, rocks, dunes, woods, and roadsides. The roadside, of course, is not a natural unit, but it is an asylum for the wild flowers, and it has immense possibilities for beauty thru planting. The beauty of the eight minor types is of the obvious and popular sort, because of their romantic or picturesque character. But the beauty of the prairie is harder to understand. It may be well for us to consider the eight minor types of scenery before we try to restore the prairie.

Restoration of the Lake Bluffs

OUTSIDE the great cities of Illinois the most valuable residential property, from the assessor's standpoint, is the shore of Lake Michigan—a great underlying cause of this value being scenery, especially the lake and the wooded ravines. The whole shore from Chicago to Wisconsin is,

broadly speaking, a steep, high, clay-bank that is continually being eaten away by the water. See Fig. 43. Fortunes have been spent to save these bluffs from further destruction, and tens of thousands of dollars have been spent on restoration schemes of every sort—the bluffs being generally thickly planted with trees and shrubs in great variety by dozens of private owners. "Unfortunately," writes E. L. Millard of Highland Park, "practically all places are still in the 'locust stage' of development, the locust being the best soil-binder at the start, but an unsightly tree owing to the attacks of borers. The highest type of beauty worked out by nature along this shore can be inferred from five priceless fragments at and near Lake Forest that should be preserved with reverential care forever. The supreme plants, in my opinion, are the white pine, red cedar, arborvitæ, and canoe birch. At my own place (see Fig. 65) I am beginning to destroy the locusts and all other plants foreign to the locality, as I believe the highest possible aim is to restore and intensify the peculiar beauty which nature adapted to the lake bluff by experiments on a scale so colossal that those which the ordinary multimillionaire

can encompass during a single lifetime sink into insignificance."

Restoration of the Ravines

THE immense popular appeal of the ravines has been fatal to their highest beauty. First, the ravines attracted many home-builders, who soon demanded storm sewers, and these, according to some authorities, carried away much of the water that formerly gave the effect of charming creeks. Second, the ravines attract great Sunday crowds from Chicago, and these have despoiled the ravines of wild flowers. Under such conditions, restoration may be impossible unless private places are closed to the public, except during certain hours when supervision can be provided. Perhaps the largest and most consistent restoration is that made by Mr. and Mrs. Julius Rosenwald of Ravinia. See Figs. 41, 42. Most of the communities between Evanston and Wisconsin aim to attract high-grade residents and to discourage factories. Obviously the ravines form one of the greatest natural assets, and the communities that formerly treated them as dumping grounds are gradually transforming them into public parks and reservations. Let the good work go on!

43-44. Many Restorations of the Lake Bluffs have been made North of Chicago

At the right is the Cyrus H. McCormick place, Lake Forest, where about 150 species, mostly natives, clothe the banks. This wide beach has been created by means of jetties and the willows in the foreground, which were originally planted at the limits of wave action. Warren H. Manning, landscape designer.

45. "Away with Gaudy Foreigners and Artificial Varieties!"

"This overgrown nursery in Humboldt Park," says the designer, "was full of brilliant 'best-sellers,' such as cut-leaved, weeping, and variegated shrubs. These may be jewels in themselves, but superb specimens of them can be seen everywhere and forever. Shall we turn the whole outdoor world into a museum?"

46. "Restore the Native Vegetation!"

"Mr. Corngrower, can you see beauty in your creek, even when there is not a single flower or striking form? If so, you understand why we swept away the showier vegetation of Fig. 45 and restored the simple beauty you often thoughtlessly destroy. If you destroy it, will your children stay on the farm?"

Restoration of the River Banks

EVERY Illinoisan knows about the three great rivers in which we have a share, the Mississippi, Wabash, and Illinois, but to realize the wonderful possibilities of our water system for use, recreation, and beauty one must see a map devoted entirely to our watercourses, showing how few and small are the areas which the people cannot reach by means of a ten-cent fare or an hour's ride in an automobile or a farm buggy. Many of these watercourses have been denuded or desecrated and all sorts of restorations have been made in various parts of the state. Perhaps the largest and most consistent restoration is the "Prairie River" in Humboldt Park, Chicago, which aims to epitomize or suggest the characteristic beauty of the Illinois rivers as a whole. See Fig. 2. The "river," which is man-made, is 1,650 feet long, and varies in width from 52 to 108 feet. It has several branches and some cascades, with rock-work modeled after that of the Rock river. See Circular 170, Fig. 105. The designer deliberately discarded all foreign materials (see Figs. 45, 46) because he was attempting to re-create a pure Illinois landscape. By so doing he denied himself many showy flowers which he believes are among the finest that can be used in ordinary landscape gardening. For example, he would not use pink or yellow water lilies in Fig. 2, because they would not be true to nature. Fortunately, we can see these beautiful foreign plants in every park, but faithful restorations of by-gone scenery are rare. Every property owner along a watercourse or drainage ditch may restore some trees, shrubs, or flowers. Every citizen has a chance to work and vote for restoration of watercourses in park and community plans.

Restoration of Ponds, Pools, and Lakes

WHILE Illinois is not as rich in small lakes as the states to her north, the total amount of still or slowly-moving waters is respectable. Moreover, many city

47-48. Restoration vs. Show, or Inspiration vs. Desecration

"I shall not allow any showy geraniums or other foreign flowers to spoil the composition made for the previous owner of my place—Mr. Harry Rubens. The aim was to re-create an Illinois water system in miniature—spring, brook, cascade, river, and lake. These pictures were taken before all the Illinois species were planted. The Japanese iris and geraniums were stop-gaps until wild iris and prairie phlox could be established."—James Simpson, Glencoe.

49-50. This Formal Garden was Destroyed by the Owner in favor of a Restoration of the Rocks

W. A. Simms of Spring Station, Kentucky, has taken the rocks beneath his lawn and, with the aid of an Illinois designer, built a miniature water system to epitomize the beauty of the ravines. K. D. Alexander has restored to a natural ravine the rock-loving flowers of his own county. No foreign flowers are tolerated. The same stratified rocks are found in Illinois and the same methods are practical where rocks and ravines occur.

residents are glad to consider a small water garden, provided the expense for water can be kept well within their means. Perhaps the most consistent restoration of the Illinois water scenery on any private place is the one at Glencoe, at the home of Mr. James Simpson. See Fig. 48. The designer of this garden says, "I aimed to reproduce in miniature the atmosphere and characteristic vegetation of Illinois rivers as a whole, especially the watercourses of the ravine country, when the ravines were young." This has been done on a piece of land 240 feet long, and from 30 to 60 feet wide, or about one-fourth of an acre. Most of the large trees in Figs. 47 and 48 were there, but everything else has been planted, including the red cedars. Numerous restored ponds of the type shown in Fig. 48 have been made, for example, such as at River Forest by Henry Babson, and at Bloomington by Spencer Ewing.

Restoration of Rocks

ROCKS are so rare in Illinois that every visible ledge is likely to have decided value. F. O. Lowden, on his place near Oregon, Illinois, has some land bordering Rock river which makes rather tame scenery, in spite of noble woods, until you come to a bold headland about thirty feet high, the beauty of which is doubled by reflection in the water. A good landscape gardener will sacrifice a good many bushes or trees to expose a

rugged and picturesque ledge. Such an act may be called restoration, even if the vegetation be destroyed, because it restores to the scenery a dramatic element that has been hidden. Many property owners along the Rock and Illinois rivers can apply this principle, especially at river bends.

Most Illinoisans have just the opposite problem, because of the scarcity of rocks. Newcomers from the East often get so homesick for the sight of a stone that they import or dig up boulders, at considerable expense, and these are often displayed in the front yard or parking as curiosities. Such features are more appropriate in back yards. The common rock garden of the East, which is copied from the Alps via England, may be justifiable in a few Illinois back yards, but mountain flowers are hardly appropriate to prairie scenery, and the plants of cool, moist climates do not thrive in our hot, dry summers. A new type of rock garden aiming to fit our scenery and climate is being evolved. One step is the stratified rockwork in the Prairie River. (Circular 170, Fig. 106.) This had to be executed in tufa, the conventional material of the trade, as there was then no Illinois quarry where suitable stone could be had at a fair price in a region devoid of all stone. The next step is exemplified by Fig. 50, where the only plants used are the simple rock-loving flowers of the neighborhood instead of those exquisite gems from the alpine regions of the world which are dear to the hearts of all good rock-gardeners. Evi-

dently the owner regards quiet scenery as a more refined type of beauty than floral display, and such is the sober judgment of most authors of books on landscape gardening.

Lately a Wisconsin limestone has become popular in northern Illinois for stepping stones, ledges, dancing springs, cascades, and other naturalistic rockwork.

Restoration of the Dunes

THE reader probably fancies that dunes and sandy soil are of little interest or importance to Illinoisans. On the contrary, a large part of Chicago is so sandy that many thousand lot owners are having great trouble and expense in growing trees and shrubs, while the key to the whole problem is at the dunes, just beyond the state line, near Gary, Indiana. A popular complaint today in a large part of Chicago is "We can't grow anything in pure sand." After failure along conventional lines, a few members of the Prairie Club began to bring back from walks to the dunes some of the celebrated beauties of that region, among which are red cedar, juniper, witch hazel, june-berry, bittersweet, wafer ash, and sumac. To their surprise the dune materials throve wonderfully without good soil, fertilizers, or continual watering. Now the members of the Prairie Club are eagerly discussing "dune borders" and "dune gardens," and a strong sentiment has developed for buying the dune species from nurserymen instead of robbing the dunes.

51-52. Scene of a Restoration of Roadside Shrubbery by Illinois Farmers, and Wild Crab Apples Suggesting the Aim

"We farmers have sometimes saved trees along the roadside, but do trees alone give all the beauty we ought to have as a foil to the rich but monotonous farm land? Are not shrubs needed? Our neighbors think so.

"So we planted half a mile of highway in October, 1913, with crabs, haws, dogwoods, etc. This is the first piece of road designed and planted according to the 'Illinois way.'"—Harvey J. Sconce, Sidell, Vermilion county, Illinois.

"Unwittingly," says a former president of the club, "the members have hit upon the solution of the home-grounds question for the sandy parts of Illinois and the discovery may eventually save $500,000 to the citizens of Chicago, or more than it will cost them to buy the dunes and keep them forever for the people. About 100 kinds of these trees, shrubs, and perennials are suitable for home grounds and obtainable from nurserymen."

"Millions of dollars can eventually be saved," says one park designer, "by applying the lesson of the dunes to Illinois city parks. For example, the park boards commonly buy whole farms at $200 an acre or thereabouts in order to skim off the top soil and move it to the Chicago parks. Some of this expense may be necessary, because it is hard to maintain a good lawn on pure sand. Much of this effort, however, is a vain attempt to maintain fertility enough to grow foreign shrubs, and that is pouring money thru a sieve of sand, for the 'best sellers' of the nurseries are mostly of the swamp type, i. e., they have been adapted by nature to moist soil and cannot make long tap-roots like the drought-resisting species. To grow swamp plants in sand is to fight nature; to grow dune plants in sand is to harness nature. The highest type of beauty Chicago parks can ever have, in my opinion, is a dune restoration. Instead of leveling the sandhills and filling the valleys, why not run the drives thru the valleys, and plant the hills with sand-loving trees? Some day we shall have a Dune Park that will give Illinois international fame.

Home gardeners who have little space and money may apply the lesson of the dunes by planting some of the sand-loving materials enumerated on page 26, under Dry Soil.

Restoration of the Woods

THE following tale is perhaps one of the forty root-stories from which, according to Mark Twain, all jokes can be derived. A newly rich Chicagoan bought and built on the "North Shore" because of a piece of woods which he considered beautiful. "Why don't you get a landscape gardener?" his neighbors asked. "I will as soon as I clean up a little," he replied. So he cut out the shrubbery, and the landscape gardener made him put it all back at a cost of $2,000. He bought the same species from nurserymen and had to wait four or five years before he got as good an effect as the one he had destroyed. Every town in Illinois that has a wooded park generally has some variant of this story, because it is the regular thing for newly elected park boards to clean out the buck-brush, and then hire an expert who opens their eyes to the beauty of buck-brush and makes them plant it.

The first thing the landscape gardener makes the millionaire do to the old cow pasture is to fringe it with wild bushes, "so as to restore privacy and charm," as the expert says. (What he means is that woods do not amount to much if you can see right thru them; they are more interesting and beautiful if something is left to the imagination.) The next step is to restore the wild flowers, and the whole family soon catches the spirit of the

thing. On their drives and walks they bring home plants and set them beside the trails, or gather seeds of wild flowers and sow them broadcast. One of the best restorations of this sort made by Illinois people is described in "Our Country Home," and "Our Country Life," by Frances Kinsley Hutchinson.

These simple methods of restoration can be used by Illinois farmers, especially when the woodlot is near the house. There may be no inducement for the farm renter to make any permanent improvements, but the average farm owner ought to care enough for his children's education in nature-lore and beauty to fence a portion of the woodlot, and let them restore the wild flowers that have been destroyed by cattle. Perhaps the first woodlot restoration made by a real farmer from a landscape gardener's design is the one made in 1915 at Sidell, by H. J. Sconce. See Figs. 37, 38. The farmers near Palestine, Illinois, also have a design for restoring shrubs and wild flowers to a piece of woodland in their country park. Henry Ford is making a woodland restoration of over 300 acres at Dearborn, Michigan. Eighty acres have already been thickly planted with trees and shrubs large enough to give in one year the effect of a forest thirty years old.

The city lot owner can, perhaps, ask his park board for a small woodland restoration, or vote for "outer park belts," and can apply the principle to his home grounds by making a "woodland border" in the shady corner.

Restoration of Roadside Beauty

MOST of the planting along the public roads of Illinois has been done by suburbanites or country gentlemen. In the wooded region north of Chicago it is not unusual to see shrubbery planted almost continuously in the parkings, or spaces between sidewalk and curb, especially in Winnetka and Highland Park, where all styles may be easily compared. Some of this has been inspired by Wildwood avenue in Graceland Cemetery. See Fig. 54. The pure spirit of restoration appears in Lake Forest, where E. L. Ryerson has planted haws, crabs, and plums, while on the prairie J. M. Cudahy has planted the same materials with red oak, hard maple, an undergrowth of common hazel, and such familiar prairie flowers as brown-eyed susan, butterfly weed, Aster laevis (the best blue aster), and the "Philadelphia lily."

One of the first

restorations made on the prairie by a large owner of farm land is near Monticello, in Piatt county. This has changed the opinion of several influential farmers about roadside planting. Some are willing to plant trees along the roadside, but more prefer shrubs because they do less harm to crops. In the wooded parts of Illinois, a mile of roadside may be planted solidly with shrubs, but on the prairie, open spaces are necessary for breezeways or to give enough sun and air to keep the road in good condition. Incidentally, these open spaces greatly improve the prairie views, because they are enframed by planting. In this and other ways all the practical difficulties commonly made by farmers, engineers, and officials can be solved to the satisfaction of all classes of road-users on at least enough of the roadside to transform it from ugliness to beauty at a cost that property owners can afford.

Perhaps the first roadside planting done in the Illinois way is that described under Figs. 51, 52. Another leader is Spencer Otis, who has planted trees and shrubs on a mile near Barrington. Both cases are pure restorations, made by men who farm at a profit, in the open country, on rich corn land; and they are not on private drives, but on public roads.

The possibilities of roadside planting are enormous, for about two and one-half percent of the state's area is in roads, and if they are all planted, Illinois may have the largest state park system in the world—larger than the whole state of Rhode Island—without the cost of buying the land.

WE WILL

☐ Help our community to re-create in park, playground, cemetery, or roadside, one or more of these eight scenic units.

53. Should Every Mile of Illinois Road be like This?
Some farmers believe that bare roads, decorated only with poles, wires, fences, and weeds have a depressing or deadening influence upon their families.

54. Or would you Like some of This Occasionally?
Some farmers can see beauty in ordinary "brush," even when the bushes are not in flower, and are willing to have trees along the roadside, trusting that the birds will keep the insects in check. (Wildwood avenue, Graceland Cemetery.) All trees and shrubs planted here are native.

55-56. Before and after Restoring the Prairie Feeling to a Park; the Broad View Conventionalized

"Here was a case of too much useless water and no chance for exercise. This shallow lake in Douglas Park had been made for show, and could not be used for canoeing or bathing. The neighborhood was densely settled and there was no place to play ball. Fortunately, there were two better lakes near by."

"So we developed those for use and beauty, and changed this to a ball field. We tried to restore the broad prairie view. It is conventionalized, for long grass would spoil a ball field. But we planted thousands of stratified Illinois shrubs. Anyone who skirts the field can get a suggestion of the prairie."—Jens Jensen.

VI—Can the Prairie be Restored?

BEFORE we can do any constructive think-ing about prairie scenery, we must define "prairie." By this we mean land that was treeless when the white man came to Illinois. It may be wild or cultivated, flat or rolling.

The first big fact to notice is that the sen-timental appeal of the wild prairie is vastly greater than that of the cultivated prairie. A popular notion about the prairie is that its wonder and beauty have gone forever, and that there is nothing to do but mourn about it. Historians, travelers, novelists, poets, and musicians have tried to express the grandeur,

loneliness, and beauty of the wild prairie, but they rarely say a kind word for the beauty of cultivated prairie. And, apparently, it never occurs to them that any restoration of wild prairie is possible. The one overwhelming im-pression that all travelers got from the wild prairie was the infinite extent of it. Nowadays people do not see how the idea of infinity can be brought home with the old-time power without the use of a tract of land so large that no individual can afford to pay taxes on it and let it lie idle. To re-create a big, wild prairie is a state-park proposition.

Wanted—a Prairie Park

"SOME day," says one far-seeing citizen, "every middle-western state will make one prairie reservation before it is too late or re-create one wild prairie for the people to enjoy forever. It would take less land than is popularly supposed. For the main purpose is to get out of sight of trees and away from every suggestion of man's work. This can perhaps be done on 1,000 acres, if the land rolls enough. A dozen parties could then be in as many different valleys, yet each could enjoy without interruption for short periods

57. The Broad View of the Prairie, Framed by Stratified Honey Locust

For constructive purposes all prairie scenery may be reduced to two units—the broad view and the long view. The broad view is the one that suggests in-finite extent, and is the more inspiring for occasional visits. See Fig. 58.

the apparent infinity of green grass and blue sky which impressed the pioneers as powerfully as the ocean. For contrast, the big open space could be skirted by the other great element of Illinois scenery—the irregular border of woodland, which originally defined the typical Illinois prairie, with its pleasant suggestion of a river hidden within the forest. Such a prairie park seems necessary to "recharge the batteries" of those who do the world's work. The millions who toil in great cities ordinarily have but two weeks' vacation. Several states now provide a chance to camp in the wilds at the least expense. Possibly prairie schooners could be used. The educational value of the park would be increased by combining with it an arboretum or botanical garden large enough to teach the people the names of the most interesting trees and wild flowers which they find in the adjacent woodland and prairie. I believe this dream can be realized at a cost which many a private citizen can afford as a gift to the people. Universities and libraries are doubtless more important to humanity, but a prairie park might touch a very responsive chord in the popular heart and ought to win the everlasting gratitude of mankind."

Miniature Prairies

CAN a bit of wild prairie be restored for the sake of beauty, even if it lacks the suggestion of infinity? Certainly. Occasionally, one hears of some old settler who, in some waste corner of the farm, saved a bit of prairie sod to remind him of old times. Or a plainsman, like Bishop Quayle's father, willed that his last resting place should be beneath a strip of Buffalo grass, and enjoined his son to see that the wild grass is never run out by the domesticated. One may respect such sentiments, but the results can hardly be called beautiful. The beauty of the wild prairie can be restored in an impressive way to one park in every Illinois city by means of a "miniature prairie" of the kind described by William Trelease.

"I wish a plan for a ten-acre prairie restoration, surrounded by trees and shrubbery, in the borders of which perennial flowers may be grown in beds for botanical students. The center is to be thickly planted with bluestem and other wild grasses, amid which the characteristic prairie flowers, like sunflowers, gaillardia, compass plant, and blazing star, are to fight for existence. How long it will take to restore anything like the thick sod of the wild prairie, no one knows. But in two or three years there should be a strong suggestion of prairie wildness, because the flowers will seem to float on a sea of grasses. This effect can hardly be produced in the ordinary hardy border, but it seems practical in any city park that can afford from two to five acres or more for such a feature."

Prairie Gardens and Prairie Borders

ILLINOISANS are now experimenting with "prairie gardens" of many kinds. The most promising type is a protest against the conventional shrubbery border which has become effeminate thru over-refinement. In order to carry the eye easily from trees to lawn and vice versa, the gardener often makes many gradations. First, he puts a row of tall shrubs, next a row of medium bushes, then low shrubs, and finally a continuous edging of perennial flowers, which may be similarly graduated. In seeking for a more virile kind of border the leader of the prairie school went for inspiration to the place where wood and prairie meet. "There," he says, "I found the strongest and most satisfactory border that nature has ever given man, so far as my observations go. The full-grown border of haws and crabs has been likened by some to mosaic, by others to lace work, while some declare it is a tone poem. By comparison the conventional shrubbery border, full of gaudy

'best sellers,' seems a kaleidoscope or crazy quilt. Stand off and view the ordinary border of shrubs, and you will see how poor a job it makes of uniting lawn and woods. It

needs small trees to bind together forest and meadow. The bold leap that nature often makes from haws and crabs down to the prairie flowers reminds me of some powerful and beautiful animal, slipping silently from forest shade into a sea of grasses. Therefore, in my new prairie gardens I make no transition between small trees and lawn, except that I have extra-wide, irregular colonies of phlox, using the wild phlox, or a variety with flattish clusters, like Rynstrom."

Those who find the preceding paragraph too poetic may at least have a practical border of prairie flowers —say 3x25 feet, choosing from Nos. 1 to 21, and 88 to 106, on page 24. Every Illinois city should have in at least one park a "prairie border"— with the grasses, composites, and other flowers labeled. It will not be like the prairie, but it will serve to teach the rising generation about the famous prairie flowers of which they read in novels and histories.

The Scenic Value of Cultivated Prairie

SO much for the wild prairie and its restoration. As to cultivated prairie, travelers generally admit that the feeling of infinity can still be had from the high spots, and they also admit that a sea of corn is beautiful. Easterners commonly acknowledge that rolling prairie is full of inspiration, but they usually say that flat prairie is not attractive. Foreign eyes are not educated to see the slight undulations in "flat" prairie that give so much quiet enjoyment every day to those who live on the land. Many plain farmers feel this beauty so deeply that they do not like to talk about it, but is repression the best attitude? Can we take any honest pride in prairie beauty if we never spend an hour or a dollar to save any of it? Is it not better to discuss and practice restoration?

Whether the prairie is a higher order of beauty than that of mountainous country we leave to popular disputation. Those who have been reared amid one type often feel uneasy in the other. But it is not safe to tell an Illinois man that flat land is unattractive and has no possibility of making one of the most beautiful regions of the world. One resident of Lake Forest is reported to have said, "The beauty of ordinary, flat, cultivated prairie is so clear to me that I was one of the first to turn away from the more obvious beauty of Lake Michigan and the wooded ravines to build on the prairie, where I run a farm that aims to make money. To unsympathetic eastern eyes our prairie view may look tame and new, but we would rather have it, even if we must wait for the trees."

58. The Long View of the Prairie
The long, narrow glimpses are more human and intimate than the broad views, like Fig. 57. The small picture above and to the left is framed by cottonwood.

Restoring the Broad View

FOR constructive purposes all prairie scenery may here be reduced to two units, the broad view and the long view. See Figs. 57, 58. The broad view is the one that suggests infinity and power, and is the more in-

59. Long View of Prairie Conventionalized
"Instead of putting a single row of trees down the center of this parking," says the designer, "I left the center open and put native shrubbery at the sides to suggest the long view of the prairie or the farm lane at its best." See page 18.

spiring for occasional visits; the long view is more human and intimate, and often more satisfactory to live with.

One of the first attempts to restore the broad view is the playground in Garfield Park. See Figs. 55, 56. Another may be summarized as follows: "I have a ten-acre pasture on which I am trying to restore as much of the wild-prairie beauty as the average farmer can afford—and no more, for I am much opposed to display. I am not prepared to advocate surrounding every field with a solid border of shrubbery, altho some authorities believe that such borders will keep down insects by attracting birds. But I do believe that the average Illinois farmer can enrich his family life greatly by bordering one field near the house with native shrubs. The financial loss is more than offset by the pleasure of seeing the flowers, berries, and birds, and above all by the chance to idealize his broad view. For example, we built in the open because we prefer farm life to lake and woods, but the ordinary broad view on Illinois farms is certainly commonplace for a good part of the year. To idealize it we have planted several elms near the door to enframe the prairie, and one big one near the middle of the pasture to suggest the solitary giants that occasionally enlivened the wild prairie. At the edge of the pasture are planted some hard maples and other trees to remind us of the distant woodlands which formerly bounded the typical prairie view in Illinois. The shrubbery surrounding the pasture consists of common wild crabs, plums, haws, sumac, hazel, sheepberry, chokecherry, witch hazel, smooth rose, etc., which will idealize the flat prairie by restoring some of the wild beauty. For this reason I would much rather have these native shrubs than miles of Japanese barberry hedges, or the showier beauty of foreign spireas, hydrangeas, and crimson ramblers, which seem to me quite out of harmony with Illinois farm scenery."

What else can the farmer do with a broad view? Luckily he does not have to own all the land and keep it idle. The important thing is to control the high place. Sometimes he may build on it, sometimes locate a drive along the top of a ridge, sometimes put a seat at the best spot. Often he can enframe the best view by pairs of trees in front of the house, beside the dining room, or along the road, as has been done near Sidell and Barrington.

Restoring the Long View

BY "long view" is meant the narrow opening between farmsteads and woodlots which often extends for several miles. See Fig. 58. It does not need to go off to infinity. Indeed, many persons prefer to have it stopped by a hazy ridge or misty piece of woods. They believe that a finite view is easier to understand and love than an infinite one. The long view is the home-like and friendly side of the prairie. Farmers have noticed the long view less, but when their attention is called to it they are often quick to see its practical advantages. For a person can often frame a long view from a home window at less cost and in less time than a broad view.

One of the most inspiring long views in America was made by Mr. Simonds in Graceland Cemetery. See Fig. 60. The famous English authority, William Robinson, greatly admired this vista. It lies within a city of two million inhabitants, yet it occupies only about 10x400 feet, or say one-tenth of an acre. One critic has called Fig. 60 "the straight way to the great hope," because it points to Nature's annual resurrection as a seeming promise of the resurrection of the soul. The next picture (Fig. 61) he calls "the straight way to bad taste," because it shows one of the many ways in which fine artworks are desecrated by a display of wealth. Can we not have in every Illinois community one cemetery of the highest type?

The farmer has a fine chance to idealize the long view. "I never frame a long prairie view with spectacular trees, like Lombardy poplar, as the eastern men do," says an Illinois landscape gardener. "Even red cedars do not look right on the Illinois farm. Nature left the exclamation point out of the prairie scenery. The kind of accent she made for the prairie is not vertical, but horizontal. Let the farmer frame his long view with a pair of vase-formed elms or cottonwoods." See Fig. 58.

In the city the long view of the prairie can be symbolized. For example, Graceland Cemetery was not consciously modeled on the prairie, but Fig. 60 suggests how it can be done in a park or cemetery on 4,000 square feet.

Has the long prairie view been conventionalized? "Yes," says one Illinois landscape gardener, "I deliberately aimed at this on Logan boulevard, Chicago, along the half-mile between Milwaukee and California avenues, and also on Humboldt boulevard. See Fig. 59. Formerly gardeners used to put a line of tall trees at uniform distances thru the middle of a parkway, or scatter shrubs for show. Nowadays, to prevent holdups and disorderly conduct, it is necessary to keep the center open, light it, and avoid all places of concealment, such as pockets of shrubbery. These conditions give a fine chance to conventionalize the long view of the prairie by planting at either side of the parking haws, crabs, and gray dogwood, which becomes stratified when old. Of course, in all conventional work, Nature's original suggestion must be hidden from the crowd, or it will be misunderstood and ridiculed. But the discerning few who look down the center of the parking will feel the long view of the prairie."

Methods of Restoration

NO methods absolutely new to the art of landscape gardening are practiced by restorers, but in the most elaborate restorations, four sciences are pursued farther than usual along the lines indicated below. Some investigation is necessary or the product cannot be called a restoration.

1. *Systematic botany.* The first step is to make a botanical survey, or list of all plant materials now growing wild on the property, or at least the most important ones. Since some desirable species are missing, the next step is to consult a county flora to find whether they grew in the vicinity originally and whether they were common and characteristic or rare and untypical. Unfortunately there is no state flora, but see page 27.

2. *State and local history.* The main types of scenery in nearly all parts of the state have been described at length by travelers or pioneers. For samples see page 27. The county courthouse should be searched for the oldest records, especially the original survey, which sometimes names and locates the finest trees that served as landmarks.

3. *Ecology.* This is a new and fascinating branch of botany that deals with plant societies. It gives combinations of plants that are far more effective in restorations than any which can be invented by man, because Nature has evolved them by ages of experiment. As an introduction to this science, see books listed on page 27.

4. *Ornithology.* Restoration of the birds should be an organic part of every scheme for reproducing Illinois scenery or vegetation. The means of attracting birds are described in an immense number of bulletins and catalogs. A letter to the U. S. Department of Agriculture or to the National Association of Audubon Societies, 1974 Broadway, New York, will put one in touch.

WE WILL

☐ Restore some feeling of the prairie to our home grounds by having an open, central lawn flanked by some stratified bushes and prairie wild flowers.

☐ Have a prairie garden, miniature prairie, or prairie border.

☐ Help Illinois create a prairie park as described on pages 16, 17.

☐ Ask our park board to frame a prairie view, like Figs. 57 to 59.

☐ Help our community secure or restore a bit of wild prairie.

60. "The Straight Way to the Great Hope"
This vista has been so called because it points to Nature's annual resurrection as a seeming promise of the resurrection of the soul. See under "Restoring the Long View."

61. "The Straight Way to Bad Taste"
Desecration of an artwork by display of wealth. Can we not have one landscape cemetery with high ideals in every Illinois community? See above.

62. Repetition of the Prairie Line on a Golf Green by Cutting Out Border Trees Less Valuable Than Haws
The golf club at Winnetka tired of hard, straight lines thru the woods, so they employed Mr. Simonds to secure more natural vistas.

VII—Everyone Can Apply the Principle of Repetition

HOW THE "PRAIRIE SPIRIT" HAS BEEN BROUGHT INTO THE DAILY LIVES OF RICH AND POOR, IN CITY, SUBURBS, AND COUNTRY, IN ALL PARTS OF THE PRAIRIE STATE

ANYONE can discover the magical part played by repetition in the Illinois landscape simply by walking or driving to the nearest high spot that commands a broad view of the prairie. How eagerly does the stranger look forward to his first glimpse of the prairie and what an unforgetable experience it is! The first thing that strikes everyone is the bigness of it, for it seems infinite, as the ocean does. But as your glance instinctively follows the gentle, wave-like roll of the land, it comes to the place where land and sky meet and there it stops. See Fig. 57. The prairie horizon has been called "the strongest line in the western hemisphere." You may try to look at something else, but your eyes will keep coming back to the horizon until you follow it around the circle. No wider view is possible on earth, when you can see all the land-circle and half of the sky-circle simply by turning on your heel. To get an experience like this people often climb high mountains, sometimes with danger, always with difficulty and expense. But the Illinois farmer can get his broad view with little effort and no expense, simply by mounting a land-wave twelve or fifteen feet high. Do we Illinoisans appreciate our privileges and enjoy to the ut-

most the inspirational value of these high places? If not, we are lucky when our memory is jogged by some traveler who says he has come 5,000 miles just to see the prairie; that Europe has nothing like it; and that the prairie is the most characteristic scenery on the American continent. But, however we Illinoisans may differ in our appreciation of scenery, we generally agree that the greatest prairie view is the one that enables you to follow the line of the horizon "clear round the world."

After discovering the overwhelming importance of the horizontal line comes the second revelation. You notice an absence of spectacular forms; there are no steep hills, pointed rocks, or spiry trees; all vertical lines are obscured. At first you are a little disappointed, because you are used to picturesque or romantic scenery, and here is something very different. Then your curiosity is aroused as to what can be the secret of the prairie's beauty. For the prairie is obviously beautiful, but its beauty is hard to define. You begin to study the main features of the scenery and find that there are usually five—land, sky, woods, crops, and water. Next you notice that the distant woodlands have level or gently

rounded tops; that the corn crop is level, as well as the ground; and if there be a lake or river, that, too, is level. If the prairie looks its best there will be fleecy clouds in the sky, sailing toward the horizon like fleets of flat-bottomed ships. Then it gradually dawns upon you that the essence of the prairie's beauty lies in all these horizontal lines, no two of which are of the same length or at the same elevation, but all of which repeat in soft and gentle ways the great story of the horizon.

Thus, you have learned straight from nature the great law of repetition, the importance of which can be quickly verified when you get back to your library. For Ruskin, in his "Elements of Drawing," explains that repetition is one of the nine laws of composition that are fundamental to all the fine arts. After describing the law of principality (by which he means making one feature more important than all the rest), he says, "Another important means of expressing unity is to mark some kind of sympathy among the different objects, and perhaps the pleasantest, because most surprising, kind of sympathy is when one group imitates or repeats another; not in the way of balance or symmetry, but subordinately, like a faraway and broken echo of it."

63-64. Before and after Repeating the Prairie on the Parking of a City Street
"The people of Highland Park planted about $700 worth of Illinois shrubs in public places in 1914. Our environment is woodland and therefore many of us believe in planting the parkings in order to intensify the sylvan charm of the town and connect all private places with the town ideal. But woodland beauty needs a foil, so we have some open spaces and many haws and crabs to suggest the great prairie beyond us."—Everett L. Millard, Highland Park, Illinois.

65. Repetition of Horizon and Whitecaps by Elders

The horizon is, perhaps, the strongest line in the prairie states. It can be beautifully repeated on the prairie or beside the lake by planting trees and shrubs with horizontal branches or flower clusters. For E. L. Millard's explanation, see page 12, column 2.

66. Repetition of Prairie by Stratified Haws in Summer

Hawthorns are still abundant along many roads in Illinois and are much admired for their deep, mysterious shadows, their flat flower clusters, red fruits, autumn colors, and the stratified branching of some species, which is most obvious in winter. They help to restore the song birds.

How far nature has carried the principle of repetition in Illinois you can easily discover on your next long drive to the country, unless you are so unfortunate as to live in one of those sections where nearly all native vegetation has been swept away by men whose souls have not yet been opened to the refining influences of beauty. In the latter case you may get some light by analyzing the list of materials on pages 24, 25. Of the 200 species of Illinois materials listed, eighty-seven are stratified in branch or flower. This is about forty-three percent, or, say, two-fifths of the native species that are in cultivation.

Has your discovery any practical value to every Illinois citizen? Certainly, provided refining influences of any kind are worth while. Of course, if life is only for dollars, we should steel our hearts against any softening influences. But if we believe in home and children and the higher life, it will be an immense help to have beautiful home grounds. Your discovery means that you can reproduce some of the effects illustrated on pages 19 to 23. It means that no two places in Illinois need look just alike, for everyone can make a different combination of the stratified materials enumerated on page 24. It means that all places can be part of one great scheme to make Illinois beautiful. It means that we Illinoisans need try no longer to imitate the East, which can always excel us in evergreens, especially rhododendrons and mountain laurel. For we have discovered a type of beauty in which the prairie states naturally excel. By working out the principle of repetition in all sorts of ways we can restore and intensify a type of beauty which mountainous, hilly, and arid regions cannot duplicate.

The full beauty of your discovery comes only when you have committed yourself to it by planting on your home grounds a considerable quantity of stratified material. Then every day brings some fresh revelation of the law of repetition. You see it in every house and statue that you admire, and hear it in every piece of music. You begin to search for the subtler forms of it in poetry, painting, and the drama. Every book you pick up seems to have some bearing on it, and if you are tempted to exaggerate its importance Ruskin restores your perspective by telling the other laws of composition, viz., principality, continuity, curvature, radiation, contrast, interchange, consistency, and harmony. All these laws are merely devices for securing unity, and the supreme pleasure connected with repetition comes when we ask, "What is the unity that underlies prairie scenery?"

When you stand upon a high place overlooking the prairie, what seems to you its deepest meaning? Some say the dominant note is peacefulness—that this middle-western country will never be invaded by a foreign foe, and the landscape expresses this sense of security. Others declare that it is an expression of God's bounty. The horizon is but a symbol of a religious idea which each person may express in his own way, just as everyone may make his own interpretation of a piece of music. Every great style in art, it is said, is based upon some religious idea. The

67. Horizontal Branches of Swamp White Oak

This circular bed of foreign flowers may be allowable in this case, but it belongs to the gardenesque style. The prairie spirit suggests American bluebells or Canada lily fringing the shrubbery. (Graceland.)

68. Repetition of Water Line by Tupelo

The tupelo or pepperidge is famed for its early red autumn color, and is even more valued for its stratification, which is probably the strongest among deciduous trees. (Graceland.)

69. At Wood-Edges Nature Suggests Prairie

"I would have planted composite flowers here to repeat the prairie, but nature restores them abundantly in the form of brown-eyed susans and asters." —A resident of Ravinia, Illinois.

70. A Subtle Case of Repetition—American Hornbeam

This small tree has slender branches, which are conspicuously horizontal only in winter, especially after rain, snow, or an ice storm. (Carpinus.)

71. Some Repeat the Horizontal Only When in Flower

Above is a thorn (Crataegus mollis) which does not have horizontal branches. The same is true of the viburnums, elders, and most shrubby dogwoods.

soul of Gothic architecture is its symbol of aspiration—the spire, which the pointed arch repeats in outline, while both forms can be reduced to a single line, the vertical. This line is repeated by the spiry evergreen trees of Europe. The ascending line characterizes the Chinese temple, and is repeated by many of the Chinese evergreens. The horizontal line characterizes the prairie style of architecture and landscape gardening, and this line is repeated by stratified hawthorns and crab apples.

The necessity of softening a dominant line by repetition is illustrated by the awe-inspiring loneliness of the wild prairie. Pioneers and travelers were at times afraid to be alone with such an infinite thing, as their records testify. Perhaps the frankest utterance of the old attitude occurs in a French traveler's account of the Russian steppes. Speaking of the eternal sameness among the people, in dress, speech, and houses, he attempts to explain their melancholy by the endless breadth of the land, and ends by exclaiming, "It is impossible to live with the Infinite and be happy." Is there any minister today who would agree to such an assertion, especially the author of "The Great Companion?" Does not every religion today emphasize love of the Infinite, rather than fear? And is not the prairie less fearful and more lovable since its sea of hissing grasses has changed to fields of corn? The

modified prairie may be less beautiful now than the wild prairie, but it is pleasanter to live with, and it may become one of the most beautiful regions in the world if we take on a missionary zeal for building houses and gardens that repeat the prairie line. For repetition translates the fearful Infinite into the friendly finite. Our stratified materials break up the horizon into bits that we can grasp and understand. They will enable Illinois to idealize the scenery of an entire state.

So, every Illinois citizen, no matter what his religion, can express the modern, intimate, and joyful relation with the Infinite by planting some stratified trees or bushes that symbolize the great horizon which in turn is but a symbol of the great reality that underlies all religions. Symbolism always has been and ever will be natural and necessary to mankind. We need something to express the infinite peace, plenty, and happiness of the prairie country. What better symbol can we have on the lawn than the stratified hawthorn, loaded in the spring with flowers and in the autumn filled with brilliant red fruits on which the birds feast? In the flower garden the first aim, of course, is flowers or color, but there may be a deeper, hidden meaning also. Gaillardias may stand for the prairie spirit and larkspurs for the Gothic. The aspiring and the stratified flowers may be regarded as religious symbols.

Each is a good foil for the other. (Fig. 73.)

Granting that repetition is an important principle, can it not be overdone or poorly done? Certainly. It is conceivable that some sentimentalist might plant only stratified material and make a mess of it, but there are too many other attractive plants to make this a serious matter. A joke may stand only one repetition, but the prairie's story will bear retelling many times. And the stratified materials of Illinois are never loud or coarse storytellers. The danger of overplanting them is practically nothing compared with the universal tendency to overdo the formal and gardenesque styles. Nature often suggests symmetry, but never pushes it to the extreme of a formal garden, in which everything is balanced. The prairie furnishes haws and crabs to accentuate her idea, but they are moderate and peaceful compared with the gardenesque style, which kills peace in home grounds because it is all accent and that of the flashiest kind, like cannas and coleus. Put your trust in the prairie. The danger of overdoing her type of beauty is remote.

WE WILL

☐ Repeat the strongest line in the prairie states by planting some of the stratified materials enumerated on page 24.

72. The Prairie Spirit in the Shady Corner

The most beautiful repeater of the prairie among woodland flowers is wild blue phlox (Phlox divaricata), here planted under shrubs at Graceland.

73. The Prairie Spirit in the Sunny Garden

The first aim in a flower garden or hardy border is flowers and color, but there may also be a deeper, hidden meaning, as explained above.

74-75. The First Principle in Adapting the Prairie Style is to Intensify each Peculiar Type of Scenery

Looking down from this bridge the ravine seems very deep, when measured by this wild grape, which has climbed from the bottom up a tall tree. E. L. Millard, Highland Park, Illinois.

Among the strongest features of woodland are the arbors of wild grape. They furnish shade, protection from rain, food for the birds, and beauty. The vines are rampant and often need restraint. Glencoe, Illinois.

VIII—Adapting the Prairie Style to Other Kinds of Scenery

HOW TO INTENSIFY THE PECULIAR BEAUTY OF EACH TYPE AND HOW TO BLEND ALL IN ONE GREAT SCHEME FOR BEAUTIFYING ILLINOIS

THOSE Illinoisans who live amid scenery that is different from the prairie will naturally ask, "Is the prairie style only for the prairie, or can it be adapted to our conditions?" The answer is that it has already been adapted to all types of Illinois scenery and by methods that can be easily illustrated.

For example, consider the wooded parts of Illinois, which comprise about fifteen to eighteen percent of the state's area, and are very attractive to home-builders. Do you think the "prairie house" shown in Fig. 76 fits the woodland? Evidently the architect did not try to make his house as conspicuous as possible —quite the opposite—for he has put the house not outside the woods but inside, and taken great pains to save the trees closest the house. For the same reason he has made the house long and low, instead of tall and narrow. Also he has used more wood and less stucco than for a house in the open. Finally he has stained the siding brown and the roof green to harmonize with tree trunks and foliage. The landscape gardener can carry the

adaptation one degree farther by planting near the house those shrubs that are so dependent upon woodland shade that they rarely thrive without it, for example, red elder, maple-leaved arrow-wood, and round-leaved dogwood. We now perceive that in woodland, and in all other kinds of Illinois scenery, adaptation consists largely in intensifying the peculiarities of each scenic type.

How to Intensify Each Scenic Type

IF you build on the lake bluffs you will naturally plant red cedar, Canadian juniper, white pine, red oak, gray poplar, hop hornbeam, Buffalo berry, red-twigged dogwood, Aster laevis, and wild grape. (Fig. 74.)

If your garden is a ravine you will naturally plant the great specialties of the ravines, namely, American linden, sugar maple, witch hazel, hepatica, bloodroot, meadow rue, trillium, and wild grape. See Fig. 75.

If you are so fortunate as to own a bit of river bottom, you will naturally plant more of the wonderful trees that reach their great-

est development on the flood plain, namely, American elm, buttonball, cottonwood, ash, walnut, butternut, tulip tree, hackberry, coffee tree, mulberry, redbud, and buckeye. Other plants that intensify the feeling of nearness to a river are the riverbank grape, wild gooseberry, American bluebell, wild blue phlox, western adder's tongue (Erythronium albidum), Jacob's ladder, and Collinsia verna.

If you live on drained land that was formerly a swamp or bog, you may be able to grow some of the finest products of that scenic type, namely, the bur, scarlet, and swamp white oaks, red maple, arborvitae, American larch, Nyssa sylvatica (Fig. 68), winterberry, red and black chokeberry, flowering currant, buttonbush, wintergreen, Rubus hispidus, cinnamon fern, royal fern, and marsh marigold.

If you live on a sandhill or dune, you can make it a beauty spot instead of a desert by planting the white pines (Fig. 77), gray pine, red cedar, bur oak, frost grape (Vitis cordifolia), chokecherry, and sand cherry.

If you live on a clay hill you may have

76. How "Prairie Architecture" has been Adapted to Woodland

House put inside the woods—not outside; trees nearest house carefully saved; house made long and low; woodwork painted brown like tree trunks, and roof green, like foliage. Needs shrubbery at foundation to connect house, woods, and prairie. (Frank Lloyd Wright, architect.)

77. White Pine is Adapted to Dunes, Bluffs, and Rocks

It also connects these types with the prairie by repeating the horizon. Longer-lived than the Scotch or Austrian pine, and looks more at home about the farmstead or at edge of woodlot. Must have drainage. Thrives better on rolling prairie than on flat land.

78-79. The Second Principle in Adapting the Prairie Style—Connect the Other Types of Scenery with the Prairie

June-berry, when old, becomes stratified, thus giving the suggestion of prairie which nature has put into the heart of every type of Illinois scenery.

The rounded tops of haws repeat the rolling land, while the species with stratified branches suggest the level prairie. "The haws are the most significant feature in our landscape."—Mrs. Lew Wallace, Gale Farm, Galesburg, Illinois.

the good fortune to preserve the original white and red oak, shell-bark hickory, sugar maple, and even the beech. If the undergrowth has been destroyed, the proper companions for the above are the dotted and scarlet haws, hazel, viburnums, yellow violet, and wood anemone.

If you live on a rocky hill you may accentuate its original picturesqueness by planting the dwarf rose (Rosa humilis), ninebark, chokeberry, staghorn sumac, and wafer ash.

If you own a bit of pond you can make a water garden containing water lily and perhaps American lotus, wild rice, pickerel weed, arrowhead, bur reed, and cat-tail.

It will be hard for man to improve on the above combinations, for they have been adapted to these scenic units thru ages of experimentation by nature. All of them are genuine Illinois examples and are reported by Henry C. Cowles in "The Plant Societies of Chicago and Vicinity."

Now, if the essence of adaptation in landscape gardening is intensification of the native flora instead of importing foreign beauty, it is obvious that the most important methods must be conservation and restoration. But these are about two-thirds of the prairie style. Therefore, the prairie style can, to this extent at least, be adapted to all parts of Illinois. In fact, it has been, as shown by Figs. 41 to 48.

How to Blend All Types of Scenery

BUT this is not all of the story, for if each scenic type were emphasized to the utmost and nothing done to connect one type with another, the contrasts would be too strong. Now comes to our assistance the law of interchange, which is explained by Ruskin as follows: "Closely connected with the law of contrast is a law which enforces the unity of opposite things, by giving to each a portion of the character of the other. * * * The typical purpose of the law of interchange is, of course, to teach us how opposite natures may be helped and strengthened by receiving each, as far as they can, some impress, or imparted power, from the other."

Let us now apply the principle of interchange to those who live amid woodland. For example, the house in Fig. 76 is not wholly of the woods, like a log cabin; it has a decided suggestion of the sunny prairie outside, owing to its style of design. Only one more touch is needed to unite the home grounds with the outside world, viz., a group of the round-leaved dogwood next to the house. For this species (Cornus circinata) clearly unites in itself two opposite types of scenery. It belongs to the woods, because it will not thrive in full sunshine, and yet its horizontal branches clearly suggest the pleasant prairie outside. Other plants that can

be used to connect woods and prairie are maple-leaved arrow-wood, witch hazel, and wild blue phlox. The two last named will grow in full sun as well as shade.

One of the most delightful themes for a walk in the country is to discover how far nature has worked out this law of interchange. At the edge of every minor type of scenery she has generally interwoven some plants that suggest the dominant type of Illinois scenery—the prairie. She has even carried the prairie spirit into the heart of the most contrasting scenery by means of stratified plants. For example, at the edge of a clearing, nature restores the brown-eyed susans and other composite flowers, as explained under Fig. 69, while in the inmost recesses of the woods she expresses the prairie spirit by red elder, maidenhair fern, meadow rue, wild spikenard (Aralia racemosa), wood aster, and wild blue phlox (Fig. 72). At Starved Rock her crowning feature is the dramatic group of white pines, thru whose stratified branches she shows you the stratified rock, while both features grandly echo the noble valley of the Illinois and the distant prairie. At the dunes near Chicago she brings another type of wild beauty to the climax shown in Fig. 77, where white pine repeats the strongest line in the Middle West. At the waterside she will teach you the prairie spirit thru tupelo (Fig. 68), swamp white oak (Fig. 67), red-twigged dogwood, blue ash, and in favored localities, thru red maple and red elder. In the exclusive precincts of the ravines she will gently suggest the democracy of the prairie thru witch hazel, round-leaved dogwood, meadow rue, spikenard, sarsaparilla, maidenhair, Aster laevis, and even by the june-berry, which becomes stratified when old, as shown in Fig. 78. But on the aristocratic bluffs poor Nature may be forced to trepan the obstinate skull and insert the prairie idea thru white pine (as she clearly does at White Pine Grove in Ogle county and at Sinnissippi Farm near Oregon, Illinois), or else by elder as in Fig. 65.

Has nature put stratified material into every kind of scenery in the world and can the prairie style be adapted to every country? No. The prairie style ought not to be copied by people who live among the mountains or in the arid regions, simply because their friends in Illinois may have something beautiful in that style. The essence of landscape gardening is the accentuation of native scenery, and the strong feature in mountainous countries is the vertical line, which mountaineers should repeat by planting their own aspiring evergreens, such as white spruce, hemlock, and balsam. We can hardly forbid them making some slight suggestion of the neigh-

boring plain. Indeed, there are enough stratified materials in the mountains to give the hint. But in no type of scenery that differs from the prairie should people plant more stratified than unstratified materials. The law of principality requires that one thing shall be dominant, and on the prairie stratified plants should probably be more in evidence than anywhere else in the world. The law of contrast shows how the true character of a dominant idea can be brought out by contrast, provided the opposing idea is subservient. Therefore, on the prairie it is right to plant a few reminders of the woods and waterside. Conversely, if you live amid different scenery from the prairie, emphasize that difference all you can, but do not forget to have some suggestion of the prairie also.

Is there any other way by which all types of Illinois scenery and all home grounds can be blended in one great scheme for beautifying the state? Obviously, we could plant our state tree, which is simply called the "native oak." (The "Act in Relation to a State Tree and a State Flower," approved February 21, 1908, appears as Chapter 57A, Sec. 16, on page 1320 of Hurd's Revised Statutes of 1913.) We are richer in oaks than in any other kind of trees, since we have eighteen species, but the most characteristic of all is the bur or mossy-cup oak, which is as rugged in appearance as Lincoln. It should be planted in every part of Illinois where it is likely to thrive. Unfortunately the state flower will not help us much, for by "prairie violet" people commonly mean the large-flowered, long-stemmed Viola cucullata, which is not peculiar to the prairie, being common in the woods and in the East. Moreover, this violet is disappointing in cultivation, making its response to rich soil by producing more leaves than flowers. Of all the plants popularly named after the prairie, the prairie rose is the most satisfactory for general cultivation thruout the state. And since Illinois is the Prairie State, we may be justified in calling it the Illinois rose, and making it a symbol of the "Illinois way of planting." But to symbolize the prairie style that is to fit the Middle West, shall we not choose that quintessence of the prairie spirit—the hawthorn?

WE WILL

☐ Intensify the peculiar scenery amid which we live by planting strong masses of the materials native to our type.

☐ Plant a few stratified materials to remind us of the bountiful prairie on which the prosperity of Illinois largely depends, and to show others that we wish to cooperate with any scheme for beautifying Illinois.

IX—Materials Used in the Prairie Style

PERMANENT ORNAMENTAL PLANTS NATIVE TO ILLINOIS WHICH CAN BE OBTAINED FROM NURSERYMEN

THIS list is not complete, but it contains nearly all native plants that are advisable for small places, as well as a good many that are suitable only for parks and large estates. It is impractical to give full descriptions of all the plants mentioned, and the garden-lover must look to horticultural publications, nursery catalogs, and local authorities for detailed information.

Nurserymen. Most good nurserymen offer some of the species mentioned in this circular. Those named below offer a considerable variety of trees, shrubs, and perennials native to Illinois. Augustine Nursery Co., Normal, Ill.; Geo. Wm. Bassett, Hammonton, N. J.; Biltmore Nursery Co., Biltmore, N. C.; H. A. Dreer, 714 Chestnut St., Philadelphia; Edward Gillett, Southwick, Mass.; F. H. Horsford, Charlotte, Vt.; Harlan P. Kelsey, Salem, Mass.; Klehm's Nurseries, Arlington Heights, Ill.; Henry Kohankie and Son, Painesville, Ohio; Leesley Bros., N. Crawford and Peterson Aves., Chicago; Naperville Nurseries, Naperville, Ill.; Swain Nelson and Sons Co., Marquette Bldg., Chicago; Peterson Nursery, 30 N. LaSalle St., Chicago; the Storrs and Harrison Co., Painesville, Ohio.

Class I. Stratified Materials or Symbols of the Prairie (All native to Illinois)

(The practical uses to which these are best suited are indicated in the article on page 26. Incidentally they may symbolize or idealize prairie scenery or Illinois surroundings. Those marked * have strong horizontal branches; the others have flat flower clusters.)

GROUP 1. PERENNIALS AND NEAR PERENNIALS.

a. For garden cultivation in full sun.
1. Asclepias tuberosa. Butterfly weed.
2. Aster lævis. Smooth aster.
3. Boltonia asteroides. Aster-like boltonia.
4. Coreopsis lanceolata. Lance-leaved tickseed.
5. Coreopsis tinctoria (*Calliopsis elegans*). Golden coreopsis. (Annual, but self-sows.)
6. Echinacea purpurea (*Rudbeckia purpurea*). Purple coneflower.
7. Eupatorium cœlestinum (*Conoclinium coelestinum*). Mist flower.
8. Euphorbia corollata. Flowering spurge.
9. Gaillardia aristata (*G. grandiflora*). Perennial gaillardia. See Fig. 73.
10. Galium boreale. Northern bedstraw.
11. Helenium autumnale. Sneezeweed.
12. Helianthus giganteus. Giant sunflower.
13. Helianthus lætiflorus. Showy sunflower.

14. Helianthus mollis. Hairy sunflower. Circular 170, Fig. 62.
15. Heliopsis lævis. Pitcher's ox-eye.
16. Phlox divaricata. Wild blue phlox. See Fig. 72 and Circular 170, Fig. 69.
Rudbeckia purpurea. See Echinacea.
17. Rudbeckia speciosa (*R. Newmanni*). Showy coneflower.
18. Rudbeckia subtomentosa. Sweet coneflower. Similar to Fig. 69.
19. Rudbeckia triloba. Thin-leaved coneflower. (Biennial, but self-sows.) Similar to Circular 170, Figs. 81, 82.
20. Sedum ternatum. Wild stonecrop.
21. Solidago Riddelli. Riddell's goldenrod. (Collect.)
21a. Solidago Virgaurea, var. nana. Dwarf goldenrod.
b. For shady places.
22. Adiantum pedatum.* Maidenhair fern.
23. Aralia racemosa.* Wild spikenard.

24. Thalictrum polygamum* (*T. Cornuti*). Fall meadow rue.
25. Thalictrum dioicum.* Early meadow rue.
c. For water gardens or wet soil.
26. Asclepias incarnata. Swamp milkweed.
27. Eupatorium perfoliatum. Boneset.
28. Eupatorium purpureum. Joe-Pye weed.
29. Eupatorium urticæfolium (*E. ageratoides*). White snakeroot.
30. Nelumbo lutea (*Nelumbium luteum*). American lotus.
31. Nymphaea odorata. Sweet-scented water lily. Figs. 2, 48.
d. For very dry soil, for example, roadsides.
32. Monarda fistulosa. Wild bergamot.
33. Silphium integrifolium. Entire-leaved rosin-weed.
34. Silphium lacinatum. Compass plant. (Often native to moist meadows.)

GROUP 2. SHRUBS.

a. Low shrubs, ordinarily 4 ft. or less in cult.
35. Ceanothus americanus. New Jersey tea.
36. Ceanothus ovatus. Illinois redroot.
37. Hydrangea arborescens. Wild hydrangea.
38. Viburnum acerifolium. Maple-leaved arrow-wood. Circular 170, Figs. 39, 40.
39. Viburnum pubescens. Downy-leaved arrow-wood. See Fig. 40 and Circular 170, Figs. 37, 38.
b. Medium-high shrubs, ordinarily 5 to 6 ft.
40. Cornus Amomum (*C. sericea*). Silky dogwood. Circular 170, Figs. 79, 80.
41. Cornus racemosa (*C. paniculata*).* Gray dogwood. Branches stratified on old plants.

42. Cornus stolonifera. Red-osier dogwood.
43. Sambucus canadensis. American black elder. Inside front cover and Figs. 4, 5, 65.
44. Sambucus canadensis, var. acutiloba. Illinois cut-leaved elder. Figs. 2, 46.
45. Sambucus pubens (*S. racemosa* of some nurseries). American red elder.
46. Viburnum cassinoides. Appalachian tea.
47. Viburnum dentatum. Arrow-wood.
48. Viburnum molle. Soft-leaved viburnum.
49. Viburnum Opulus. High-bush cranberry. (The native form, known as *V.

americanum, is said to be freer from plant lice than the European). Circular 170, Figs. 77, 78.
c. Tall shrubs, ordinarily 7 to 10 ft. in cult.
50. Aralia spinosa.* Hercules' club.
51. Cornus alternifolia.* Alternate-leaved dogwood.
52. Cornus rugosa (*C. circinata*).* Round-leaved dogwood.
53. Hamamelis virginiana.* Witch hazel.
54. Physocarpus opulifolius (*Spiraea opulifolia. Opulaster opulifolia*). Ninebark.
55. Viburnum Lentago. Sheepberry. Circular 170, Figs. 55, 56.
56. Viburnum prunifolium. Black haw.

GROUP 3. SMALL TREES.

57. Aesculus glabra.* Ohio or fetid buckeye.
58. Amelanchier canadensis* (*A. Botryapium*). June-berry. (Stratified when old.) See Fig. 78.
59. Amelanchier lævis (*A. canadensis* of some nurserymen).* Smooth june-berry.
60. Carpinus caroliniana.* American hornbeam. Blue beech. Fig. 70.

61. Cornus florida.* Flowering dogwood. Not hardy north. Circular 170, Fig. 110.
62. Crataegus Crus-galli.* Cockspur thorn.
63. Crataegus mollis. Red-fruited thorn. Red haw. Fig. 71.
64. Crataegus Phaenopyrum (*C. cordata*). Washington thorn.
65. Crataegus punctata.* Dotted haw.

66. Crataegus tomentosa.* Pear thorn. (Branches sometimes stratified.)
Hawthorns. See Figs. 1, 3, 7, 12, 62, 64, 66, 71, 79, 91.
67. Pyrus ioensis* (*Malus ioensis*). Prairie or western crab apple. Fig. 52. Sometimes cataloged as P. coronaria.
68. Sorbus americana (*Pyrus americana*). American mountain ash.

GROUP 4. TALL AND MEDIUM-HIGH TREES.

69. Acer rubrum.* (Thrives in some parts of Illinois, but rarely colors highly, and needs moist soil.)
70. Acer saccharum.* Sugar maple.
71. Aesculus octandra.* Sweet buckeye.
72. Fagus grandifolia (*F. americana*).* American beech. Generally fails on prairie and near Chicago, but thrives in some parts of Illinois.)

73. Fraxinus americana (*F. alba*).* White ash.
74. Fraxinus lanceolata.* Green ash.
75. Fraxinus quadrangulata.* Blue ash.
76. Gleditsia triacanthos.* Honey locust.
77. Liquidambar styraciflua.* Sweet gum.
78. Nyssa sylvatica.* Tupelo, pepperidge, or black gum. Fig. 68.

79. Quercus alba.* White oak. Circular 170, Figs. 23, 58, 60.
80. Quercus coccinea.* Scarlet oak.
81. Quercus imbricaria.* Shingle oak.
82. Quercus palustris.* Pin oak.
83. Quercus bicolor (*Q. platanoides*).* Swamp white oak. See Fig. 67.
84. Quercus rubra.* Red oak.
85. Sassafras officinale.* Sassafras.

GROUP 5. EVERGREENS.

86. Juniperus communis, var. depressa (*J. canadensis*).* Canadian juniper.

87. Pinus Strobus.* White pine. (Needs drainage.) See Figs. 77, 87.

Class II.   Non-Stratified Materials that are Reminders of Illinois

(For their practical uses see page 23.   Incidentally they may remind one of Illinois, because they are native to the state.)

GROUP 1.   PERENNIALS AND NEAR-PERENNIALS.

a. For garden cultivation in full sun.
88. Anemone canadensis (*A. pennsylvanica*). Round-leaved anemone.
89. Baptisia australis. Blue wild indigo.
90. Baptisia tinctoria. Yellow indigo.
91. Camassia esculenta (*C. Fraseri*). Prairie hyacinth.
92. Cassia marylandica. American senna.
93. Dodecatheon Meadia. Shooting star.
94. Erysimum asperum, var. arkansanum (*E. arkansanum*). Prairie wallflower.
95. Hibiscus Moscheutos. Swamp rose mallow. Circular 170, Fig. 105.
96. Liatris pycnostachya. Prairie button.
97. Liatris scariosa. Large button snakeroot.
98. Lilium philadelphicum. Wild red lily, (Bulb.)
99. Lobelia cardinalis. Cardinal flower.
100. Pentstemon laevigatus, var. Digitalis (*P. Digitalis*). Foxglove beard-tongue.

101. Phlox maculata. Early phlox. (Miss Lingard the favorite variety.)
102. Phlox paniculata. Garden or perennial phlox.
103. Physostegia virginiana. Obedient plant.
104. Sanguinaria canadensis. Bloodroot.
105. Tradescantia virginiana. Spiderwort.
106. Ulmaria rubra (*Spiraea lobata, S. palmata*). Queen-of-the-prairie.
b. For shady places.
107. Aquilegia canadensis. Wild columbine.
108. Asarum canadense. Wild ginger.
109. Campanula rotundifolia. Harebell.
110. Cimicifuga racemosa. Black snakeroot.
111. Collinsia verna. Blue-eyed Mary. (Biennial but self-sows.)
112. Erythronium albidum. White adder's tongue. (Bulb.)
113. Hepatica triloba. Hepatica.
114. Lilium canadense. Wild yellow lily. (Bulb.)
115. Lilium superbum. American turk's cap lily. (Bulb.)

116. Mertensia pulmonarioides (*M. virginica*). American bluebell. Fig. 38. Circular 170, Fig. 67.
117. Silene virginica. Fire pink.
118. Trillium grandiflorum. Large-flowered trillium.
c. For water gardens or moist places.
119. Acorus Calamus. Sweet flag. (Collect.) Fig. 36.
120. Arisaema triphyllum. Jack-in-the-pulpit.
121. Calamagrostis canadensis. Blue-joint. (Collect.) Fig. 48.
122. Caltha palustris. Marsh marigold.
123. Iris versicolor. Larger blue-flag.
124. Lobelia cardinalis. Cardinal flower.
125. Sagittaria latifolia (*S. variabilis*). Arrowhead. (Collect.) Fig. 46.
126. Sparganium eurycarpum. Broad-fruited bur reed. (Collect.)
127. Typha angustifolia. Narrow-leaved cattail. (Collect.) Fig. 2.

GROUP 2.   SHRUBS.

a. Low shrubs, ordinarily 4 ft. or less in cult.
128. Amelanchier alnifolia. Northwestern june-berry. Dwarf june-berry.
129. Amelanchier alnifolia, var. pumila.
130. Diervilla Lonicera (*D. trifida*). Northern bush honeysuckle.
131. Evonymus obovatus. Running strawberry bush. See 163.
132. Prunus pumila. Sand cherry.
133. Rhus canadensis (*R. aromatica*). Fragrant sumac.
134. Ribes americanum (*R. floridum*). American black currant.
135. Rosa virginiana (*R. blanda*). Smooth rose.
136. Rosa carolina. Swamp rose.
137. Rosa humilis. Low rose.
138. Rosa lucida. Glossy rose.
139. Rosa setigera. Illinois or prairie rose.

Figs. 14, 39. Circular 170, Figs. 44, 76, 83.
140. Rubus hispidus. Running swamp blackberry.
141. Symphoricarpos occidentalis. Wolfberry.
142. Symphoricarpos vulgaris. Indian currant.
b. Medium-high shrubs, ordinarily 5 to 6 ft. in cultivation.
143. Corylus americana. American hazel.
144. Evonymus americana (*Evonymus*). Strawberry bush.
145. Ilex verticillata. Winterberry.
146. Rhus copallina. Black sumac.
147. Rhus glabra. Common sumac.
148. Ribes aureum (*R. odoratum*). Flowering currant.
149. Ribes Cynosbati. Wild gooseberry.
149½. Salix interior (*S. longifolia*). Sunset willow. (Collect.)

150. Spiraea alba (*S. lanceolata*). Western meadow-sweet.
151. Symphoricarpos racemosus. Snowberry.
152. Xanthoxylum americanum. Prickly ash. See No. 159.
c. Tall shrubs, ordinarily 7 to 10 ft. in cult.
153. Aronia arbutifolia (*Pyrus arbutifolia, Sorbus arbutifolia*). Red chokeberry.
154. Aronia melanocarpa (*Pyrus nigra, Sorbus melanocarpa*). Black chokeberry.
155. Benzoin aestivale (*B. odoriferum, Lindera Benzoin*). Spicebush.
156. Cephalanthus occidentalis. Buttonbush.
157. Rhus typhina (*R. hirta*). Staghorn sumac. Fig. 22.
158. Staphylea trifolia. American bladdernut.
159. Xanthoxylum americanum (*Zanthoxylum*). Prickly ash. For screens and barriers. See No. 152.

GROUP 3.   VINES.

160. Ampelopsis cordata (*Vitis indivisa*). Simple-leaved ampelopsis. *Ampelopsis Engelmanni* and *quinquefolia*. See Parthenocissus.
161. Celastrus scandens. Bittersweet. Circular 170, Fig. 47.
162. Clematis virginiana. Wild clematis.
163. Evonymus obovatus. Running strawberry bush. See No. 131. *Grape, wild.* Figs. 74, 75.
164. Lonicera sempervirens. Trumpet honeysuckle. (Southern and central Illinois.)
165. Lonicera Sullivantii. Minnesota honeysuckle.
166. Parthenocissus quinquefolia (*Ampelopsis quinquefolia*). Circular 170, Fig. 45.
167. Parthenocissus quinquefolia, var. Engelmanni (*Ampelopsis Engelmanni*). Illinois creeper or Engelmann's ivy.
168. Rosa setigera. Illinois or prairie rose.

See Fig. 39 and Circular 170, Figs. 14, 42, 43, 71.
169. Rubus hispidus. Running swamp blackberry.
170. Tecoma radicans. Trumpet creeper. Circular 170, Fig. 66.
171. Vitis aestivalis. Summer grape.
172. Vitis bicolor. Northern fox grape.
173. Vitis cinerea. Sweet winter grape.
174. Vitis cordifolia. Winter or frost grape.
175. Vitis vulpina (*V. riparia*). Riverbank grape.

GROUP 4.   SMALL TREES.

176. Cercis canadensis. Redbud.
177. Prunus americana. Wild plum.

178. Ptelea trifoliata. Wafer ash. Hop tree.

179. Pyrus coronaria. Narrow-leaved or eastern crab apple.

GROUP 5.   TALL AND MEDIUM-HIGH TREES.

180. Betula papyrifera. Canoe birch.
181. Catalpa speciosa. Western catalpa.
182. Celtis occidentalis. Hackberry. Fig. 24.
183. Gymnocladus dioica (*G. canadensis*). Kentucky coffee tree.
184. Juglans nigra. Walnut. Fig. 17.
185. Liriodendron Tulipifera. Tulip tree. Circular 170, Fig. 110.
186. Magnolia acuminata. Cucumber tree.

187. Morus rubra. Red mulberry.
188. Platanus occidentalis. Buttonball. Sycamore.
189. Populus grandidentata. Gray poplar.
190. Populus deltoides. Cottonwood.
191. Prunus serotina. Wild black cherry.
192. Prunus pennsylvanica. (*Cerasus pennsylvanica*). Wild red cherry.

193. Quercus macrocarpa. Bur or mossy-cup oak.
193½. Salix vitellina. Yellow willow.
194. Taxodium distichum. Bald cypress.
195. Tilia americana. American linden or basswood. Fig. 3.
196. Tilia heterophylla. White basswood.
197. Ulmus americana. American elm. Fig. 3. Circular 170, Fig. 59.

GROUP 6.   EVERGREENS.

198. Juniperus virginiana. Red cedar. Fig. 47. Circular 170, Figs. 9, 30.

199. Thuya occidentalis. American arborvitae. Circular 170, Fig. 10.

X—Some Uses for Illinois Materials

I. THE COMMON PROBLEMS OF SMALL HOME GROUNDS

1. Foundation Planting

THE nearer the house the more exacting are the conditions and the more conventional must be the planting materials. A higher percentage of foreign and horticultural varieties is permissible here than anywhere, save in the garden. Unfortunately, the favorites are grossly overplanted, especially the "inevitable three"—Japanese barberry, Van Houtte's spirea, and Hydrangea paniculata, var. grandiflora, all of which are foreign. Their brilliancy soon becomes commonplace, or tiresome, especially when a house is surrounded by barberry or spirea alone. It is better to have variety enough to furnish some flowers or color for every month. Try to have half the materials or more native to Illinois. In arranging the materials leave one or more attractive parts of the foundation unplanted. Put the tallest shrubs at the corners, angles, and against high foundations. In front of windows a carpet of trailing juniper may be suitable. The plants marked ‡ are often called "coarse" by some landscape gardeners, who consider them unsuitable for the most refined surroundings. Others declare that ordinary foundation planting is pitifully weak, thru over-refinement, and that large buildings require large shrubs with large leaves for proper proportion. They prefer more virility and therefore believe in using hawthorns and even sumacs against some foundations, especially farmhouses and tall buildings. If more flowers are desired than bushes furnish, the shrubbery can be edged or carpeted in places with trailing myrtle and daffodils or Darwin tulips.

FOR THE SUNNY SIDE OF THE HOUSE

Low Shrubs.—(About 3 to 4 feet high.) Native: Rosa setigera, Rosa nitida, Rhus aromatica, Rosa lucida,‡ Diervilla Lonicera‡ and sessilifolia,‡ Hydrangea arborescens and var. grandiflora. Foreign: Berberis Thunbergii, Spiraea japonica, var. alba, Taxus cuspidata and var. brevifolia.

Medium shrubs.—(About 5 to 6 feet high.) Native: Viburnum dentatum, Rhus copallina. Foreign: Berberis vulgaris, Forsythia intermedia, Ligustrum Ibota, var. Regelianum, Lonicera Morrowi, Rosa rugosa, Spiraea arguta, Magnolia stellata.

High shrubs.—(About 8 to 10 feet high.) Native: Viburnum prunifolium, Lentago, and Opulus.‡ Foreign: Forsythia intermedia, var. Fortunei, Lonicera tatarica, Philadelphus coronarius, Syringa vulgaris,‡ Viburnum tomentosum, Viburnum Lantana.

FOR THE SHADY SIDE OF THE HOUSE

Low shrubs—(About 3 to 4 feet high.) Native: Rhus aromatica, Hydrangea arborescens, Symphoricarpus vulgaris, Ceanothus americanus, Taxus canadensis. Foreign: Spiraea japonica, var. alba.

Medium shrubs.—(About 5 to 6 feet high.) Native: Cornus racemosa, Viburnum cassinoides, Symphoricarpus racemosus, Ribes aureum.‡ Foreign: Aralia pentaphylla, Forsythia intermedia, Ligustrum Ibota, var. Regelianum.

High shrubs.—(About 8 to 10 feet high.) Native: Viburnum Opulus,‡ Physocarpus opulifolia.‡ Foreign: Forsythia intermedia, var. Fortunei, Ligustrum Ibota, Ligustrum amurense, Cornus alba, var. sibirica.‡

2. Vines for Porches and House Walls

For full lists of native vines, see page 25, Nos. 160-175.

On brick, stone, or rough concrete, use the self-supporting kinds, like Ampelopsis Engelmanni, which is hardier than A. Veitchii.

On a wooden house avoid the above and use a trellis or strong wire fastened with hooks so that vines can be laid down when the house is painted. Ampelopsis quinquefolia, Celastrus scandens, Clematis virginiana, Rosa setigera.

For front porch or refined surroundings, Akebia quinata, Clematis paniculata, Rambler and Memorial rose hybrids (not very hardy in northern Illinois), Rosa setigera, Wistaria chinensis.

On back porch. The following may be too coarse for the front of a fine house. Celastrus scandens,‡ Tecoma radicans,‡ wild grapes,‡ and Lonicera japonica, var. Halliana.‡

On the shady side. Ampelopsis Engelmanni and quinquefolia, Lonicera Halliana, Vitis Labrusca, Vinca minor.

3. To Frame the View of the House

For small houses, hawthorns and Cornus florida. For large houses, Ulmus americana, Quercus rubra, Acer saccharum, Tilia americana.

4. Borders

(Numbers refer to species on pages 24, 25.) Perennials for sunny borders: 1-21, 88-106. Perennials for shade: 22-25, 107-118. Low shrubs: 35-39, 128-142. Medium shrubs: 40-49, 143-159. Tall shrubs: 50-56, 153-159. Small trees: 57-68, 176-179.

II. SPECIAL PROBLEMS

(Numbers refer to species on pages 24, 25.)

Arbors and Pergolas

Hawthorns (62-66) make natural arbors of great beauty in Illinois. Climbers for arbors and pergolas 160-162, 164, 166-168, 170-175.

Banks

Shrubs and creepers are cheaper to maintain than grass, for banks are hard to mow. To hide useless terraces and bad grading, arching shrubs like 139 and 142, and rampant vines like 166 and 168, and 170-175, are useful.

Bird Gardens

Elders attract and feed with their berries sixty-seven species of birds; shrubby dogwoods, forty-seven; sumacs, forty-four; juneberries, twenty; and hawthorns, twelve. Other important groups are Junipers, Ribes, Rosa, Viburnum, and Vitis. See Farmers' Bulletin 621, U. S. Department of Agriculture.

Bluffs

For permanent effect 87, 195, 196, 198. For immediate effect, plant thickly cheap native stock in variety, especially suckering plants like locust, 42, 43, 142, 148, 157, 159, and rampant vines like 161-162, 166, 171-175. Plants that lean over the top of bluffs are 57-61, and 176, while 149 and 166 hang far down.

Clay Soils (Heavy)

Trees: 70, 84. Shrubs: 46-49, 135, 137-139.

Color

Middle-western perennials are classified by color and season of bloom in Bailey's "Standard Cyclopedia of Horticulture," vol. 3, pp. 1469, 1470.

Cut Flowers

Perennials: 4, 9-20, 96-97, 101-102. For lightening bouquets of sweet peas, 10 is a good substitute for Gypsophila paniculata, which fails in Illinois, according to Augustine.

Dry Soil

The following are great drought-resisters, most of them growing wild in sandy soil. Perennials: 2, 8, 20, 21, 32-34, 89. Shrubs: 35, 132, 133, 137, 143, 146-147, 157. Vines: 161, 166, 174. Trees: 58, 76, 79, 84-85, 178, 180. Evergreens: 86, 198.

Edging

Flower beds: 104. Shrubbery beds: 133, 142.

Meadows

Bulbs for naturalizing in meadows: 91, 93, 98, 114-115.

Poor Soil

See Dry Soil for many that will grow in sand. Juniper dislikes rich soil.

Screens

Rhus typhina. Morus rubra.

Shade

Perennials: 22-25, 107-118. Shrubs for shady side of house, see above under Foundation Planting. The following rarely thrive without shade: 38, 45, 52.

Street Trees

No species comes near perfection, but a satisfactory tree can generally be found in this short list: Red oak, American elm, Norway maple, oriental plane, sugar maple, pin oak, white ash, American linden, European small-leaved linden, horse chestnut. Avoid the short-lived box elder, soft maple, and poplars. "Green ash is better than white ash."—Burrill.

Trees for Northern Illinois

The following trees are characteristic of northern Illinois, but not of the central and southern parts, according to Burrill, and therefore should be planted freely in northern Illinois to intensify the natural beauty of that region: White pine, arborvitae, canoe birch, black ash, mountain ash, wild red cherry.

Trees for Central Illinois

The following trees are characteristic of central Illinois, but not of northern, according to Burrill, and may be planted to intensify the natural character of central Illinois: flowering dogwood, pin oak, shingle oak, sassafras.

Trees for Southern Illinois

The following trees are characteristic of southern Illinois, according to Burrill, and therefore, they may be planted to intensify the natural beauty of this section. American beech, sweet gum, bald cypress, western catalpa, silver-bell tree, basket oak, willow oak, cucumber tree, tulip tree.

Water Gardens and Water-Loving Plants

Perennials: 26-31, 119-127. Shrubs: 40-42, 136, 140, 145, 149½, 150. Vines: 169, 175. Trees: 69, 76-78, 193½, 194. Evergreens: 199.

Windbreaks

Instead of short-lived evergreens, like Norway spruce, Scotch pine, and Austrian pine, plant long-lived evergreens like white pine and hemlock. Instead of short-lived deciduous trees, like willows, soft maple, box elder, and poplars, plant long-lived trees like sugar maple, red oak, scarlet oak, or pin oak. "It may often be best to plant quick-growing trees, but if so, put them in separate rows so that they can be removed easily without destroying the more permanent trees."—Burrill.

XI—Literature of the Prairie Style of Landscape Gardening

THE following list makes no pretense of completeness. The subject is so new that the literature is fragmentary. The relation of each item to the prairie style or Illinois way is indicated. Where no name is given the author is the writer of this circular.

Agriculture

The Illinois System of Permanent Fertility. Cyril G. Hopkins. Circular 167, Illinois Agricultural Experiment Station. The Illinois system of permanent agriculture, when fully developed, will include permanent farm buildings and permanent planting materials, as well as permanent fertility of the soil. Often the orchards and the layout of the farm will be permanent. The Illinois way of planting is part of this larger scheme, since it uses permanent ornamental plants.

The Development of American Agriculture, what it is and what it means. Eugene Davenport in Report of the Illinois Farmers' Institute, 1909, pages 101-121. Contains on pages 108 and 109 a plea for the country beautiful, including a suitable country architecture and long-lived trees.

The Prairie Farmer's Creed. Clifford V. Gregory. Prairie Farmer Publishing Company, Chicago, 1912. Inspirational matter on a 9x12-inch poster.

Botany

An Illustrated Flora of the Northern United States. Britton and Brown. Scribner, 1913. Three volumes. Describes and illustrates all plants native to Illinois.

Catalog of the Flowering and Higher Flowerless Plants of Illinois. T. J. Burrill, in Ninth Report of the Board of Trustees of the Illinois Industrial University, 1878. The nearest approach to a Flora of Illinois. Though out of date, it is still helpful. A flora of the state is greatly needed.

The Flora of Cook County, Illinois. Higley and Raddin. Bulletin of the Chicago Academy of Sciences, 1891. Has been much used for restoration work in northern Illinois.

Flora Peoriana. Frederick Brendel. Valuable for restoration work in central Illinois.

Illinois As It Is. Frederick Gerhard, 1857. Chapter on climate, soil, plants, and animals by Frederick Brendel, pages 230 to 258. Describes plant societies of central Illinois.

Climate

Life Zones and Crop Zones. C. Hart Merriam, Bulletin 10, Division of Biological Survey, U. S. Department of Agriculture, 1898. Gives a scientific classification of American climates, including the three zones in Illinois, and names characteristic trees and crops of each zone.

Conservation

Report of the Illinois Park Commission for 1912, Springfield. Describes Starved Rock, White Pine Forest, and Cahokia Mound.

The White Pine Forest of Ogle County, Illinois. Free booklet published by the White Pine Forest Association, Mrs. J. C. Seyster, Secretary, Oregon, Illinois.

Ecology

The Plant Societies of Chicago and Vicinity. Henry C. Cowles. Bulletin 2, Geographic Society of Chicago, University of Chicago Press, 1901. Names the characteristic plants of fourteen environments, such as the ravine, river bluff, flood plain, prairie, etc.

The Prairies. B. Shimek in Bulletin of State University of Iowa, vol. 6, pages 169-240 (1911). Gives in tabular form over two hundred typical prairie plants of Iowa, and indicates the frequency with which they are found on flat and rolling prairie, ridges, openings, alluvial soil, and sand dunes. Explains treeless character by exposure to evaporation. Bibliography on origin of prairie.

General

How the Middle West Can Come Into Its Own. Country Life in America, September 15, 1912, pages 11-14. Mentions about fifty characteristic plants of the region from the Alleghenies to Omaha and from the Great Lakes to the Ohio river.

How to Heighten Western Color. Country Life in America, April, 1913, pages 80, 82, 84. Names twenty-seven species of permanent plants native to Illinois and the Middle West. Mentions twelve motives for unique gardens and cites western examples.

The Illinois Way of Beautifying the Farm. Wilhelm Miller. Circular 170, Illinois Agricultural Experiment Station, 1913. Names and illustrates many permanent planting materials native to Illinois, suitable for country and city planting. Has 112 illustrations.

The Illinois Way of Roadside Planting. Wilhelm Miller in Fourth Report of the Illinois Highway Commission, 1913, pages 334-345. Two illustrations.

The Illinois Way of Foundation Planting. Wilhelm Miller and F. A. Aust in Arbor and Bird Days, 1914. Department of Public Instruction, Springfield, Illinois, pages 7 to 19. Advocates foundation planting for school grounds and describes in tabular form twenty-six Illinois shrubs, giving season of flowers and berries, together with autumn or winter colors. Six illustrations.

Billerica. The North Shore Illinois Edition, issued monthly, beginning April, 1915, contains climatic charts, maps, and tables prepared under the direction of Warren H. Manning, Tremont building, Boston, and articles by W. C. Egan, E. O. Orpet, Emil Bollinger, Stephen F. Hamblin, and others. Concerns the region from Evanston to Waukegan.

Landscape Extension. Bailey's Standard Cyclopedia of Horticulture, vol. 4, 1915, pages 1813 to 1814. States aims, methods, and results in university extension work in landscape gardening, and cites several plans and plantings done by the Division of Landscape Extension, University of Illinois.

Illinois Examples of Landscape Gardening

An American Idea in Landscape Art. Country Life in America, vol. 4, 1903, pages 349-350. Describes and illustrates Graceland Cemetery, Chicago.

Reports of the West Chicago Park Commissioners, 1905 to 1908. Early illustrations of the Prairie River restoration and Rose Garden in Humboldt Park, and of the Conservatories in Garfield Park. Lists of materials planted and quantities used.

Landscape Gardening under Glass. Country Life in America, December 15, 1911, pages 10-11 and 50-51. Describes and illustrates Conservatories at Garfield Park, Chicago.

What Is the Matter With Our Water Gardens? Country Life in America, June 15, 1912, pages 23-26. Describes and illustrates the Rubens garden, Glencoe, Illinois, which is a spring, brook, and lake modeled on a prairie water system. This is also a restoration of vegetation native to the "North Shore" of Illinois.

A New Kind of Western Home. Country Life in America, April, 1913, pages 39-42. This article describes farm of F. O. Lowden, Oregon, Illinois, as type of country gentleman's estate in Middle West.

Bird Gardens in the City. Country Life in America. October, 1914, pages 58-59. Describes gardens of Albert H. Loeb and Julius Rosenwald in Chicago. The former is a restoration of plants native to Cook county.

Gartenkunst in Städtebau. Hugo Koch. Berlin, Wasmuth, 1914. Describes and illustrates work in Humboldt and Garfield Parks, Chicago.

Planting Materials

List of Perennials and Shrubs for Planting in Illinois. A. M. Augustine in Transactions Illinois Horticultural Society, 1913, vol. 47, pages 22-34. Gives in tabular form hardiness, method of propagation, value for cut flowers, etc.

Western Perennials for Western Gardens. Miller, Foglesong, and Aust, in Bailey's Standard Cyclopedia of Horticulture, 1915, vol. 3, pages 1469-1471.

Forest Planting in Illinois. R. S. Kellogg. Circular 81, Forest Service, U. S. Department of Agriculture, 1910. Describes the Urbana plantation and names, on page 30, the long-lived species for shelter belts.

Poetry

The Prairies. William Cullen Bryant.

The Plains. Lawrence Hope in "India's Love Lyrics." John Lane, 1908.

The Proud Farmer, The Illinois Village, and On the Building of Springfield. Nicholas Vachel Lindsay in "General William Booth," Kennerley, New York, 1913, pages 111-119.

Prairie Songs, especially The Call of the Wind, by Joseph Mills Hanson in Frontier Ballads. McClurg, 1910.

Scenery

Many contemporary descriptions of the wild prairie may be found with the aid of Buck's Travel and Description, 1765-1865, published by the Illinois State Historical Library, Springfield.

The Middle West—Heart of the Country. Hamlin Garland in Country Life in America, September 15, 1912, pages 19 to 24, 44, and 46. Popular account of the geologic origin of the Middle West and brief but comprehensive description of the following regions: Rolling prairie, Great Lakes, lake region, Dells, and coulees of Wisconsin and Mississippi river.

The Plains and Prairies. Emerson Hough in Country Life in America, October 1, 1912, pages 27 to 32, 50, 52, 54, and 56. Contrasts the humid and arid regions, describes some of the chief floral effects on the wild prairie, and declares that the landscape has had an important influence on human character.

Illinois Fifty Years ago. William Cullen Bryant, Prose Writings, Appleton, 1901, vol. 21, pages 13-22. Describes prairie near Jacksonville in 1832.

The Far West. Edmund Flagg, 1838. Reprinted in Thwaites' "Early Western Travels," vol. 26, pages 340-342.

The Homes of the New World, Fredrika Bremer, 1853, vol. 1, pages 601-603.

Illinois As It Is. Fred Gerhard, 1857. Chapter on "The Prairies."

Boy Life on the Prairie. Hamlin Garland. Macmillan, 1899. Describes Iowa scenes, but is largely applicable to Illinois.

The Prairie and the Sea. Wm. A. Quayle. Eaton and Mains, New York, 1905.

XII—The Showiest Plants in the World

GARDENESQUE MATERIALS ARE APPROPRIATE FOR GARDENS
BUT SHOULD BE USED SPARINGLY, IF AT ALL, ON LAWNS

MOST people are eager to avoid serious mistakes in landscape gardening, because no one likes to be accused of bad taste, and it is not pleasant to have one's home ridiculed. Singularly enough, most of the adverse criticism of home grounds comes from using the very plants that are generally considered to be most attractive in the world. People sometimes go so far as to impugn the motive of a lady whose home grounds are exceedingly brilliant. "She wants to appear richer than she is," they say. But is this fair and friendly? We doubt whether most people are really "guilty of insincerity," or "deliberately try to deceive," or "wish to make a vulgar display of wealth." On the contrary, we believe all their motives can generally be reduced to four innocent desires that may be grounded in instinct. For everybody loves flowers and color; everyone likes to have shade and beauty as quickly as possible; everybody likes a little variety or spice in life; and everyone has at least a rudimentary respect for neatness and order. Is it not possible that most of the alleged vulgarity is simply an excess of these virtues? At least the heart often tempts us to overdo a good thing. Suppose, then, we make the charitable assumption. Let us say that the motives are honorable, and the plants are attractive, and the whole question of good taste is simply one of self-restraint or of fitness. Figs. 82, 92. It may help us to understand why experienced gardeners sometimes abuse the very plants that seemed best to them as beginners, and it may be interesting to discover what plants these knowing ones now prefer. First, then, let us see how an innocent love of color leads beginners to buy the five classes of plants which commonly provoke the charge of bad taste or insincerity.

1. Bedding Plants

SUPPOSE you are an inexperienced homemaker—one of the thousands who are beginning family life every year in Illinois. You are afraid the place will not look well the first year. Even if you set out trees and shrubs it is obvious that the place lacks flowers. The florist tells you that tender plants will give more color than hardy ones. So you buy cannas, geraniums, begonias, or coleus, and in the kindness of your heart you put them in the middle of the front lawn so that every passer-by may enjoy them. How

cruel, then, for more experienced gardeners to say that you are trying to get the biggest show for the money! The kindlier thing is to explain to a beginner that tropical plants do not harmonize with a northern landscape, as hardy plants do (see Figs. 80, 81), and therefore it is more fitting to put tender plants in a garden and hardy plants on the lawn, for the garden or back yard is private, while the lawn or front yard is public. The showier the plants, the less we should expose them to every passer-by. It is a generous impulse that prompts us to share our greatest joys with everybody, but experience teaches that it is better to reserve them for family and friends than to force them on the public. It saves rebuffs. The quieter thing is in better taste.

2. Annual Flowers

A SECOND excess into which we are led by our innocent desire for color is to put too many annual flowers into the front yard. People who regard everything that is cheap and popular as "vulgar" sometimes speak slightingly of annuals, as if they represented a low degree of taste. Surely there is nothing inherently bad about the famous annual flowers, such as China asters, cornflowers, calliopsis, cosmos, pinks, pansies, poppies, stocks, and zinnias. On the contrary, refined people consider them quite appropriate to gardens. They are invaluable because they are the cheapest flowers of all and give results the first season. Every child should have a chance to grow the flowers that have charmed humanity for centuries, but the place to do it is in the flower garden, not in the front yard. Pure pink petunias may look very well when edging a garden path, but do they on a front walk? A straight line of scarlet sage may fit a garden, but does it look right when stretched across the front of a house? A bed of annuals may look very well at the edge of the lawn, but how about the middle?

3. Flowers of the Brightest Colors

A THIRD excess to which we are often impelled by this same innocent love of color, is the use of too many plants that have the strongest colors. One of the commonest complaints that ladies make is that "magenta flowers won't harmonize with anything in the house or outdoors, and we can't wear them." Gardening writers often express

the utmost animosity against magenta, as if it were a bad color in itself. Is any color inherently bad, or is it largely a question of combination? Most of the color discords in gardens are caused by the near-magenta colors, such as purple, crimson, and crimson-pink. So notorious are these "troublesome colors" that careful gardeners have a rule not to buy a phlox, peony, iris, or chrysanthemum from a catalog, even when they are advertised as being delicate colors like pink and lavender. Sad experience teaches that it is safer to select such varieties when they are in flower. If there is some plant of this color-group which you love very much, can you not harmonize it by surrounding it with a white-flowered variety, since white is the peace-making color among flowers? If not, it is easy to refine any near-magenta flowers simply by putting them in deep shade. But would the world come to an end if these "dangerous colors" were omitted altogether? What if a certain garden contained no cockscomb, Joseph's coat, spider flower, blue hydrangea, purple althea, Douglas spirea, Eva Rathke weigelia, Anthony Waterer spirea, or kochia? Would it be forever ugly, or are there enough other flowers in the world?

4. Showy Foliage Plants

A FOURTH excess to which many people are led by the desire for color is the use of too many plants that have extremely showy foliage, like the golden-leaved elder, golden mock orange, golden ninebark, and golden privet. Why do people who once grew these plants call them "yellow journalists?" Is there anything essentially criminal or low in them? On the contrary, they will produce more color at less expense than flowers, and at a distance they look like flowers. The first time we track down one of these gorgeous color masses and discover it is a showy-leaved variety of some familiar shrub, we are greatly interested. The next time there is a little disappointment to find that the wonderful new "flowers" are only leaves. After half a dozen experiences of the kind people begin to feel tricked, and some are so unkind as to call it a cheap way of making a big show of color. Flowers are finer products of nature than abnormally colored leaves. For example, coleus is probably the most efficient colorist the poor man can buy, and crotons are perhaps the most brilliant foliage plants that the wealthy put in their

80-81. Bedding Plants make the Biggest Show the First Year, but does Tropical Vegetation Harmonize with a Northern Landscape?
The bedding system gives more color than shrubbery during summer, but has no winter beauty, and the expense must be renewed every year. Fancy flower beds in the middle of a lawn make a home stand out in gaudy contrast to the surroundings; native trees and shrubs blend it with the landscape.

82-83. Good Taste in Landscape Gardening is largely a Matter of Fitness

These flowers are good, but are they not more appropriate in the back yard?   In front yards, neighbors can cooperate to get long views, like the one at
One's taste cannot be questioned if the private part of the lot is screened.   the right, by keeping them free from flower beds and by foundation planting.

lawns, but their flowers are inconspicuous or lacking, and so refined people say that coleus and crotons are like showily dressed people who are deficient in character.

So, too, with variegated plants, which have the leaves striped, barred, or spotted with white or yellow, like the famous little white-edged geranium we see in every park, which devotes itself so conscientiously to showy leaves that it hardly ever produces a flower. Why does the author of "The English Flower Garden" stigmatize them all as "variegated rubbish?" Because they are cheap? No, because rich people are much given to planting golden evergreens. Is it because variegation is often considered a sort of disease, since variegated plants are often less robust than their original forms? Not altogether.

The real objection is that plants with abnormally colored foliage often make a place too stimulating, the weight of authority being in favor of a restful place rather than an exciting one. Clear proof of this is furnished by places that are rich in magnificent specimens of copper beech, purple maple, and golden oak. Even the worst scolds among the critics concede that such plants are absolutely perfect of their kind. Yet the lawns of the newly rich are often overpowered by these superb trees —so much so that some unkind persons call them "purple cow places."

One of the most refined shrubs is the red-leaved rose (Rosa rubrifolia), a single bush of which makes an exquisite accent, while twelve in a mass are merely showy. Almost as charming is a single purple-leaved barberry in the border, but what about a hedge of it across the front of the average city lot? And how would you like to have a nursery-man scatter over your lawn six or eight specimens of the purple-leaved plum which he calls Prunus Pissardi?

Probably the hardest plant for beginners to resist is the blue Colorado spruce, which is undoubtedly the showiest and most popular evergreen in the world. It is said that one eastern millionaire has planted $50,000 worth of it on his place. But in the communities that have had the longest experience with showy plants there is a quiet reaction against Colorado spruce, because so many places have been overdressed with it, just as some people have overloaded their persons with faultless jewelry. Around Boston, which is very rich in fine old examples of landscape gardening, the leaders declare that a single blue spruce is enough for a large estate and too much for the average city lot.

5. Everblooming Flowers

THE fifth excess into which we are betrayed by our natural love of color is the use of too many everblooming plants. Yet some of these often seem absolutely necessary for certain spots which ought to look neat and attractive all summer. That is why every formal garden is likely to contain a bed of cannas, geraniums, or begonias. People who want a change from these sometimes use hardy plants that bloom two months or more, e. g., the Belladonna larkspur, Miss Lingard phlox, Napoleon III pink, Stokesia, Veronica subsessilis, or everblooming Lychnis. Those who like to have the prairie suggestion for a long time can get it from phlox, gaillardias, and mist flower (Eupatorium cœlestinum). This is quite right, but should it be carried to the point of having more everblooming flowers than short-lived ones? If so, we have a show garden instead of a garden of sentiment. Which is better for the average family?

Have you ever seen a rich man's show garden dominated by everbloomers, such as cannas, geraniums, and begonias? It is certainly more gorgeous in summer than the ordinary hardy garden. And the longer the florists' creations bloom the more we admire their efficiency. But do they stir the imagination or touch the heart like the first glimpse of "daffodils that come before the swallow dares, and take the winds of March with beauty?"

"Fair daffodils, ye haste away too soon," mourns Herrick, and this is true of nearly every hardy flower, from spring crocus to autumn chrysanthemum. The very fact that they are short-lived is a part of their charm. The pang of parting with one favorite soon gives way to the pleasure of greeting the next friend in the procession. The garden of sentiment is dominated by hardy perennials like

84-85. Before and after Learning how to Arrange Showy Plants

"Like most people who move from a great city to a wooded suburb, I tried   "Finally I realized that an open, central lawn, flanked by masses of native
to save all the crooked, diseased, and short-lived trees. After losing four years   trees, is better than a museum of costly curiosities. I now grow showy plants
I cut them down and filled the lawn with showy flower beds, trees, and shrubs."   at the edge of the lawn only."—Wm. C. Egan, Highland Park, Illinois.

86. Mr. Farmer, why don't you Restore Illinois Trees to your Farmstead instead of Spoiling Illinois Scenery with Foreign Trees?
The settlers were excusable for planting the "cheapest evergreens" like Norway spruce, but can't you see how these spiry trees fail to harmonize with the characteristic beauty of middle-western woodlots and the dignity of your own pasture oaks? If you need evergreens, why not plant white pine? See Figs. 87, 88.

tulips, iris, peonies, phlox, pinks, foxgloves, Canterbury bells, sweet william, oriental poppies, larkspurs, and chrysanthemums. The flowers are all short-lived, but the succession is generally satisfactory. If not, perhaps it can be supplemented from the lists of perennials on pages 24, 25. The great thing for the millions is not the showy garden of temporary plants, which must be renewed every year. The great thing is the hardy garden of permanent plants. The fleeting flowers make less display than the everbloomers, but are they not in better taste?

If restraint be desirable in a private flower garden, how about the front yard? The beginner's ideal is to have a big show of flowers from spring to frost in both places. But is this either practical or desirable? If you go away for a summer vacation, what becomes of flowers in the front yard? Beginners commonly put an everblooming bed in front of the house, but it is generally more practical and in better taste to place it at the rear or side. The commonest mistake we make in America with everbloomers, especially near the front door, is to overdo the shrub that gives the most bloom for the money, viz., Hydrangea paniculata, var. grandiflora, a name which is contemptuously shortened by some to "p. g." But there is nothing to sneer at in a hydrangea, especially if it be put in a garden and allowed to assume its natural form of a small tree. Unfortunately, most beginners prefer to make a bigger show, and by following the florists' advice to prune heavily, they get a small bush that is covered with enormous, topheavy bunches of bloom. Look along an average American street next September and consider how much restraint has been used in planting the showiest shrub in cultivation. What about the walks, drives, and boundaries double-lined with hydrangea and nothing else? How about the front of a

house planted with hydrangea and nothing else? Can you not make the front door sufficiently attractive and more dignified by planting near it shrubs and vines that are presentable longer than flowers, such as the Illinois creeper or Engelmann's ivy and others recommended for foundation planting on page 26?

So, too, with the shrubbery border. There are comparatively few summer-blooming shrubs, but it is possible to keep up a show by using Hydrangea arborescens, var. grandiflora. The newly rich often try to beat nature in this way, but older families generally acquiesce in nature's suggestion that a place which is green in summer is more restful than one which strains to keep up a display of flowers. A famous example is the place which is often said to be the best example of landscape gardening in America, the Sargent home at Brookline, Massachusetts. It is natural for the beginner to think that flowers are more important than foliage, and to the heart they are. Consequently people often plant only golden bells, spirea, mock orange, lilac, and hydrangea, all of which are lovely in flower, but have little autumn color, and are devoid of color all winter. A week or two of bloom is about all you get from the ordinary shrub, and what you live with for six months is foliage. Consequently, landscape gardeners have a saying that "foliage is more important than flowers." The people are right in feeling that the average home place does not have color enough. Right here is where the expert planner does better than the beginner. He gives you more color thruout the year, but distributes it more evenly by using shrubs that have the triple attractions of flower, autumn color, and brightly colored berries or branches. Thus, on a well-planned place everyone's taste in color naturally becomes refined, and the eyes are opened to the quieter delights of form and texture in foliage.

Quick Growers

QUITE as laudable as the universal love of color is the universal desire for quick results, since speed has something to do with efficiency. Moreover, the quickest-growing plants generally cost the least, and are therefore doubly attractive to beginners. Unfortunately, the speediest plants are generally of short-lived efficiency or beauty. For example, the farmers must protect house and stock from the winter wind as soon as possible, so they commonly plant Norway spruce, Austrian pine, and Scotch pine, which generally lose their most valuable branches (the lower ones) before they are twenty years old, and turn a dingy brown or look unhappy. See Fig. 88. Granting that some of these temporary evergreens may be necessary, why not also plant some permanent evergreens, like white pine and hemlock?

With these evergreens the old-time farmer commonly planted box elder, soft maple, or willows to shelter house or cattle from the winter winds. The new-time farmer will avoid these temporary trees, if he can, and if not he will plant near them some long-lived trees such as sugar maple, and pin, red, or scarlet oaks.

City people want shady spots in their yards for rest and play, so they often plant soft maple or box elder or Carolina poplar, which are soft-wooded, like all quick growers, and therefore likely to be ruined by ice or wind storms soon after they attain a good size. Can they not get the shade they require in some other way, e. g., by means of a screened porch or summer house, or a large permanent tree?

Home-makers like to get rid of the bare look as soon as possible, so they often put a California privet hedge next to the sidewalk or at the sides of the lot, or they surround the house with privet. Unfortunately the California privet often dies to the ground in Illinois, and even where it is hardy it has little flowering, autumnal, or winter beauty. It is better to put the same money into three- to four-foot plants of Japanese barberry, Van Houtte's spirea, and golden bells, and set them against foundations.

Those who like to reap the rewards of foresight may congratulate themselves if they resist the allurements of quick-growers. And they will not have to wait twenty years to get satisfaction. Every day they see a town full of soft maple or box elder they will be glad they planted sugar maples or oaks.

Spectacular Forms

QUITE as natural as the love of color and speed is the craving for that variety which is the spice of life. Anyone who wishes to attract the attention of every passer-by to his place can easily do so by planting in his front yard one or more trees that stand up like flag poles. The most celebrated of these columnar trees is the Roman cypress, which is the spectacular feature of the famous old Italian gardens. The spectacular

87-88. Which Looks Better on Prairie, Long-Lived White Pine or—
Consider the value of these pines for windbreaks and winter beauty on this Iowa farm. There is enough roll here for drainage, which white pine demands.

Short-Lived Norway Spruce
Cheap, showy, and quick, but soon gets thin and brown.

tree of eastern formal gardens is the red cedar.

The cheap substitute for these evergreens is the Lombardy poplar, which will shoot up faster, probably, than any other ornamental tree in the temperate zone. It will screen unsightly objects at the least cost and in double-quick time. It will grow on a city lot that is too small for an ordinary tree. Moreover, it often gives a pleasing note of uplift, which is a refreshing change in a monotonous environment. Even its short term of life can often be ignored, because the tree can be replaced cheaply and quickly. Any plant with such extraordinary virtues will always be a leading favorite, and, of course, it has been grossly overplanted. People naturally suppose that if one poplar makes a good accent, a dozen will look better, but is it so? One exclamation point may look well, but are not twelve in a row ridiculous? What about the ordinary city lot outlined with twelve to thirty Lombardy poplars? See Fig. 90. Too much accent is no accent, as the real estate dealer quickly discovers when he plants half a mile of street with nothing but Lombardy poplars. Overplanting of the Lombardy and Bolles' poplar is a city man's vice.

The corresponding vice of the country man is overplanting of Norway spruce. One of the leading landscape gardeners in the Middle West says, "The Illinois farmers often spoil the beauty of their farms by planting Norway spruce around their houses. See Figs. 86, 88. I call it the 'rip saw' because the ascending branches of this evergreen tear thru the sky-line of the deciduous trees in his grove or woodlot. I like evergreens and have planted thousands in Illinois, but the only one that harmonizes with the prairie is white pine, and that does not thrive everywhere. See Fig. 87. The crowning glory of the eastern scenery may be the army of evergreen spears that pierce the roof of the forest. Every landscape gardener who has come to Illinois has tried to reproduce that effect and failed, for Illinois cannot grow evergreens as well as the East. But this limitation is a blessing in disguise, for it gives us a chance to discover the peculiar beauty of western woodlands, which is the comparatively level sky-line and soft, billowy texture of our deciduous woods. This type of beauty is less spectacular, and may be poorer in species of trees, but it is exquisitely appropriate to so rich and peaceful a land as the prairie. To city people from the East it may be an acquired taste, but the farmers feel it. It is part of their faith that Illinois will become one of the most beautiful regions in the world. And that is why I wish the farmers would chop down, as soon as they can spare them, the Norway spruces that murder our Illinois scenery."

"Another assassin is the Lombardy poplar (Fig. 90), which I call the 'butcher knife,' and I beg our wealthy people who plant it on their country estates to kill it without delay. It is impossible to find any plants that will make a more violent contrast with prairie scenery than the Norway spruce and Lombardy poplar. They are like the clash of drum and cymbals, for they demand instant attention from everybody. What they give to the prairie landscape is not accent, but shock. Accent is, or should be, intensification of the original note—not something surprisingly different. The accent-marks designed for the prairie by nature are horizontal haws and crabs, not spectacular poplars. (Figs. 90, 91.) It almost seems as if the great artist, Nature, purposely omitted plants with strong upright lines when putting the finishing touches on her most exquisite creation, the prairie. Even the red cedar, which is native to Illinois, hugs the lake shore or hides in wooded river bottoms; it will not thrive in the open, as it does in the East. My advice to clients is usually to kill Lombardy and Norway and plant prairie haws and crabs!"

Is it not barely possible that there are other ways of getting variety in home grounds than by planting Lombardy poplars? Two hundred kinds of permanent plants native to Illinois are mentioned on pages 24 and 25, about four times as many as a landscape gardener usually considers enough for the average city lot. Cannot those who want a change from the prairie get it by making their home grounds a snug harbor or retreat, instead of a museum? Why not surround farmstead or back yard with trees and shrubs, mostly native, and have a private outdoor living-room where one may entertain friends? Will not the prairie seem more beautiful to the city man by contrast with his home grounds? And will not home look twice as good to the farmer after a day outdoors?

89. Order is a Virtue, but Artificiality an Excess

Is not Catalpa Bungei overdone here and in many front yards, especially when double-lining walks and drives? Is it well to surround a house or lot with trees of one kind, set at equal distances in straight rows? (See Fig. 90.)

Weeping Trees and Shrubs

ONE degree less spectacular than sky-rocket trees are plants that seem to grow upside down, like the Camperdown elm or Teas' weeping mulberry. These are certainly legitimate in back yards, especially when trained for children's play houses, but are they usually appropriate in front yards? No doubt they attract more attention there, but they also provoke more ridicule.

There is nothing essentially ridiculous in a weeping willow, for a single specimen of the Babylonian or Napoleon beside the water may have considerable dignity, but a row of them has been compared to "hired mourners." Probably the most efficient of these professionals is the Kilmarnock weeping willow, which is the poor man's favorite, but equally absurd is the rich man's lawn if overdressed with costly specimens of weeping spruce, dogwood, and Japanese maples and cherries.

Such forms originated in the garden, as Manning says, and they belong there, not on the lawn. The weeping, cut-leaved, and spectacular plants are mostly horticultural varieties rather than natural species, and they are generally perpetuated by artificial means, such as grafting. They are one degree removed from nature, and to that extent may be considered artificial. For this reason, people prefer plants that are naturally pendulous, rather than artificially so. For example, they like the Wisconsin willow better than the Kilmarnock willow, which is so radically different from the normal willow. On the other hand, the cut-leaved weeping birch seems merely to intensify the peculiar grace of its prototype, the European birch. It is probably the most popular of all weeping plants and deservedly so, in spite of its rather short

90-91. Which is the Better kind of Accent for the Prairie, Vertical or Horizontal—Foreign Poplars or Native Haws?

A little accent is a good thing, but how about thirty Lombardy poplars surrounding a city lot? "All accent is no accent." Nature left the exclamation point out of Illinois scenery.

Some landscape gardeners will never plant the Lombardy poplar on the prairie. They say it makes too strong a contrast, while the haw and crab delicately accent the native beauty of the scenery. (A hawthorn in bloom.)

92-93. Good Taste in Landscape Gardening consists largely in Self-Restraint about the Showiest Plants in the World

"We made the usual mistake of planting too many rare, costly, foreign trees. When we learned better, two weeping trees equal to the above hid a view."

"Finally we cut them out. (The ring in the grass shows one scar.) The finest specimens in the world are less important than good views."—Wm. C. Egan.

life. No wonder we see six trees of it in a city yard where one would be better, for it is easy to overplant the exquisite thing.

How many weeping plants can the average city lot contain with good effect? Some critics say "none at all." Others say "one—and that in the back yard.".

Cut-Leaved Plants

LESS spectacular, perhaps, than columnar or weeping trees are cut-leaved plants. Certainly they are not so liable to criticism, and they are supposed to give refinement or elegance to a place. The standard of beauty in this group is the fern-leaved beech. Eastern people often are exceedingly proud of their fancy beeches, as if they had done a great deal to make them perfect specimens, whereas it is hard to fail with them. Unfortunately, beech rarely thrives in Illinois.

The excessive use of finely cut foliage often tends to make a place look effeminate, weak, over-refined. This is especially true of the front yard that contains half a dozen Wier's cut-leaved maple or cut-leaved birch.

The first time one meets a refined stranger on the lawn, it is pleasant to discover that he belongs to a respectable family, like the sycamores, lindens, alders, or hawthorns. But go to any big nursery and you will see that these supposed rarities are rather common, for most trees and shrubs of importance have their cut-leaved editions. Then comes a revulsion of feeling against reducing all of nature's distinct leaf forms to a mass of shredded vegetable matter.

The reaction against "horticulturals" brings people back to nature with the question, "Is there not some simpler way of getting refinement in foliage?" Nature replies that she has adapted to Illinois the following trees with pinnate or feathery foliage: walnut, ash, Kentucky coffee, mountain ash, honey locust, and bald cypress. With shrubs of this sort she has not been so generous, but a variety of cut-leaved elder originating in Illinois is becoming a special favorite of our people. See Figs. 2 and 10. This plant is Sambucus canadensis, var. acutiloba.

Formal or Geometrical Plants

QUITE as natural as the love of color, speed, and variety is the love of order. A certain amount of formality is necessary, especially amid conventional surroundings. Unfortunately, this love of order runs to great excesses of artificiality, especially in the East, where rich men's gardens are often loaded with globes, cones, pyramids, cubes, and columns of evergreen foliage. The time-honored way of relieving flatness in formal gardens is to use bay trees in tubs. A cheap

substitute for these is California privet trained like a bay tree, and another is Catalpa Bungei, sometimes derisively called the "lollipop" or "all-day sucker." This has a legitimate use in formal gardens, but does it fit the front yards of Illinois? What about drives and walks planted with Catalpa Bungei and nothing else? See Fig. 89.

Double Flowers

A SUBTLER case of formalism which is overdone in many front yards in Illinois is the use of double flowers, such as flowering almond, flowering peach, Bechtel's crab, double lilacs, Paul's scarlet hawthorn, snowballs, altheas, and hydrangeas. Double flowers bloom longer than single ones and are, therefore, invaluable in formal gardens, especially in beds where a continual show of color must be maintained, but professionals generally agree that they are "too gardenesque for the lawn." Their single-flowered forms seem more appropriate to nature-like surroundings. Double flowers are artificial in the sense that their fullness is dependent upon man, for they go back to single forms if planted in the wild. Moreover, they generally tend toward one form—that of the ball—thus obliterating the individuality of the original flower. Consequently, many who retain the double flowers in the garden make it a point to have only single flowers on the lawn, e. g., single hydrangeas and single white altheas. Instead of the common and Japanese snowballs they plant the single-flowered originals of these, Viburnum Opulus and V. tomentosum.

In some cases, however, everybody acknowledges that the double flowers make a stronger human appeal, especially the "queen of flowers." It is the most natural thing in the world to put the common double roses in the front yard, but practical conditions are against that location. Garden roses have to be heavily fertilized and one does not like to have manure under the parlor window. The bushes must be pruned so severely that they are not presentable near the front door. Many beginners line their front walks with double roses, but is that the place to wage war on aphids, thrips, and rose-bugs? If we put double roses in the shrubbery, they will not hold their own against the bushes. Most people, after trying every location in the front, have taken their double roses to the back, but they preserve the rose sentiment in the front yard by planting the wild or single roses, of which a list is given on page 25 (Nos. 135-139).

The Evolution of Taste

IN short, the whole story of good taste in landscape gardening is chiefly one of fitness and self-restraint in the use of showy ma-

terials—plenty of them in the garden, but less on the lawn. It would be easy for us to betray the people's interests by encouraging beginners to plant anything they fancy in any way they like. But there is a chance to save the people of Illinois much money and time by pointing out the evolution of taste which communities and individuals commonly experience. To summarize it all, people generally pass in their appreciation from the temporary to the permanent, from the spectacular to the restful, from the showy to the quiet, from the artificial to the natural, from rare to common, from foreign to native. See Figs. 84, 85, 92, 93.

What can be done with costly specimens that are out of place? This is a painful question to those who have just learned that naturalistic surroundings are in better taste than the gardenesque. Three courses are possible: (1) remove them to the garden or back yard; (2) sell them or give them away; (3) use the axe. As an older editor once told an eager recruit, "The public may object to what you leave in, but they never miss what you cut out."

WE WILL

☐ Try not to overplant the things we love most, especially in the front yard.
☐ Plant our home grounds in the naturalistic style—not in the gardenesque.
☐ Move gardenesque materials from lawn to garden.

ACKNOWLEDGMENTS

Landscape Gardeners. The work of Jens Jensen is shown in Figs. 1, 2, 8, 10, 25 to 34, 36, 39, 42, 46, 48, 50, 56, 59, 69. The work of O. C. Simonds is shown in Figs. 3, 54, 60, 62, 67, 68, 71, 72, 94, 98. The work of W. H. Manning is shown in Fig. 44.

Architects. The house in Fig. 1 is by Louis H. Sullivan, who is generally considered the founder of the middle-western school of architects. Fig. 76 is by Frank Lloyd Wright, who first developed the type of domestic architecture which is called in these pages the "prairie style." (Mr. Wright declines to give or recognize any name for this work.) For the work of Robert C. Spencer, see front cover. Figs. 5 and 17 are by William Drummond. Fig. 11 is by Hewitt & Brown.

Photographers. The front cover, frontispiece, and Figs. 2, 3, 5, 6, 7, 10, 12, 17, 18, 24, 25 to 34, 36, 38, 39, 46, 52, 54, 57, 58, 60, 61, 62, 65, 67, 68, 69, 71, 72, 74, 75, 76, 88, 90, 94, 97 are by A. G. Eldredge. Figs. 9, 35, 41, 42, 45, 50, 53, 55, 56, 66, 86 are by or from Jens Jensen. Figs. 4, 13, 14, 73, 87, 89, 92 are by the J. Horace McFarland Co. Figs. 1, 8, 47, 48, 59 are by Henry Fuermann & Sons. Figs. 16, 82, 83, 95, 96 by B. A. Strauch. Figs. 15, 37 by H. J. Sconce. Figs. 19, 20 by L. D. Seass. Fig. 21 by L. E. Foglesong. Fig. 22 by C. N. Brown. Fig. 23 by A. G. Eldredge and F. A. Aust. Fig. 40 by Alfred Rehder. Figs. 43, 44 from Warren H. Manning. Fig. 49 from W. A. Simms. Figs. 63, 64 by O. B. Brand. Figs. 51, 70 by F. A. Aust. Fig. 77 by A. E. Ormes. Fig. 78 by Carl Krebs. Fig. 79 by Mrs. Lew Wallace. Figs. 84, 85, 93 from W. C. Egan. Fig. 91 by B. S. Pickett. Fig. 98 by Wasson.

Drawings on pages 4, 5 and "Done in Illinois" by L. D. Tilton.

The Illinois Citizen's Oath

Suggested by the Famous Athenian Oath Which Was Taken by Every Young Man When He Came of Age and Received the Suffrage

It has been proposed that graft can be largely prevented and the best citizenship promoted by a dramatic ceremony connected with the bestowal of political power. Every large park has some broad lawn suitable for public gatherings, such as ball games, folk dances, pageants, and political meetings. The youths and maidens, clad in flowing robes, may assemble in such a spot and make their vows of good citizenship according to the form in which each city chooses to express its ideals. At least one Illinois city is considering the best possible setting for great public gatherings where the city's aims may be expressed in dramatic ways upon occasion. Some of the sentiments expressed below have little to do with home gardening, but they have much to do with park design, which used to be the most important part of a landscape gardener's practice, and all must be considered in city planning, which is commonly regarded as the most important branch of landscape gardening today. The following is not recommended for any particular locality, but merely suggests some of the civic ideals that are commonly proposed by city clubs, chambers of commerce, and other bodies that usually attempt to express the aims of a community. Each town, of course, will wish to formulate its aims in its own way.

I will receive the right to vote as a sacred trust and always use it for the good of the whole community, instead of my own selfish interest.

I will vote for the liberty, health, and happiness of all my fellow citizens, not for the privilege of any class.

I will separate local issues from national ones and vote for the best man for each job, regardless of party politics.

I will assume all men to be honest and try to cooperate with public servants before criticizing them adversely.

I will strive unceasingly against graft, corruption, and inefficiency.

I will work for peace and try to prevent war—military, economic, and social.

I will practice moderation in speech and will urge toleration in matters of conscience.

I will help Illinois enlarge and improve her cities by promoting cooperation or emulation among neighboring communities, and I will not work against nearby towns.

I will help Illinois preserve and restore her sacred shrines of native beauty by extending the state and local park system for the recreation of soul and body.

I will do what I can to develop a living civic art, as the Athenians did.

I will endeavor to make my community so comfortable and beautiful that her children will always wish to live here and share in the perfecting of our civilization.

I will try to build a permanent home surrounded by many permanent plants native to Illinois.

As a public token of my loyalty I will plant beside the foundation of my home some Illinois roses to remind me and others of the "Illinois spirit."

I will work persistently to express the highest ideals of all citizens in a comprehensive city plan for extending, developing, and beautifying the city.

The Illinois Spirit in Landscape Gardening—Developing the Native Beauty instead of Copying a Foreign Type

Italy has her cypresses, Scotland has her pines, the East has her mountain laurel, and Illinois has her hawthorns, crab apples, bur oaks, and prairie rose. Does your community own a spot like this, which can be used for pageants, folk dances, readings, religious meetings, and the citizen's oath? (A scene in Graceland.)

Rogers & Hall Co., Printers, Chicago, Illinois

I Defy Anyone to Sell These Houses at a Profit

"This block of 'stickers' is the despair of every real-estate dealer. Not a tree or shrub. Telephone poles in the parking instead of in the back yards. You cannot expect to sell a bare property without serious loss."—F. M. Vanneman, real-estate dealer, Urbana.

All Houses on This Street are Readily Salable

"People are eager to live under these elms. I have sold these four properties a total of thirteen times. Each sale was at an increased price. It pays to plant permanent trees and shrubs according to a well-considered plan."—F. M. Vanneman, real-estate dealer, Urbana.

The Prairie Spirit

I BELIEVE that one of the greatest races of men in the world will be developed in the region of the prairies. I will help to prove that vast plains need not level down humanity to a dead monotony in appearance, conduct, and ideals.

I feel the uplifting influence of the rich, rolling prairie and will bring its spirit into my daily life. If my home surroundings are monotonous and ugly, I will make them varied and beautiful. I will emulate the independence and progressiveness of the pioneer.

I will do what I can to promote the prosperity, happiness, and beauty of all prairie states and communities.

I will try to open the eyes of those who can see no beauty in the common "brush" and wild flowers beside the country roads. If any souls have been deadened by sordid materialism I will stand with these people on the highest spot that overlooks a sea of rolling land, where they can drink in the spirit of the prairies.

I will fight to the last the greed that would destroy all native beauty. I will help my state establish and maintain a prairie park, which will restore for the delight of future generations some fragment of the wild prairie—the source of our wealth and civilization.

I will plant against the foundations of my house some bushes that will remind me of the prairie and be to my townsfolk a living symbol of the indomitable prairie spirit.

"Short Ballot" for Illinois Citizens

Let each family unite on some of the following propositions and record the resolution here as a reminder of the ideals they wish to accomplish during the coming year.

WE WILL

☐ Keep our home grounds clean, and screen unsightly objects by planting.

☐ Save old trees and plant long-lived species.

☐ Have an informal shrubbery border for year-round beauty instead of a trimmed hedge.

☐ Plant shrubs and vines against the foundations of our house. Plant permanent materials mostly native to Illinois. (See pages 24, 25.)

☐ Design and plant our home grounds or get the best advice we can.

HOW THE BALLOT-SIGNERS KEPT THEIR PROMISES

At the end of the second year the Division of Landscape Extension had 5,200 pledges "to do some permanent ornamental planting within a year." The signers were then asked to tell how they had kept their promises. Replies were received from 991, or 19 percent. of the signers. Of these, 785 spent a total of $75,117 on materials, plans, grading, lawn tools, etc. The average for the whole group of 991 was nearly $76. The average expenditure of 642 persons who spent less than $100 was $22. Let us hope that all readers of this circular will do as well or better.

What a Difference it makes in the Appearance of a Street if the Houses have Foundation Planting!

Shrubs are needed to remove the bareness and make a house look like a home. Sometimes neighbors cooperate and tie a whole street together by low shrubbery in the parking, as in the next picture.

Foundation planting gives a park-like appearance, especially when a block at a time is done. Around these foundations are many Illinois shrubs, especially roses. (Moeller and McClelland homes, Decatur.)

Index

Page references to illustrations are in *italics*.

Personal names following site names denote persons involved in the design of the site.

INDEX

INDEX

Eckbo, Garrett, 31–39, 42, 45
    Alcoa Forecast Garden, Eckbo Residence, Los Angeles, Calif., *38, 39,* 38–39
    Sudarsky House, Bakersfield, Calif., *35*
    Zimmerman House, Los Angeles, Calif., *37*
eclecticism, 11
Eisenman, Peter, and Hanna/Olin, Ltd., Wexner Center for the Visual Arts, Ohio State University, Columbus, Ohio, 260–62, *261–62,* 269
Eldredge, Arthur, 113
Emerson, George Barrel, 71
Emerson, Ralph Waldo, 71–75, 78, 84, 93, 98, 214
    "The Young American," 74, 74 n. 28
England, 128–34, 173, 191, 216, 246, 264, 265–66, 272
    Blenheim, 129
    Chelsea (Gough House), *148*
    Cliveden, Buckinghamshire, 129, *130*
    influence on garden design in the United States, 23, 135, 142–45, 147–54
    Kent Garden, Rousham, 42
    Manchester, 205
    Richmond, Surrey, 129, 131–33, 139–40
    Thames River, 129–34, 139–40, 146–47
    Twickenham, 129–33, 140
    see also London
Entenza, John, 26

Fagan residence, Woodside, Calif., Bernard Maybeck, 57, 59, *60*
Fairmount Park, Philadelphia, Pa., 205
Felton, C. C., 75
Filoli, Woodside, Calif., Bruce Porter, *13*
Fitzhugh, William, 126
Five of Clubs, 73
Folwell, William Watts, 82, 83 n. 64
Ford Estate (Fair Lane), Jens Jensen, 114
Frampton, Kenneth, 22, 269, *see also* critical regionalism
Fremont, John Charles, 47
Fremont Estate, Mariposa, Calif., F. L. Olmsted, 47–48, 211
French, William Merchant Richardson, 78–80, 82–83
French parterre tradition, 175
front lawn, 29, 128
Frost, Robert, 216, 252

garden, definition of, 7, 42, 169, 173
Garden, Hugh M. G., Refectory Building, Humbolt Park, Chicago, Ill., *105*
Garden and Forest, 95, 97
Garden District, New Orleans, La., 165, 167, 177–90
Garden Magazine, 113, 272–73, 275
gardenesque, 198

Garland, Hamlin, 101
Gebhard, David, 11
Gibbs, James, 131, 133
Glassie, Henry, 244–45
Goldsmith, Oliver, *The Deserted Village,* 193
Governor's Palace, Williamsburg, Va., 142
Graceland Cemetery, Chicago. Ill., H. W. S. Cleveland and O. C. Simonds, 78, *79,* 83, 95, 96 n. 106, 98, *100,* 103, *103,* 272 n. 3
Greece, 45, 47, 250
    Athens, 56, 65, 158
    influence on garden design in the United States, 135, 144, 154–59
Green-Wood Cemetery, Brooklyn, N.Y., 197
Greenbelt House (Case Study House No. 4; unrealized), Ralph Rapson, *30*
Greene, Charles, and Henry Greene (Greene and Greene), 45, 246, 269
Gregg, John, 45
Griffin, Walter Burley, 69, 69 n. 3, 97, 99 n. 2, 102, 273, 274
Grove, William Hugh, 139
Guerin, Jules, 64
Guevrekian, Gabriel, 31
    Villa Noailles, Hyères, France, *33*
Gunston Hall, Va., 148–50, 154, 155

Haag, Richard, 249, 250, 256, 269
Habermas, Jurgen, 269
Hall, William Hammond, 235
Halprin, Lawrence, 250
Hanna, Robert, 259
Hanna/Olin, Ltd., 243, 251–70
    Battery Park City, New York, N.Y., 255–56, *257*
    Canary Wharf, London, 255, *255,* 266
    Codex Corporation Headquarters, Canton, Mass., 251–52, 265
    Kitzmiller Residence (Abigail House), New Albany, Ohio, 263–65
    Pitney Bowes Headquarters, Stamford, Conn., 252, *253*
    Playa Vista, Los Angeles, Calif., 252, *254,* 255
    Sixteenth Street Transitway Mall, Denver, Colo., 256–59
    Westlake Park, Seattle, Wash., 256, *258,* 259–60, 267
    Wexner Center for the Visual Arts, Ohio State University, Columbus, Ohio, 260–62, 269
Hanson, A. E., Lloyd Estate, 11
Hawthorne, Nathaniel, 71, 73, 84
Hearst, William Randolph, 65
Hearst Gymnasium and Memorial Complex, University of California at Berkeley, Bernard Maybeck, 64–65, *66*
Henderson Residence, Hillsborough, Calif., Thomas Church, 31, *32*

INDEX

Loring (Central) Park, Minneapolis, Minn., H. W. S. Cleveland, *87,* 88–90
Los Angeles, Calif., 14, 253, 255, 265
    Alcoa Forecast Garden, Eckbo Residence, 38–39
    Barnsdall House (Hollyhock House), Frank Lloyd Wright, 24–26
    May Residence, Cliff May, 17, *18*
    Playa Vista, Hanna/Olin, Ltd., 252, 254–55
    Schindler House, Rudolph M. Schindler, 27
    Union Station, John and Donald Parkinson, 246–48
    Zimmerman House, Garrett Eckbo, 37
Loudon, John Claudius, 104, 195, 197–98, 200, 207
Lowell, James Russell, 75

Magnus Estate, Winnetka, Ill., Jens Jensen and Robert Spencer, 102, 109, *113,* 274 n. 12
Mall, Washington, D.C., 197–201, 205
Marble Hill, 132, *133,* 134
Mariposa, Calif., Fremont Estate, F. L. Olmsted, 47–48, 211
Mason, George, 148, 154
Massachusetts Horticultural Society, 193, 202
Mathews, Arthur and Lucia, 45, 54–55, 57
    Youth, 55
Mattaponi River, 139
May, Cliff, 17
    May Residence, Los Angeles, Calif., 17, *18*
    ranch house, Keene, Calif., *18*
    Sunset offices, Menlo Park, Calif., Cliff May and Thomas Church, 17, *19*
Maybeck, Bernard, 44–68 passim, 249
    Fagan residence, Woodside, Calif., 57, 59, *60*
    Hearst Gymnasium and Memorial Complex, University of California at Berkeley, 64, 65, *66*
    Hospital (unrealized), University of California at Berkeley, *58*
    Mills College campus design, Oakland, Calif., 56–57
    Oakland Packard Showroom, Oakland, Calif., 50, *52*
    Palace of Fine Arts, San Francisco, Calif., 50, *51,* 59–65
    Phoebe Apperson Hearst Memorial, University of California at Berkeley, *53,* 65, *67*
    Senger House, Berkeley, Calif., 50, *54*
    Stanford University campus design, Palo Alto, Calif., 47
    Strawberry Canyon Bath House, University of California at Berkeley, *58*
McHarg, Ian L., *Design with Nature,* 248–49
McLaren, John, 45
Meade Estate (Maycox Plantation), 138

Mediterranean influence, 47, 56, 57, 64, 65, *see also* Italy, influence of
Mexico, 9 n. 4, 10
Miami, Fla., Vizcaya, F. Burrell Hoffman and Diego Suarez, 21, *21*
Michigan State University campus, O. C. Simonds, 119
Middle West, 69–98, 99–123, 260, 263–65, 273
Mies van der Rohe, Ludwig, German Pavilion, Barcelona, 23–24, *24*
Mill, John Stuart, 214
Millard House (La Miniatura), Pasadena, Calif., Frank Lloyd Wright, 24, *25*
Miller, Philip, *The Gardeners Dictionary,* 135, 147
Miller, Wilhelm (William), 69, 95, 99, 106, 110–12, 117, 122, 271–75
    "An American Idea in Landscape Art," 272
    "The Prairie Spirit in Landscape Gardening," 99, *100,* 122, 271, 273, 277–81
    What England Can Teach Us About Gardens, 272
Mills, Robert, 198–201
    Bunker Hill Monument, Boston, Mass., 198
    Plan of the Mall, Washington, D.C., *199,* 200–1
    Smithsonian Institution, Washington, D.C., 198, *199*
Mills College campus design, Oakland, Calif., Bernard Maybeck, 56–57
Minneapolis, Minn., 85–90, 93, 96–97
    Central (Loring) Park, H. W. S. Cleveland, 85–90, *91*
    Minnehaha Park/Falls, H. W. S. Cleveland, 86, 90–93, 94 n. 102, 98
    Mississippi River, 72, 86, 93
Miró, Joan, 39
missions, influence on regional garden design in the United States, 9, 14, 247, 248, 250
Moholy Nagy, Sybil, *Matrix of Man,* 260
Monroe, Harriet, 101
Monticello, Va., 145, 154, 157–61
Moore House, Ojai, Calif., Richard Neutra, 27
Morgan, Julia, 45
    Berkeley City Club, Berkeley, Calif., 64
    Oakland Chapel of Chimes, Oakland, Calif., 64
Morris, Robert, 132
Morris, William, 48
Moser, William, Santa Barbara County Courthouse, 11
Mount Airy, Va., 150–51, *152–53*
Mount Auburn Cemetery, Cambridge, Mass., General Henry Dearborn, 75, 193–97, 205
Mount Deposit, Md., *144*
Mount Vernon, 144, 154–55, *156–57,* 160
Mudd, Ignatius, 200
Muir, John, 45, *46,* 48, 50

INDEX

INDEX

INDEX

Contributors

Ackerman, James S.
Professor Emeritus, Department of Fine Arts, Harvard University, Cambridge, Massachusetts.

Beveridge, Charles E.
Series Editor, The Frederick Law Olmsted Papers, Department of History, The American University, Washington, D.C.

Brown, C. Allan
Landscape architect and landscape historian, Charlottesville, Virginia.

Grese, Robert E.
Associate Professor, Landscape Architecture Program, School of Natural Resources and Environment, University of Michigan, Ann Arbor.

Harris, Dianne
Doctoral candidate in architectural history, Department of Architecture, College of Environmental Design, University of California, Berkeley.

Hunt, John Dixon
Chair, Department of Landscape Architecture, University of Pennsylvania, Philadelphia.

Neckar, Lance M.
Associate Professor, Department of Landscape Architecture, College of Architecture and Landscape Architecture, University of Minnesota, Minneapolis.

Olin, Laurie
Principal, Hanna/Olin, Ltd., Philadelphia, Pennsylvania.

O'Malley, Therese
Associate Dean, Center for Advanced Study in the Visual Arts, National Gallery of Art, Washington, D.C.

Treib, Marc
Professor, Department of Architecture, College of Environmental Design, University of California, Berkeley.

Turner, Suzanne
Professor, School of Landscape Architecture, College of Design, Louisiana State University, Baton Rouge.

Vernon, Christopher
Assistant Professor, Department of Landscape Architecture, College of Fine and Applied Arts, University of Illinois, Urbana-Champaign.